YO &!

14

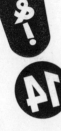

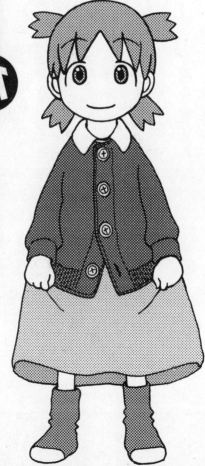

KIYOHIKO AZUMA

CONTENTS

YOTSUBA&!
KIYOHIKO AZUMA

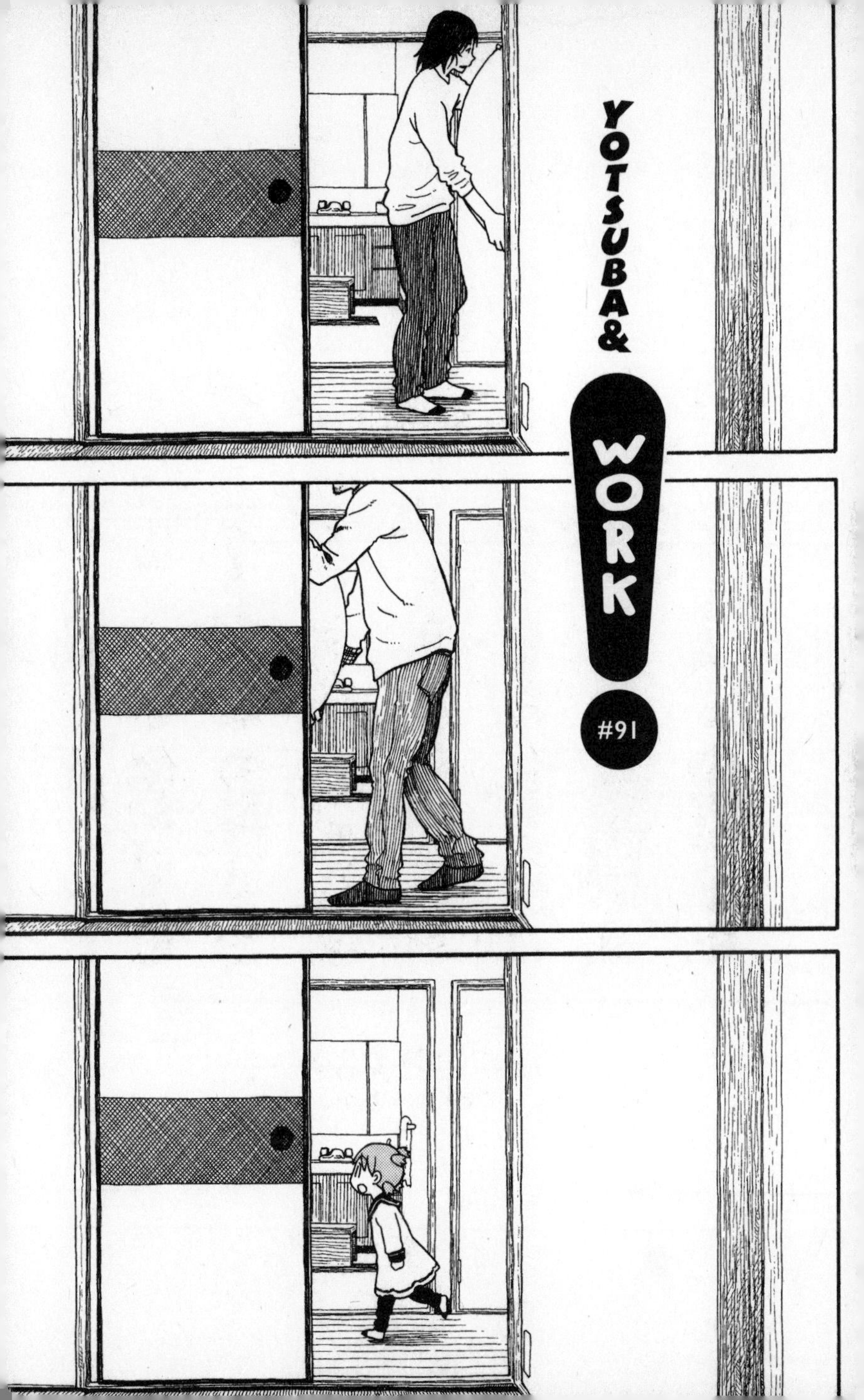
YOTSUBA&
WORK!
#91

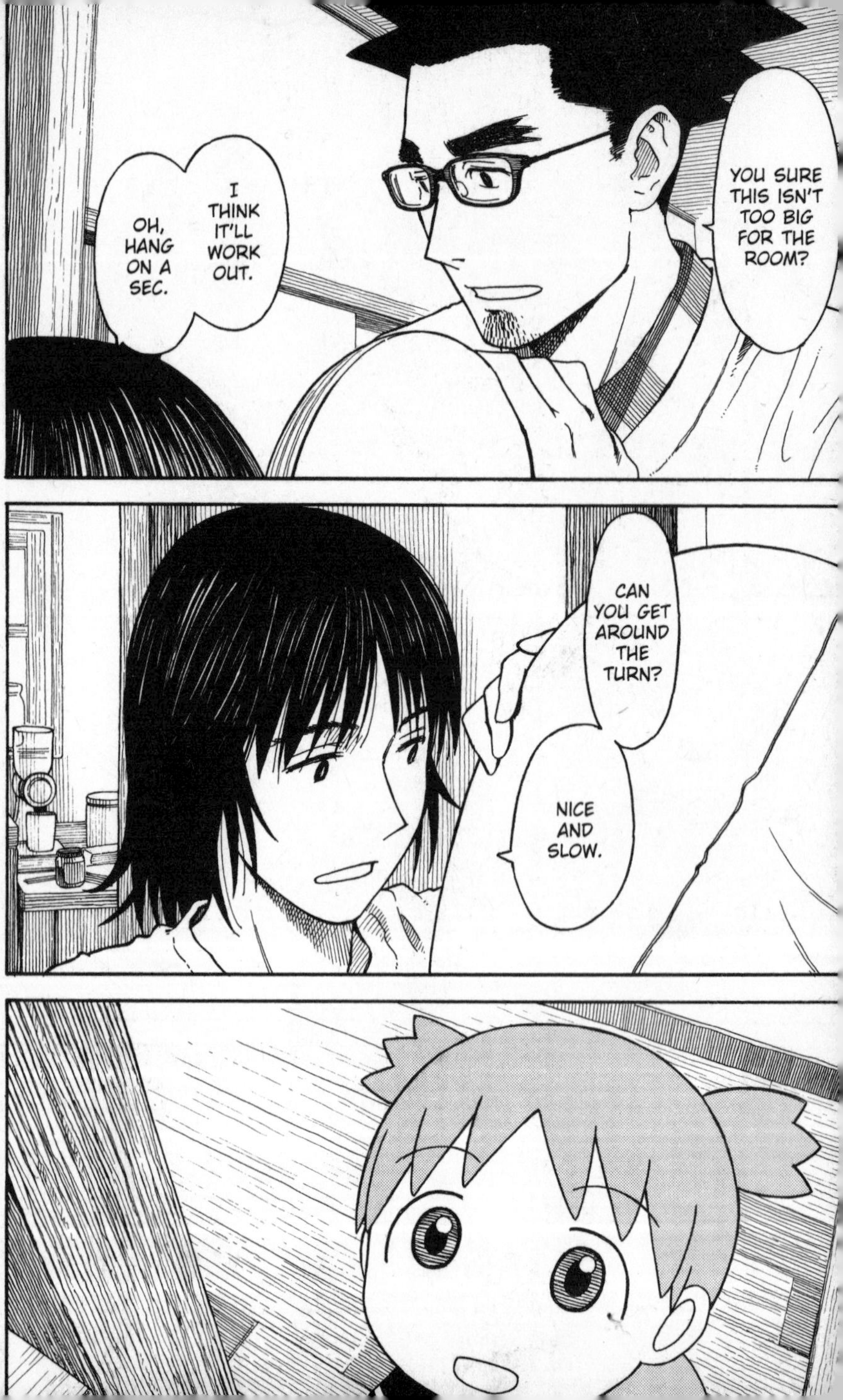
YOU SURE THIS ISN'T TOO BIG FOR THE ROOM?
I THINK IT'LL WORK OUT.
OH, HANG ON A SEC.
CAN YOU GET AROUND THE TURN?
NICE AND SLOW.

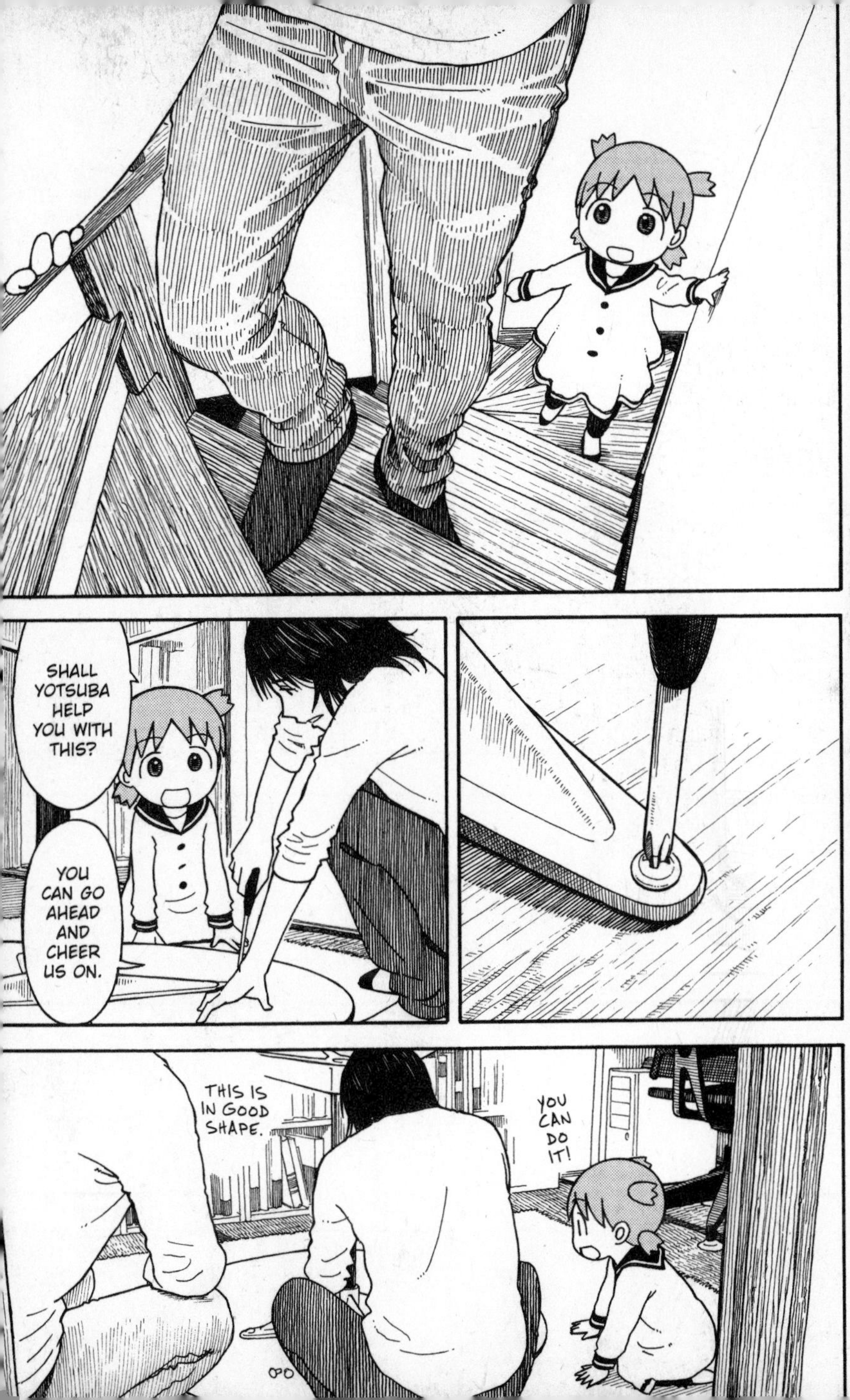
SHALL YOTSUBA HELP YOU WITH THIS?
YOU CAN GO AHEAD AND CHEER US ON.
YOU CAN DO IT!
THIS IS IN GOOD SHAPE.

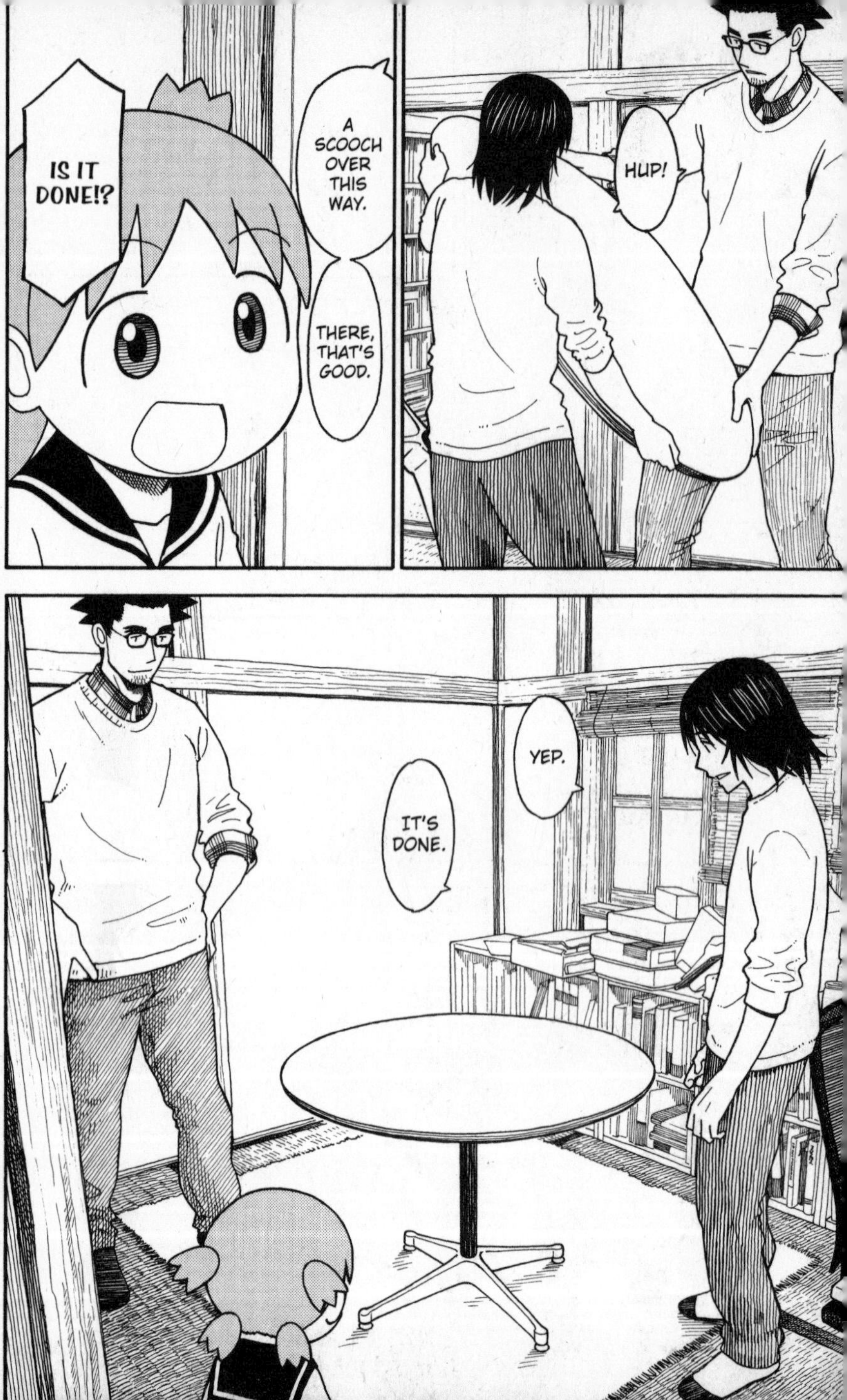
HUP!
A SCOOCH OVER THIS WAY.
THERE, THAT'S GOOD.
IS IT DONE!?
YEP.
IT'S DONE.

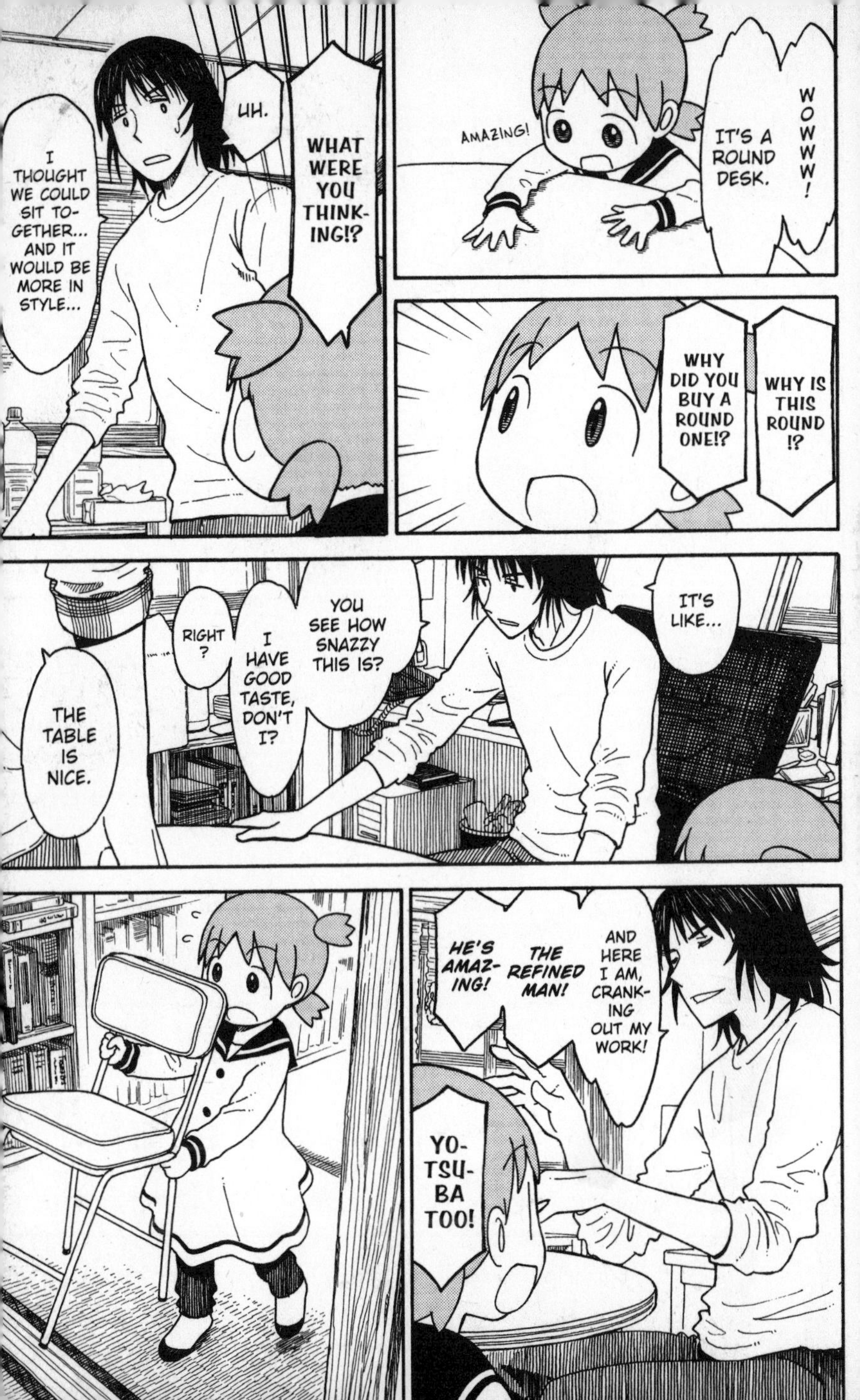
WOWWW!
IT'S A ROUND DESK.
AMAZING!
WHY IS THIS ROUND!?
WHY DID YOU BUY A ROUND ONE!?
WHAT WERE YOU THINKING!?
UH.
I THOUGHT WE COULD SIT TOGETHER... AND IT WOULD BE MORE IN STYLE...
IT'S LIKE...
YOU SEE HOW SNAZZY THIS IS?
I HAVE GOOD TASTE, DON'T I?
RIGHT?
THE TABLE IS NICE.
AND HERE I AM, CRANKING OUT MY WORK!
THE REFINED MAN!
HE'S AMAZING!
YOTSUBA TOO!

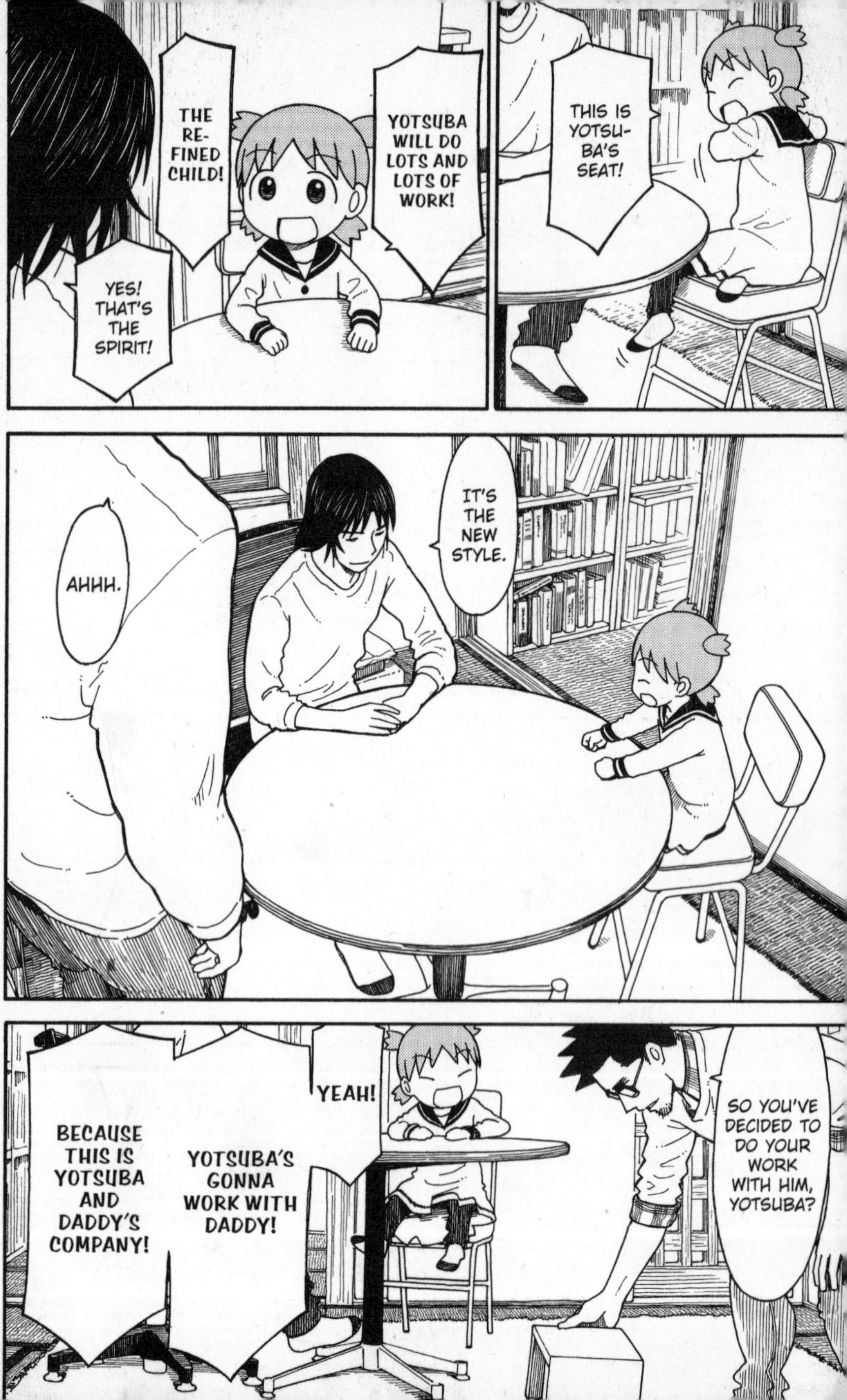
THIS IS YOTSUBA'S SEAT!
YOTSUBA WILL DO LOTS AND LOTS OF WORK!
THE REFINED CHILD!
YES! THAT'S THE SPIRIT!
IT'S THE NEW STYLE.
AHHH.
SO YOU'VE DECIDED TO DO YOUR WORK WITH HIM, YOTSUBA?
YEAH!
YOTSUBA'S GONNA WORK WITH DADDY!
BECAUSE THIS IS YOTSUBA AND DADDY'S COMPANY!

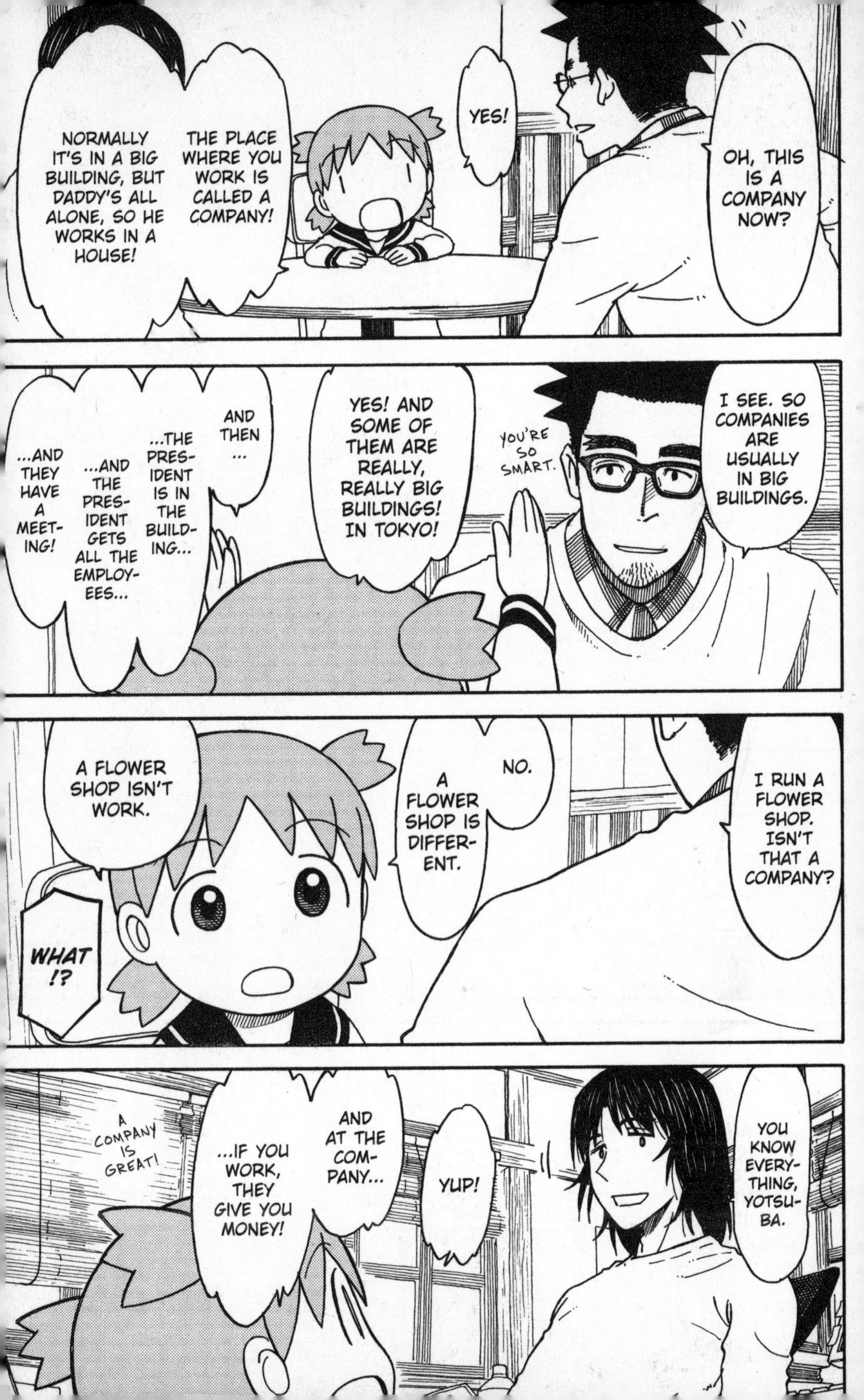
OH, THIS IS A COMPANY NOW?
YES!
THE PLACE WHERE YOU WORK IS CALLED A COMPANY!
NORMALLY IT'S IN A BIG BUILDING, BUT DADDY'S ALL ALONE, SO HE WORKS IN A HOUSE!
I SEE. SO COMPANIES ARE USUALLY IN BIG BUILDINGS.
YOU'RE SO SMART.
YES! AND SOME OF THEM ARE REALLY, REALLY BIG BUILDINGS! IN TOKYO!
AND THEN...
...THE PRESIDENT IS IN THE BUILDING...
...AND THE PRESIDENT GETS ALL THE EMPLOYEES...
...AND THEY HAVE A MEETING!
I RUN A FLOWER SHOP. ISN'T THAT A COMPANY?
NO.
A FLOWER SHOP IS DIFFERENT.
A FLOWER SHOP ISN'T WORK.
WHAT!?
YOU KNOW EVERYTHING, YOTSUBA.
YUP!
AND AT THE COMPANY...
...IF YOU WORK, THEY GIVE YOU MONEY!
A COMPANY IS GREAT!

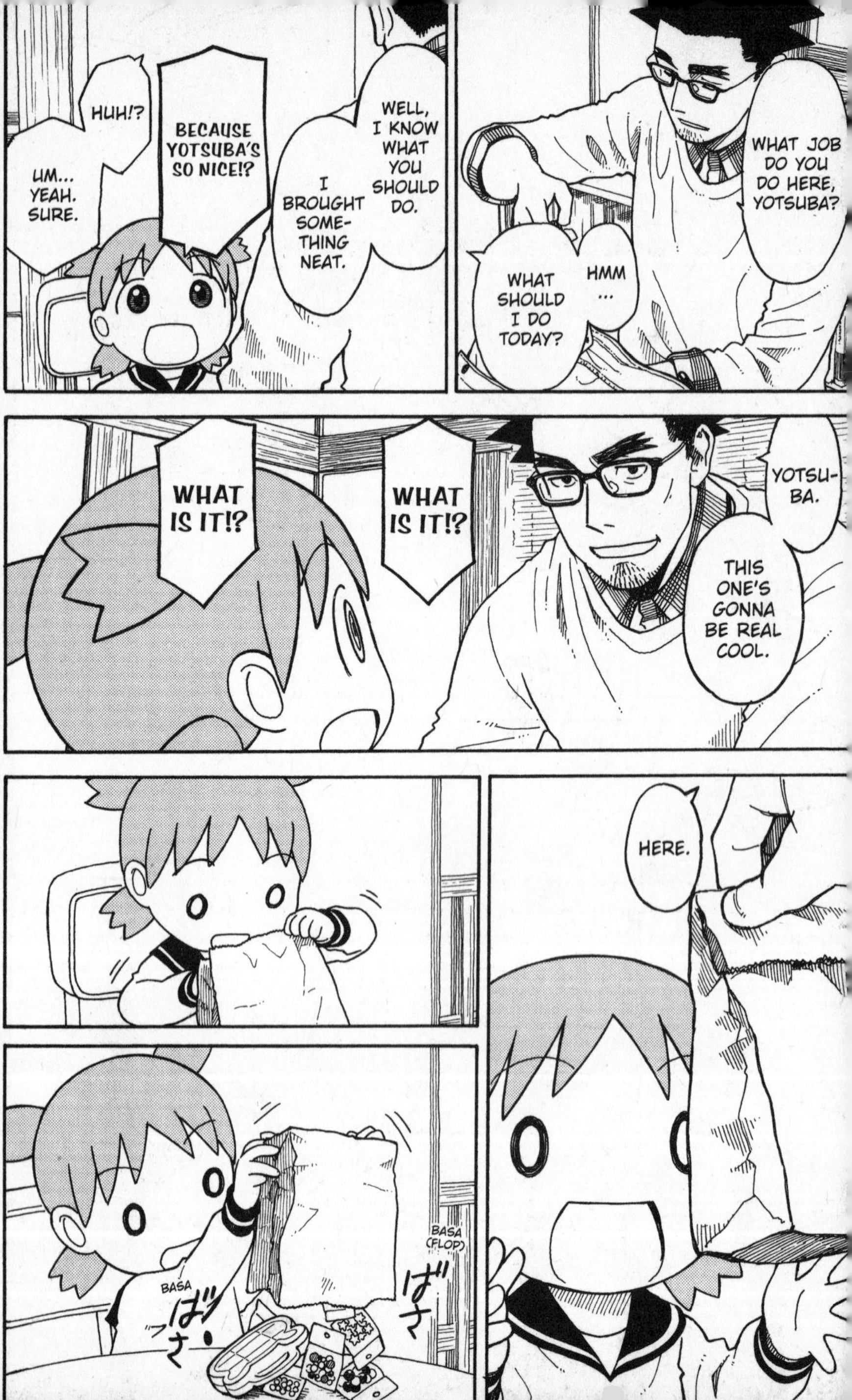
WHAT JOB DO YOU DO HERE, YOTSUBA?
HMM ...
WHAT SHOULD I DO TODAY?
WELL, I KNOW WHAT YOU SHOULD DO.
I BROUGHT SOME-THING NEAT.
BECAUSE YOTSUBA'S SO NICE!?
HUH!?
UM... YEAH. SURE.
YOTSU-BA.
THIS ONE'S GONNA BE REAL COOL.
WHAT IS IT!?
WHAT IS IT!?
HERE.
BASA (FLOP)
BASA

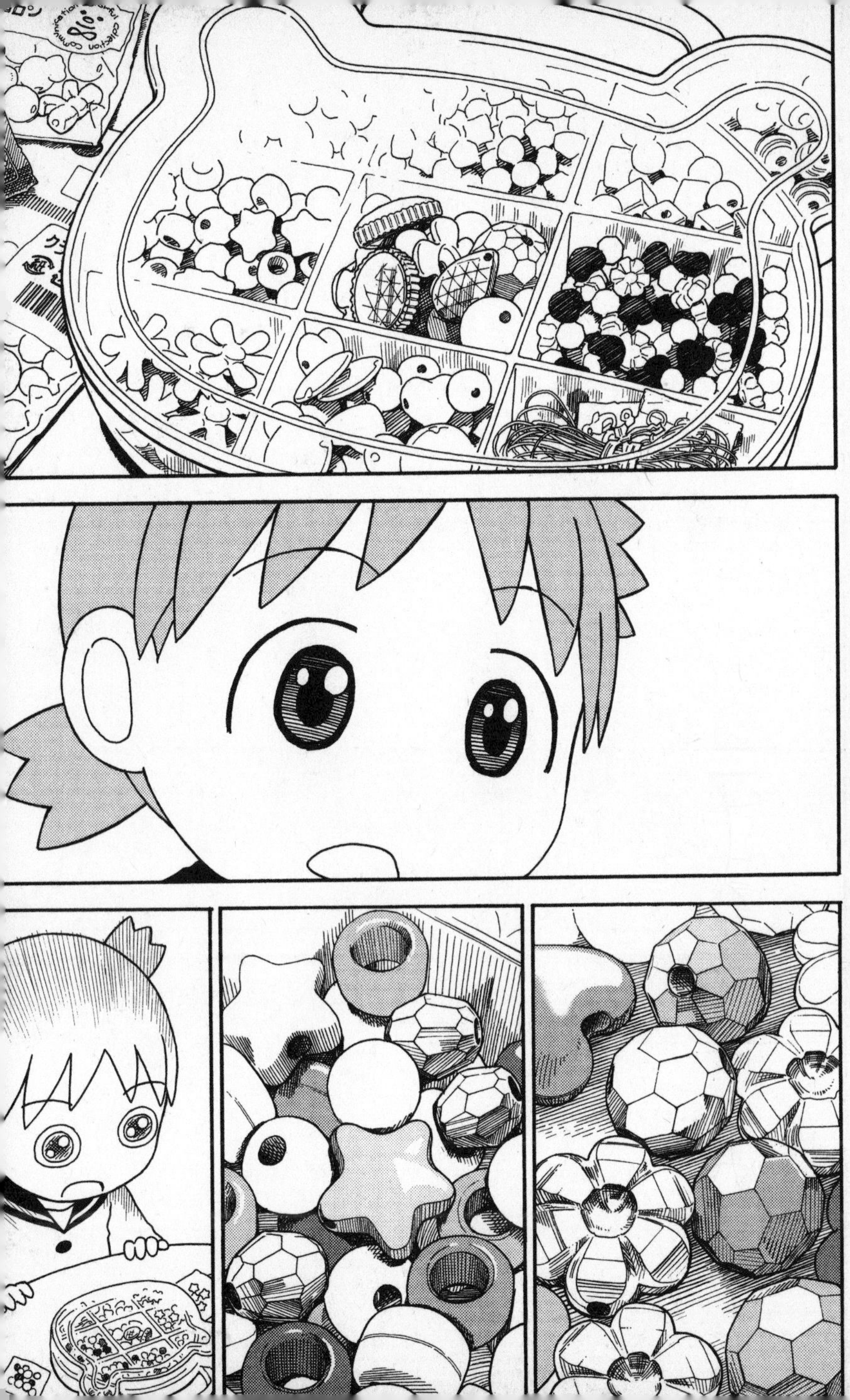

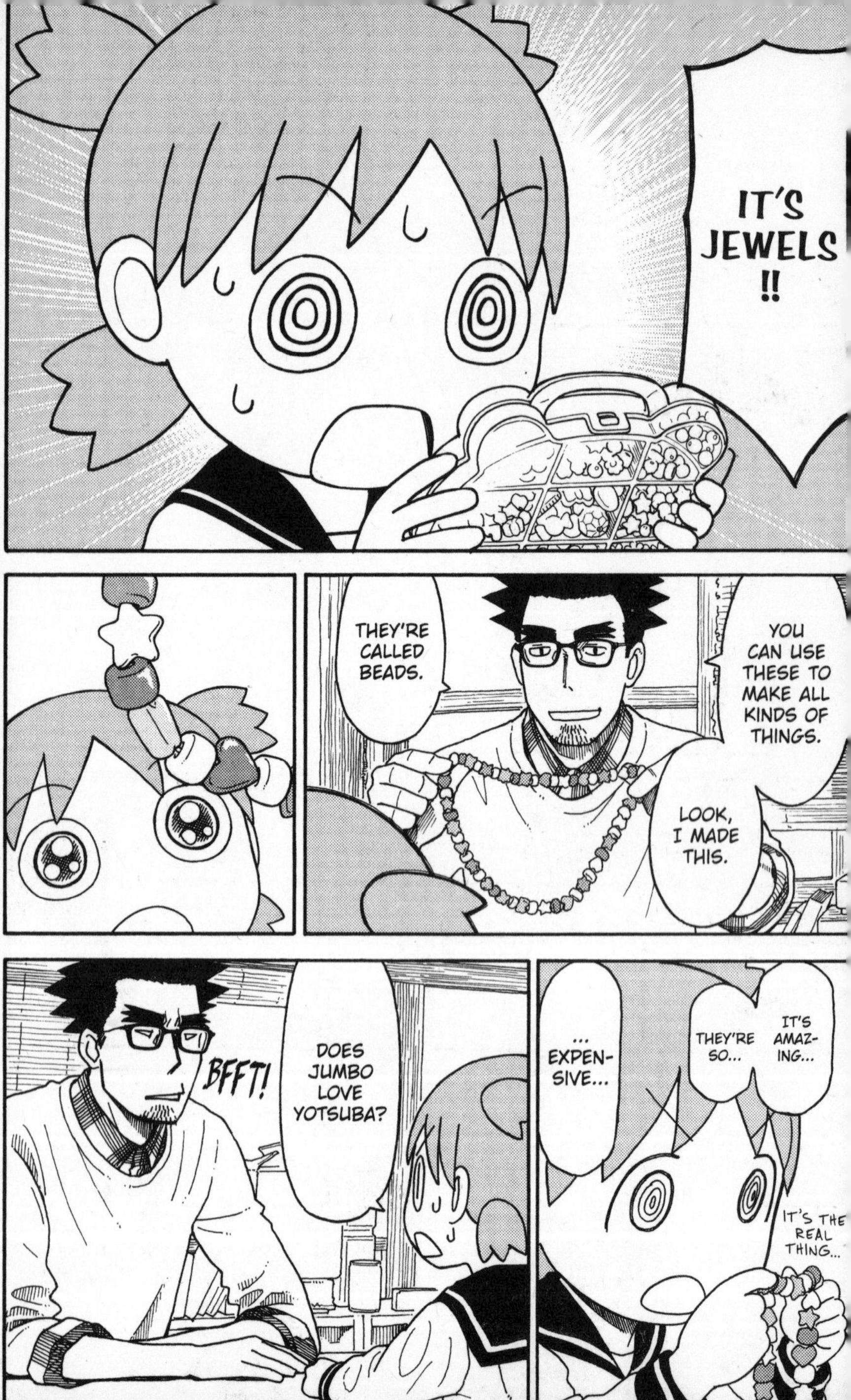
IT'S JEWELS !!
THEY'RE CALLED BEADS.
YOU CAN USE THESE TO MAKE ALL KINDS OF THINGS.
LOOK, I MADE THIS.
IT'S AMAZ-ING...
THEY'RE SO...
... EXPEN-SIVE...
IT'S THE REAL THING...
DOES JUMBO LOVE YOTSUBA?
BFFT!

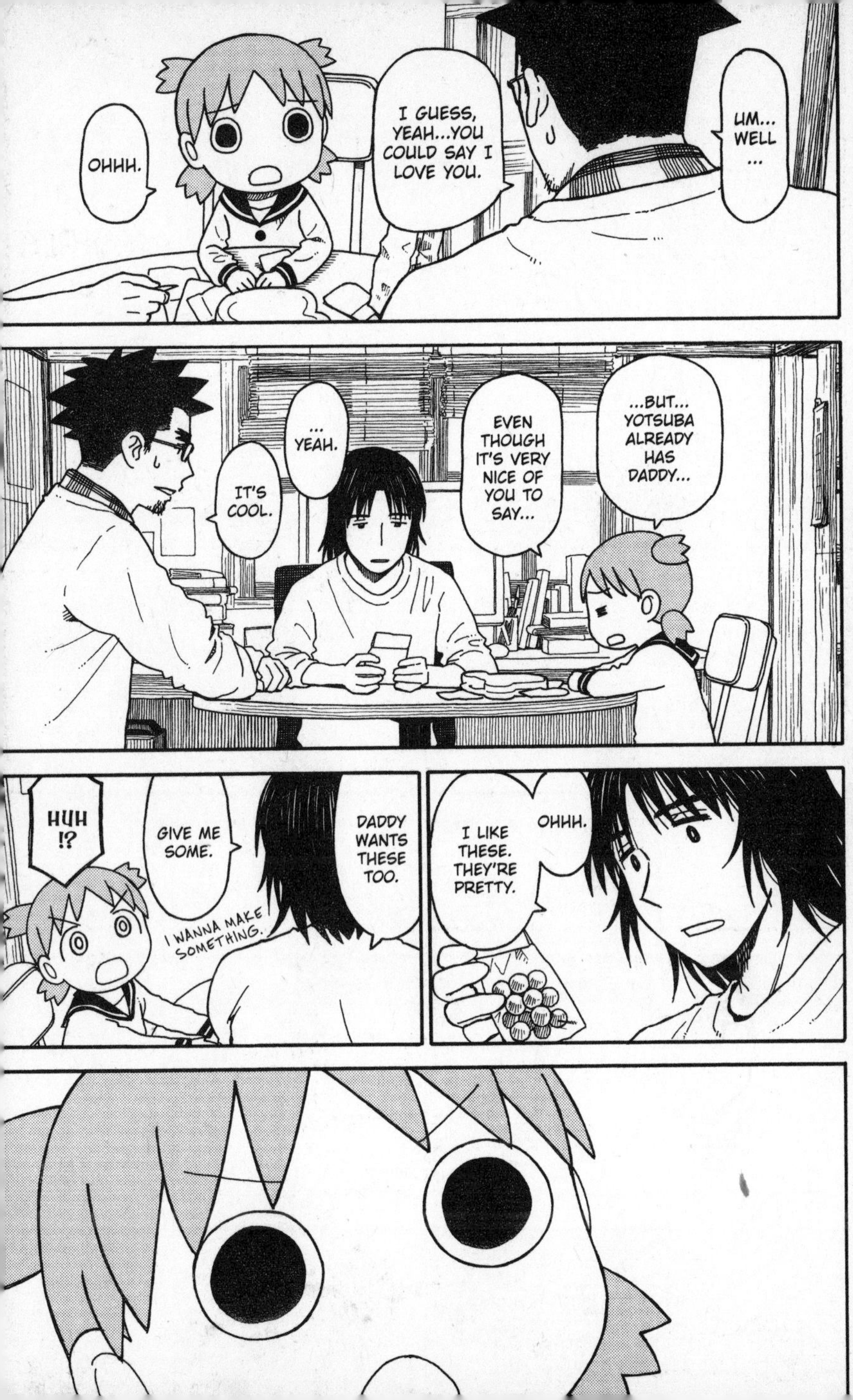
UM... WELL ...
I GUESS, YEAH...YOU COULD SAY I LOVE YOU.
OHHH.
...BUT... YOTSUBA ALREADY HAS DADDY...
EVEN THOUGH IT'S VERY NICE OF YOU TO SAY...
... YEAH.
IT'S COOL.
OHHH.
I LIKE THESE. THEY'RE PRETTY.
DADDY WANTS THESE TOO.
GIVE ME SOME.
HUH !?
I WANNA MAKE SOMETHING.

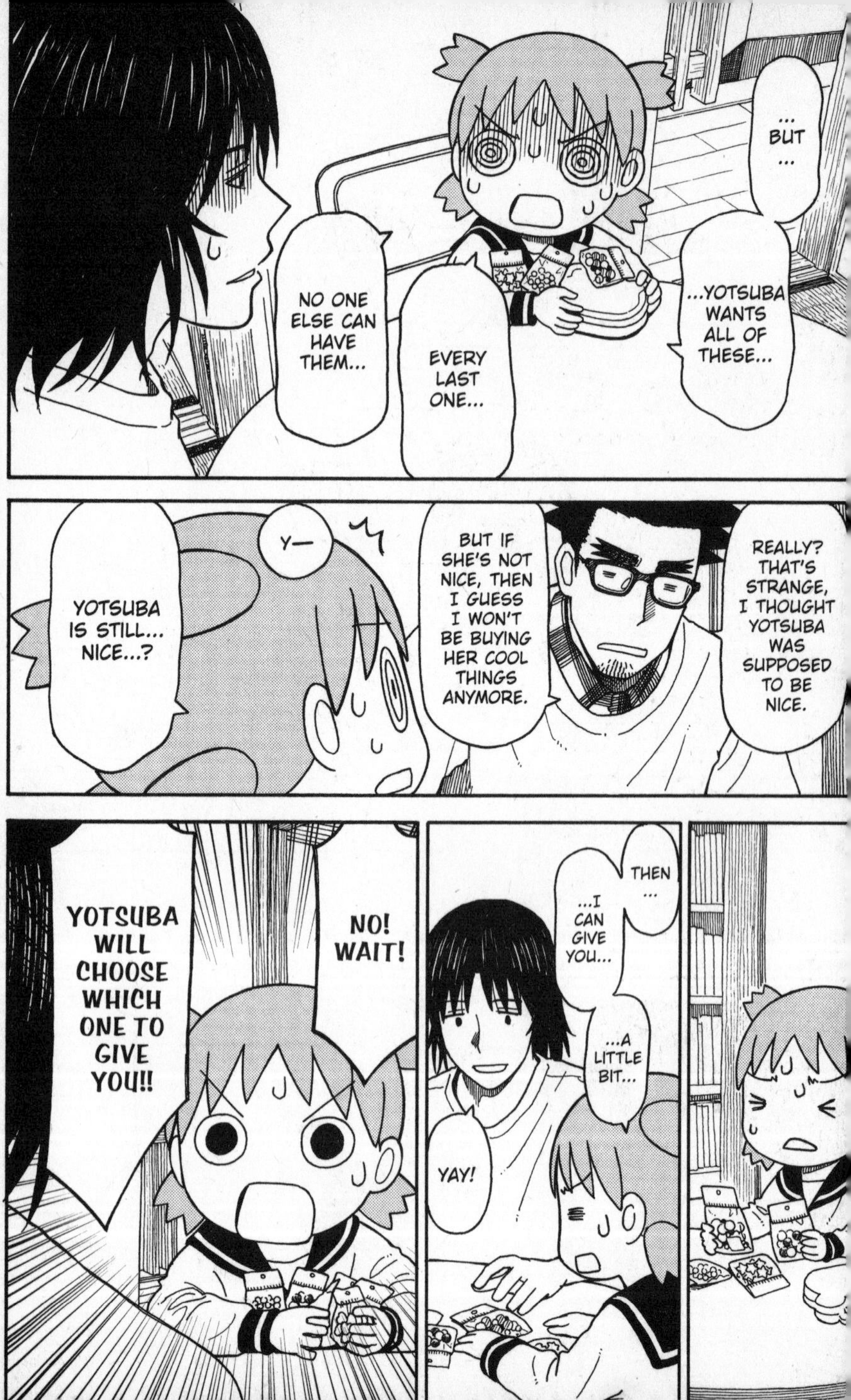
... BUT ...
...YOTSUBA WANTS ALL OF THESE...
EVERY LAST ONE...
NO ONE ELSE CAN HAVE THEM...
REALLY? THAT'S STRANGE, I THOUGHT YOTSUBA WAS SUPPOSED TO BE NICE.
BUT IF SHE'S NOT NICE, THEN I GUESS I WON'T BE BUYING HER COOL THINGS ANYMORE.
Y—
YOTSUBA IS STILL... NICE...?
THEN ...
...I CAN GIVE YOU...
...A LITTLE BIT...
YAY!
NO! WAIT!
YOTSUBA WILL CHOOSE WHICH ONE TO GIVE YOU!!

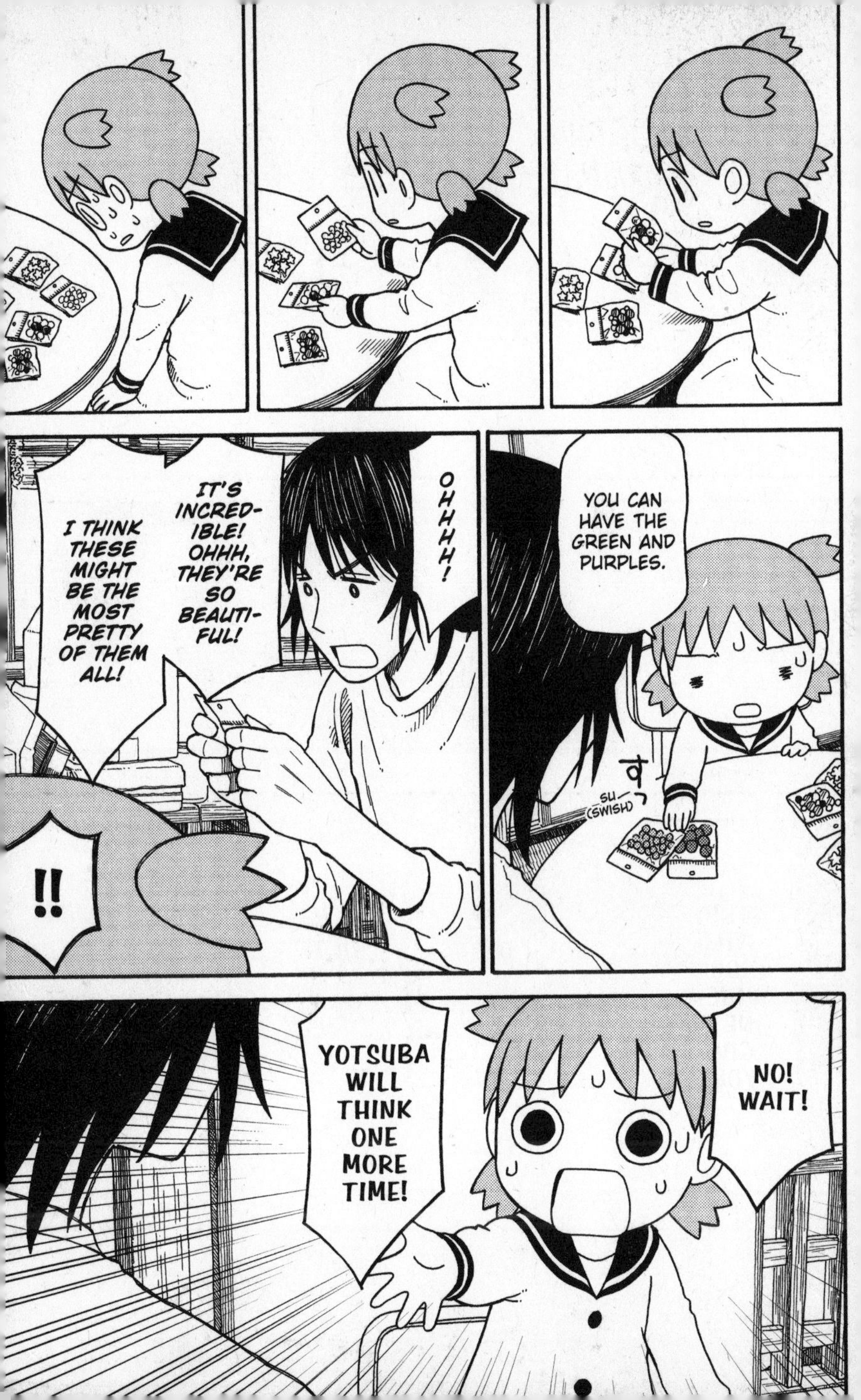
YOU CAN HAVE THE GREEN AND PURPLES.
す
SU (SWISH)
OHHHH!
IT'S INCREDIBLE! OHHH, THEY'RE SO BEAUTIFUL!
I THINK THESE MIGHT BE THE MOST PRETTY OF THEM ALL!
!!
NO! WAIT!
YOTSUBA WILL THINK ONE MORE TIME!

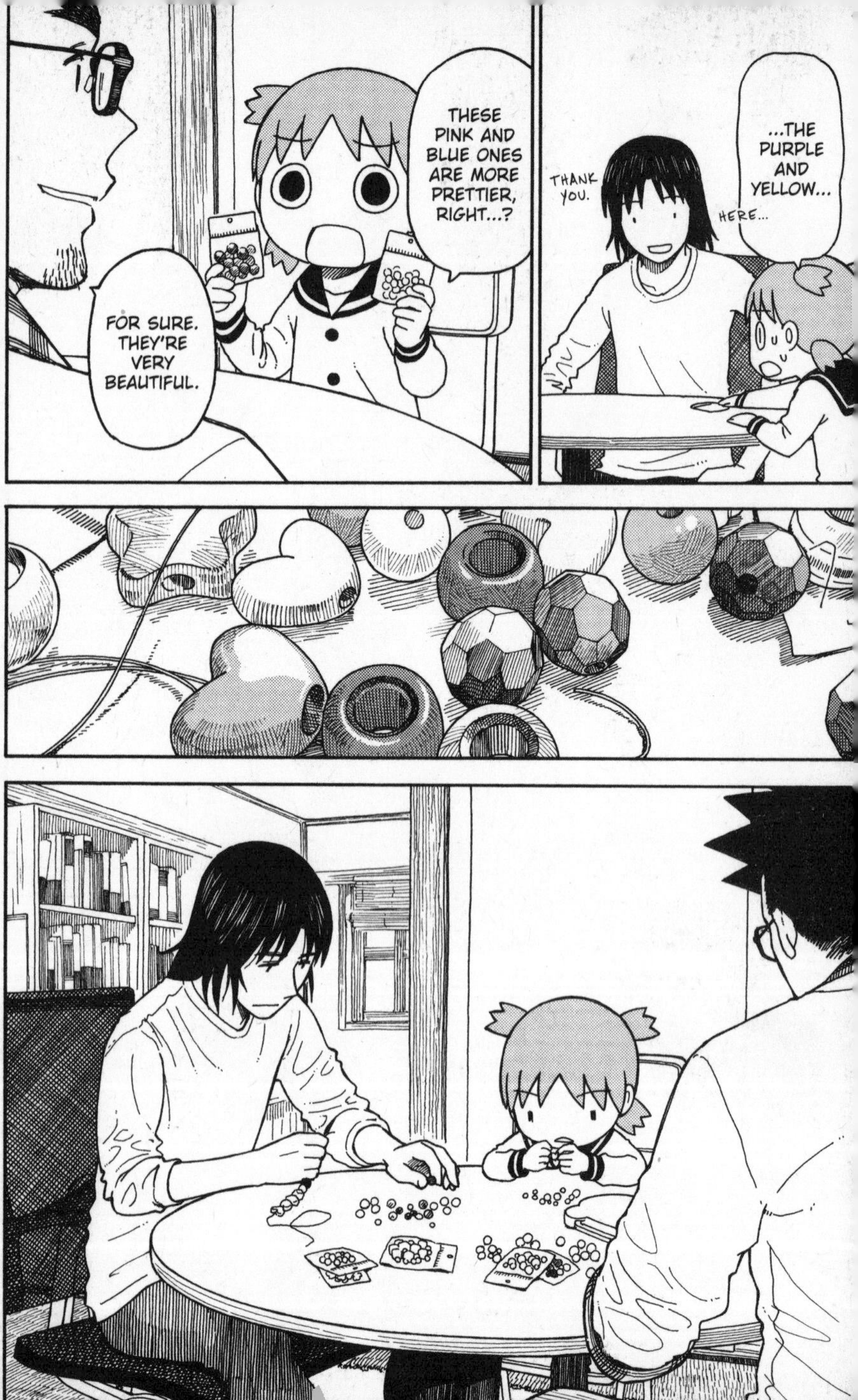
...THE PURPLE AND YELLOW...
HERE...
THANK YOU.
THESE PINK AND BLUE ONES ARE MORE PRETTIER, RIGHT...?
FOR SURE. THEY'RE VERY BEAUTIFUL.

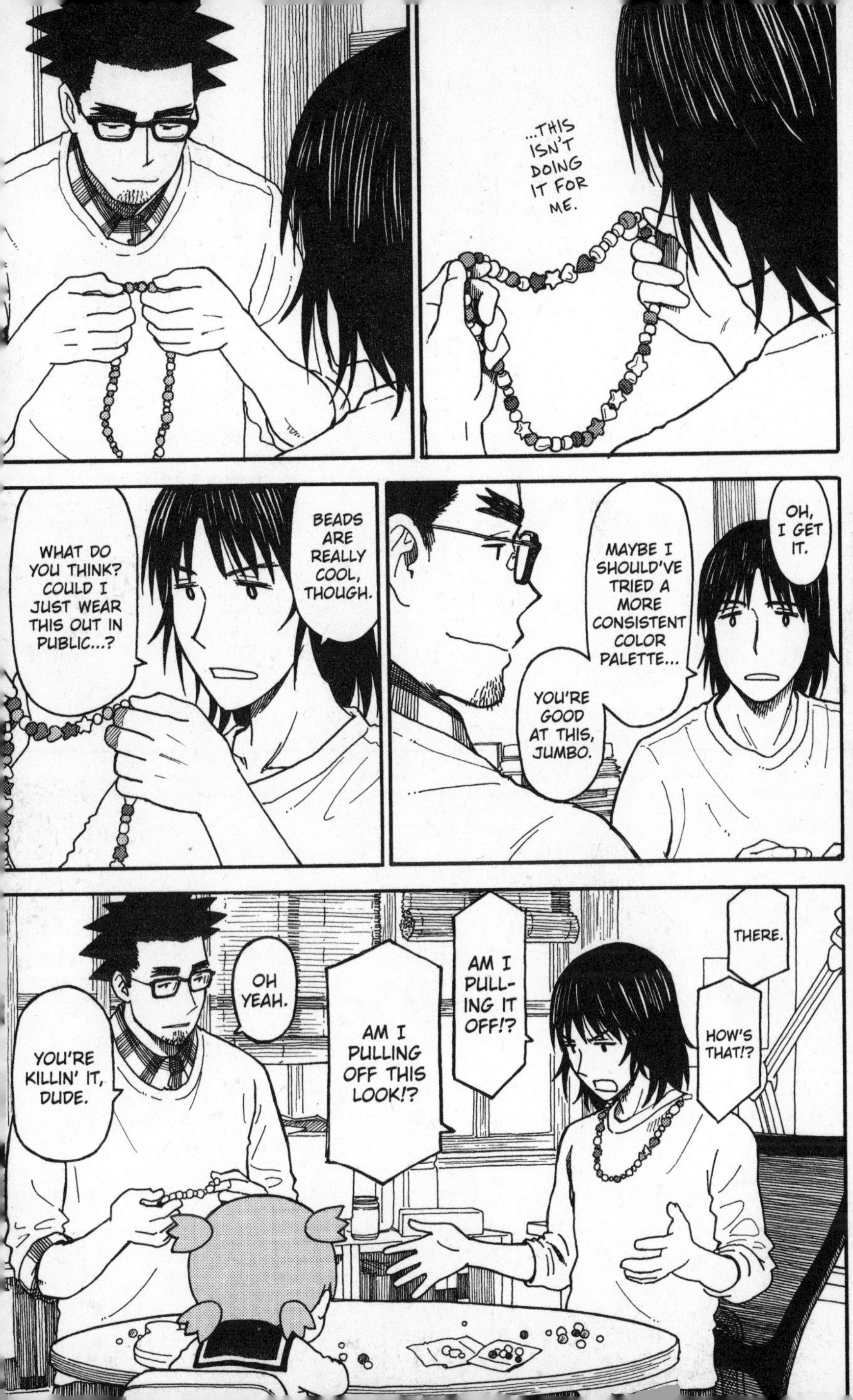
...THIS ISN'T DOING IT FOR ME.
OH, I GET IT.
MAYBE I SHOULD'VE TRIED A MORE CONSISTENT COLOR PALETTE...
YOU'RE GOOD AT THIS, JUMBO.
BEADS ARE REALLY COOL, THOUGH.
WHAT DO YOU THINK? COULD I JUST WEAR THIS OUT IN PUBLIC...?
THERE.
HOW'S THAT!?
AM I PULLING IT OFF!?
AM I PULLING OFF THIS LOOK!?
OH YEAH.
YOU'RE KILLIN' IT, DUDE.

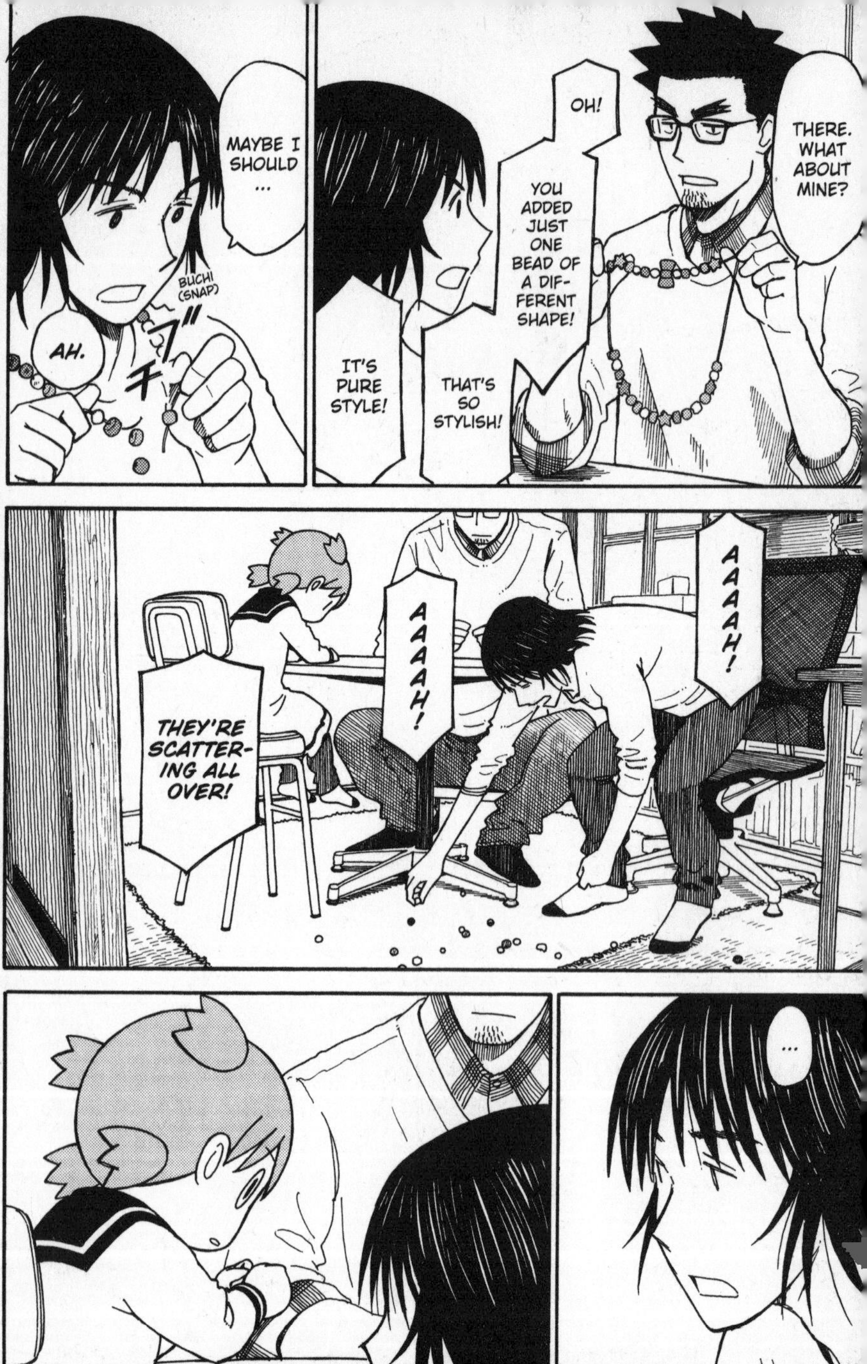
THERE. WHAT ABOUT MINE?
OH!
YOU ADDED JUST ONE BEAD OF A DIF-FERENT SHAPE!
THAT'S SO STYLISH!
IT'S PURE STYLE!
MAYBE I SHOULD ...
BUCHI (SNAP)
AH.
AAAAH!
AAAAH!
THEY'RE SCATTER-ING ALL OVER!
...

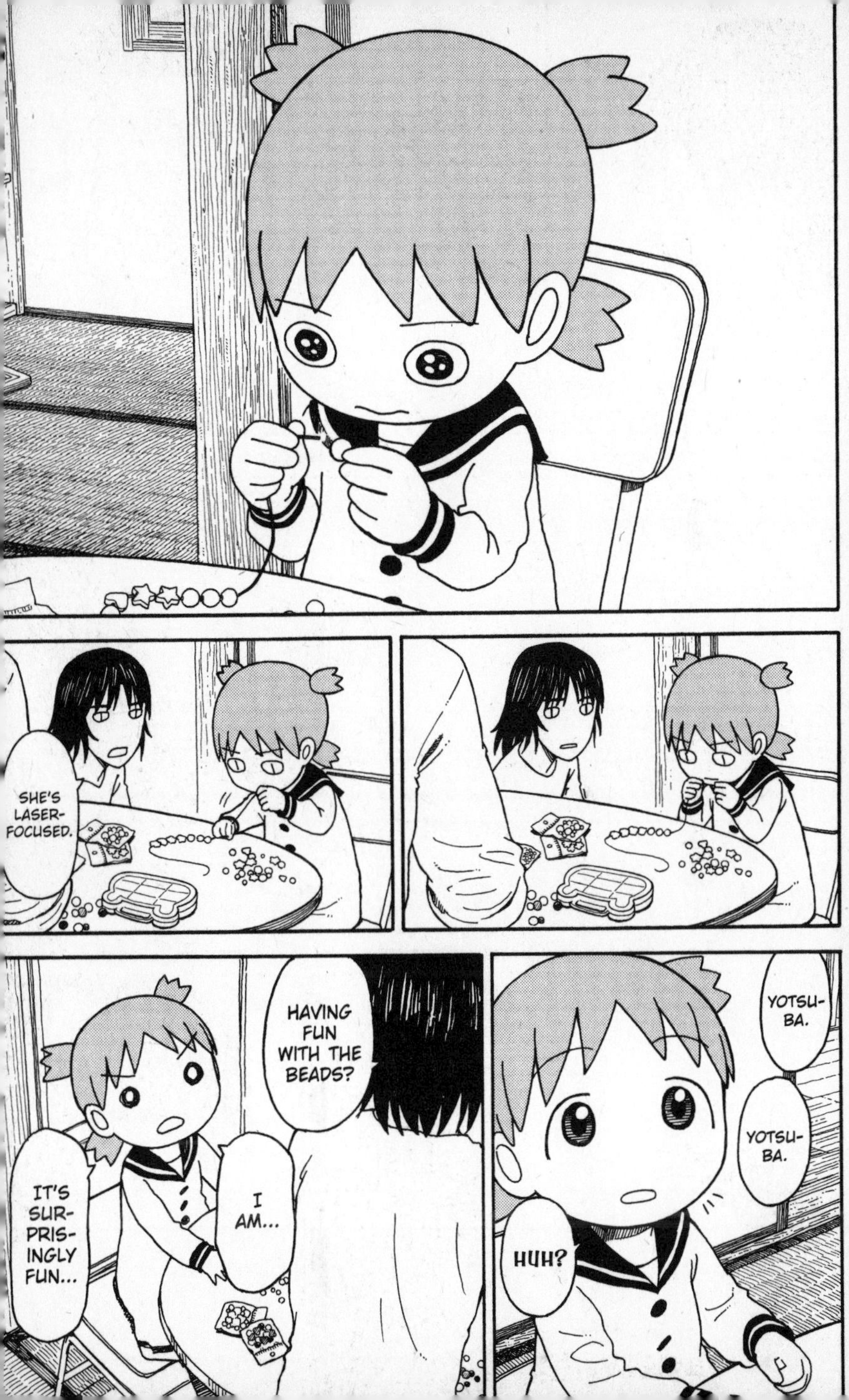
SHE'S LASER-FOCUSED.
YOTSU-BA.
YOTSU-BA.
HUH?
HAVING FUN WITH THE BEADS?
I AM...
IT'S SURPRISINGLY FUN...

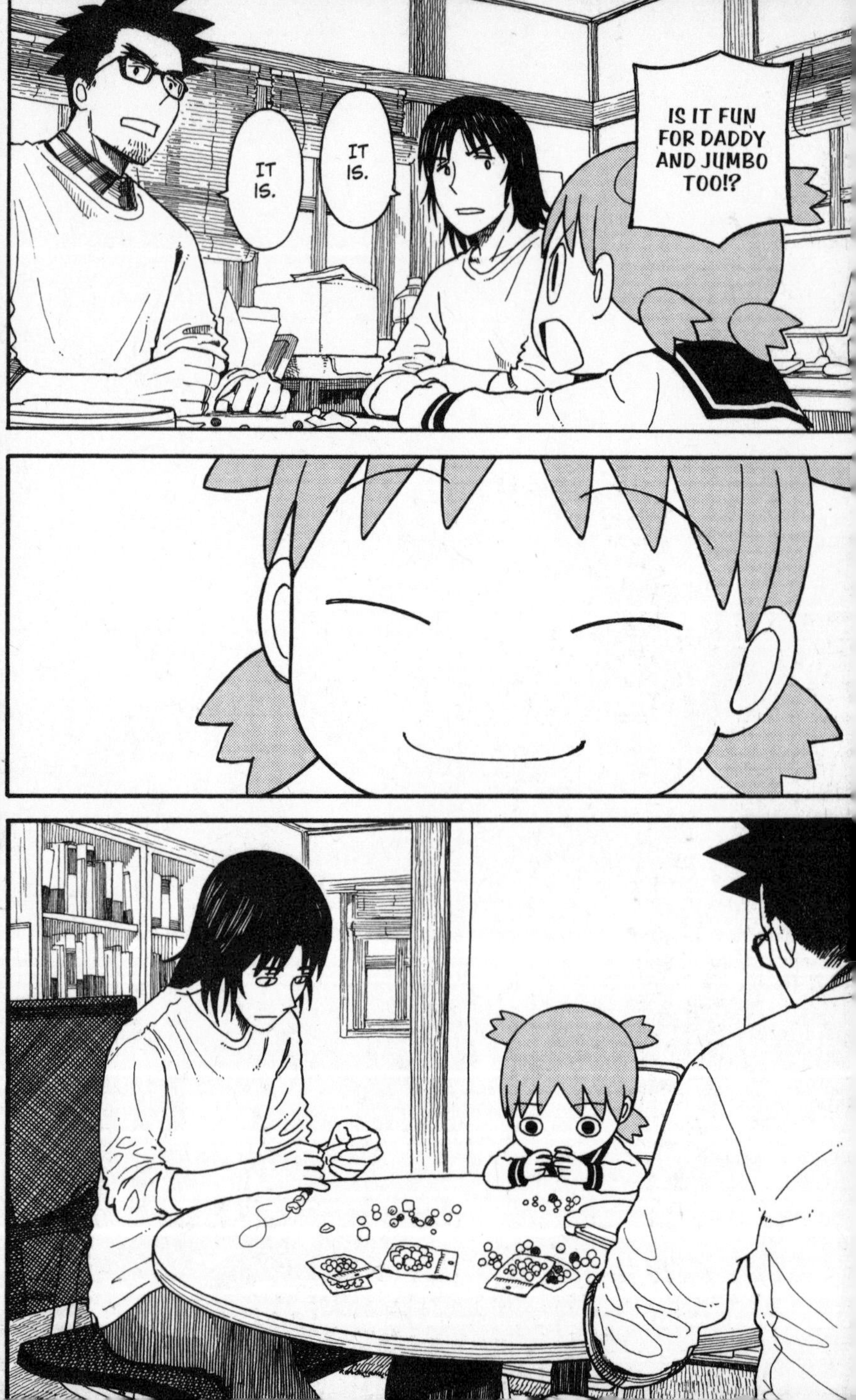
IS IT FUN FOR DADDY AND JUMBO TOO!?
IT IS.
IT IS.

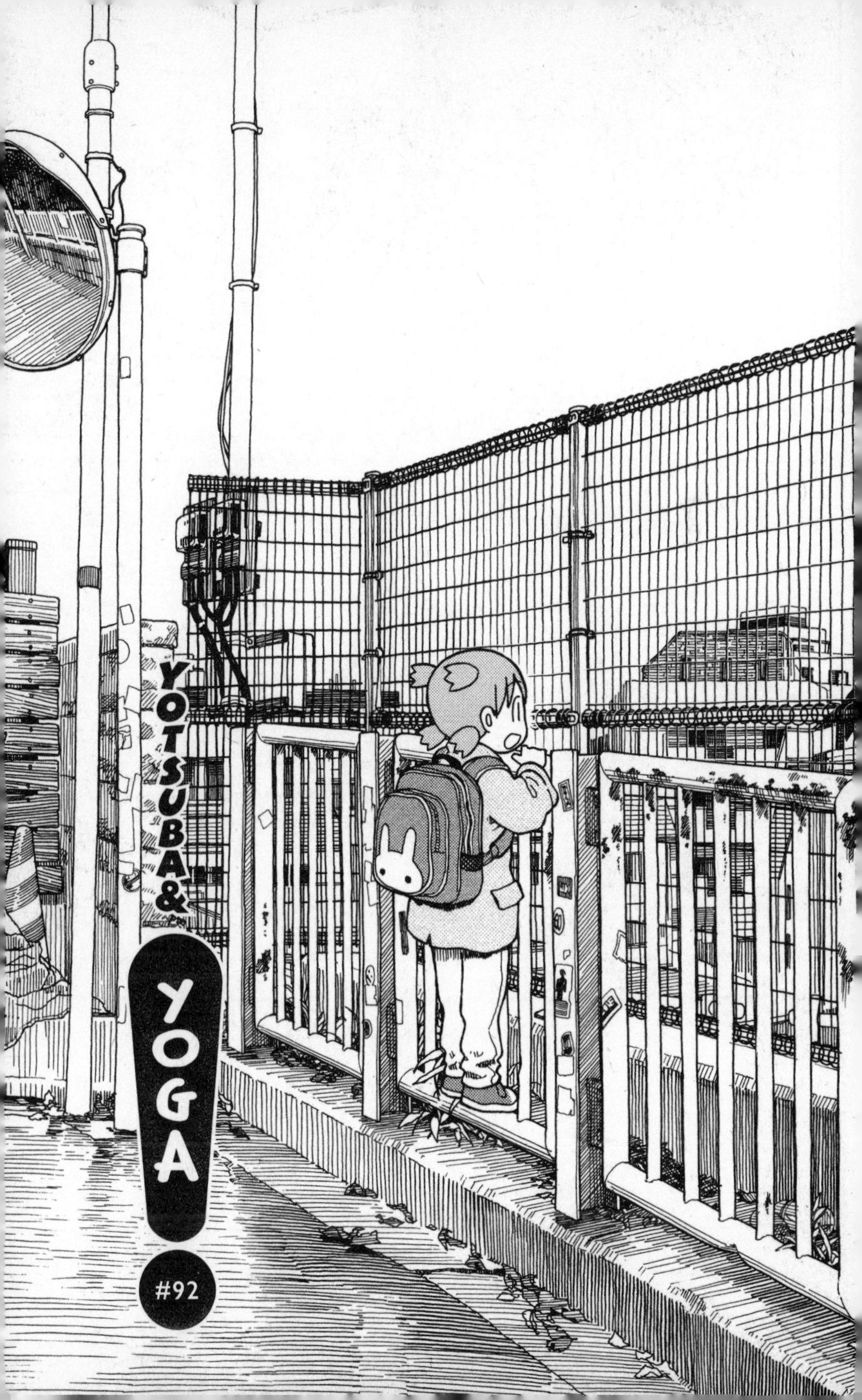
YOTSUBA&
YOGA
#92

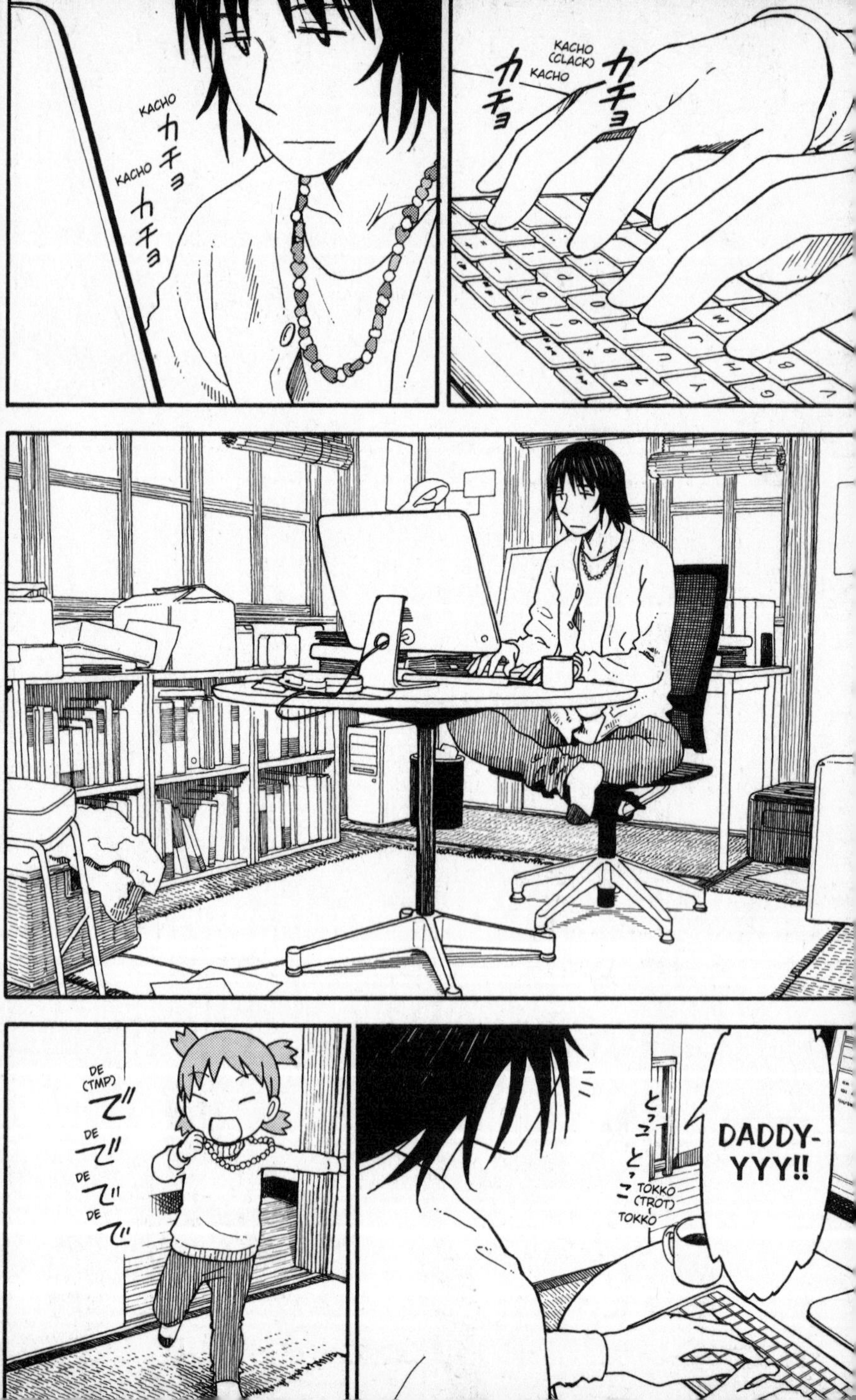
KACHO (CLACK)
カチョ
KACHO
カチョ
KACHO
カチョ
KACHO
カチョ
DADDY-YYY!!
とっこ
とっこ
TOKKO (TROT) TOKKO
DE (TMP)
で
DE
で
DE
で
DE
で

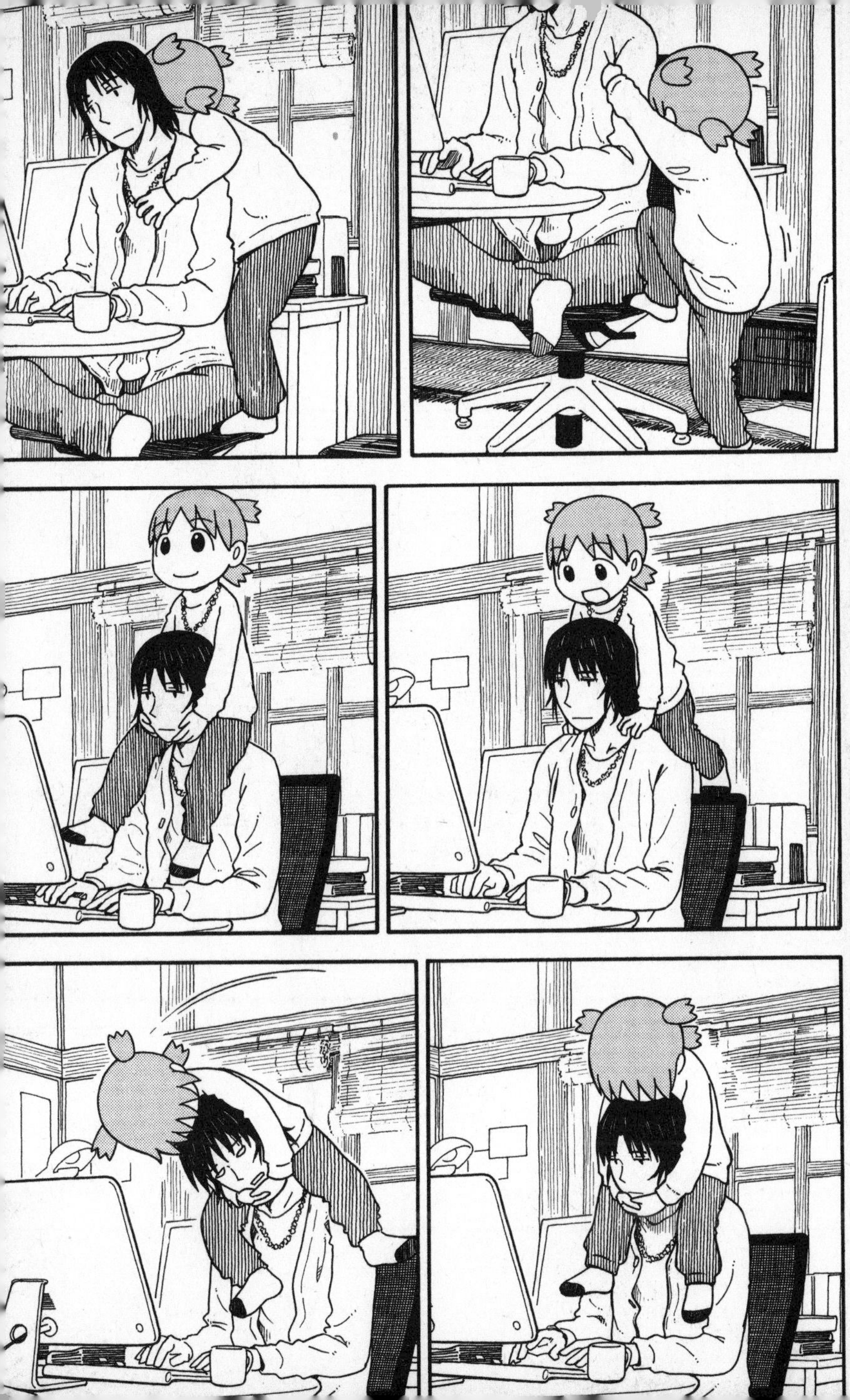

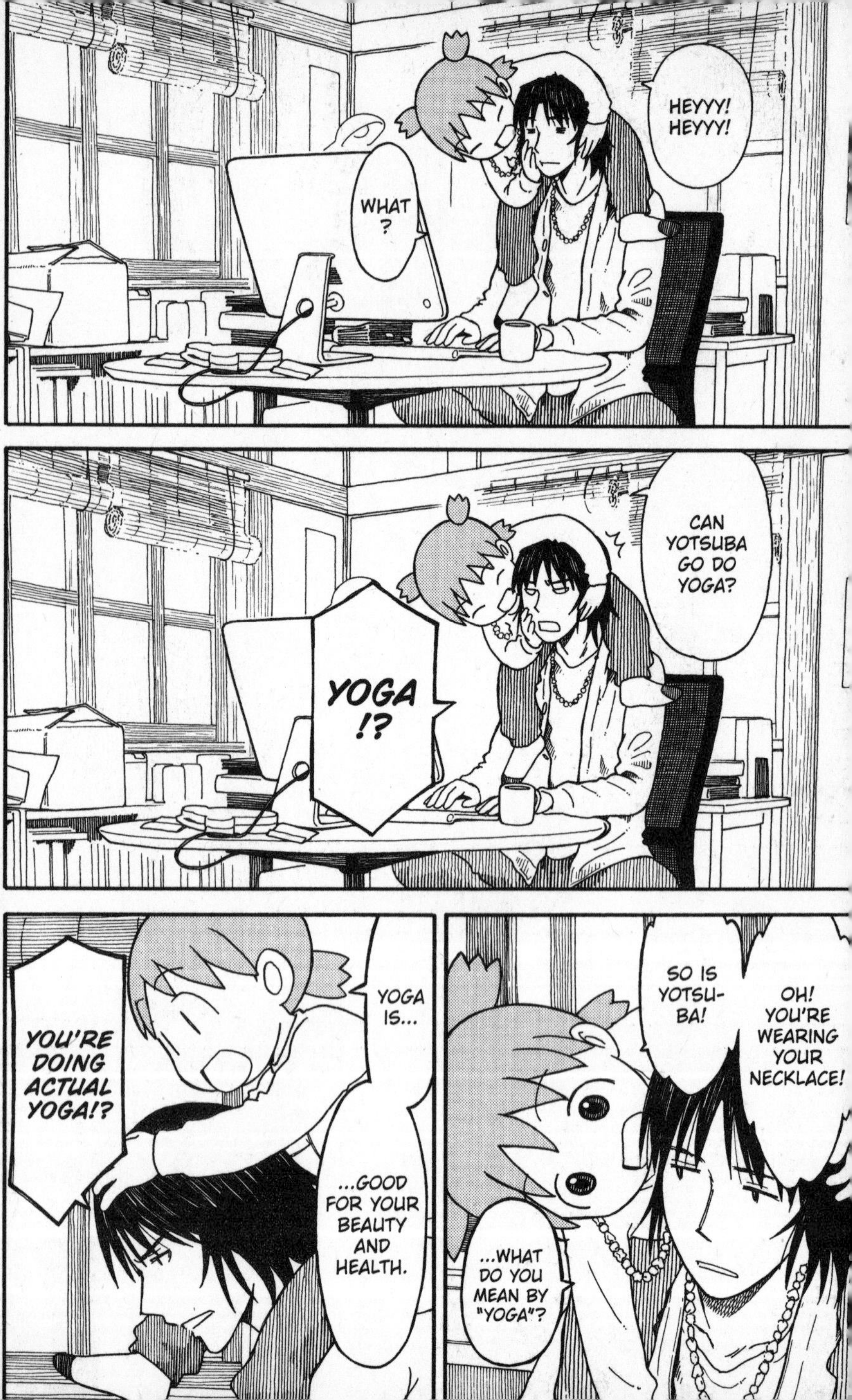
HEYYY! HEYYY!
WHAT?
CAN YOTSUBA GO DO YOGA?
YOGA!?
OH! YOU'RE WEARING YOUR NECKLACE!
SO IS YOTSU-BA!
...WHAT DO YOU MEAN BY "YOGA"?
YOGA IS...
...GOOD FOR YOUR BEAUTY AND HEALTH.
YOU'RE DOING ACTUAL YOGA!?

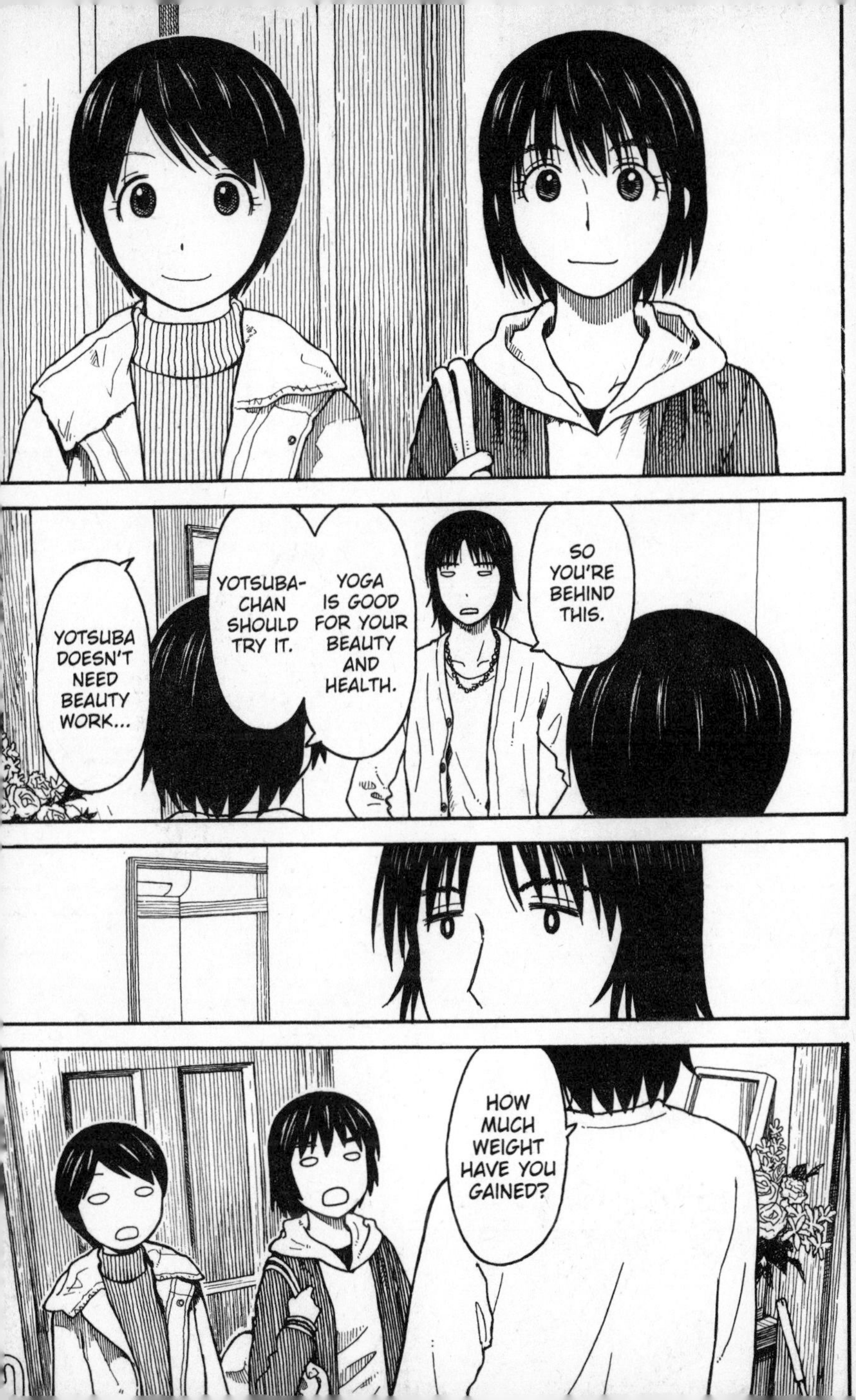
SO YOU'RE BEHIND THIS.
YOGA IS GOOD FOR YOUR BEAUTY AND HEALTH.
YOTSUBA-CHAN SHOULD TRY IT.
YOTSUBA DOESN'T NEED BEAUTY WORK...
HOW MUCH WEIGHT HAVE YOU GAINED?

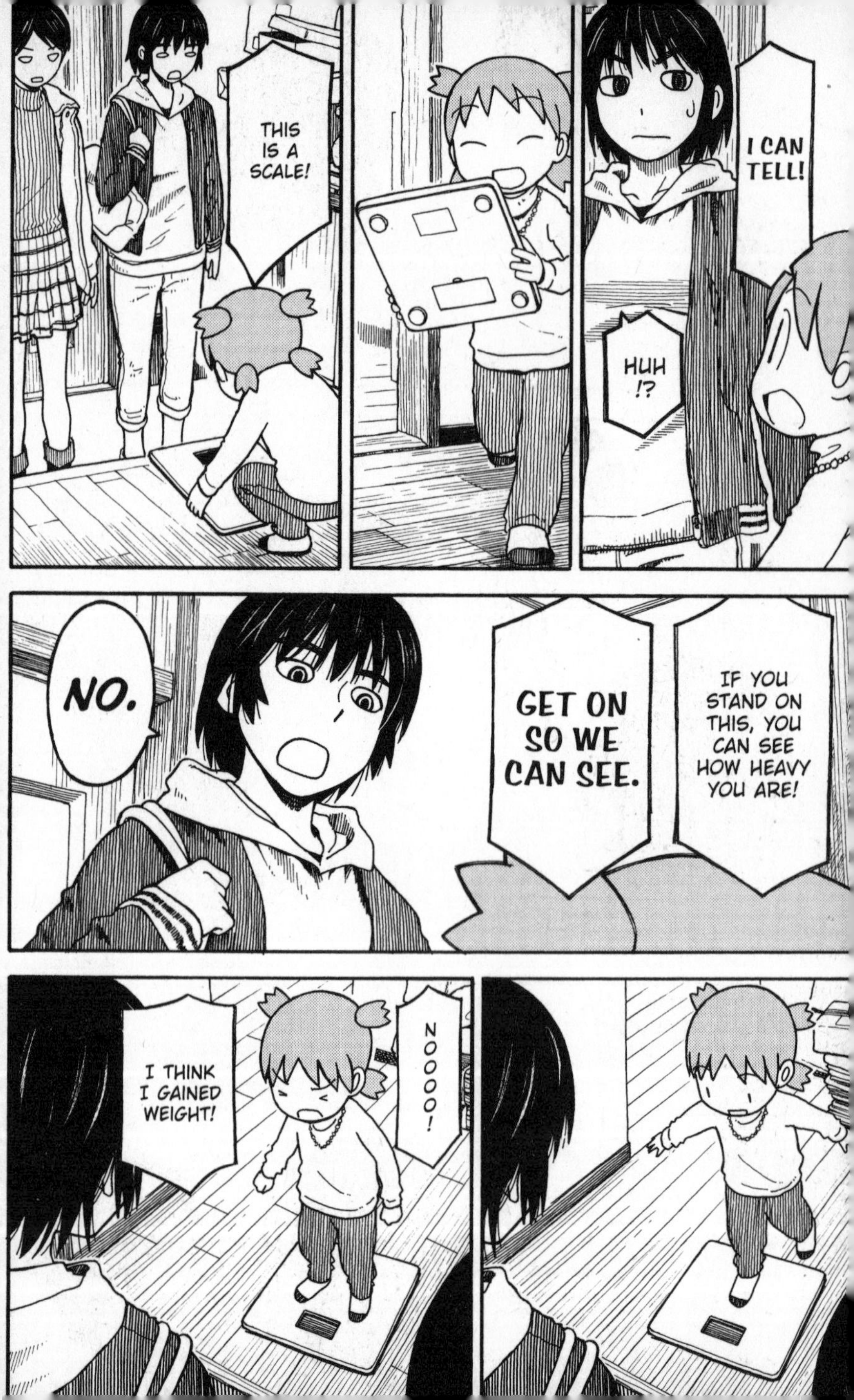
I CAN TELL!
HUH!?
THIS IS A SCALE!
IF YOU STAND ON THIS, YOU CAN SEE HOW HEAVY YOU ARE!
GET ON SO WE CAN SEE.
NO.
NOOOO!
I THINK I GAINED WEIGHT!

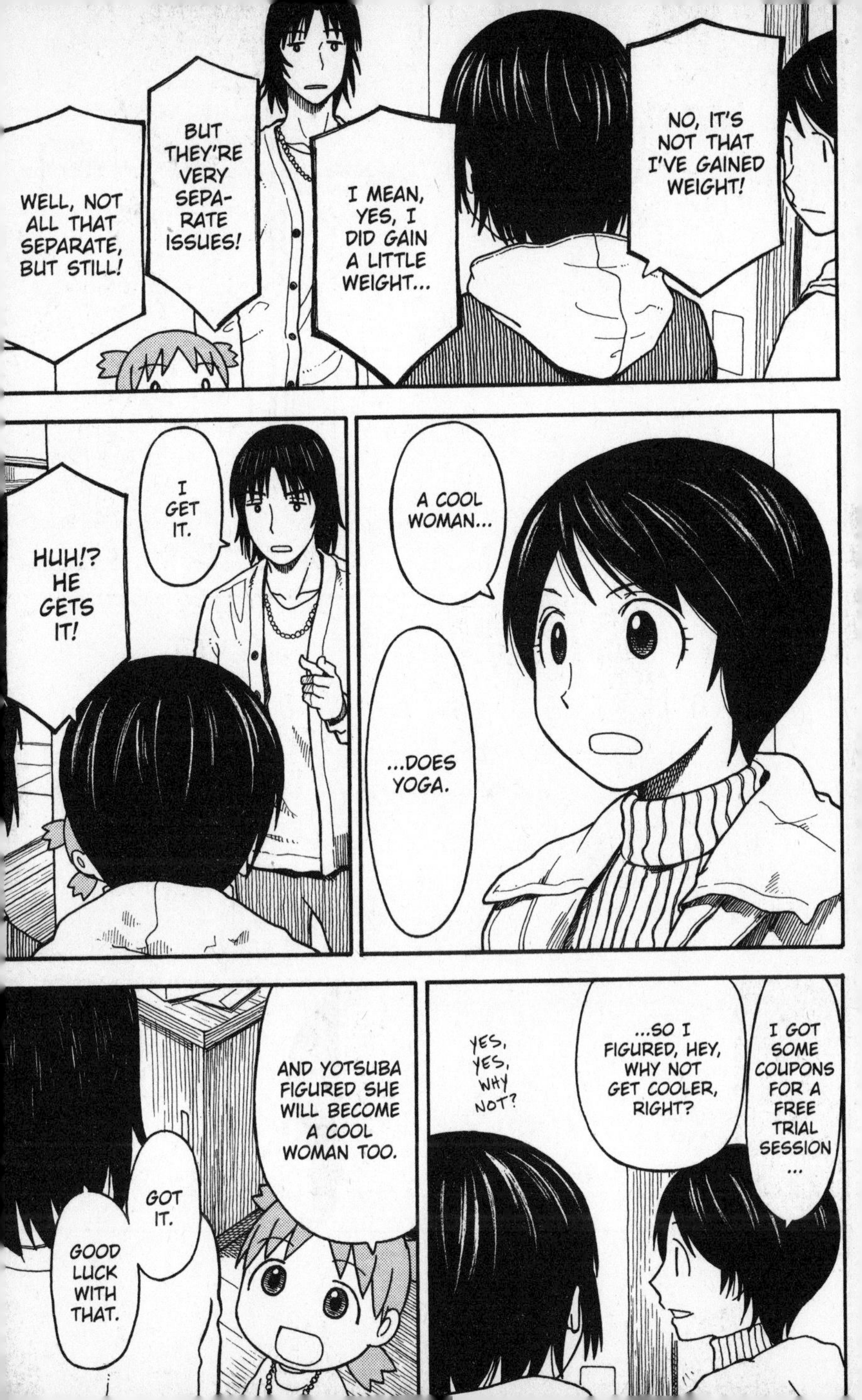
NO, IT'S NOT THAT I'VE GAINED WEIGHT!
I MEAN, YES, I DID GAIN A LITTLE WEIGHT...
BUT THEY'RE VERY SEPA-RATE ISSUES!
WELL, NOT ALL THAT SEPARATE, BUT STILL!
A COOL WOMAN...
...DOES YOGA.
I GET IT.
HUH!? HE GETS IT!
I GOT SOME COUPONS FOR A FREE TRIAL SESSION...
...SO I FIGURED, HEY, WHY NOT GET COOLER, RIGHT?
YES, YES, WHY NOT?
AND YOTSUBA FIGURED SHE WILL BECOME A COOL WOMAN TOO.
GOT IT.
GOOD LUCK WITH THAT.

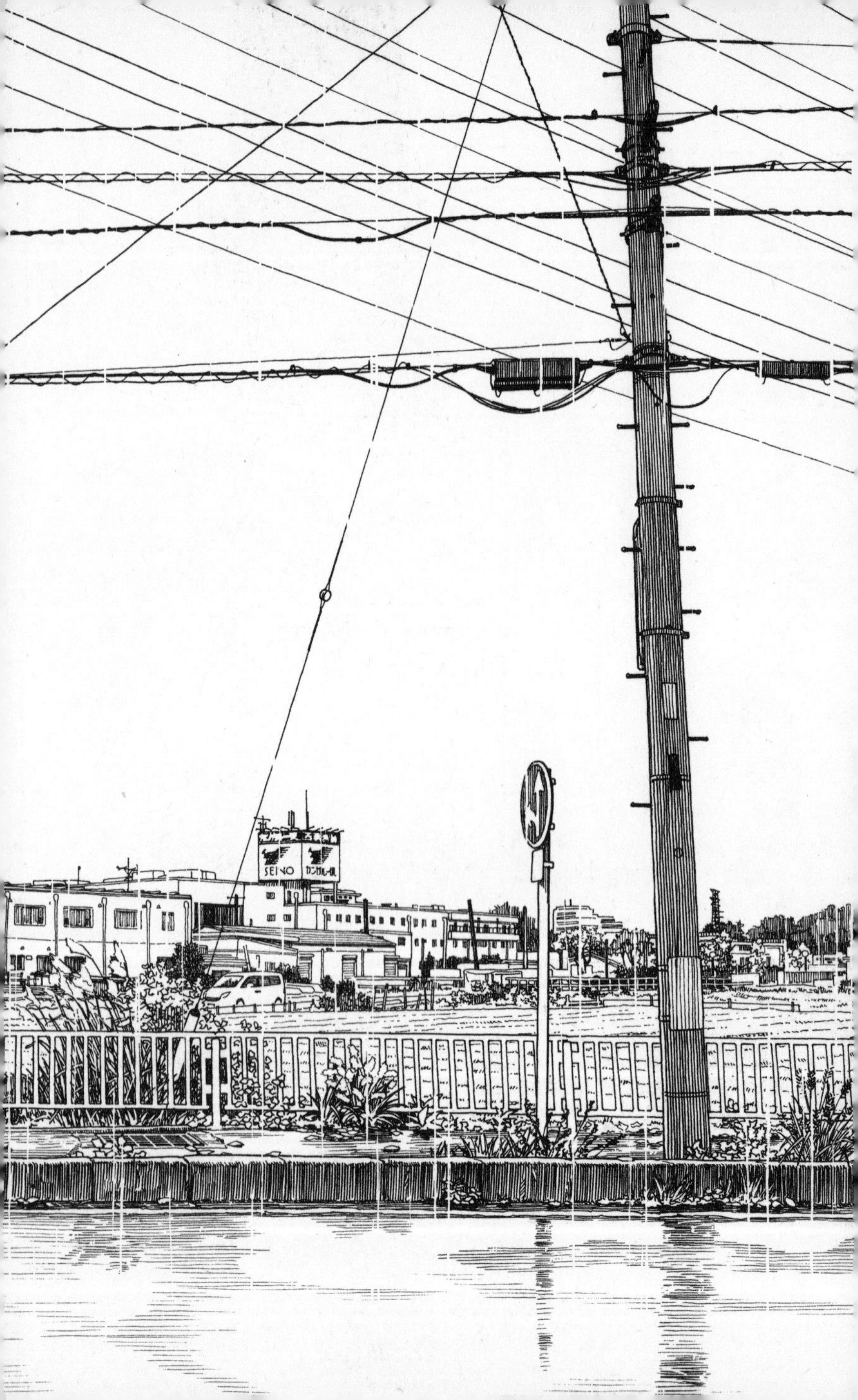
SEINO
カンガルー便

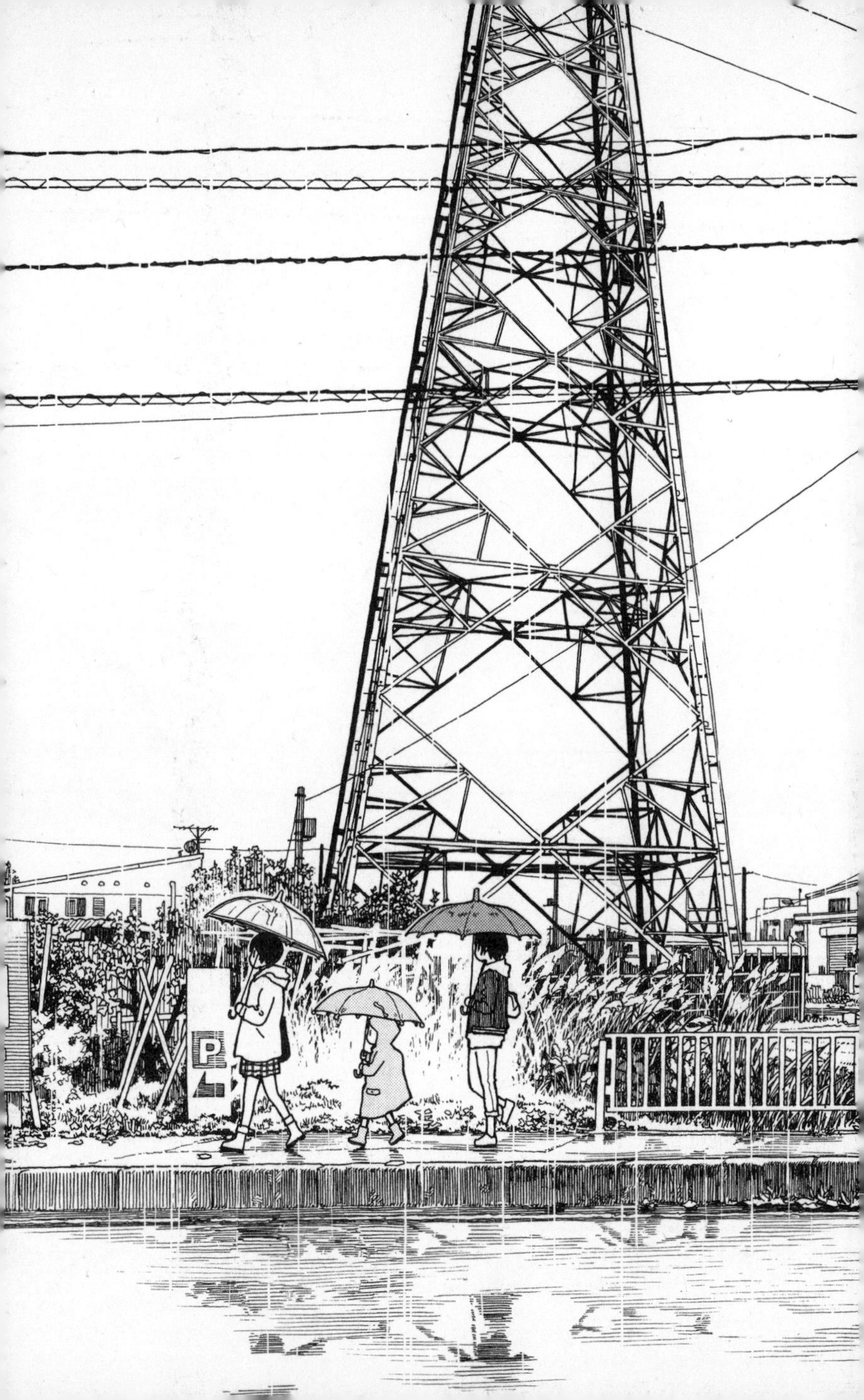
P

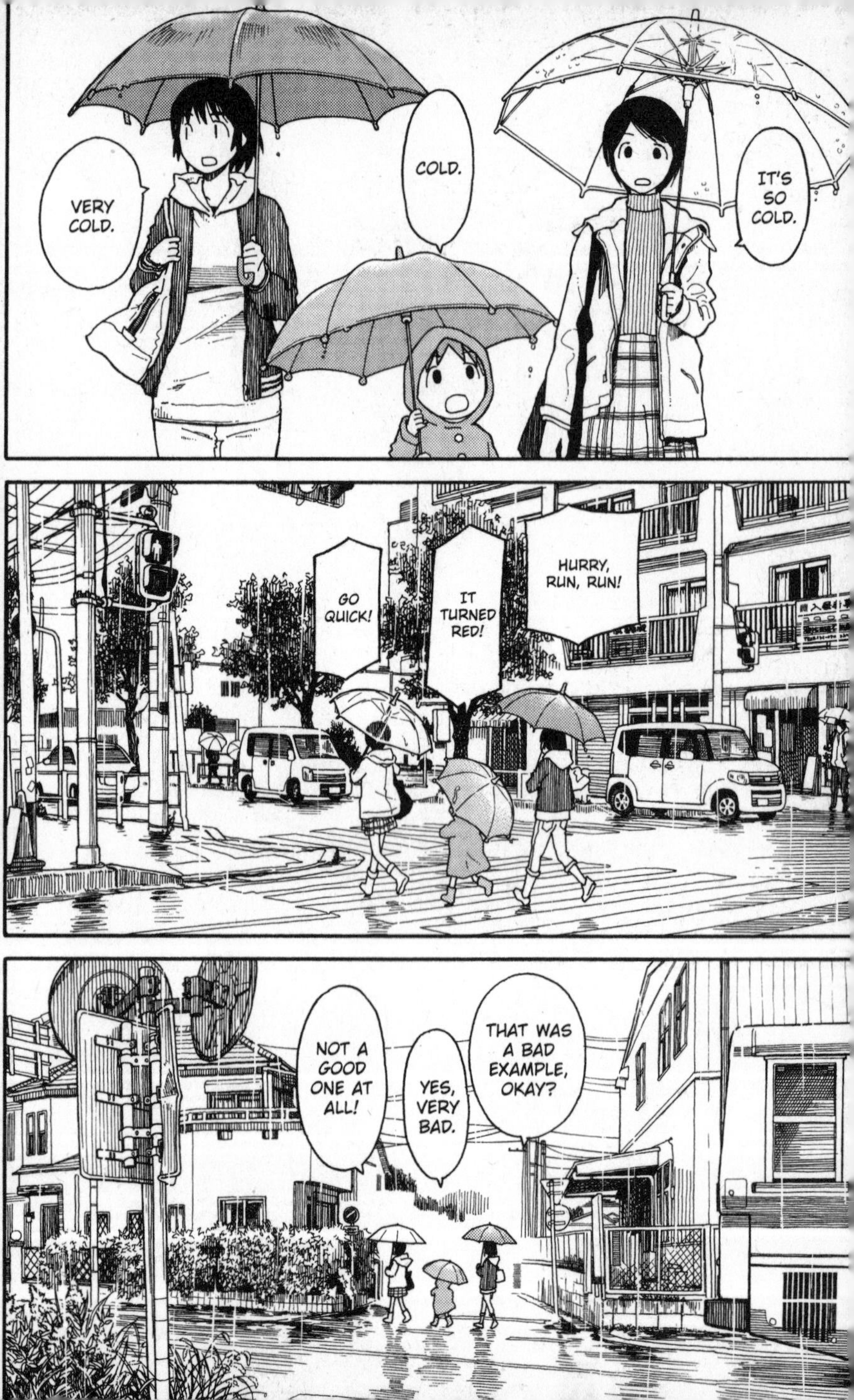
IT'S SO COLD.
COLD.
VERY COLD.
HURRY, RUN, RUN!
IT TURNED RED!
GO QUICK!
THAT WAS A BAD EXAMPLE, OKAY?
YES, VERY BAD.
NOT A GOOD ONE AT ALL!

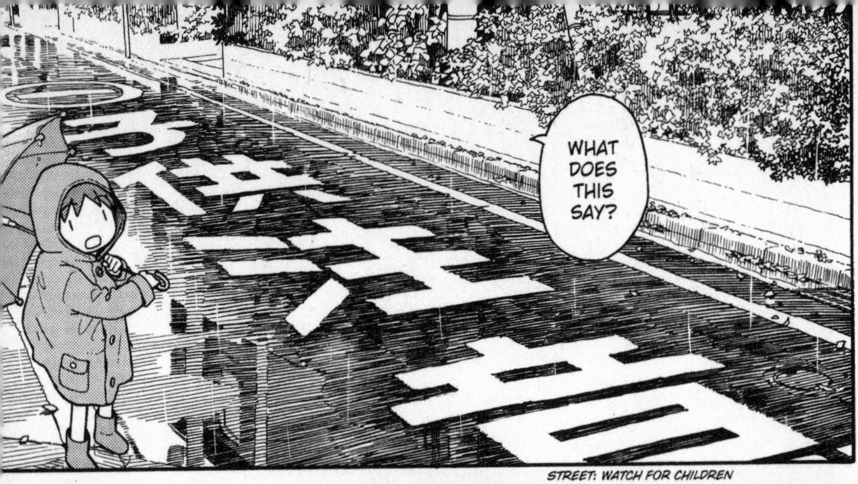
WHAT DOES THIS SAY?

STREET: WATCH FOR CHILDREN

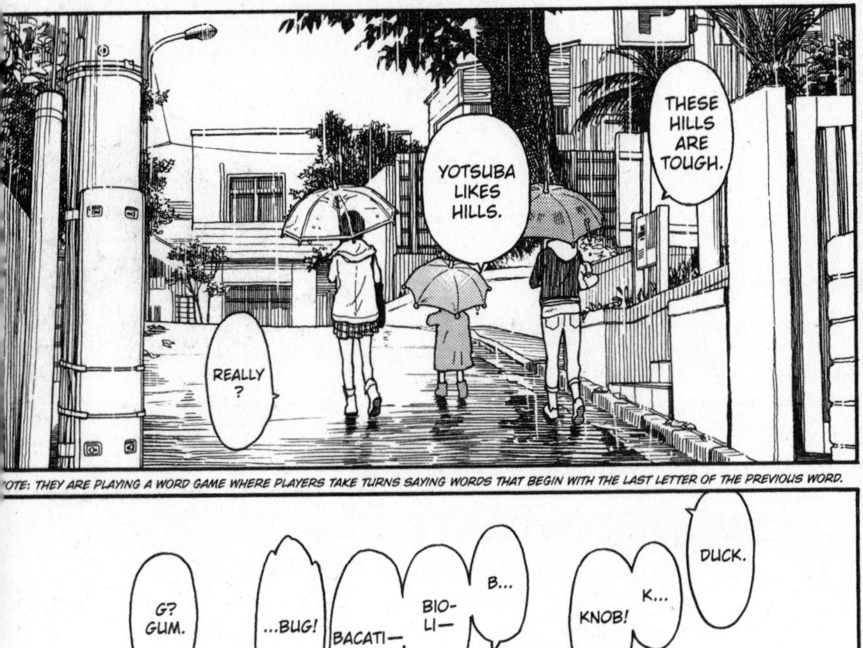
THESE HILLS ARE TOUGH.
YOTSUBA LIKES HILLS.
REALLY?

OTE: THEY ARE PLAYING A WORD GAME WHERE PLAYERS TAKE TURNS SAYING WORDS THAT BEGIN WITH THE LAST LETTER OF THE PREVIOUS WORD.

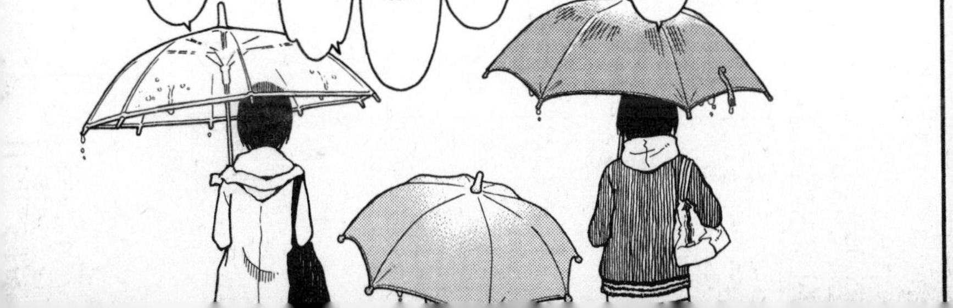
DUCK.
K...
KNOB!
B...
BIO-LI—
BACATI-NO...
...BUG!
G? GUM.

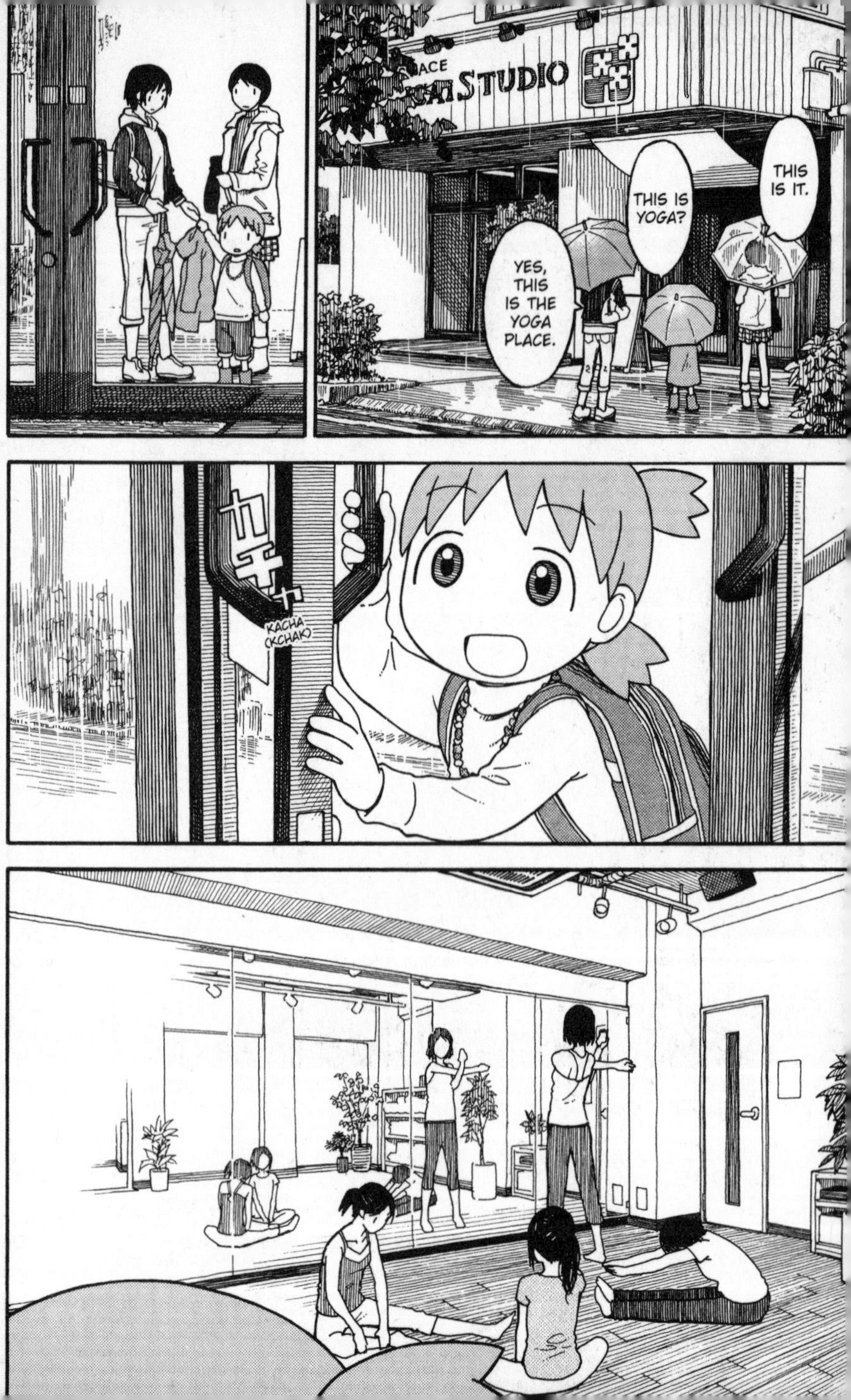
STUDIO
THIS IS IT.
THIS IS YOGA?
YES, THIS IS THE YOGA PLACE.
カチャ
KACHA (KCHAK)

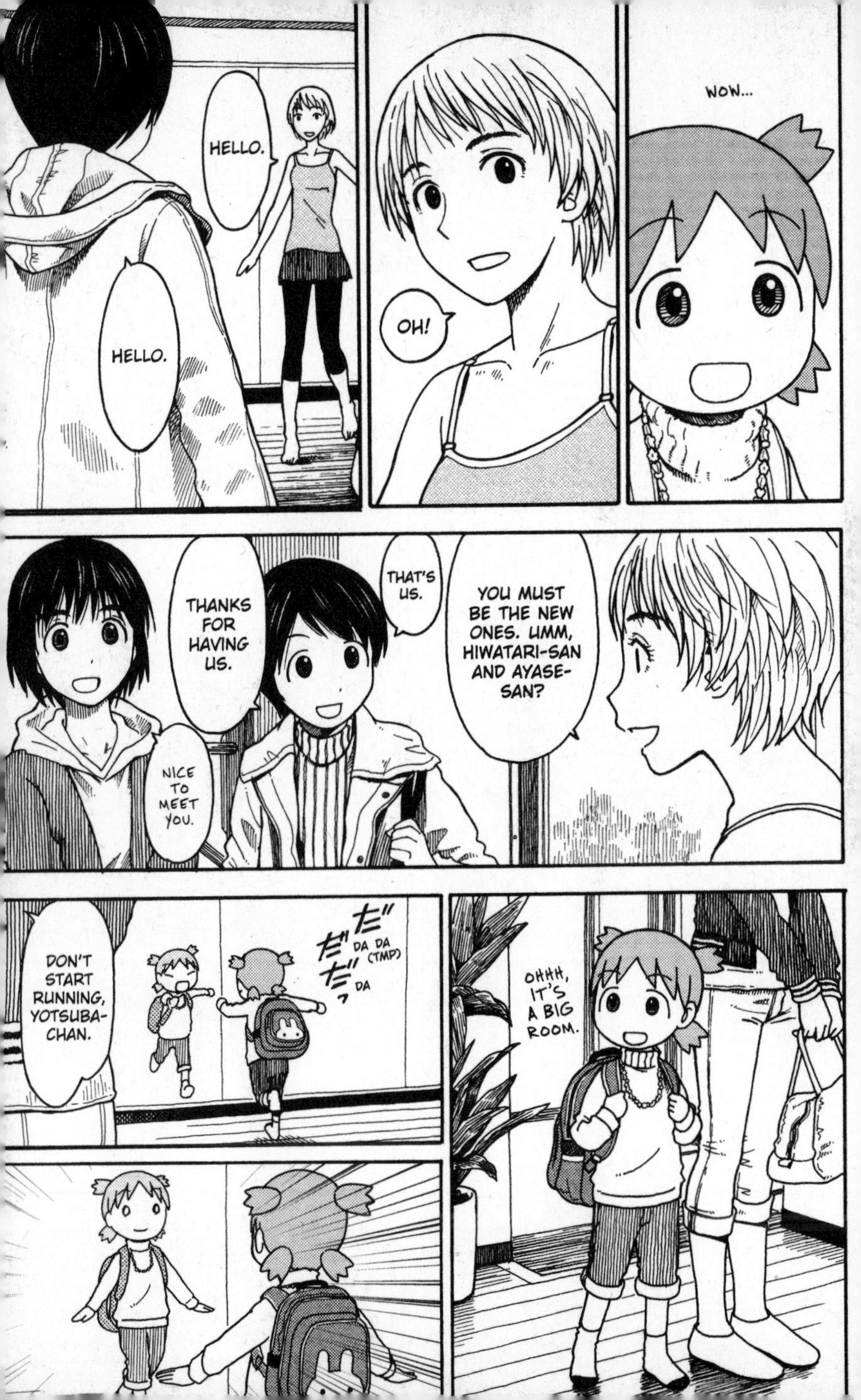
WOW...
OH!
HELLO.
HELLO.
YOU MUST BE THE NEW ONES. UMM, HIWATARI-SAN AND AYASE-SAN?
THAT'S US.
THANKS FOR HAVING US.
NICE TO MEET YOU.
OHHH, IT'S A BIG ROOM.
DA DA (TMP) DA
DON'T START RUNNING, YOTSUBA-CHAN.

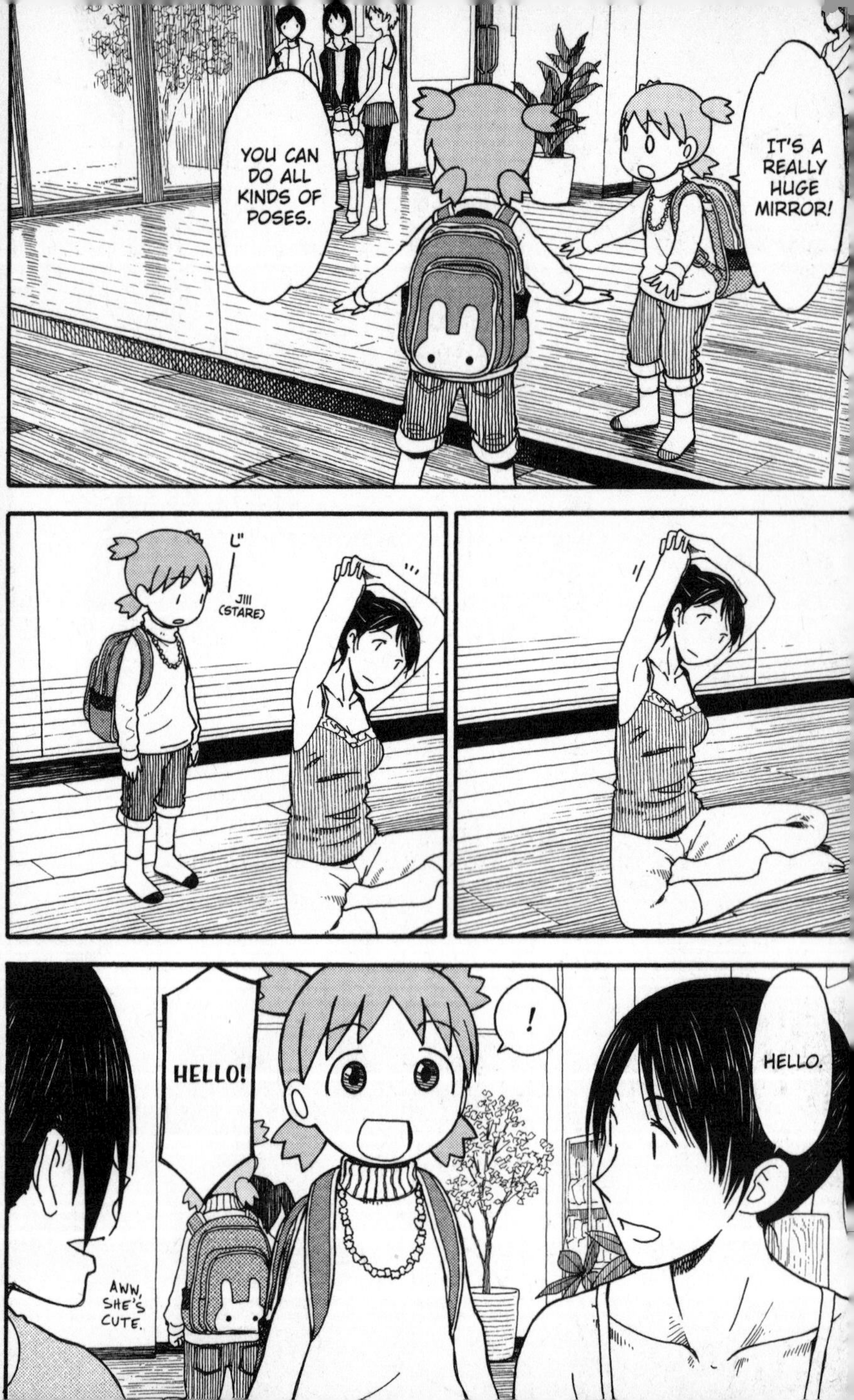
IT'S A REALLY HUGE MIRROR!
YOU CAN DO ALL KINDS OF POSES.
じ
JIII (STARE)
HELLO.
!
HELLO!
AWW, SHE'S CUTE.

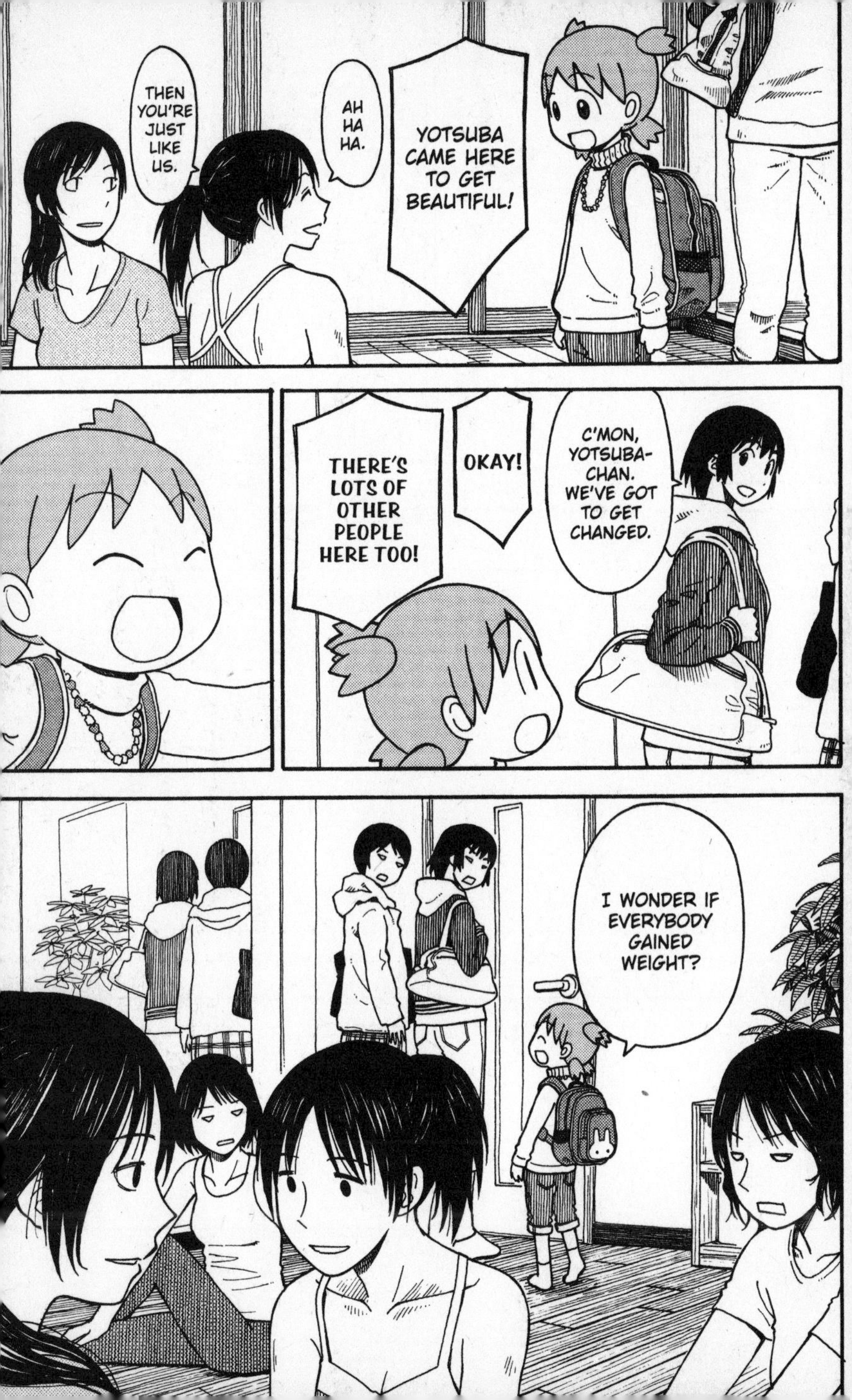
YOTSUBA CAME HERE TO GET BEAUTIFUL!
AH HA HA.
THEN YOU'RE JUST LIKE US.
C'MON, YOTSUBA-CHAN. WE'VE GOT TO GET CHANGED.
OKAY!
THERE'S LOTS OF OTHER PEOPLE HERE TOO!
I WONDER IF EVERYBODY GAINED WEIGHT?

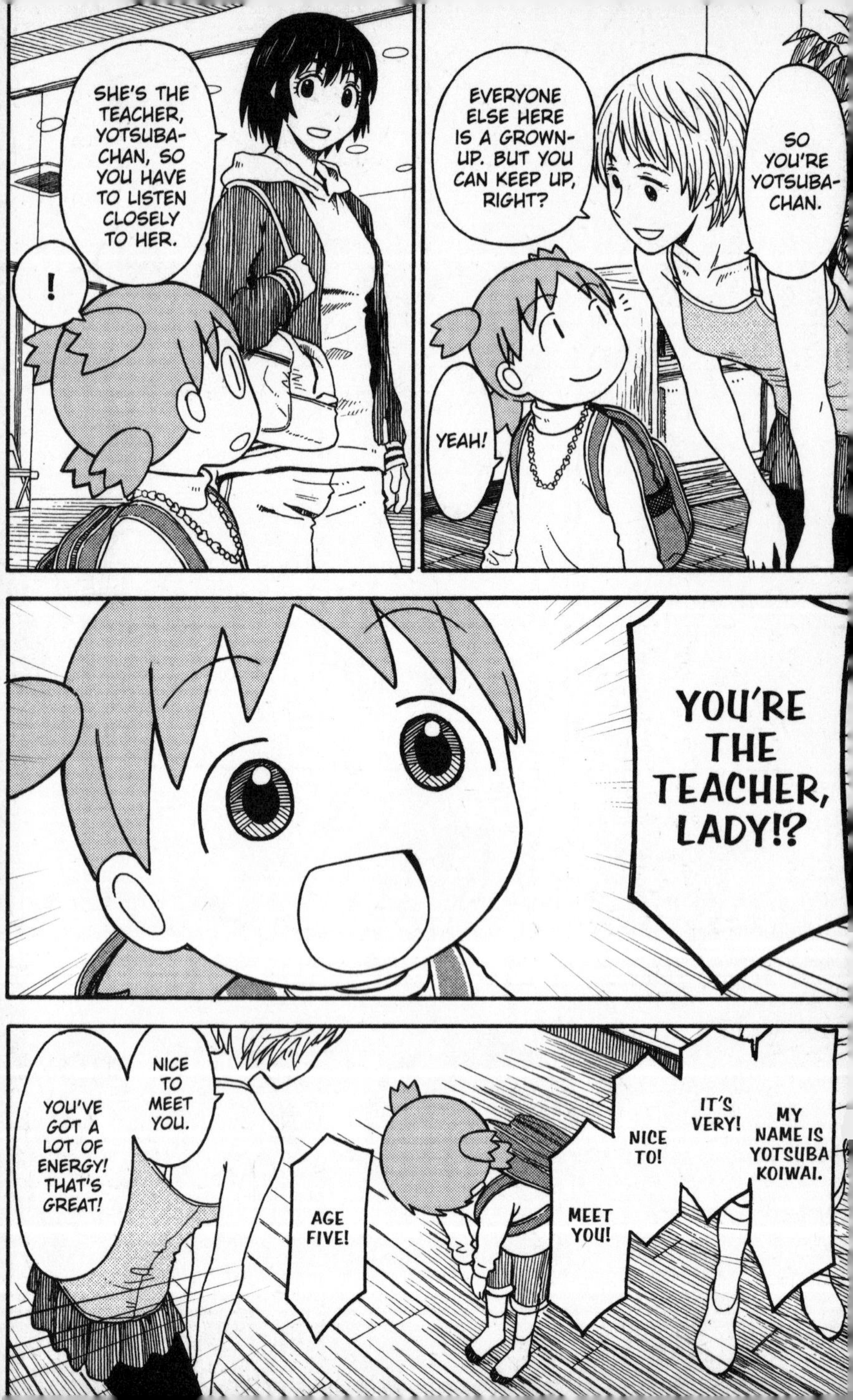
SO YOU'RE YOTSUBA-CHAN.
EVERYONE ELSE HERE IS A GROWN-UP. BUT YOU CAN KEEP UP, RIGHT?
YEAH!
SHE'S THE TEACHER, YOTSUBA-CHAN, SO YOU HAVE TO LISTEN CLOSELY TO HER.
!
YOU'RE THE TEACHER, LADY!?
MY NAME IS YOTSUBA KOIWAI.
IT'S VERY!
NICE TO!
MEET YOU!
AGE FIVE!
NICE TO MEET YOU.
YOU'VE GOT A LOT OF ENERGY! THAT'S GREAT!

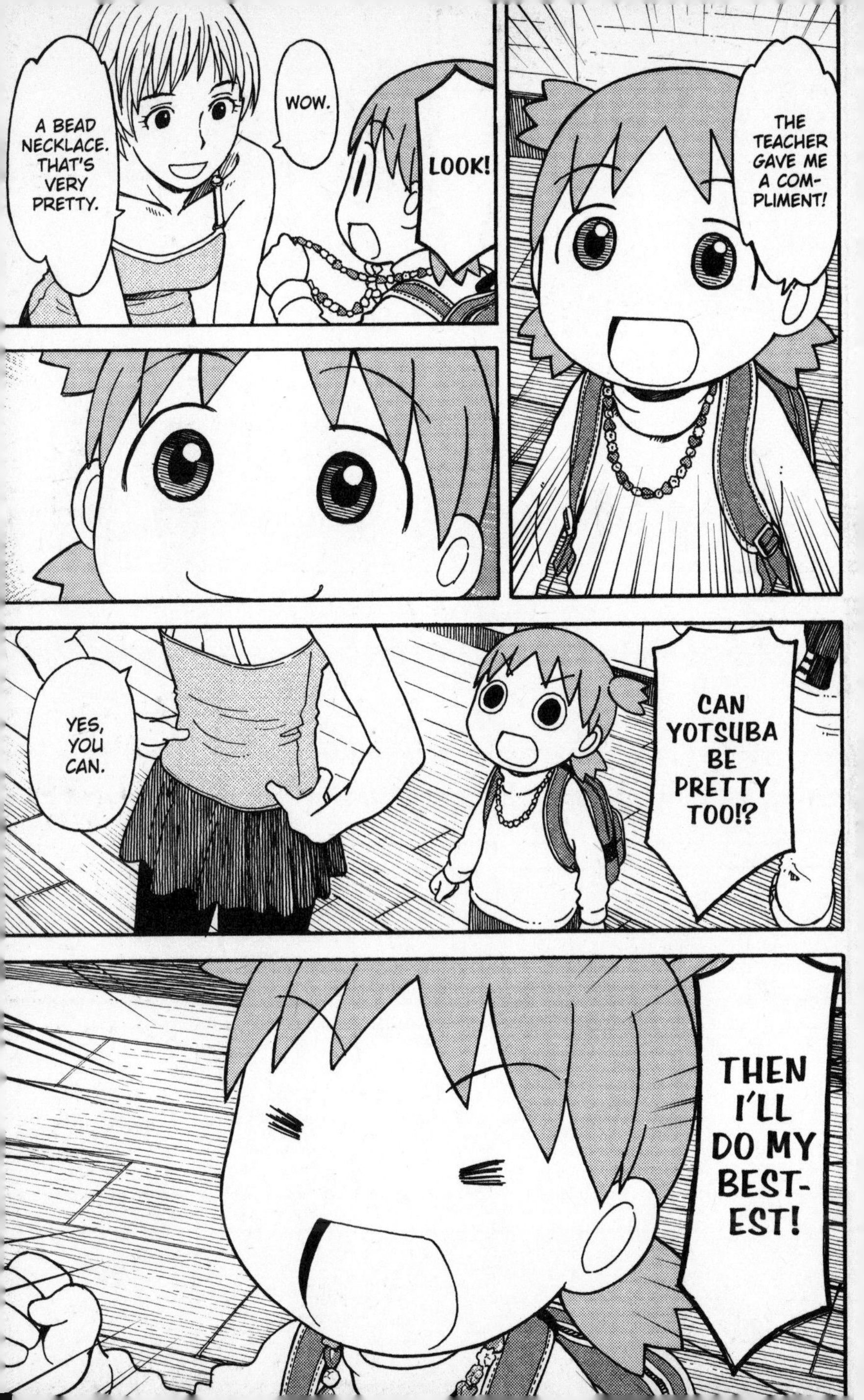
THE TEACHER GAVE ME A COM-PLIMENT!
LOOK!
WOW.
A BEAD NECKLACE. THAT'S VERY PRETTY.
CAN YOTSUBA BE PRETTY TOO!?
YES, YOU CAN.
THEN I'LL DO MY BEST-EST!

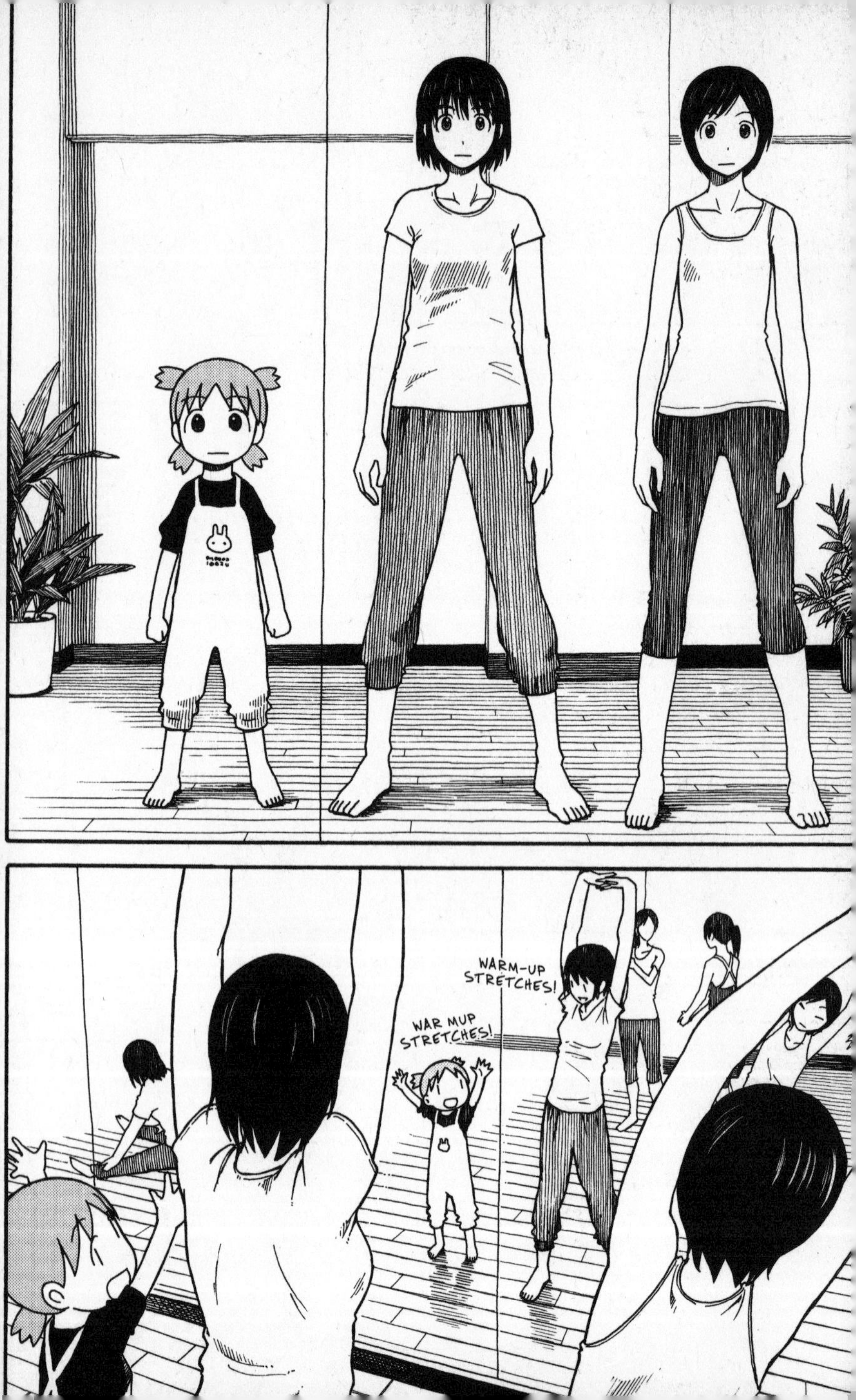
WARM-UP STRETCHES!
WAR MUP STRETCHES!

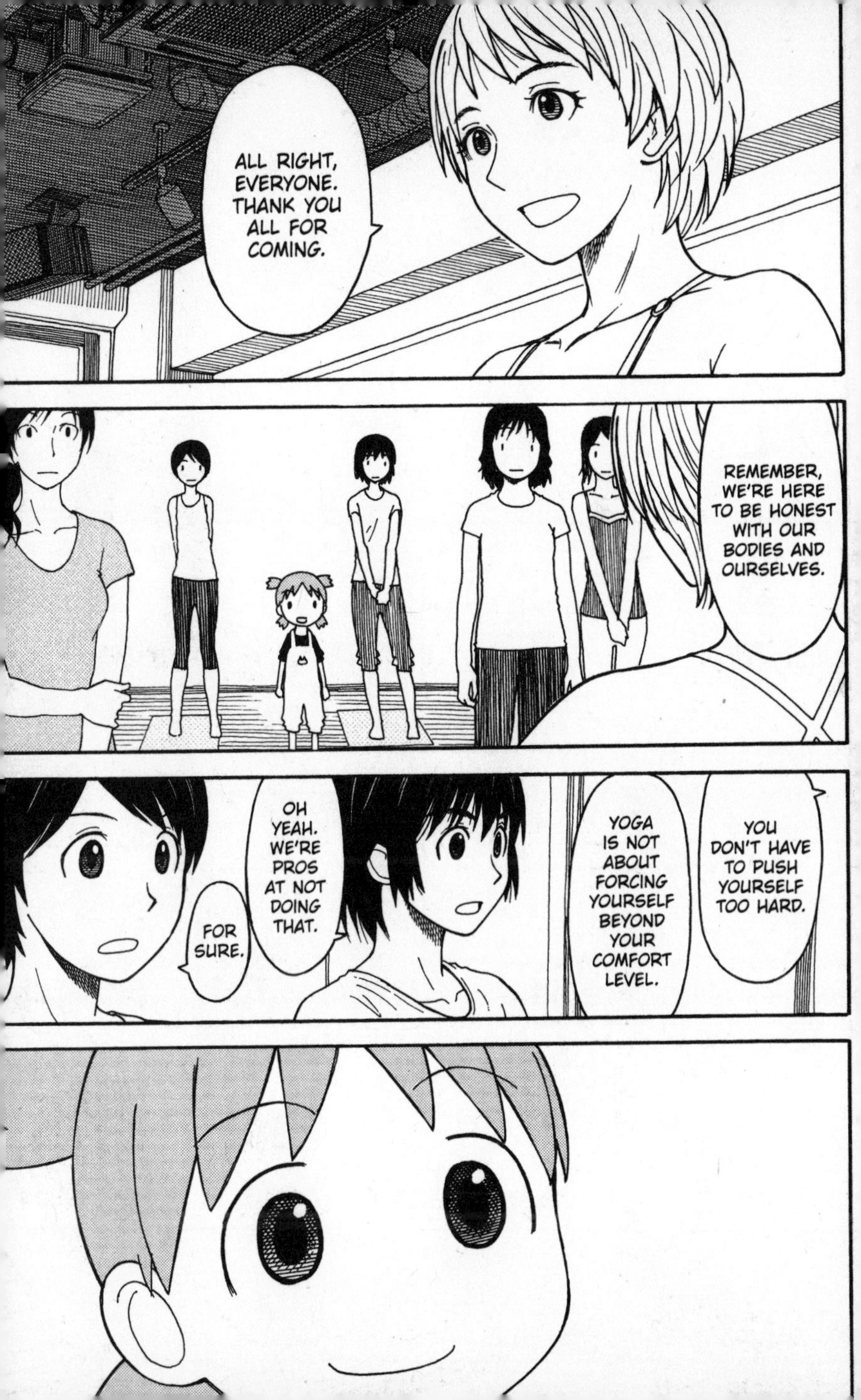
ALL RIGHT, EVERYONE. THANK YOU ALL FOR COMING.
REMEMBER, WE'RE HERE TO BE HONEST WITH OUR BODIES AND OURSELVES.
YOU DON'T HAVE TO PUSH YOURSELF TOO HARD.
YOGA IS NOT ABOUT FORCING YOURSELF BEYOND YOUR COMFORT LEVEL.
OH YEAH. WE'RE PROS AT NOT DOING THAT.
FOR SURE.

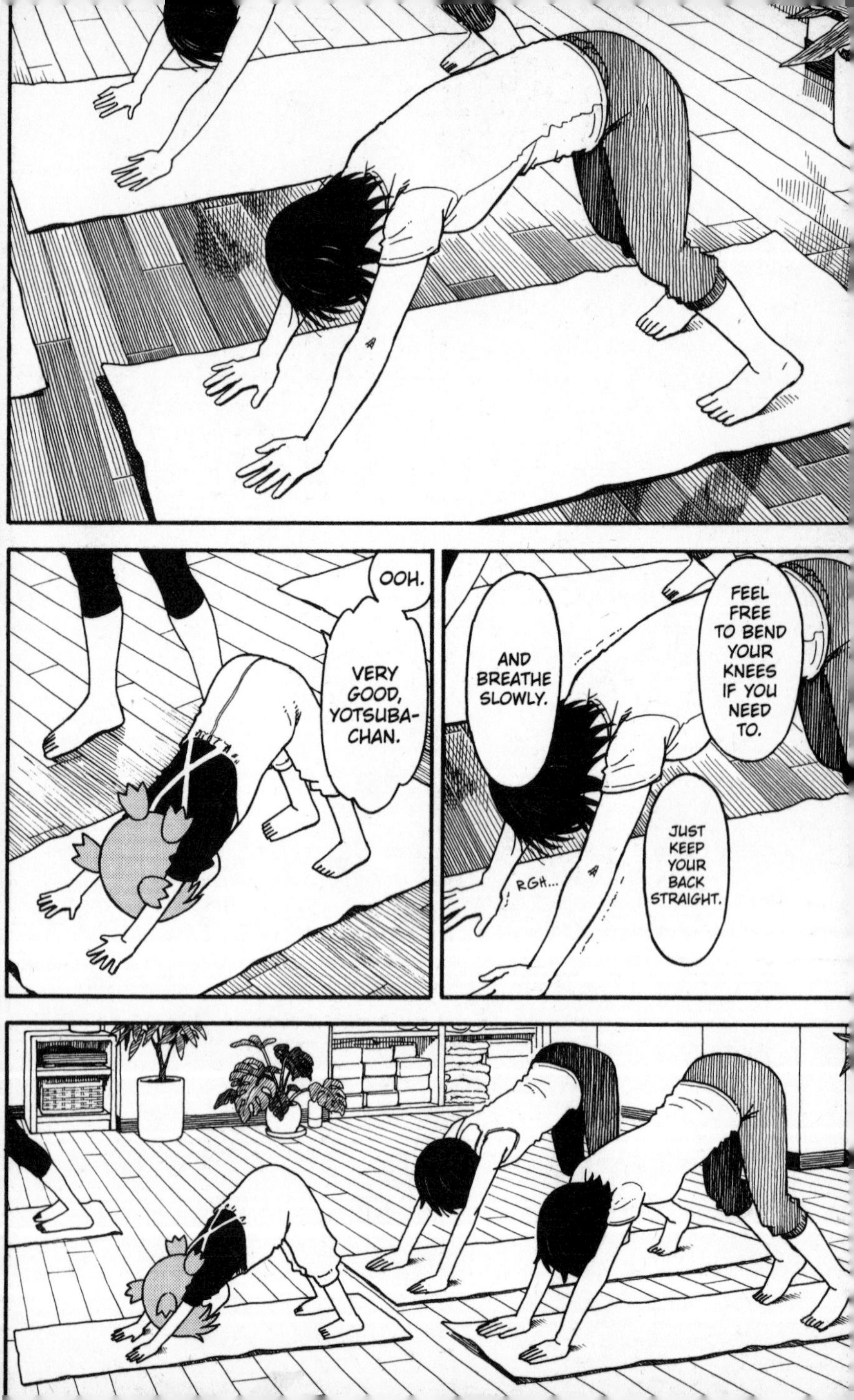
FEEL FREE TO BEND YOUR KNEES IF YOU NEED TO.
AND BREATHE SLOWLY.
JUST KEEP YOUR BACK STRAIGHT.
RGH...
OOH.
VERY GOOD, YOTSUBA-CHAN.

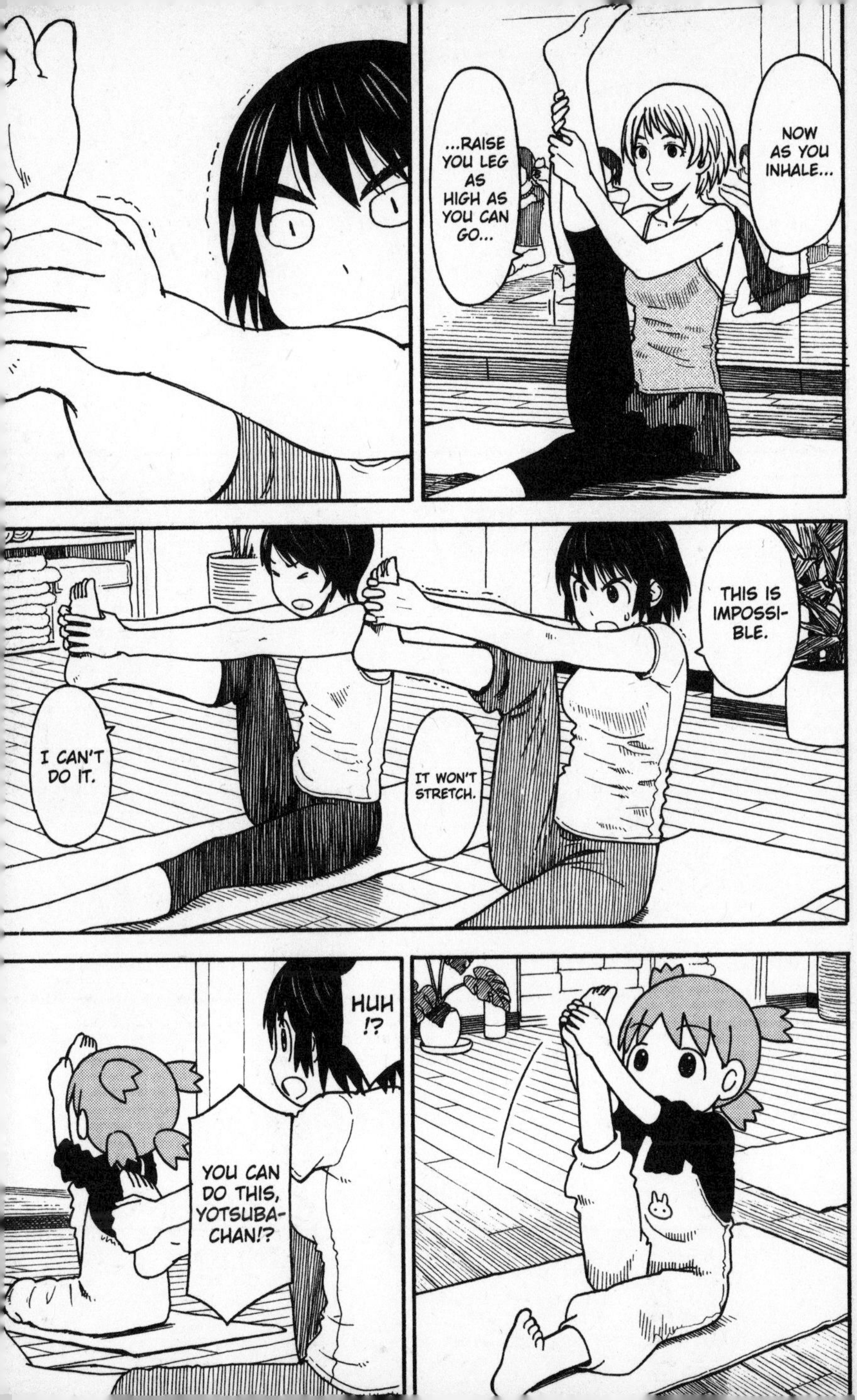
NOW AS YOU INHALE...
...RAISE YOU LEG AS HIGH AS YOU CAN GO...
THIS IS IMPOSSIBLE.
IT WON'T STRETCH.
I CAN'T DO IT.
HUH!?
YOU CAN DO THIS, YOTSUBA-CHAN!?

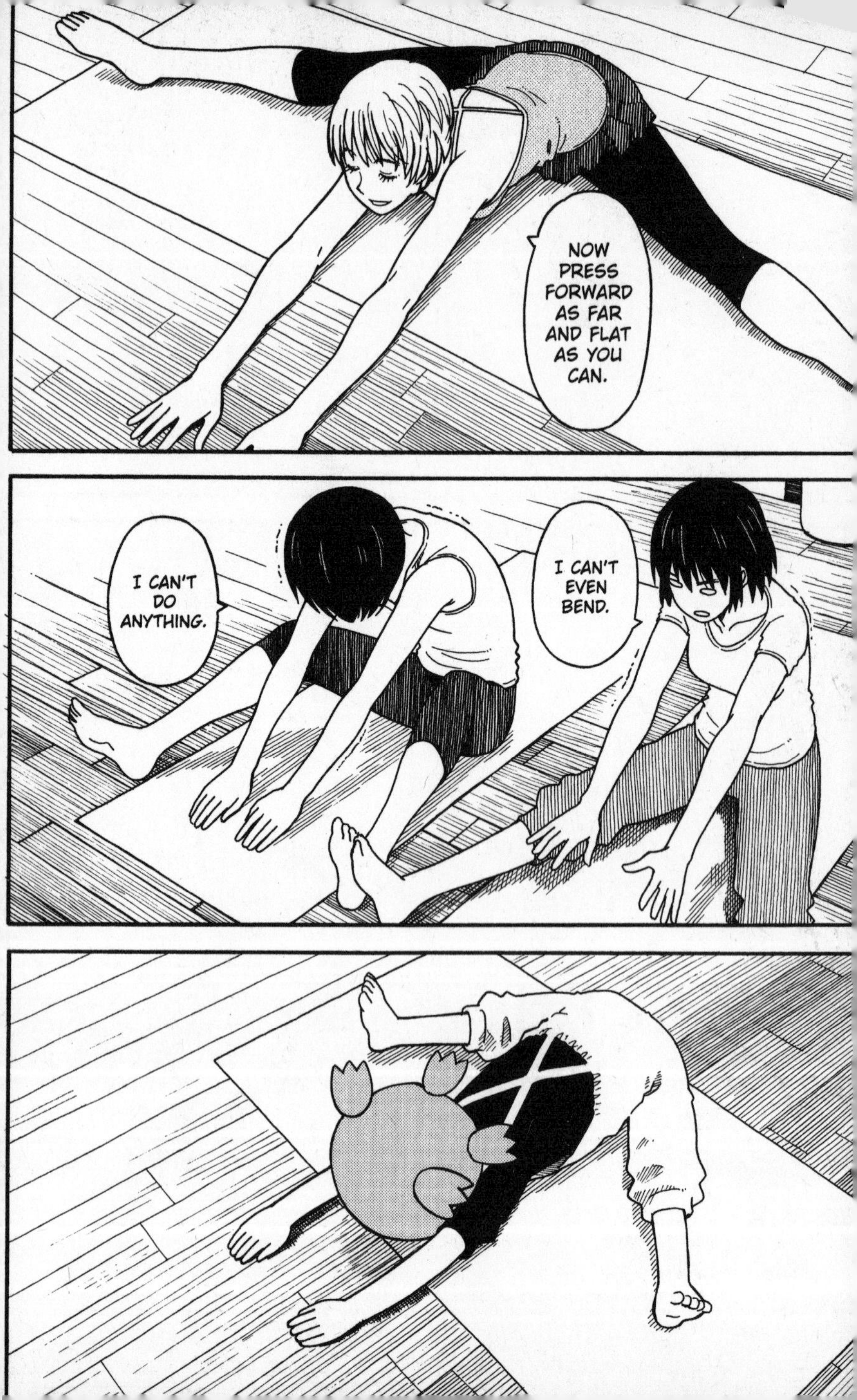
NOW PRESS FORWARD AS FAR AND FLAT AS YOU CAN.
I CAN'T EVEN BEND.
I CAN'T DO ANYTHING.

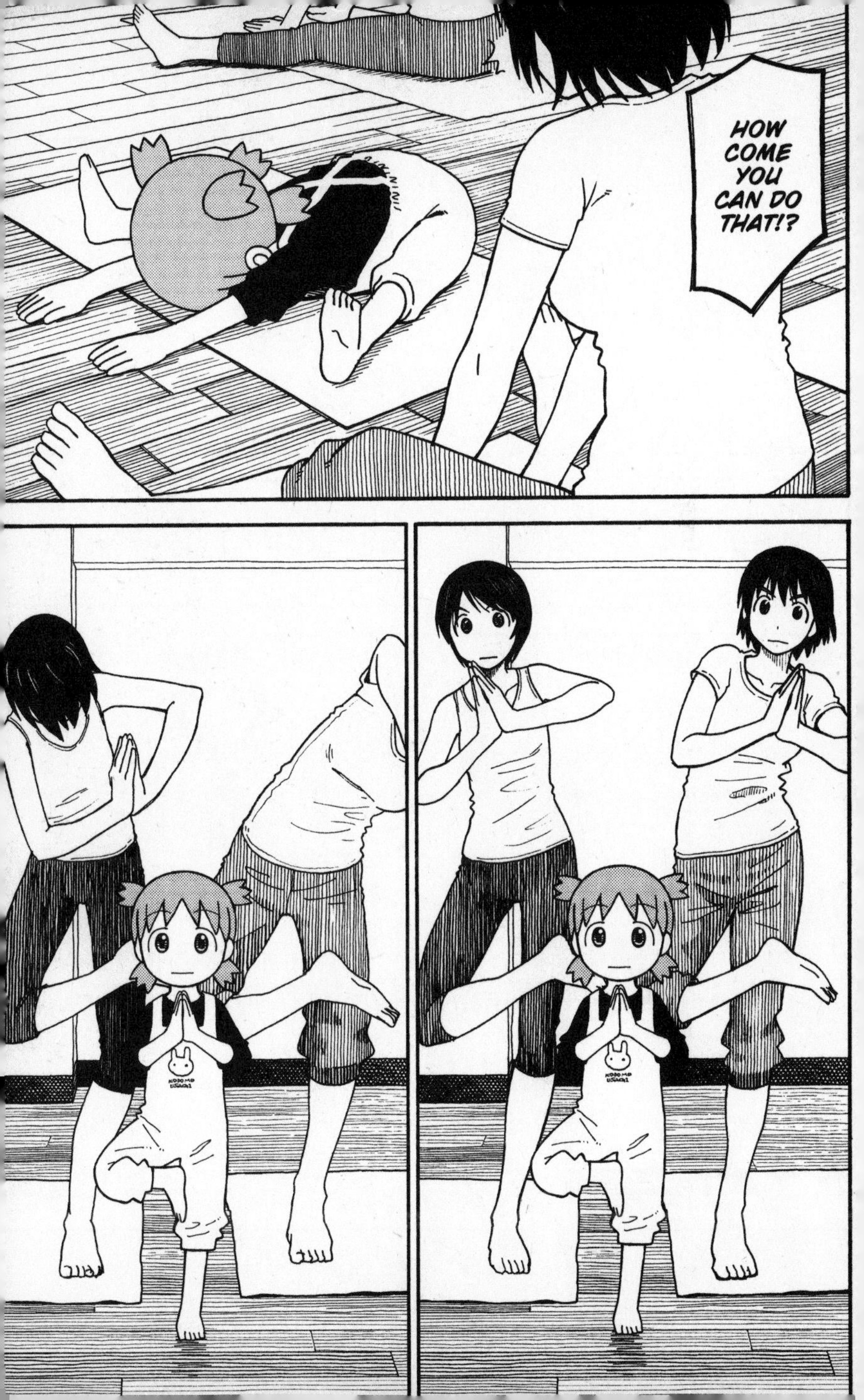
HOW COME YOU CAN DO THAT!?

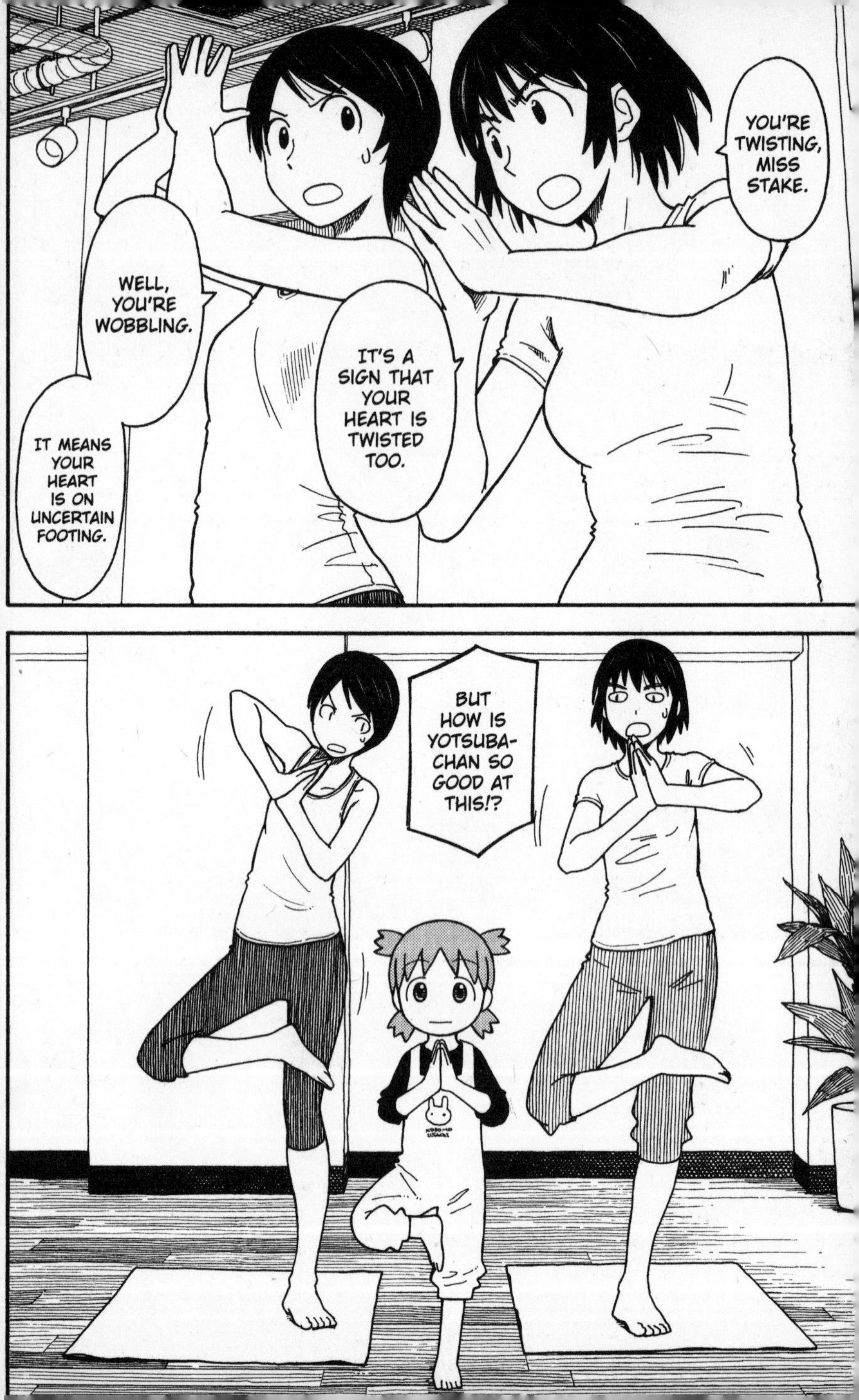

YOU'RE TWISTING, MISS STAKE.
IT'S A SIGN THAT YOUR HEART IS TWISTED TOO.
WELL, YOU'RE WOBBLING.
IT MEANS YOUR HEART IS ON UNCERTAIN FOOTING.
BUT HOW IS YOTSUBA-CHAN SO GOOD AT THIS!?

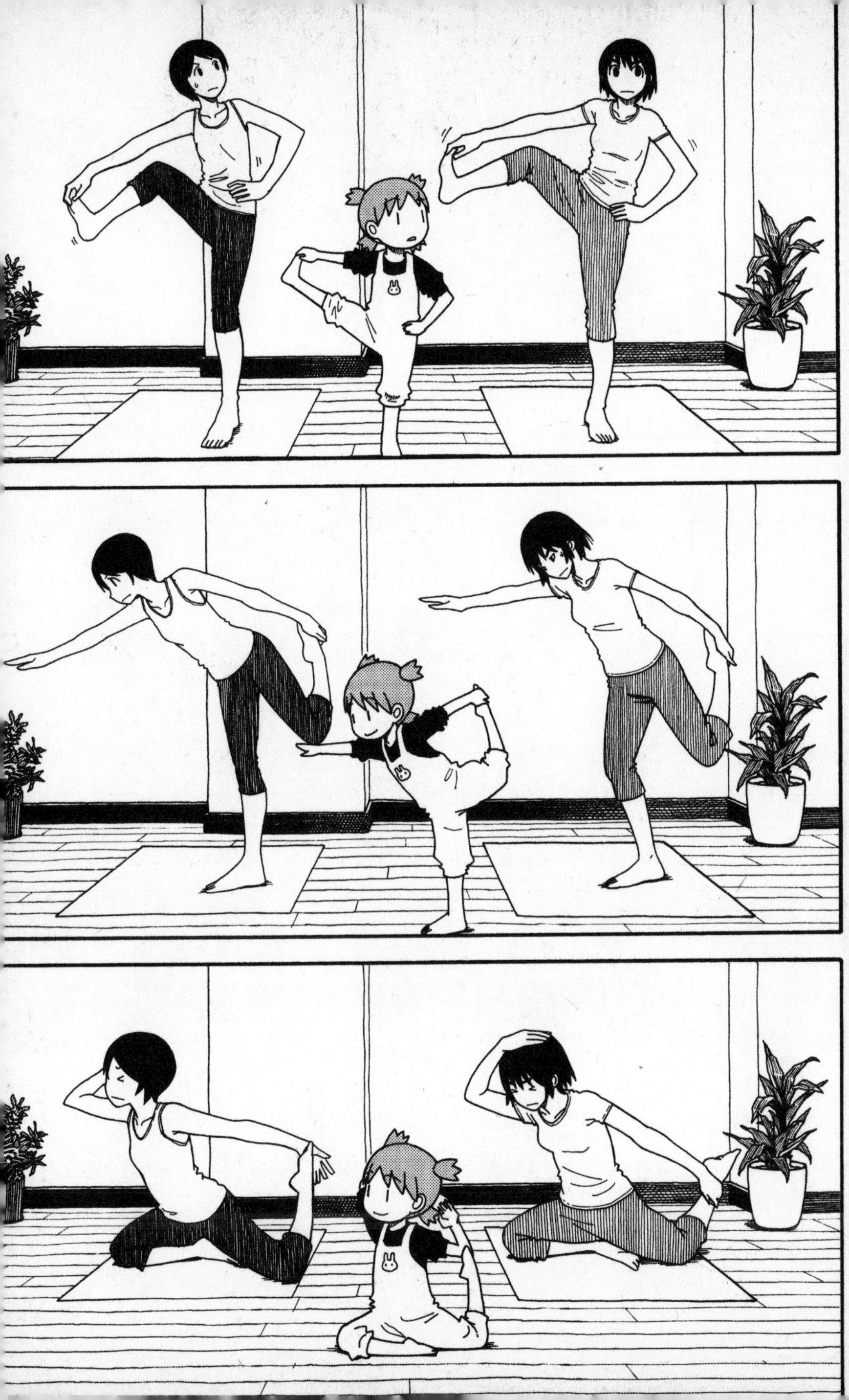

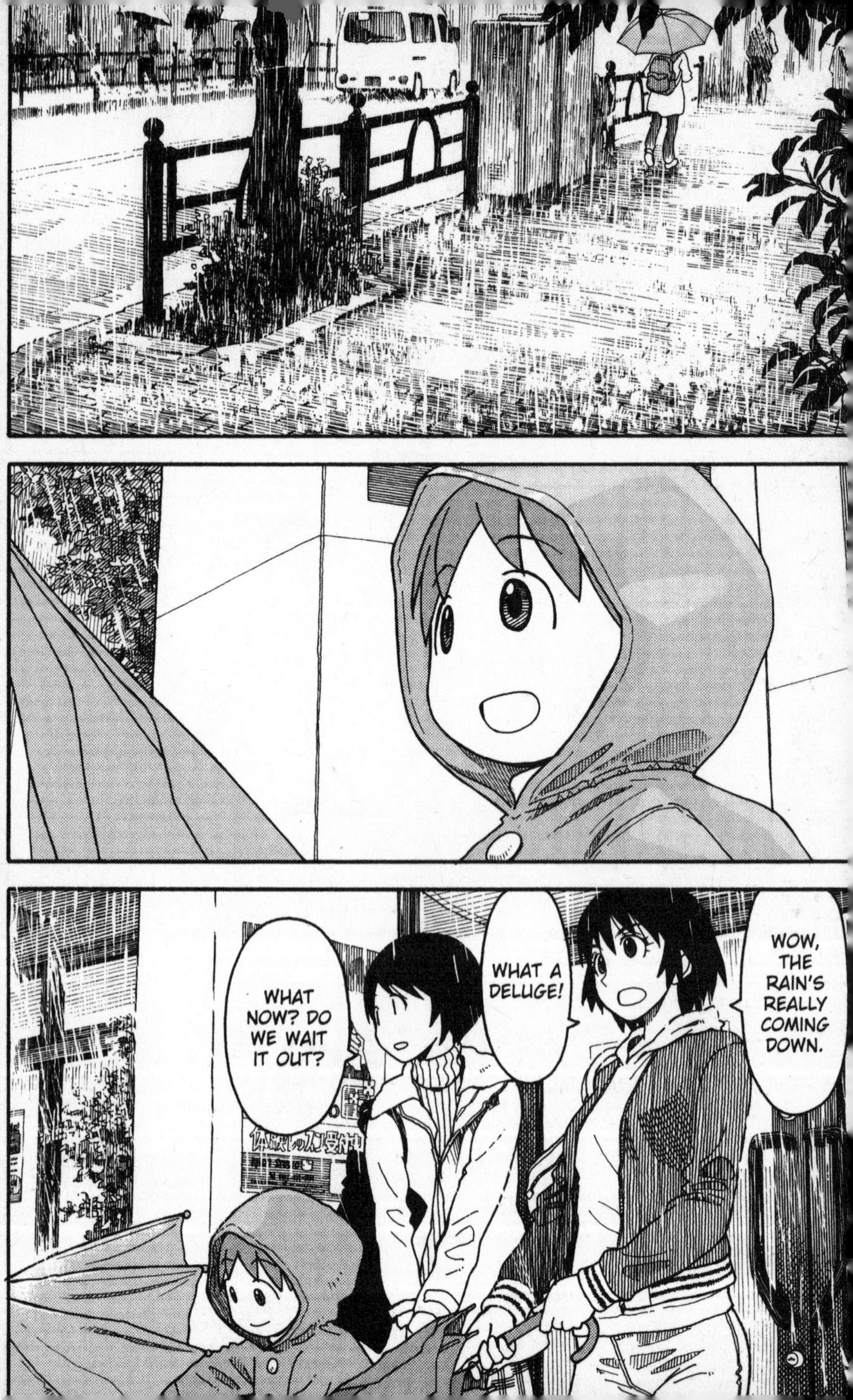
WOW, THE RAIN'S REALLY COMING DOWN.
WHAT A DELUGE!
WHAT NOW? DO WE WAIT IT OUT?

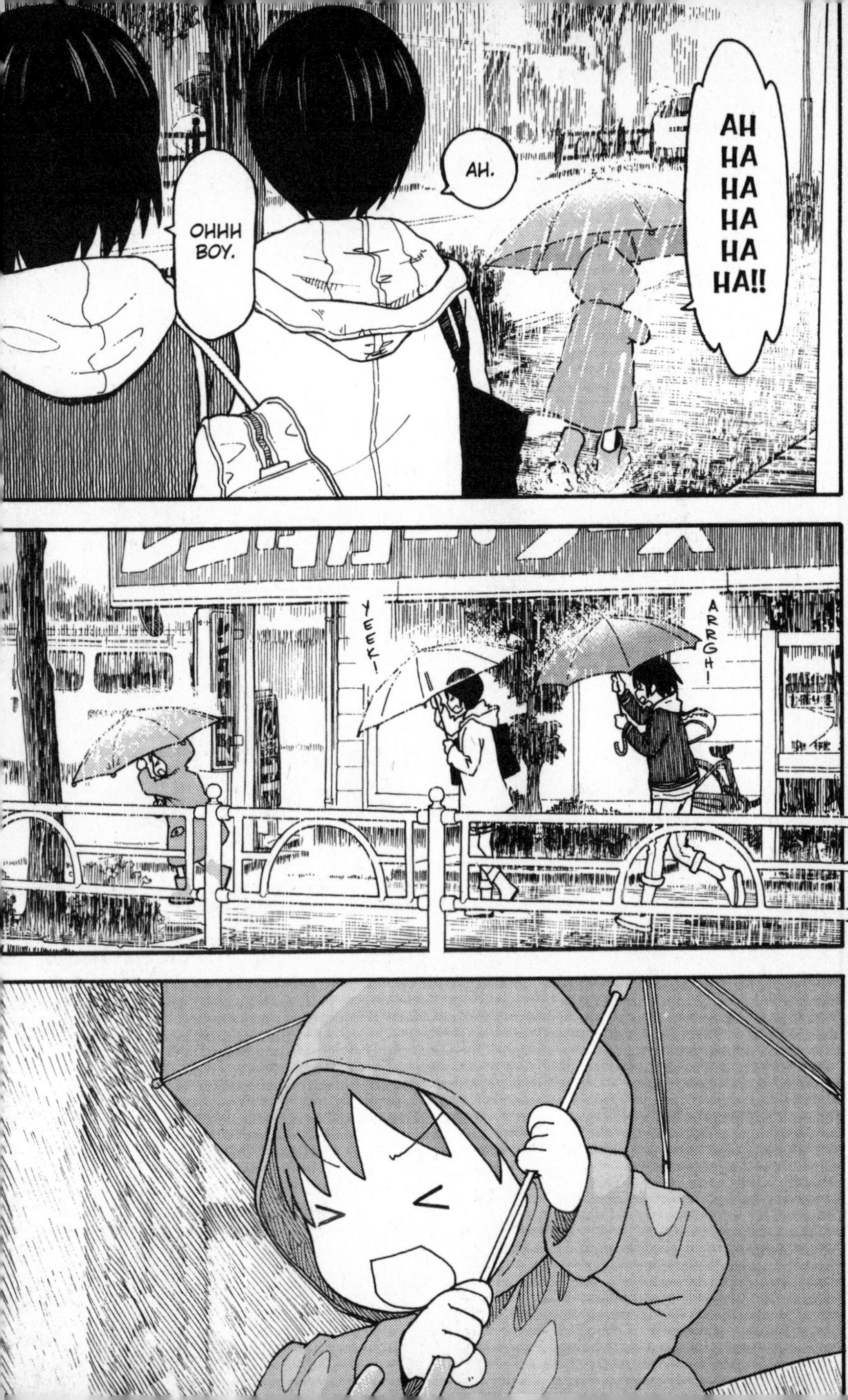
AH HA HA HA HA HA HA!!
AH.
OHHH BOY.
ARRGH!
YEEK!

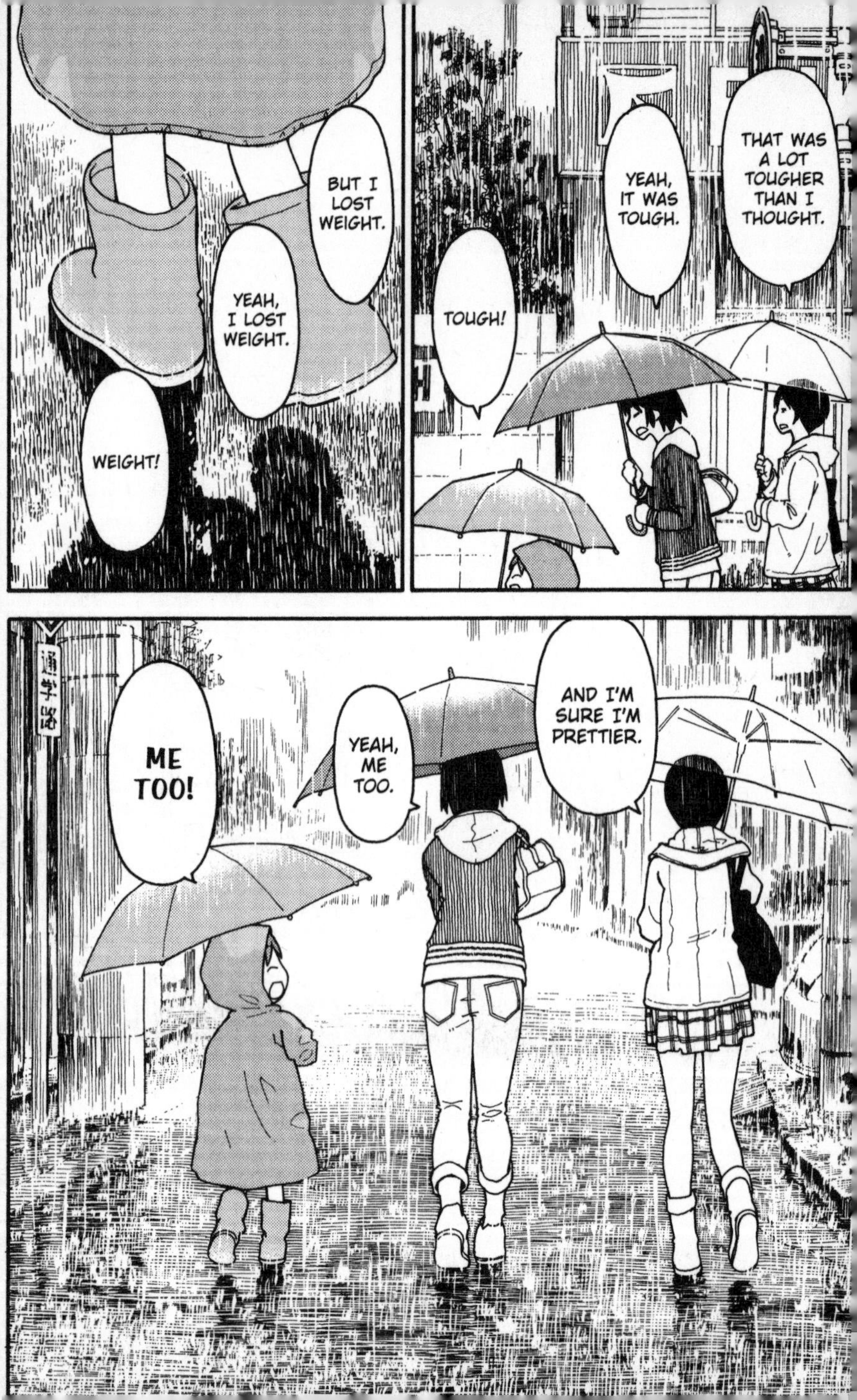
THAT WAS A LOT TOUGHER THAN I THOUGHT.
YEAH, IT WAS TOUGH.
TOUGH!
BUT I LOST WEIGHT.
YEAH, I LOST WEIGHT.
WEIGHT!
AND I'M SURE I'M PRETTIER.
YEAH, ME TOO.
ME TOO!
通学路

YOTSUBA&!

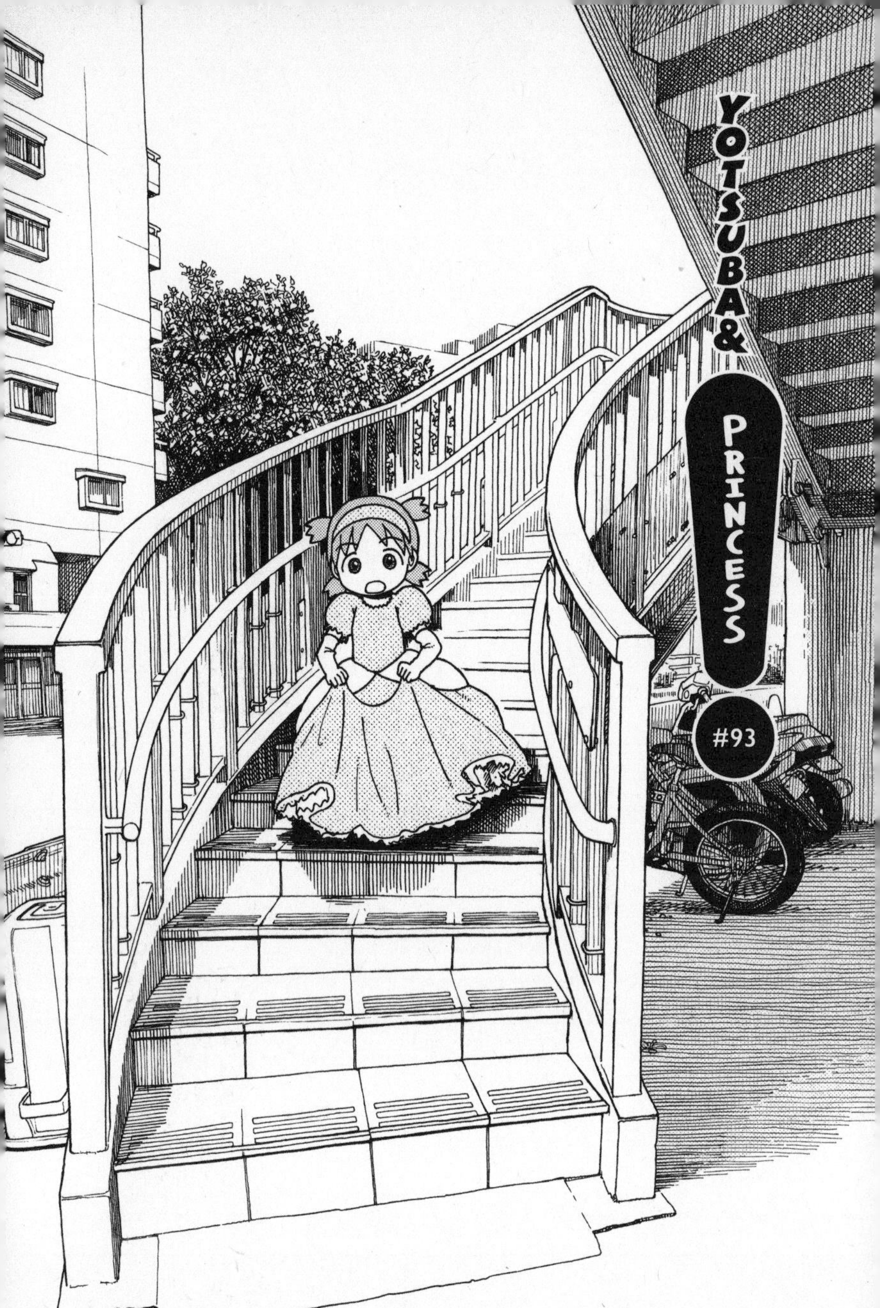
YOTSUBA&
PRINCESS!
#93

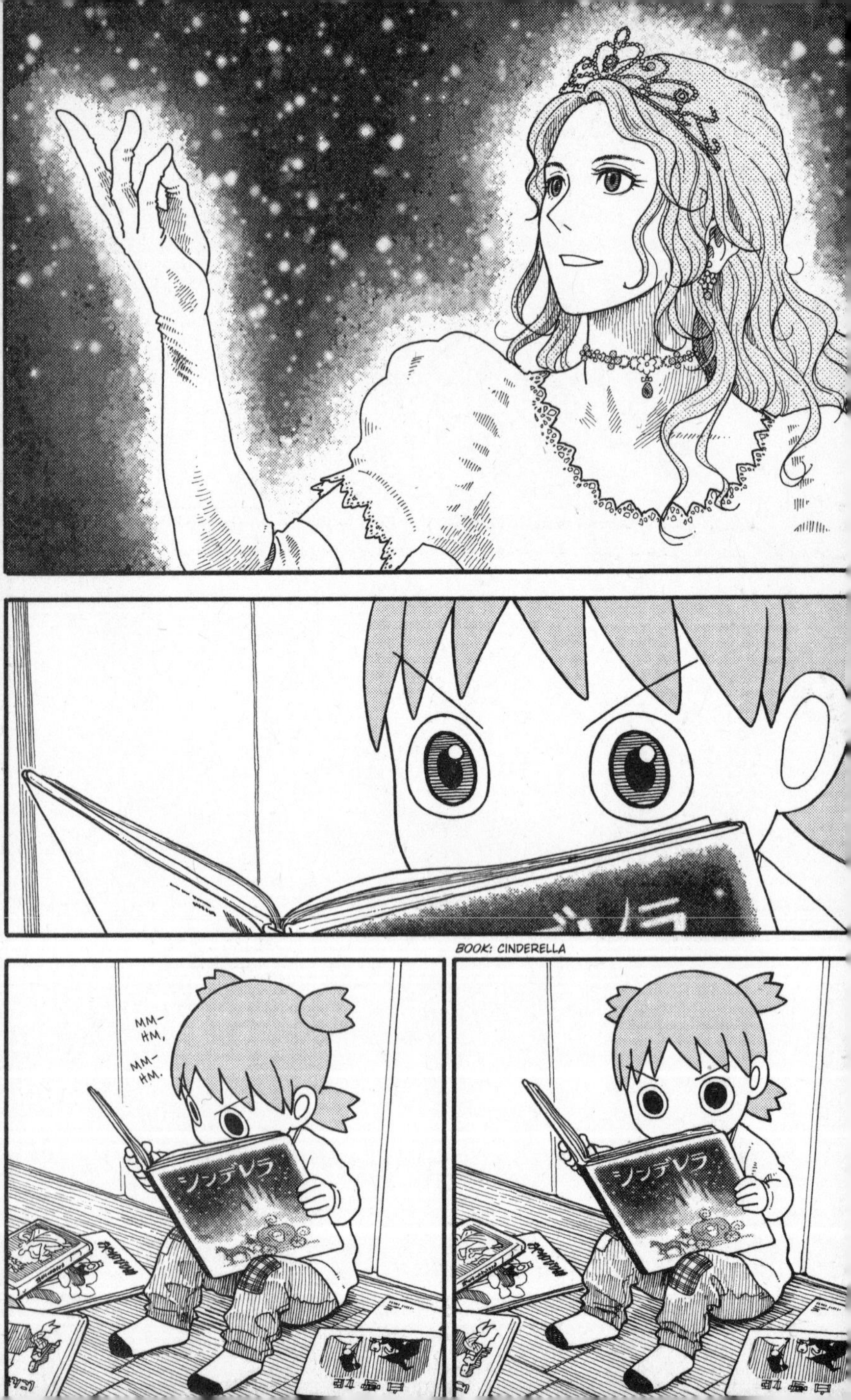
BOOK: CINDERELLA
シンデレラ
MM-HM,
MM-HM.

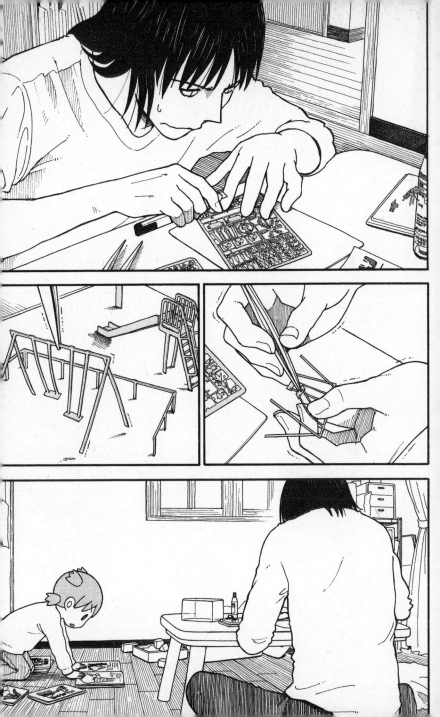

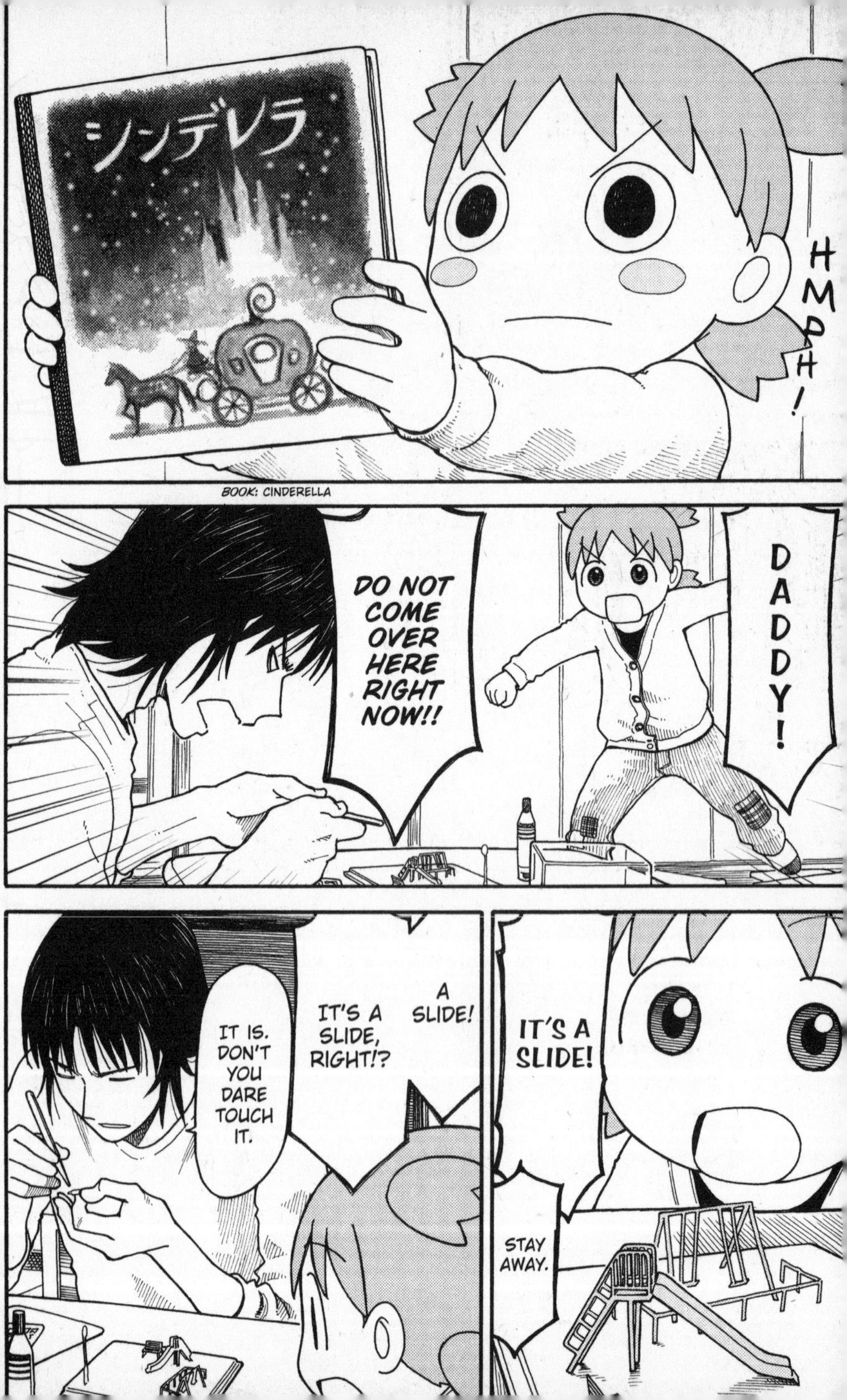
シンデレラ
HMPH!
BOOK: CINDERELLA
DADDY!
DO NOT COME OVER HERE RIGHT NOW!!
IT'S A SLIDE!
STAY AWAY.
A SLIDE!
IT'S A SLIDE, RIGHT!?
IT IS. DON'T YOU DARE TOUCH IT.

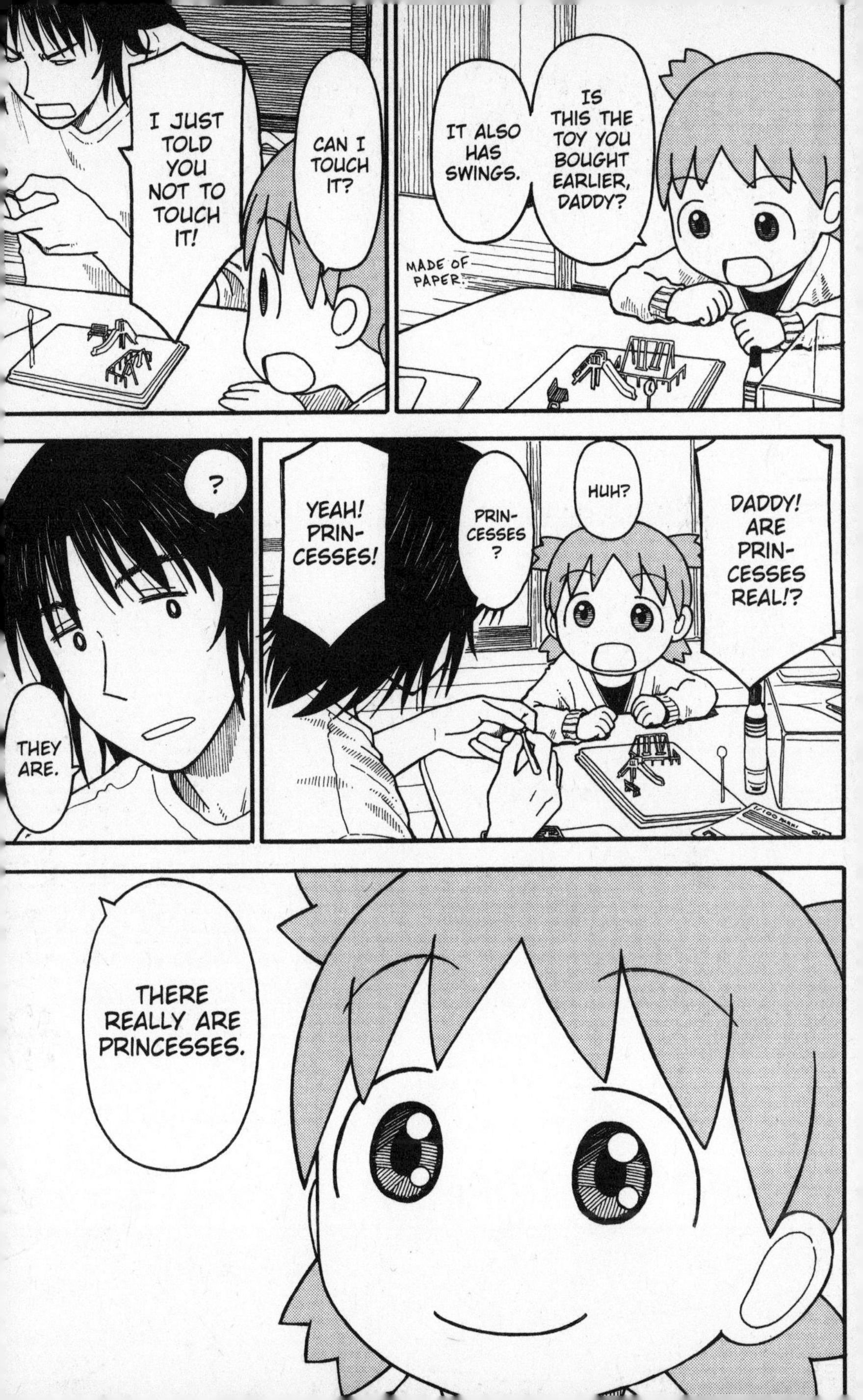
IS THIS THE TOY YOU BOUGHT EARLIER, DADDY?
IT ALSO HAS SWINGS.
MADE OF PAPER.
CAN I TOUCH IT?
I JUST TOLD YOU NOT TO TOUCH IT!
DADDY! ARE PRIN-CESSES REAL!?
HUH?
PRIN-CESSES?
YEAH! PRIN-CESSES!
?
THEY ARE.
THERE REALLY ARE PRINCESSES.

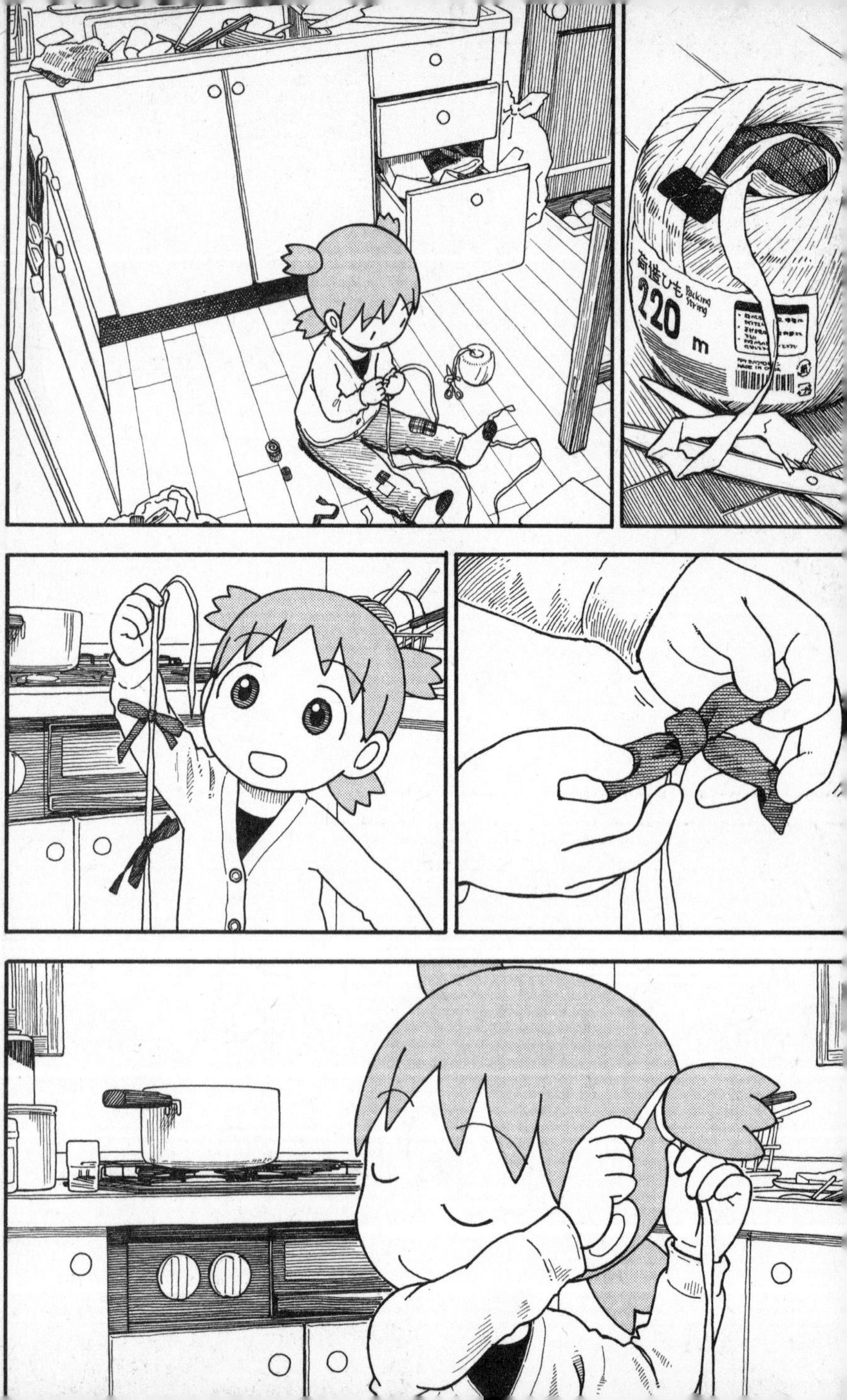
荷造ひも Packing String
220 m

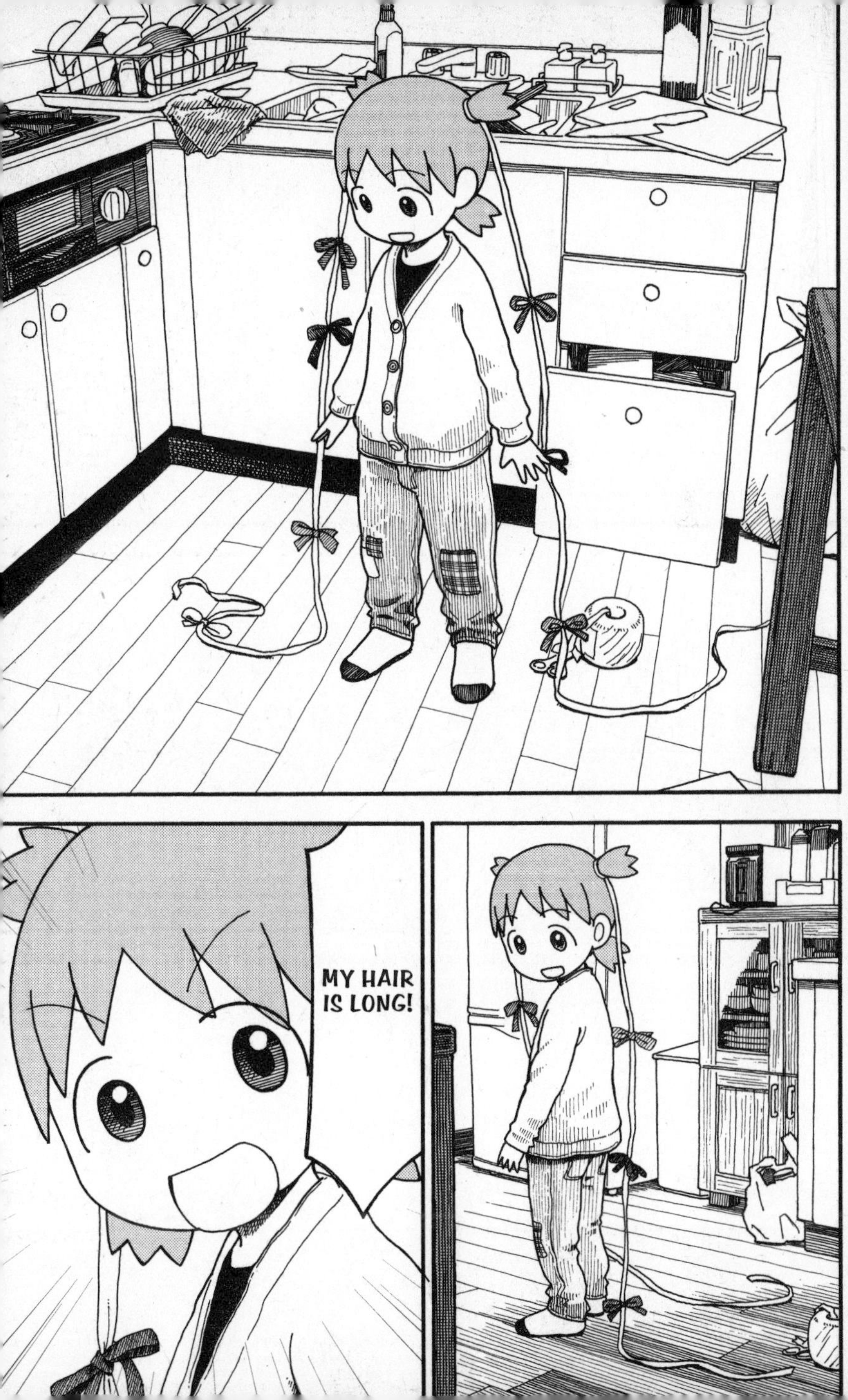
MY HAIR IS LONG!

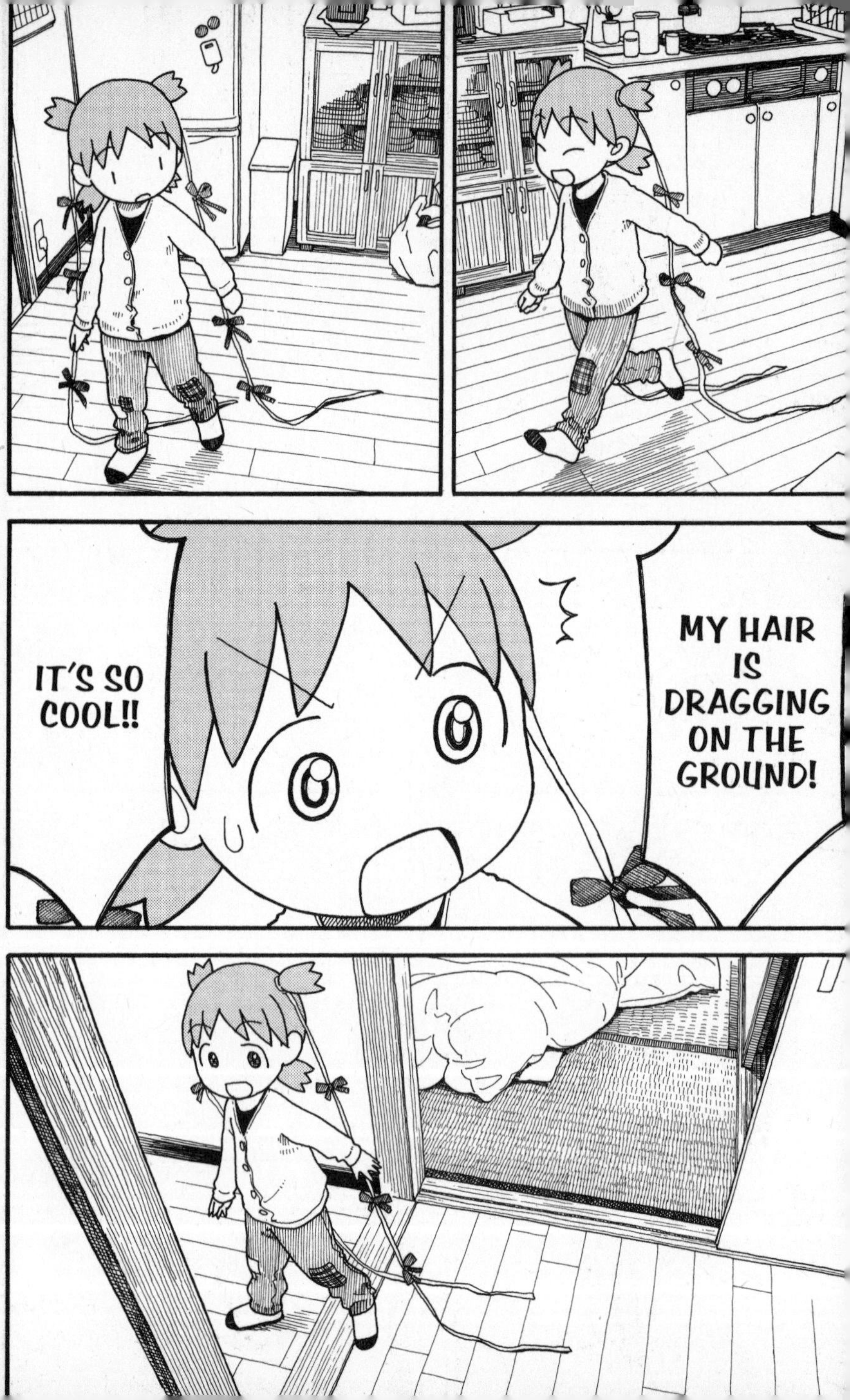
MY HAIR IS DRAGGING ON THE GROUND!
IT'S SO COOL!!

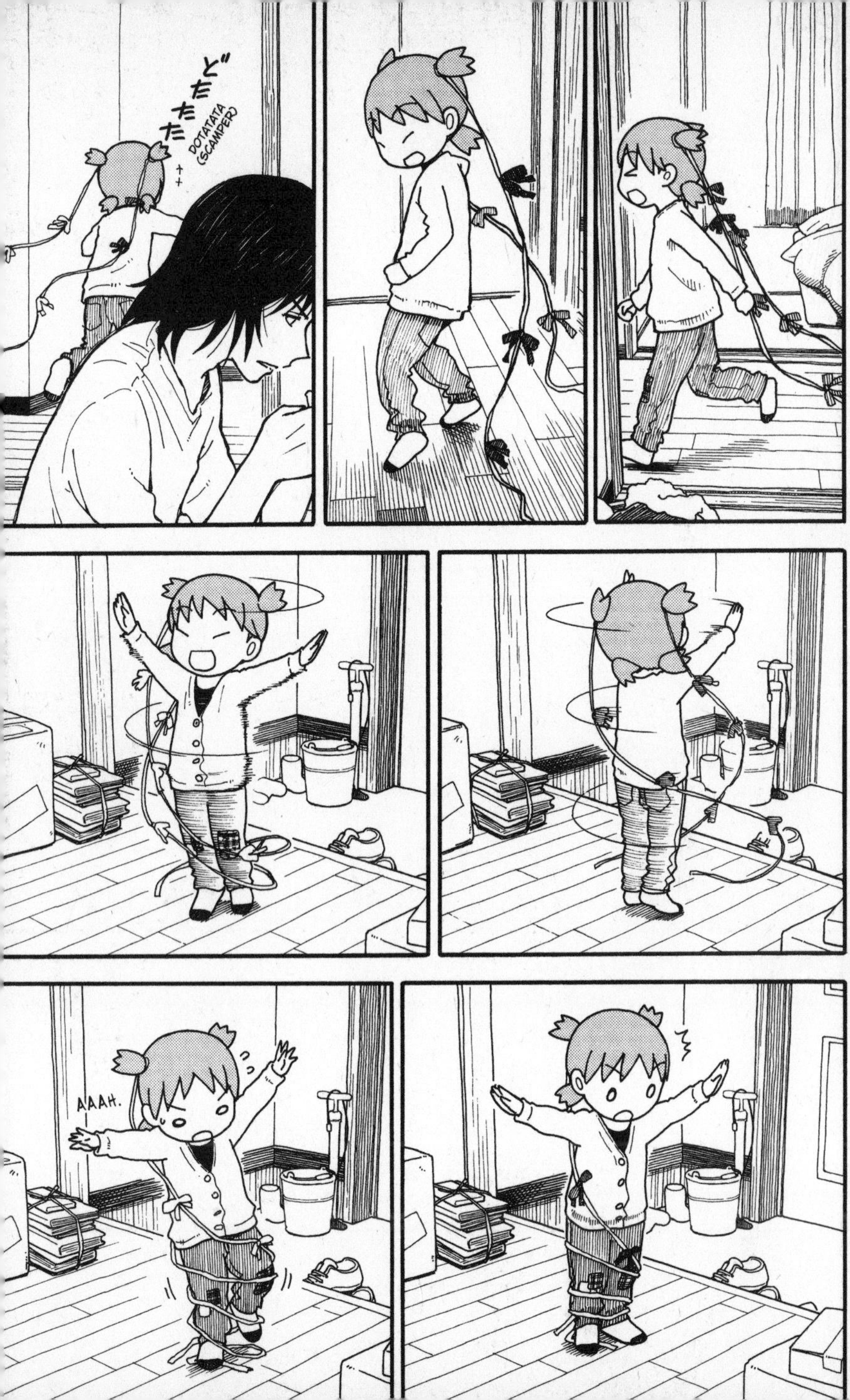
どたたた
DOTATATA (SCAMPER)
AAAH.

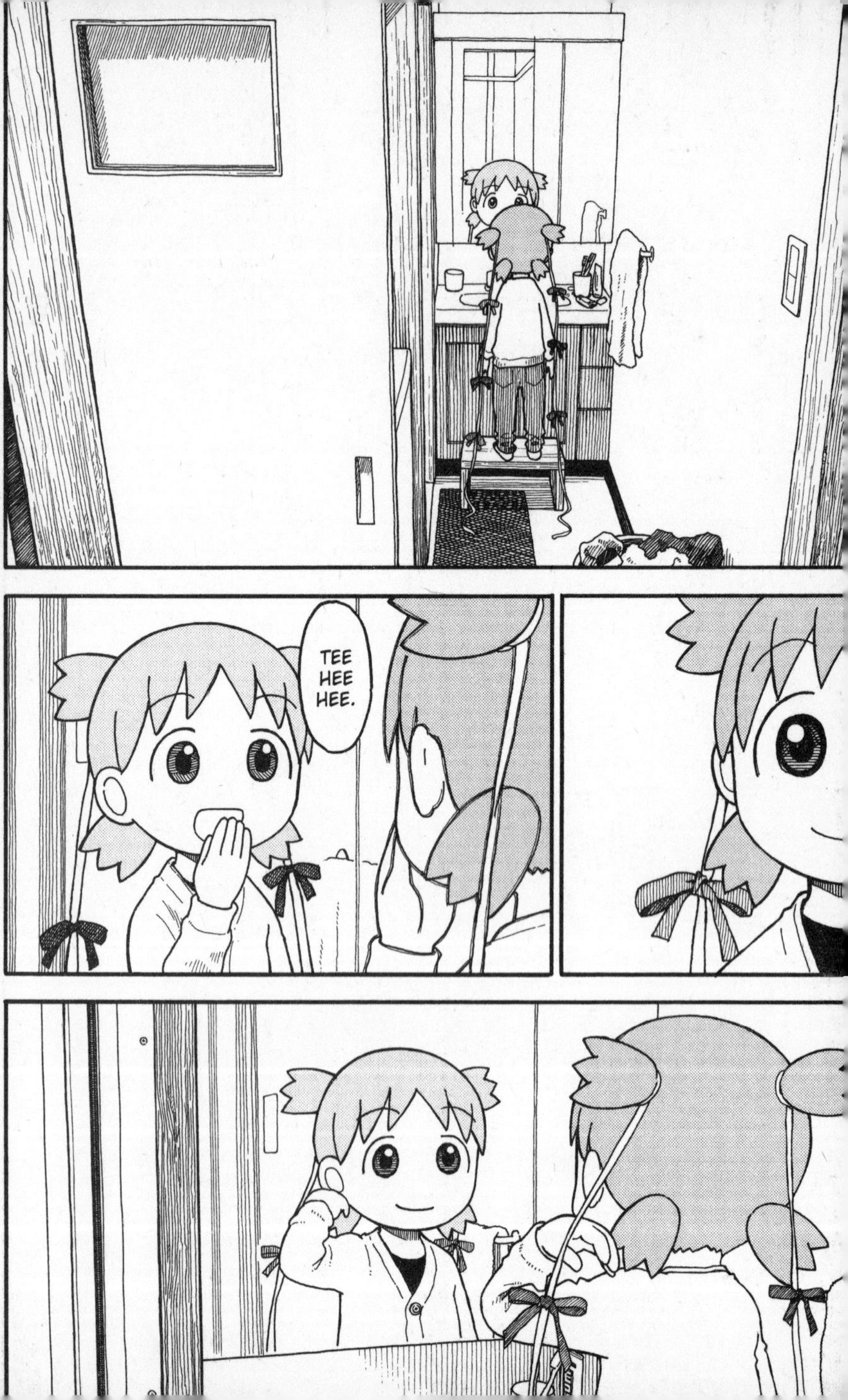
TEE HEE HEE.

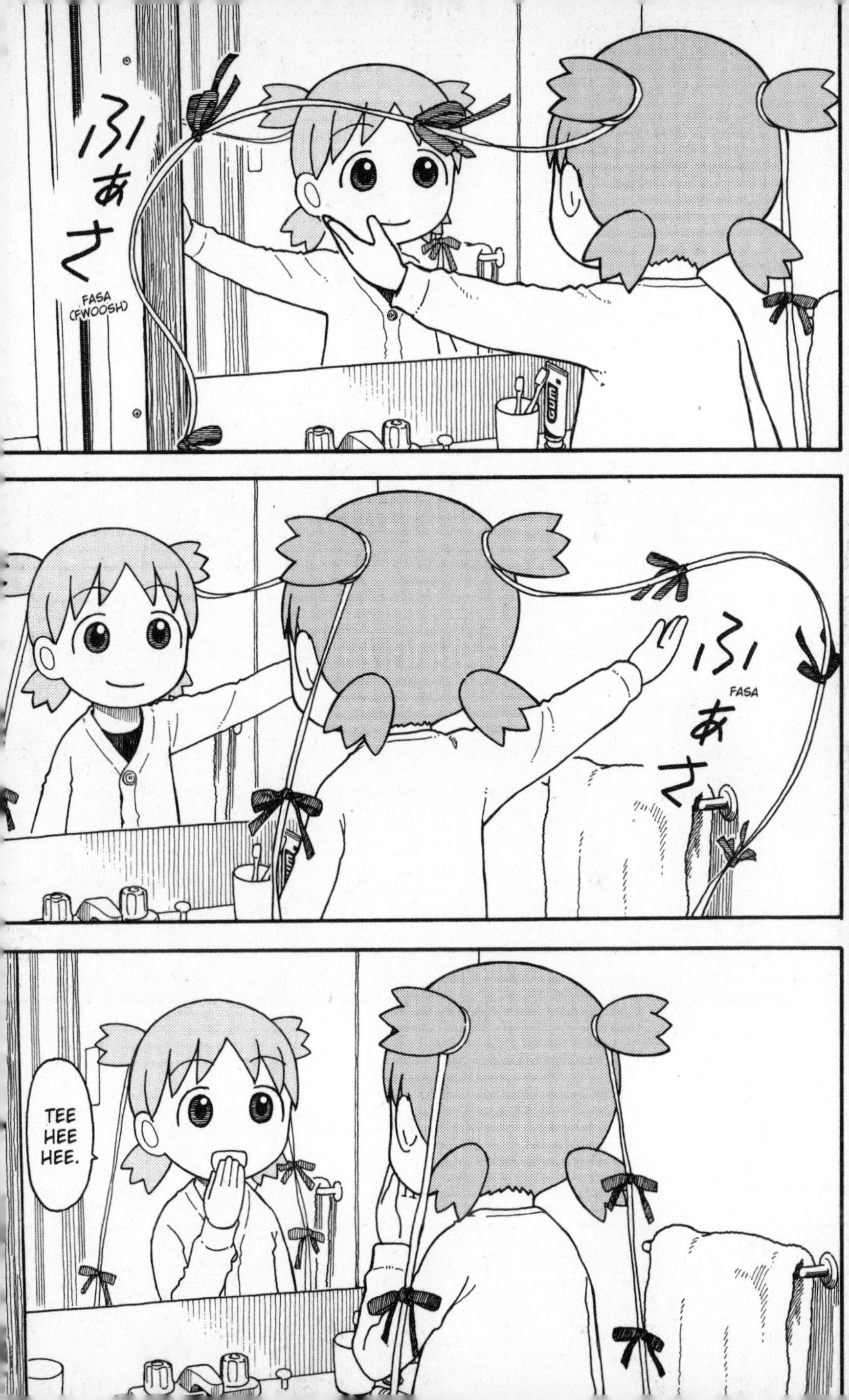
ふぁさ
FASA (FWOOSH)
ふぁさ
FASA
TEE HEE HEE.

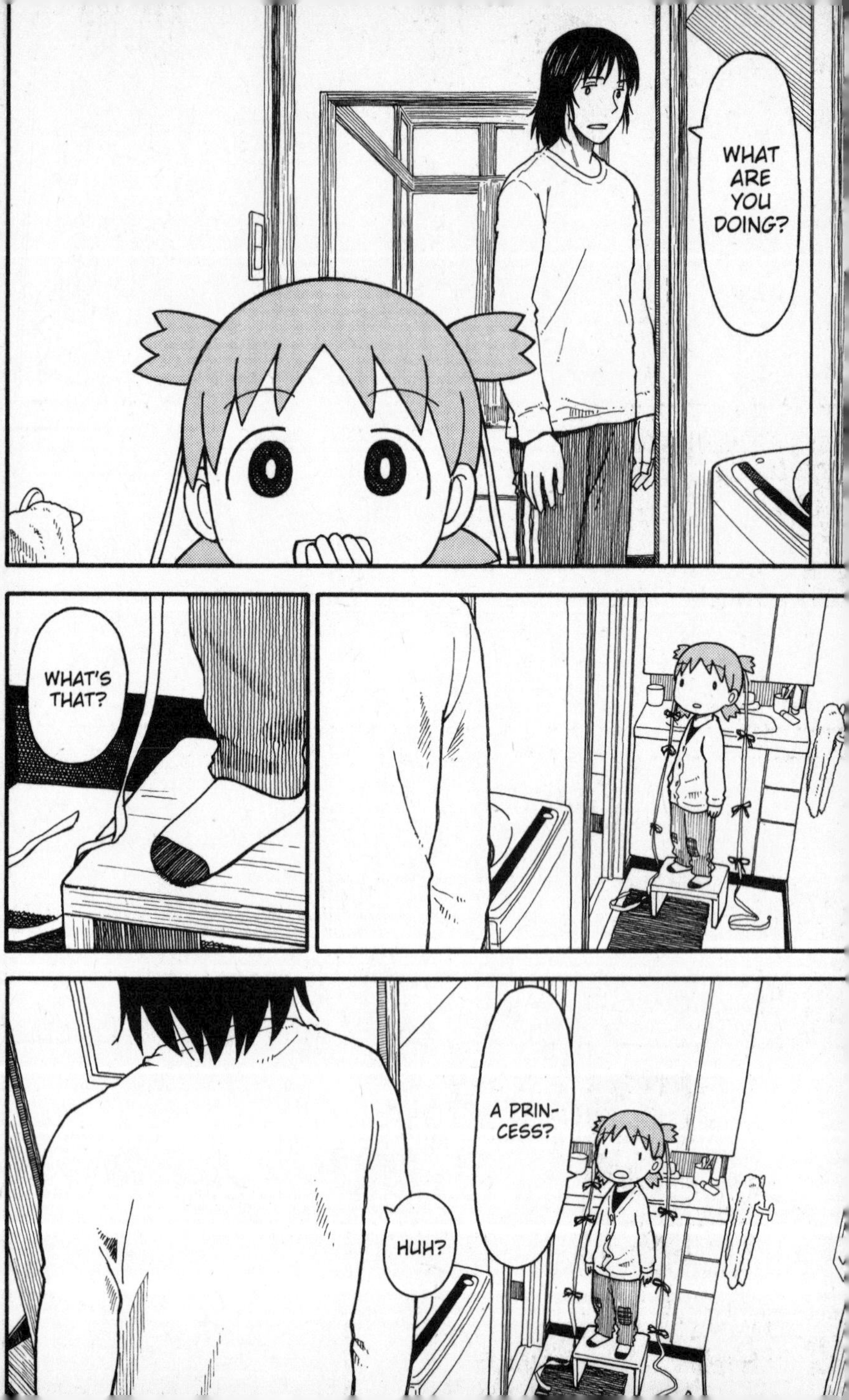
WHAT ARE YOU DOING?
WHAT'S THAT?
A PRIN-CESS?
HUH?

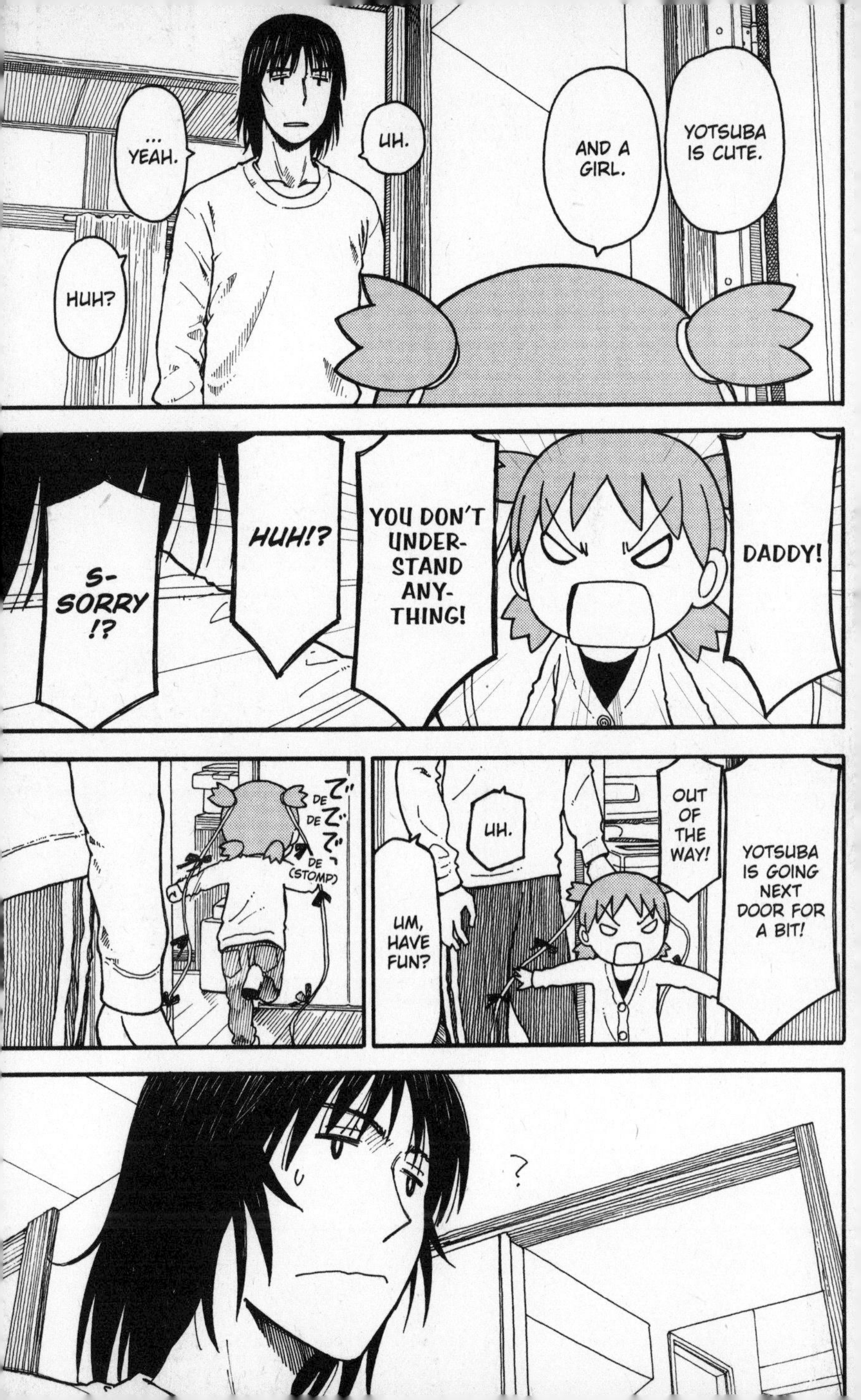
YOTSUBA IS CUTE.
AND A GIRL.
UH.
... YEAH.
HUH?
DADDY!
YOU DON'T UNDER-STAND ANY-THING!
HUH!?
S-SORRY!?
YOTSUBA IS GOING NEXT DOOR FOR A BIT!
OUT OF THE WAY!
UH.
UM, HAVE FUN?
で DE で DE で DE (STOMP)
?

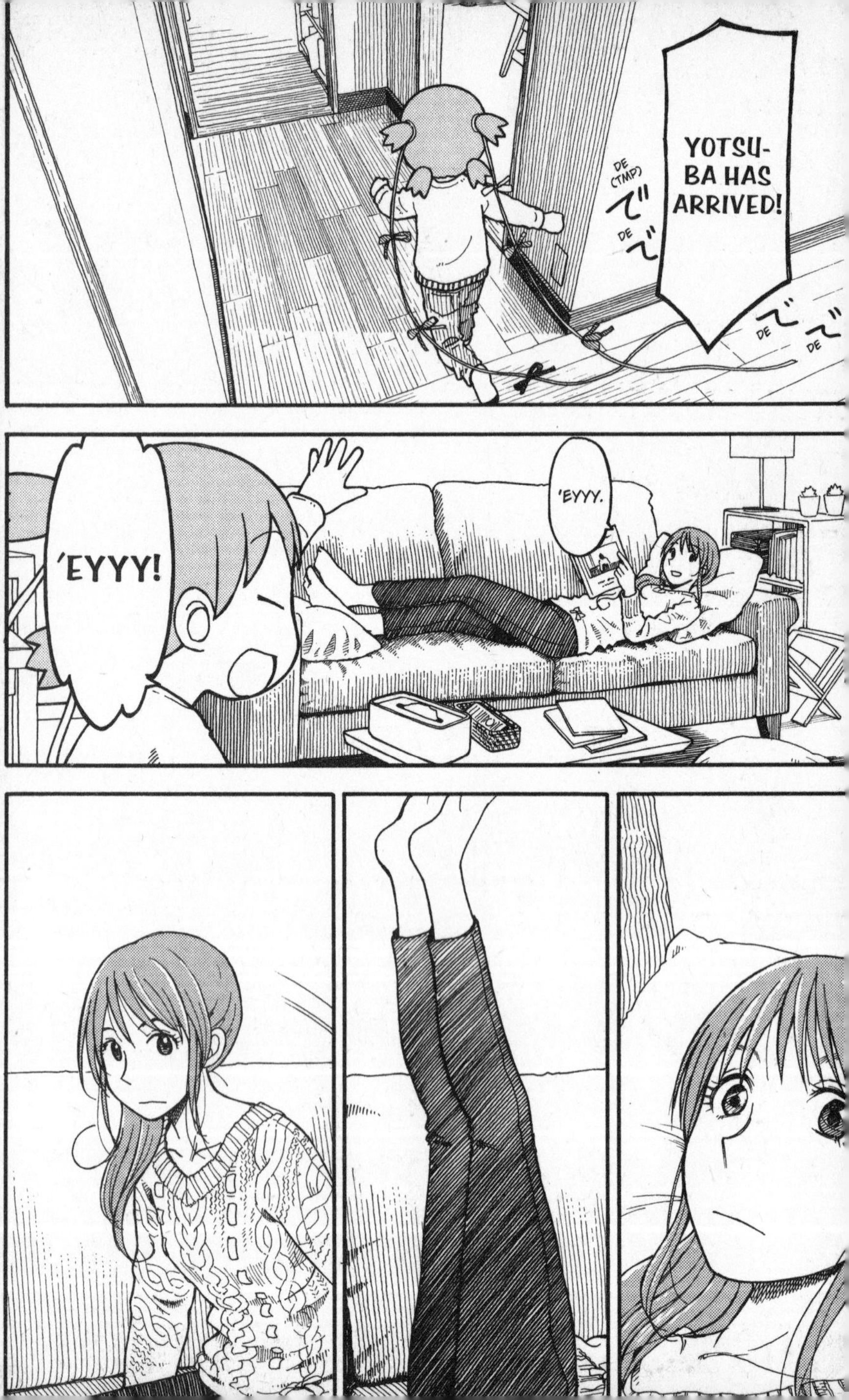
YOTSUBA HAS ARRIVED!
DE (TMP) で
DE で
DE で
DE で
'EYYY.
'EYYY!

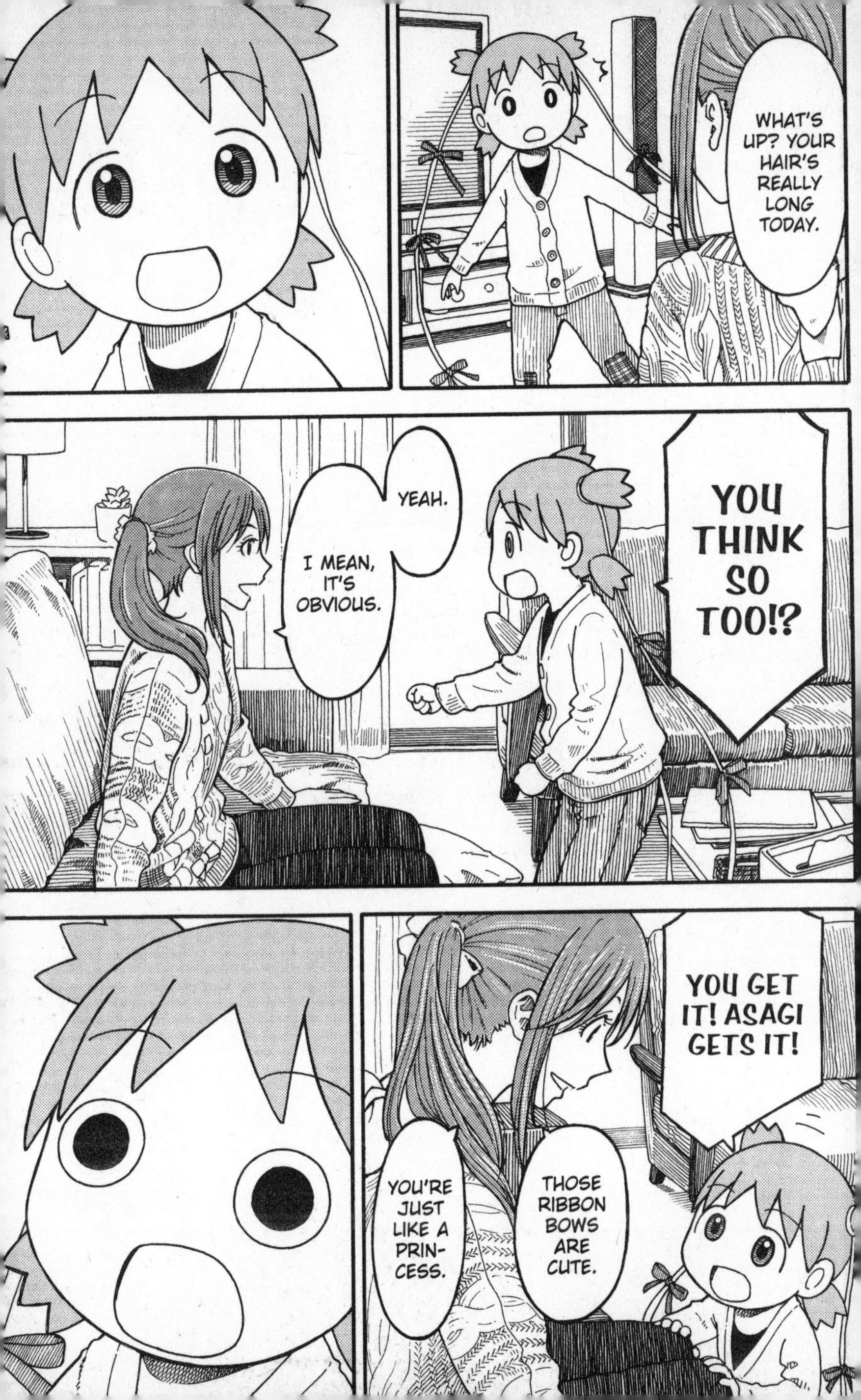
WHAT'S UP? YOUR HAIR'S REALLY LONG TODAY.
YOU THINK SO TOO!?
YEAH.
I MEAN, IT'S OBVIOUS.
YOU GET IT! ASAGI GETS IT!
THOSE RIBBON BOWS ARE CUTE.
YOU'RE JUST LIKE A PRIN-CESS.

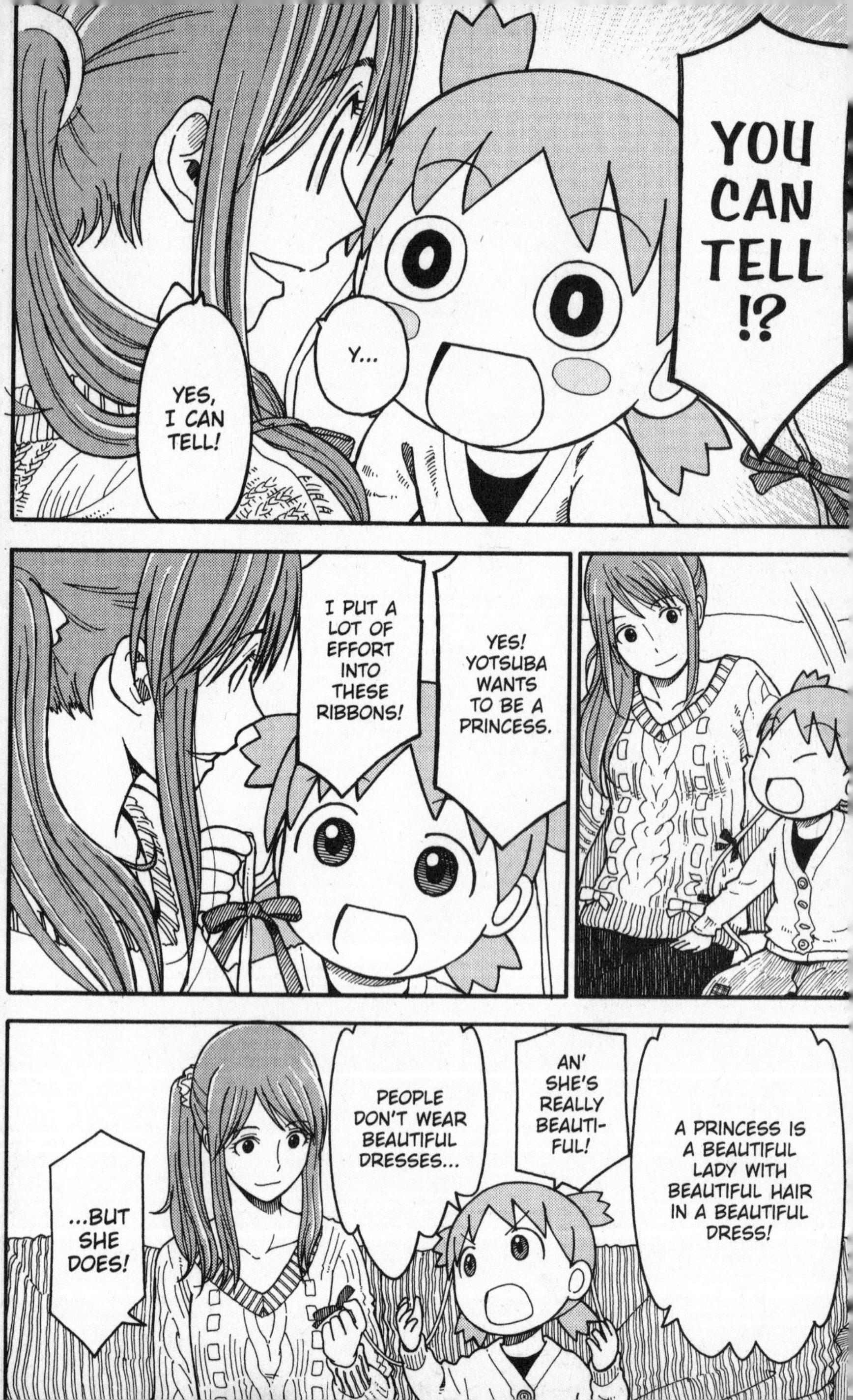
YOU CAN TELL!?
Y...
YES, I CAN TELL!
YES! YOTSUBA WANTS TO BE A PRINCESS.
I PUT A LOT OF EFFORT INTO THESE RIBBONS!
A PRINCESS IS A BEAUTIFUL LADY WITH BEAUTIFUL HAIR IN A BEAUTIFUL DRESS!
AN' SHE'S REALLY BEAUTI-FUL!
PEOPLE DON'T WEAR BEAUTIFUL DRESSES...
...BUT SHE DOES!

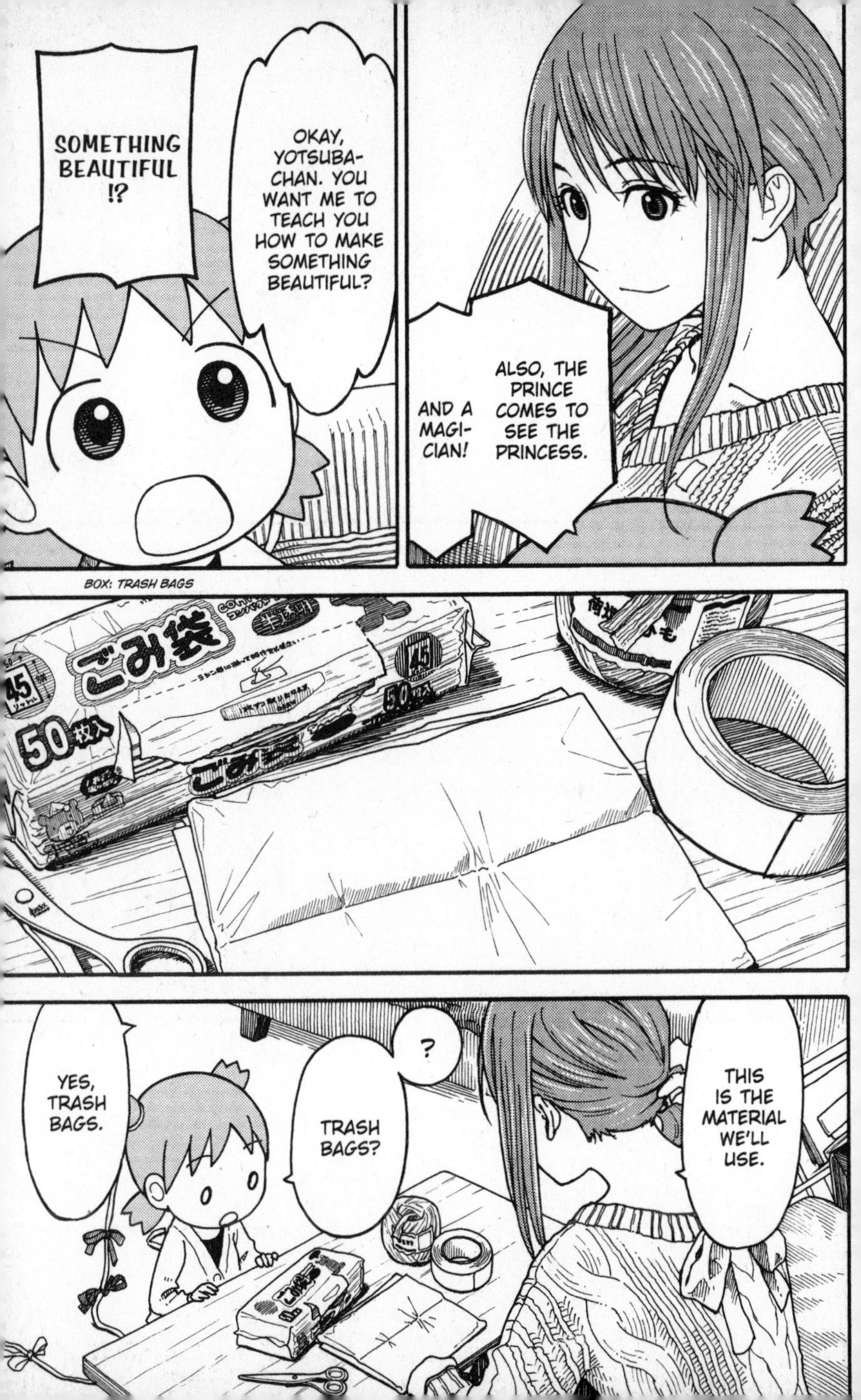
ALSO, THE PRINCE COMES TO SEE THE PRINCESS.
AND A MAGI-CIAN!
OKAY, YOTSUBA-CHAN. YOU WANT ME TO TEACH YOU HOW TO MAKE SOMETHING BEAUTIFUL?
SOMETHING BEAUTIFUL!?
BOX: TRASH BAGS
ごみ袋
50枚入
THIS IS THE MATERIAL WE'LL USE.
?
TRASH BAGS?
YES, TRASH BAGS.

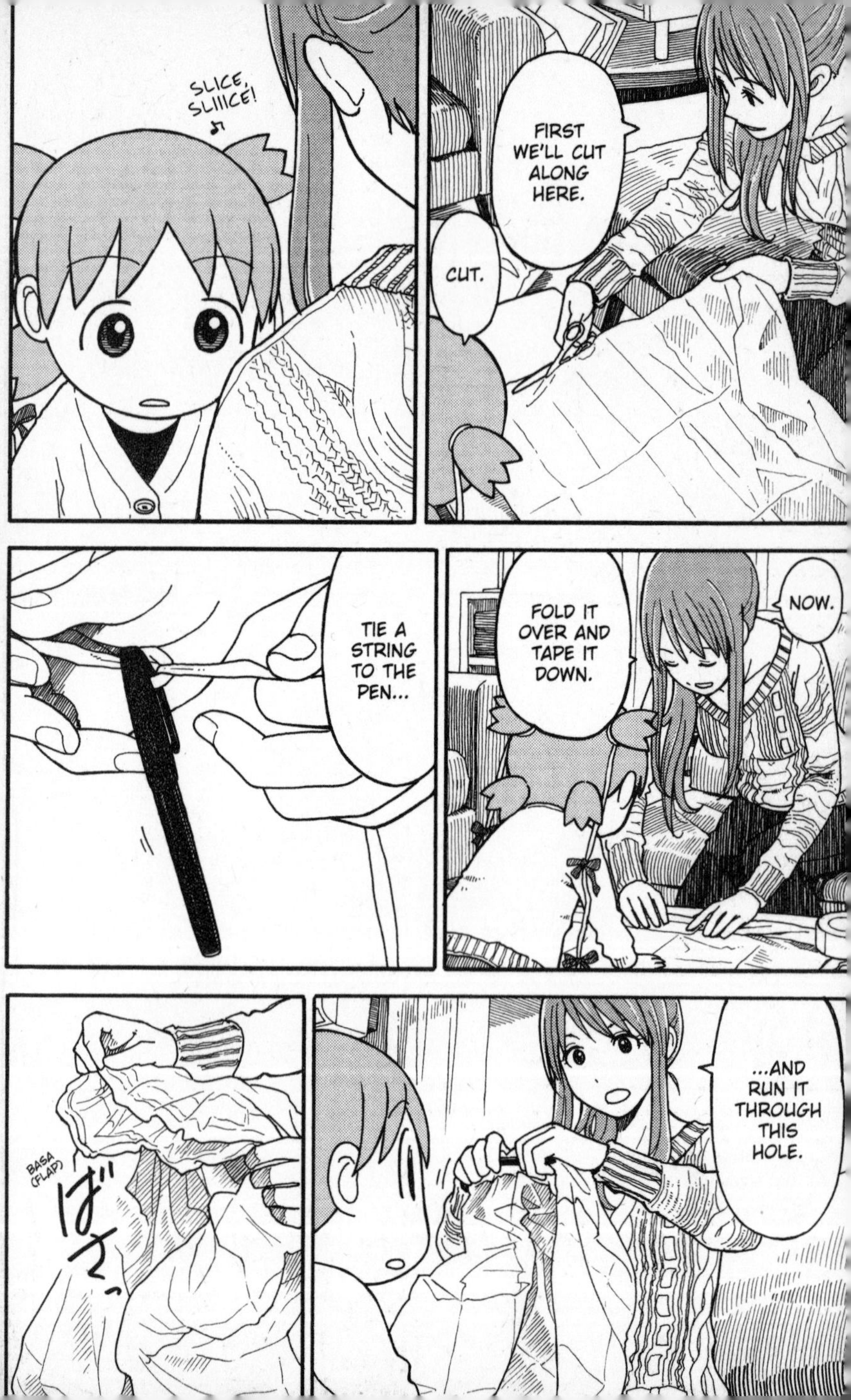
FIRST WE'LL CUT ALONG HERE.
CUT.
SLICE, SLIIICE! ♪
NOW.
FOLD IT OVER AND TAPE IT DOWN.
TIE A STRING TO THE PEN...
...AND RUN IT THROUGH THIS HOLE.
ばさっ
BASA (FLAP)

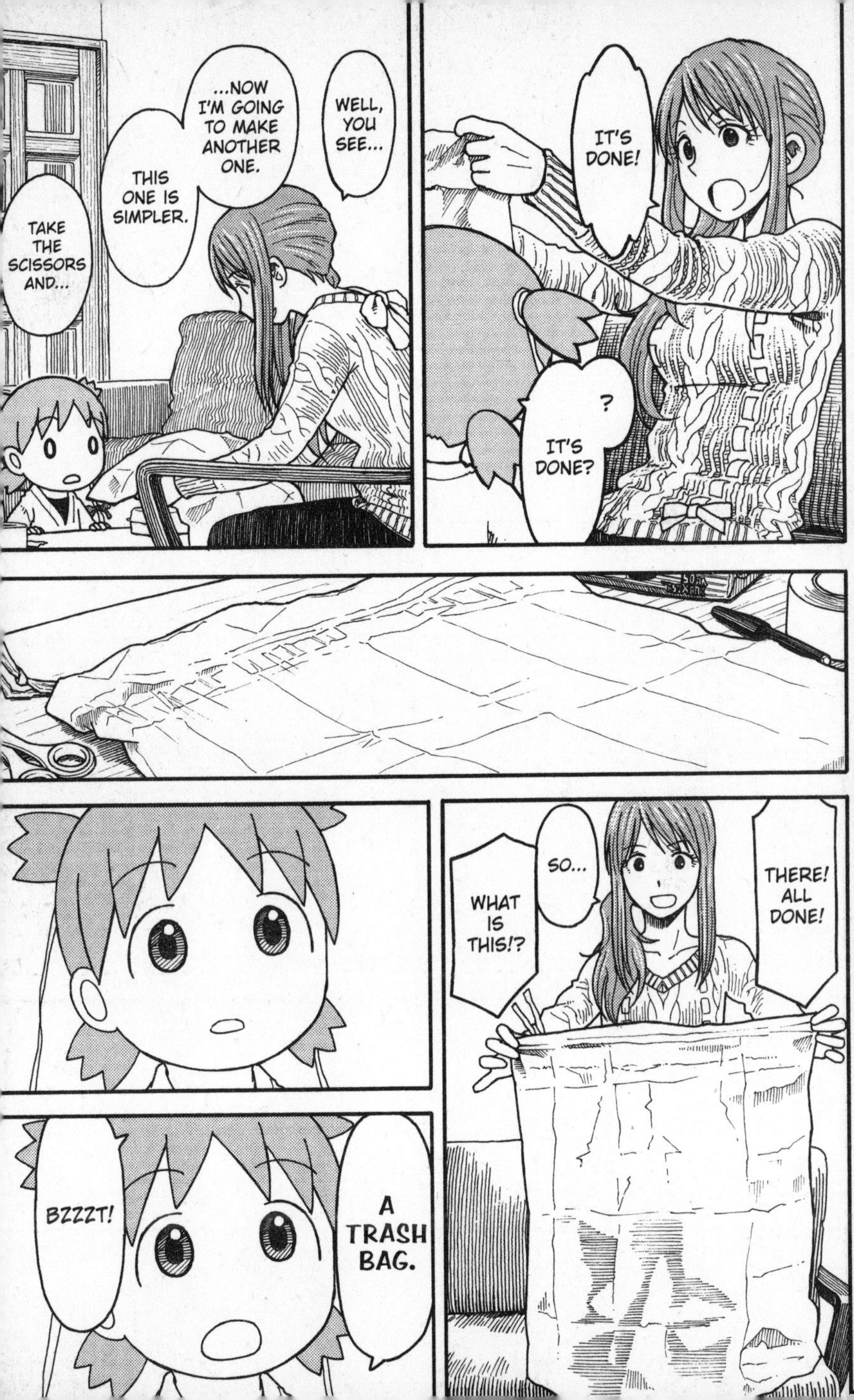
IT'S DONE!
?
IT'S DONE?
WELL, YOU SEE...
...NOW I'M GOING TO MAKE ANOTHER ONE.
THIS ONE IS SIMPLER.
TAKE THE SCISSORS AND...
THERE! ALL DONE!
SO...
WHAT IS THIS!?
A TRASH BAG.
BZZZT!

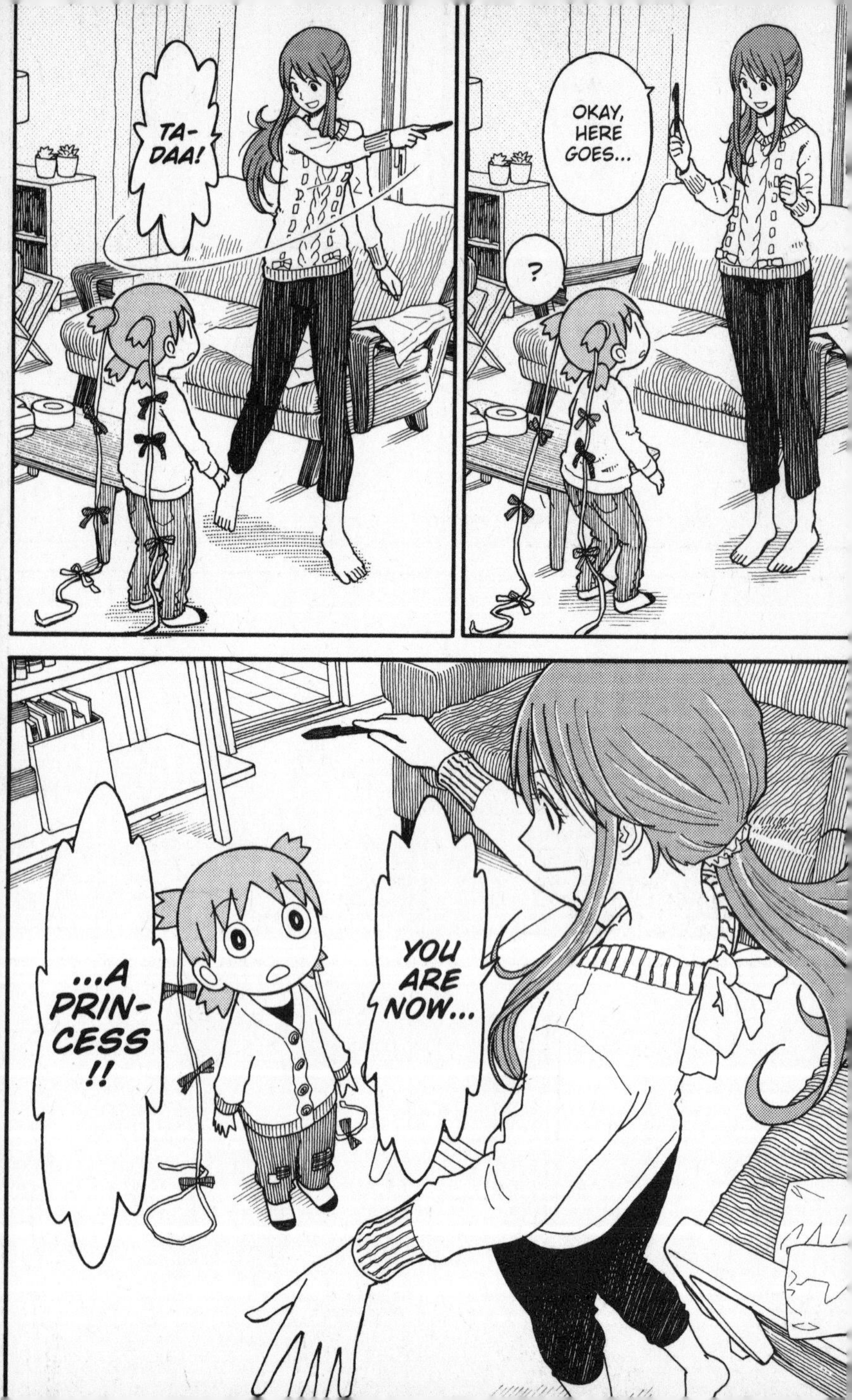
OKAY, HERE GOES...
?
TA-DAA!
YOU ARE NOW...
...A PRIN-CESS!!

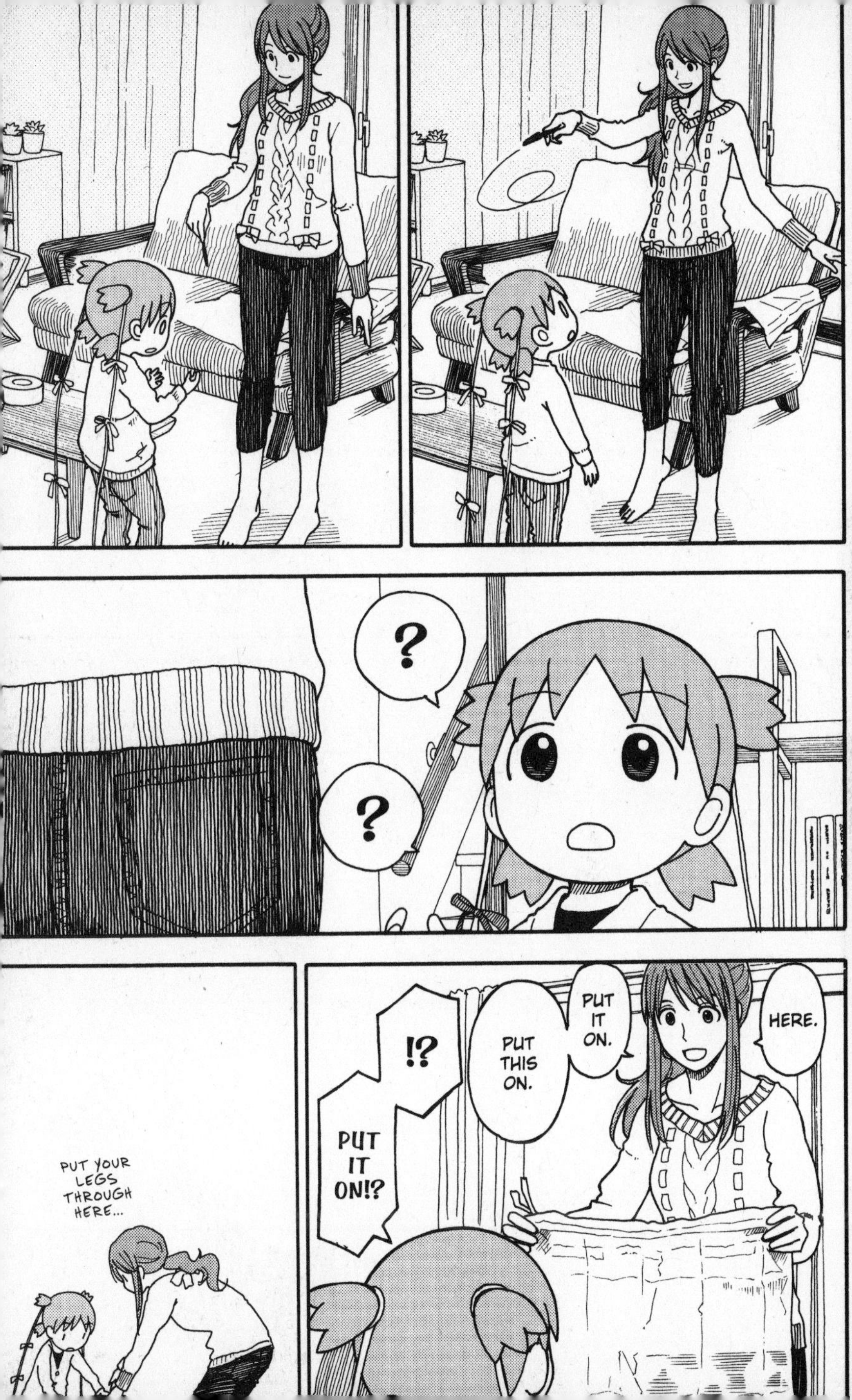
?
?
HERE.
PUT IT ON.
PUT THIS ON.
!?
PUT IT ON!?
PUT YOUR LEGS THROUGH HERE...

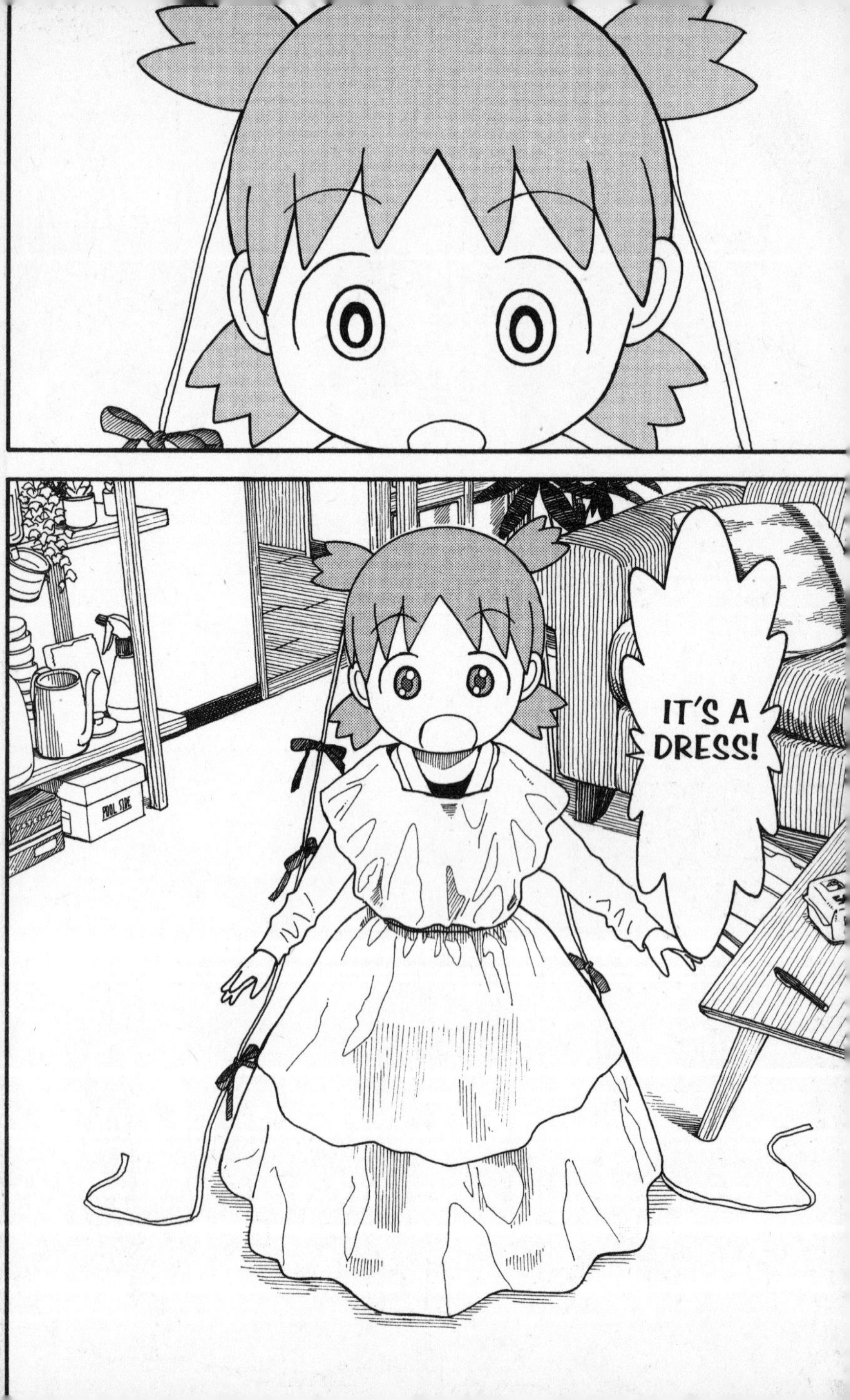
IT'S A DRESS!

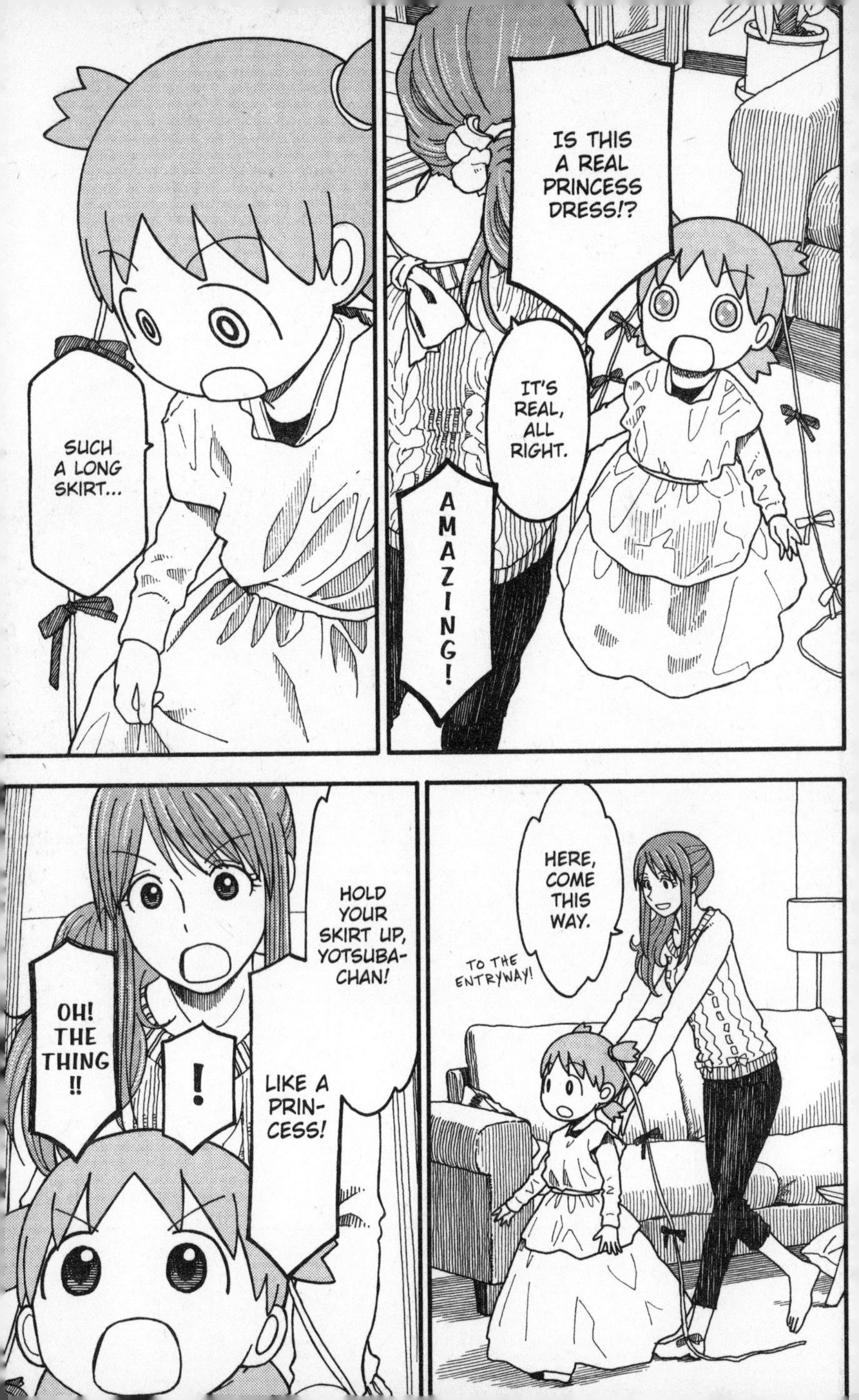
IS THIS A REAL PRINCESS DRESS!?
IT'S REAL, ALL RIGHT.
AMAZING!
SUCH A LONG SKIRT...
HERE, COME THIS WAY.
TO THE ENTRYWAY!
HOLD YOUR SKIRT UP, YOTSUBA-CHAN!
LIKE A PRIN-CESS!
!
OH! THE THING!!

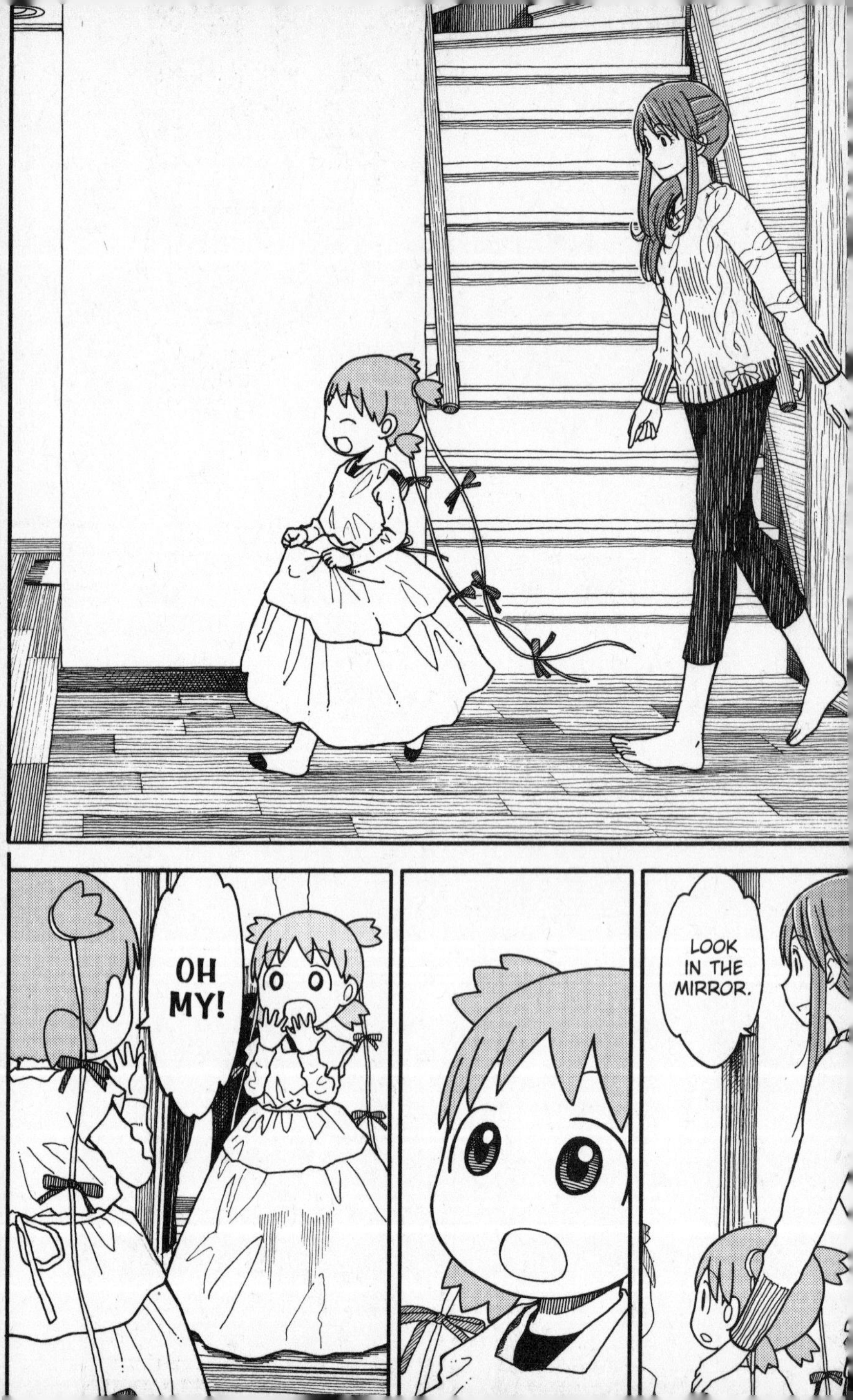
LOOK IN THE MIRROR.
OH MY!

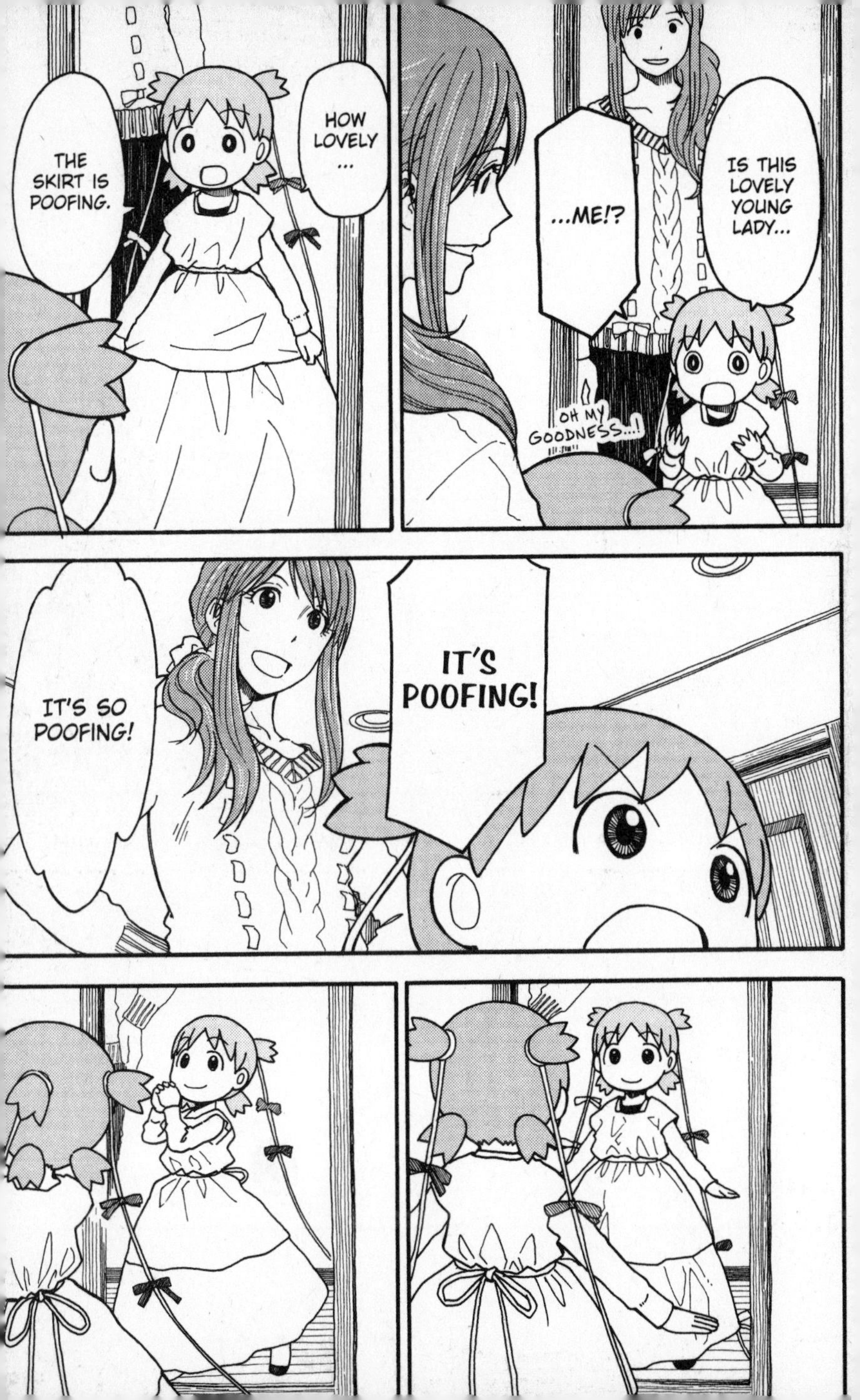
IS THIS LOVELY YOUNG LADY...
...ME!?
OH MY GOODNESS...!
HOW LOVELY ...
THE SKIRT IS POOFING.
IT'S POOFING!
IT'S SO POOFING!

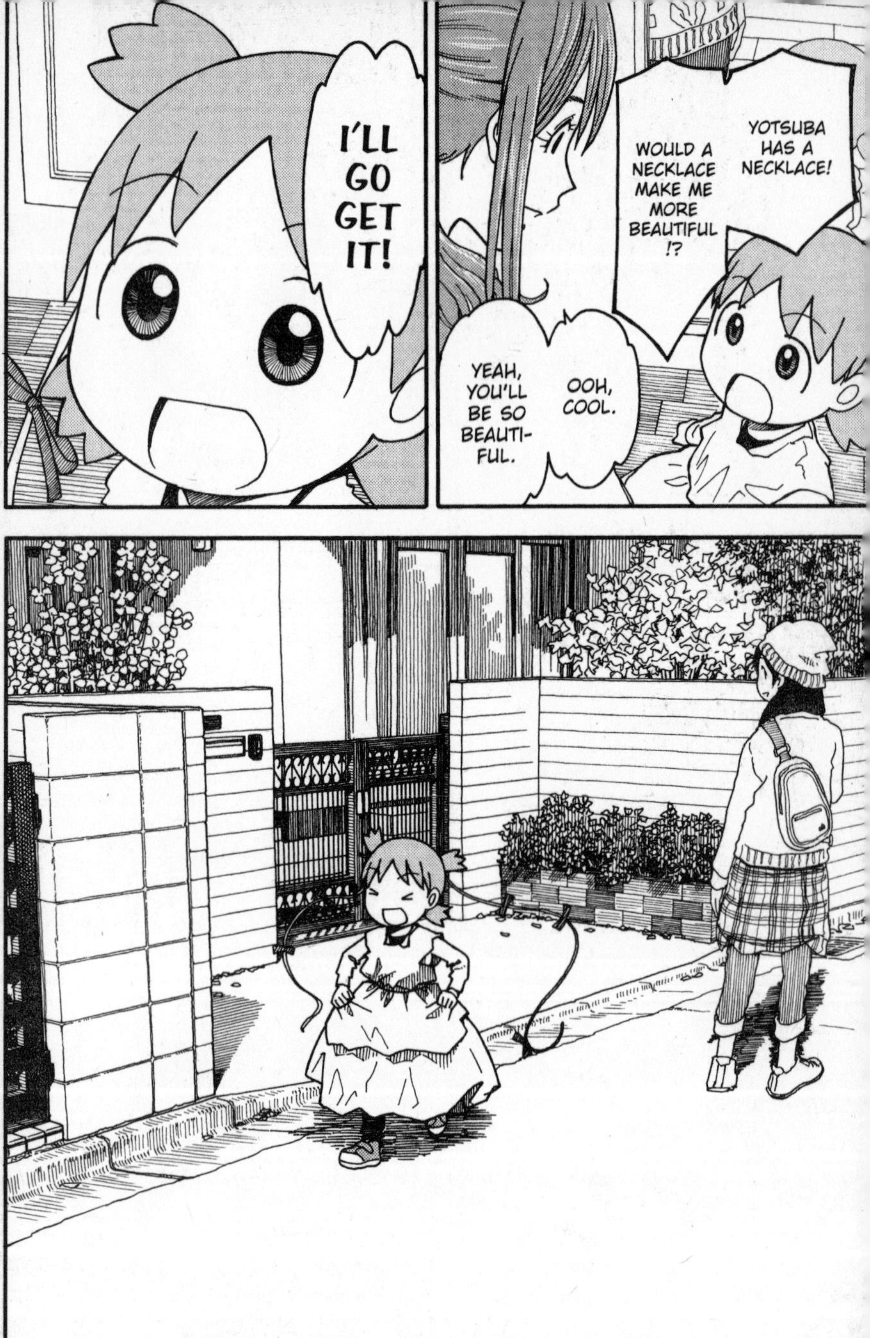
YOTSUBA HAS A NECKLACE!
WOULD A NECKLACE MAKE ME MORE BEAUTIFUL!?
OOH, COOL.
YEAH, YOU'LL BE SO BEAUTIFUL.
I'LL GO GET IT!

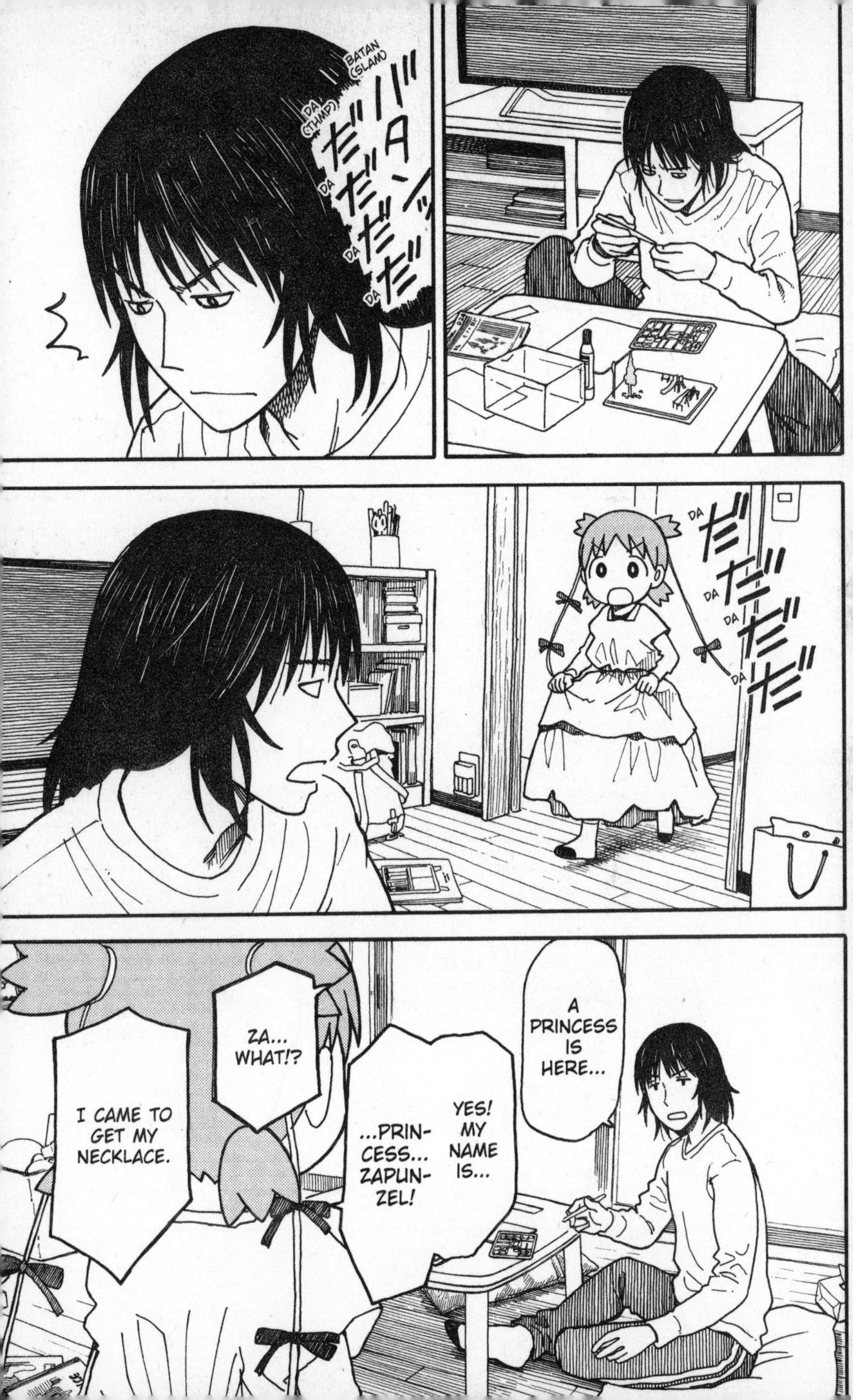
BATAN (SLAM)
DA (THMP)
DA
DA
DA
DA
DA
DA
DA
A PRINCESS IS HERE...
YES! MY NAME IS...
...PRIN-CESS... ZAPUN-ZEL!
ZA... WHAT!?
I CAME TO GET MY NECKLACE.

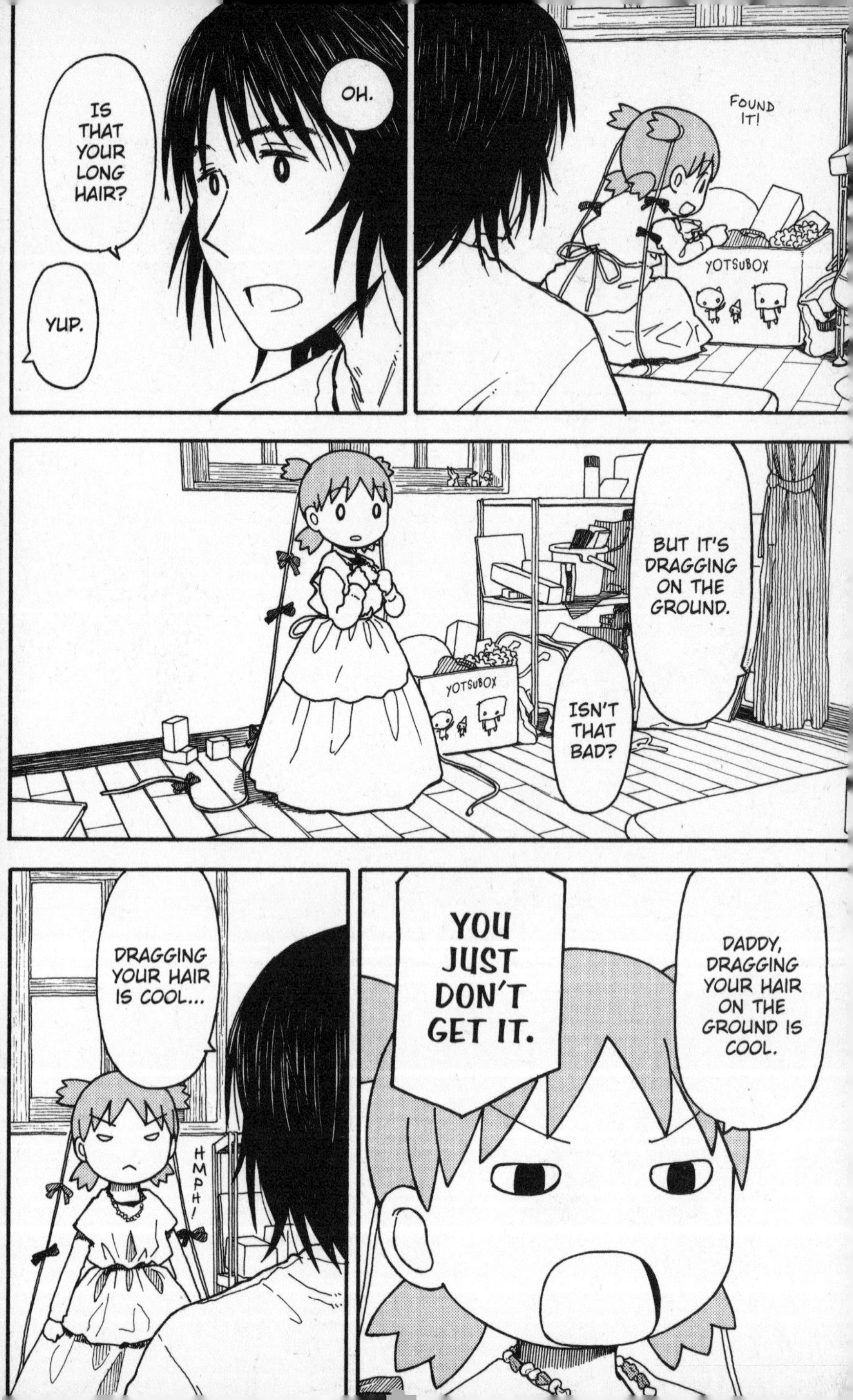
FOUND IT!
YOTSUBOX
OH.
IS THAT YOUR LONG HAIR?
YUP.
BUT IT'S DRAGGING ON THE GROUND.
ISN'T THAT BAD?
YOTSUBOX
DADDY, DRAGGING YOUR HAIR ON THE GROUND IS COOL.
YOU JUST DON'T GET IT.
DRAGGING YOUR HAIR IS COOL...
HMPH!

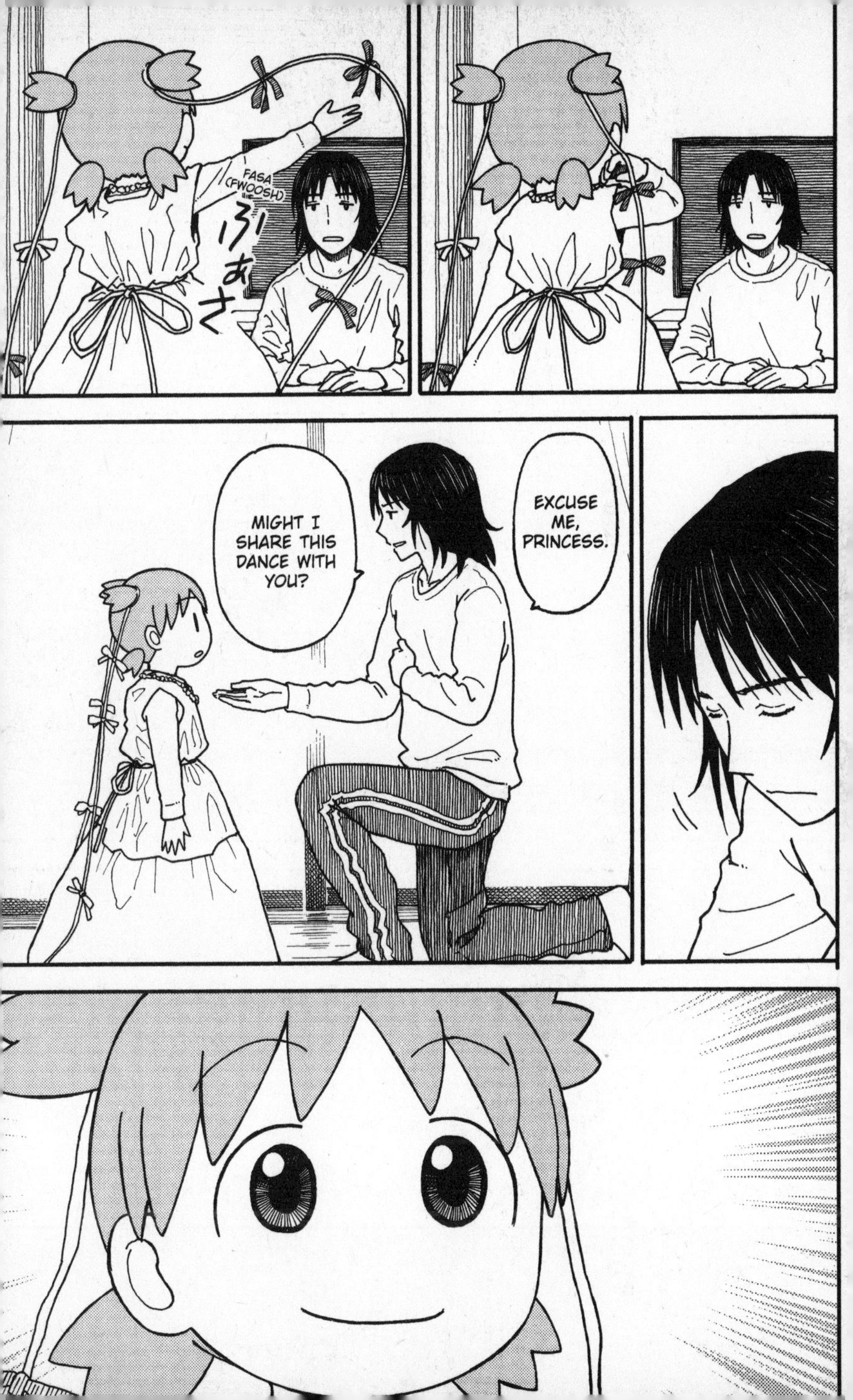

FASA
(FWOOSH)
EXCUSE ME, PRINCESS.
MIGHT I SHARE THIS DANCE WITH YOU?

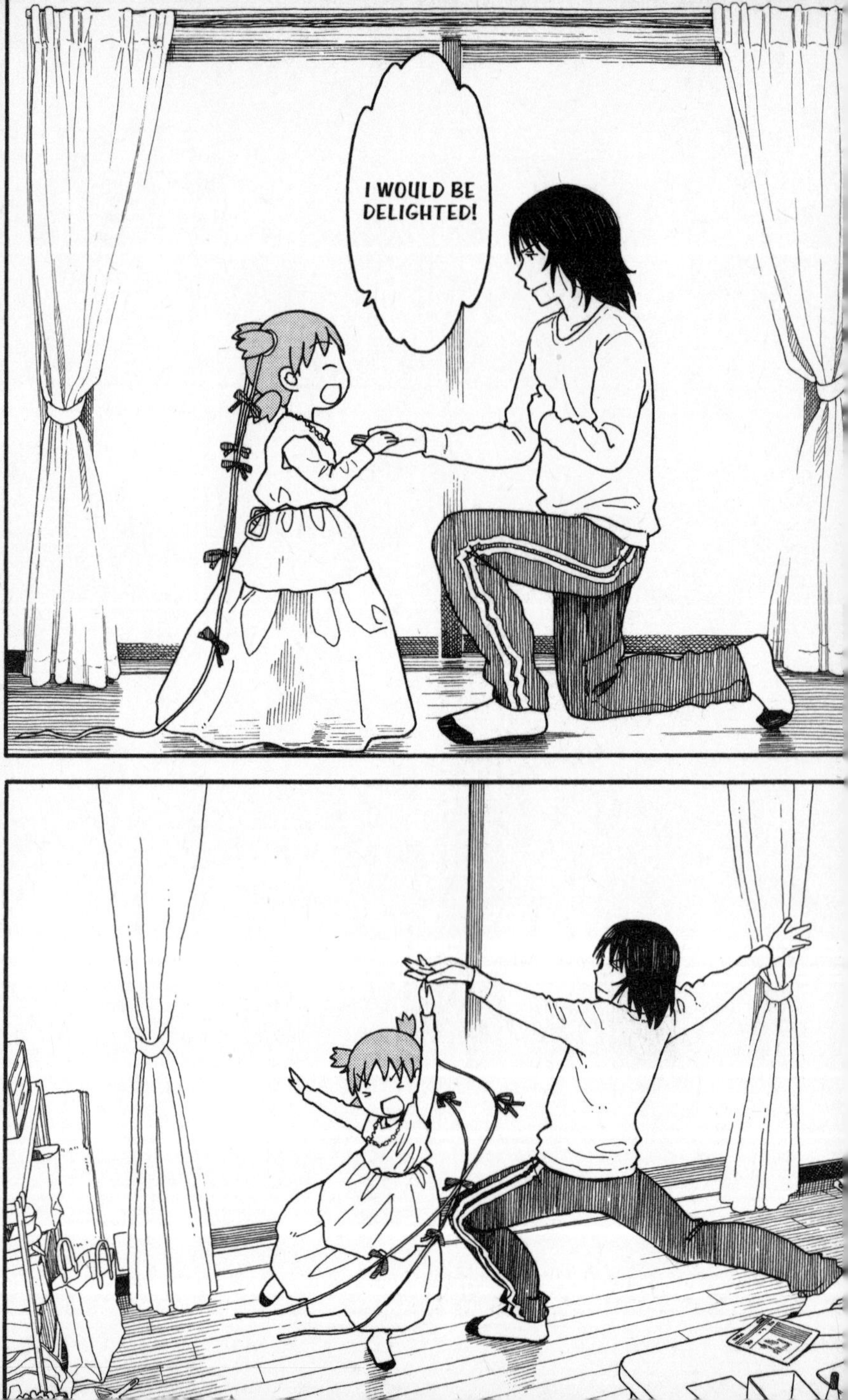
I WOULD BE DELIGHTED!

YOTSUBA&!

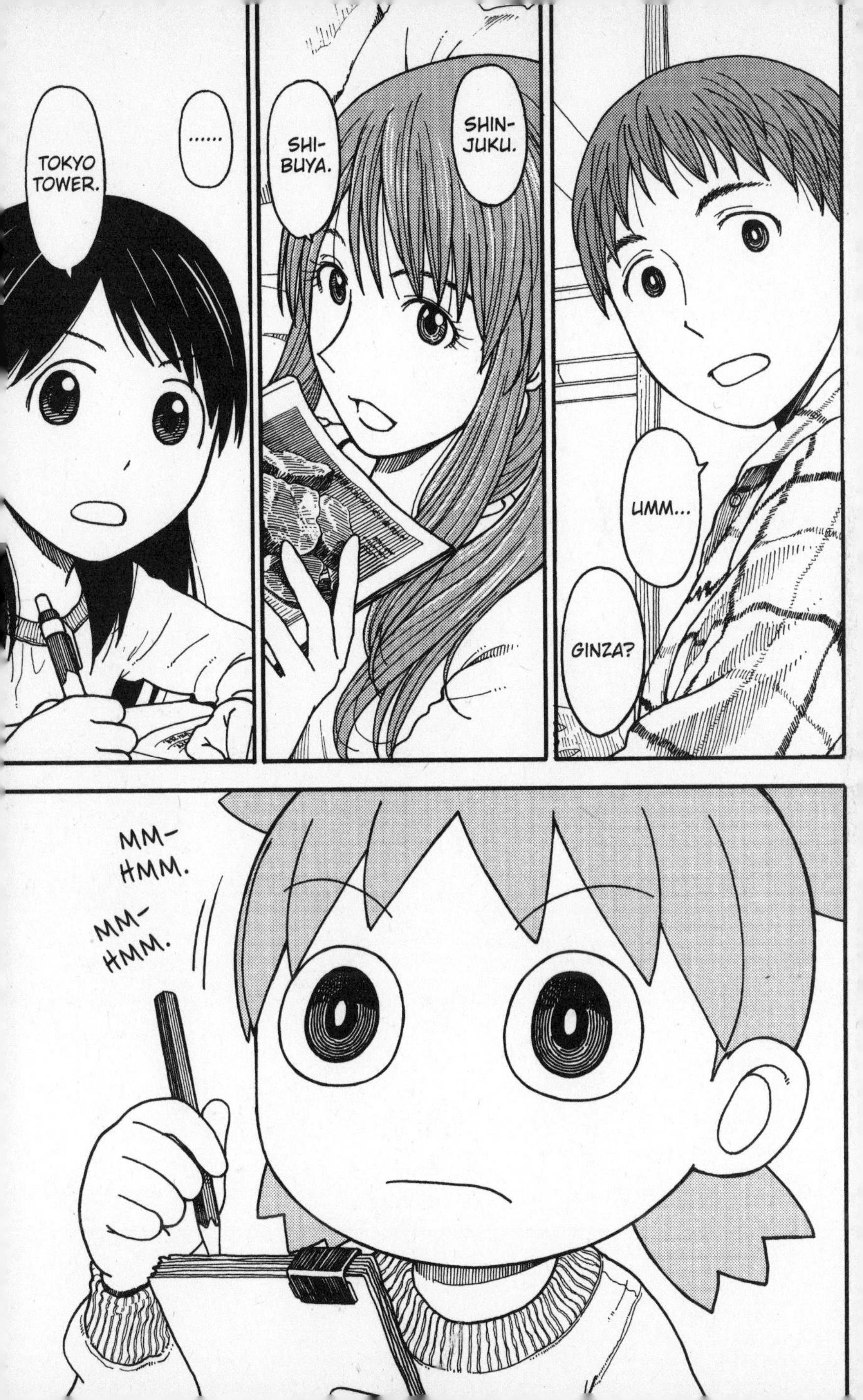
UMM...
GINZA?
SHIN-JUKU.
SHI-BUYA.
......
TOKYO TOWER.
MM-HMM.
MM-HMM.

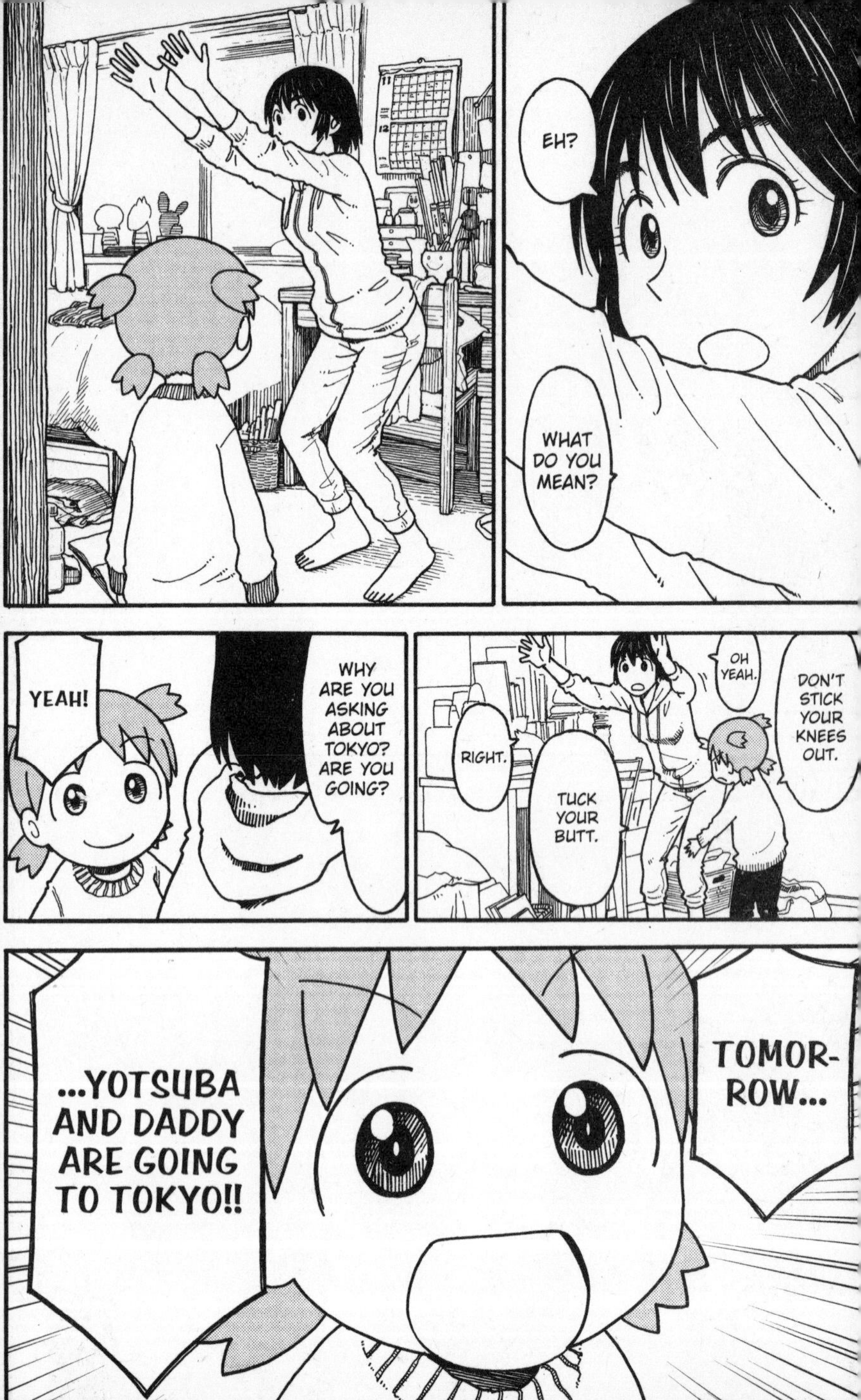
EH?
WHAT DO YOU MEAN?
DON'T STICK YOUR KNEES OUT.
OH YEAH.
TUCK YOUR BUTT.
RIGHT.
WHY ARE YOU ASKING ABOUT TOKYO? ARE YOU GOING?
YEAH!
TOMOR-ROW...
...YOTSUBA AND DADDY ARE GOING TO TOKYO!!

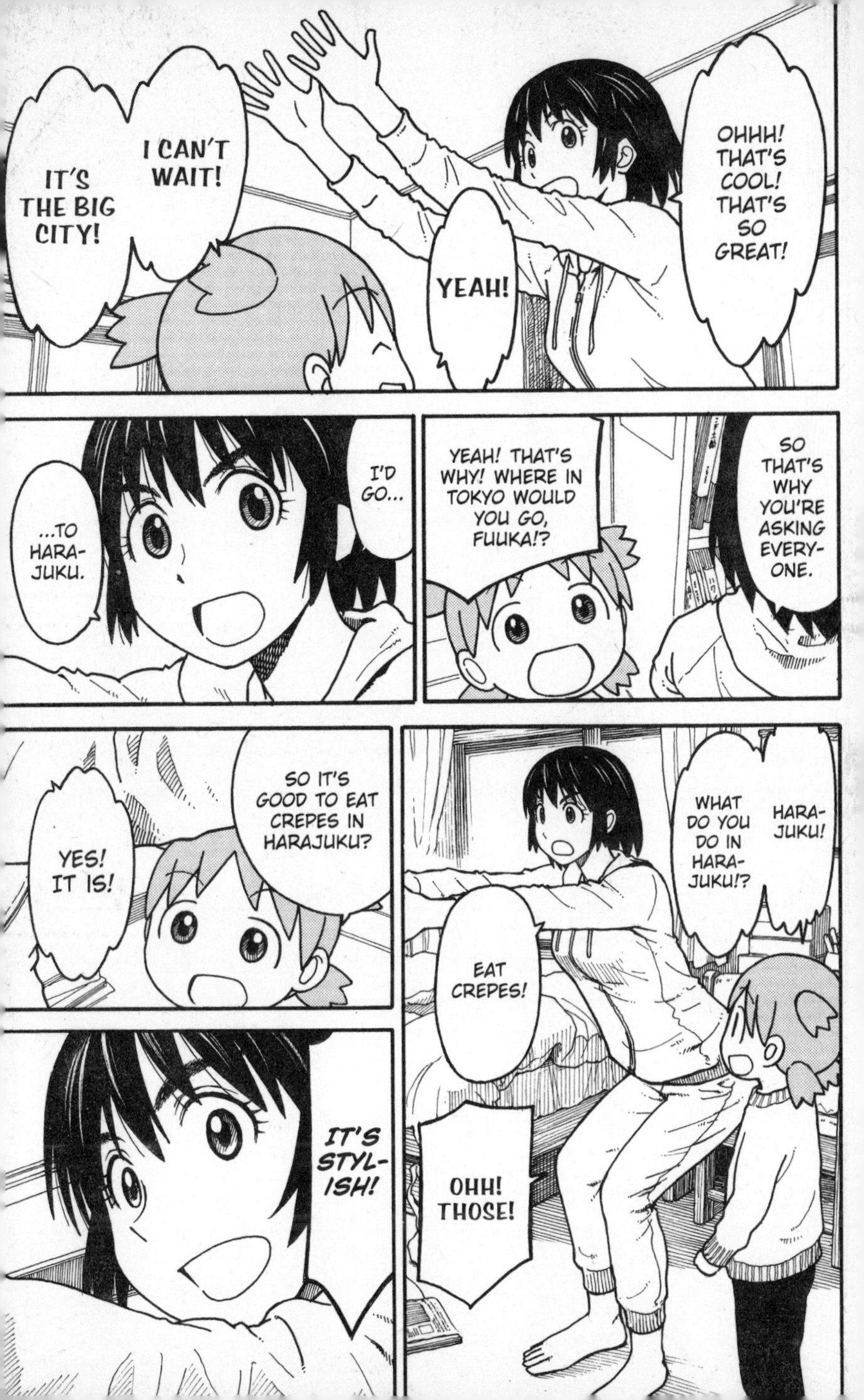
OHHH! THAT'S COOL! THAT'S SO GREAT!
YEAH!
I CAN'T WAIT!
IT'S THE BIG CITY!
SO THAT'S WHY YOU'RE ASKING EVERY-ONE.
YEAH! THAT'S WHY! WHERE IN TOKYO WOULD YOU GO, FUUKA!?
I'D GO...
...TO HARA-JUKU.
HARA-JUKU!
WHAT DO YOU DO IN HARA-JUKU!?
EAT CREPES!
OHH! THOSE!
SO IT'S GOOD TO EAT CREPES IN HARAJUKU?
YES! IT IS!
IT'S STYL-ISH!

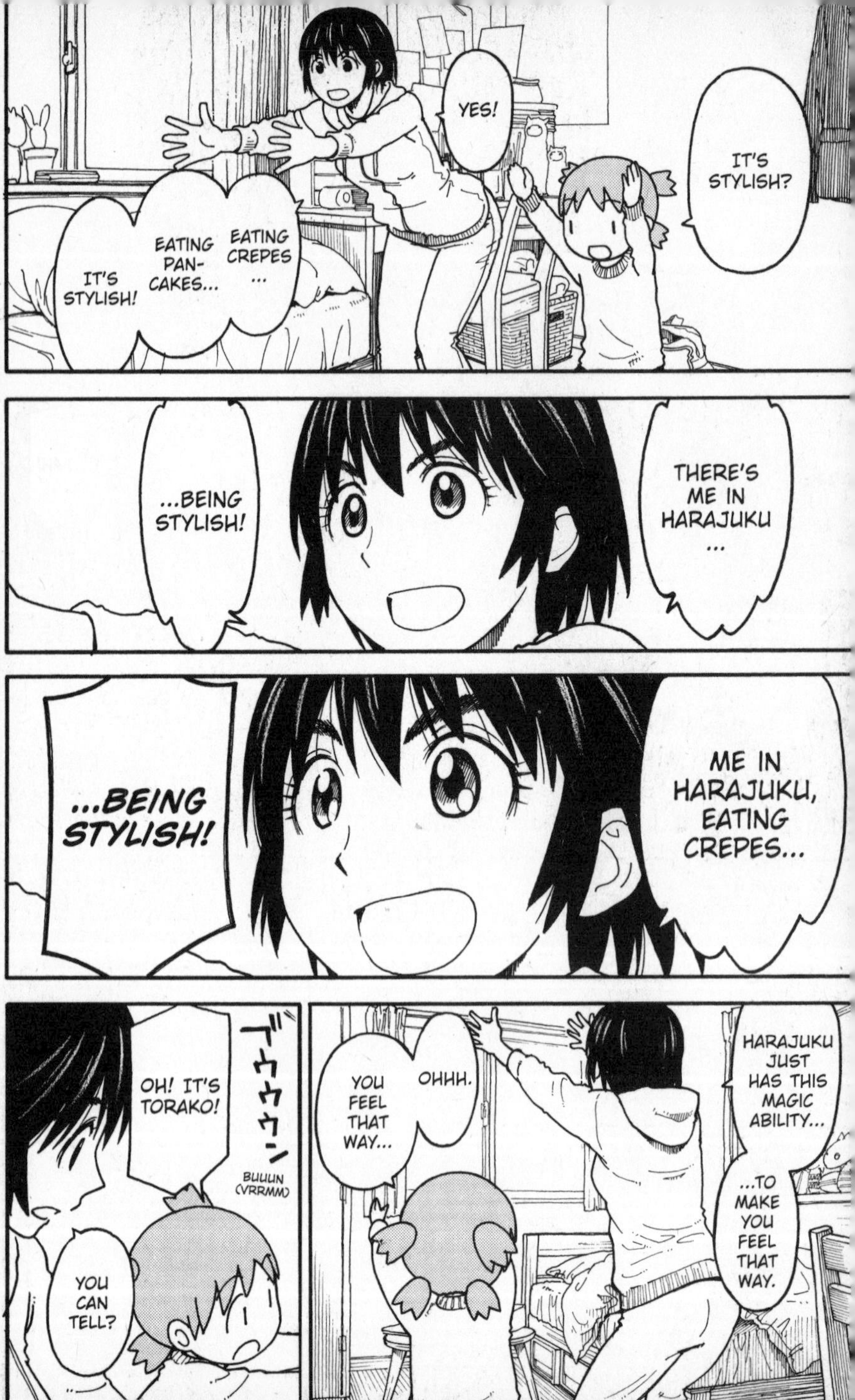
IT'S STYLISH?
YES!
EATING CREPES... EATING PAN-CAKES... IT'S STYLISH!
THERE'S ME IN HARAJUKU...
...BEING STYLISH!
ME IN HARAJUKU, EATING CREPES...
...BEING STYLISH!
HARAJUKU JUST HAS THIS MAGIC ABILITY...
...TO MAKE YOU FEEL THAT WAY.
OHHH.
YOU FEEL THAT WAY...
ブウウウン
BUUUN (VRRMM)
OH! IT'S TORAKO!
YOU CAN TELL?

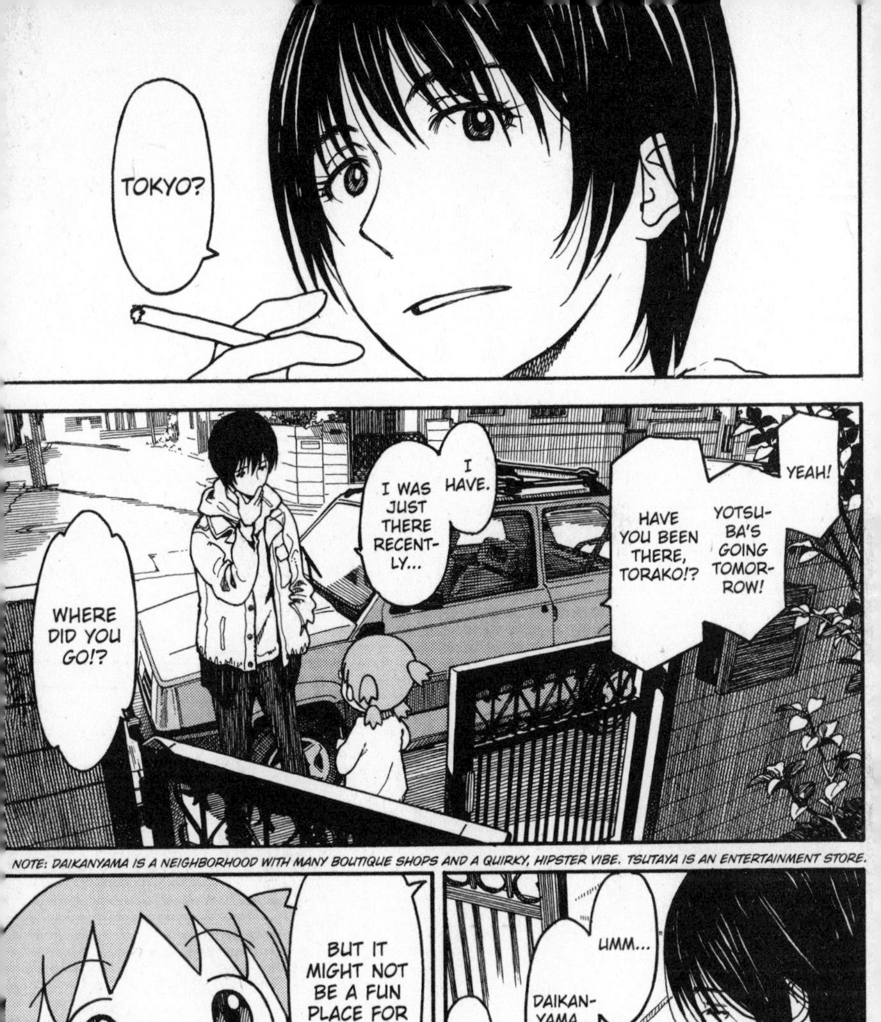
TOKYO?
YEAH!
YOTSU-BA'S GOING TOMOR-ROW!
HAVE YOU BEEN THERE, TORAKO!?
I HAVE.
I WAS JUST THERE RECENT-LY...
WHERE DID YOU GO!?

NOTE: DAIKANYAMA IS A NEIGHBORHOOD WITH MANY BOUTIQUE SHOPS AND A QUIRKY, HIPSTER VIBE. TSUTAYA IS AN ENTERTAINMENT STORE.

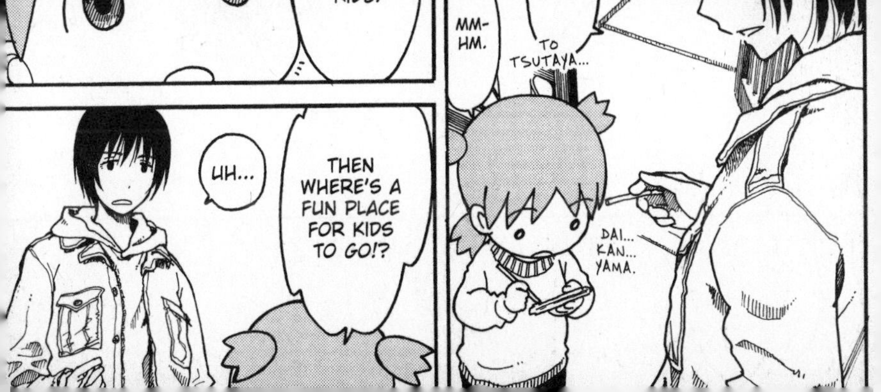
UMM...
DAIKAN-YAMA...
TO TSUTAYA...
MM-HM.
DAI... KAN... YAMA.
BUT IT MIGHT NOT BE A FUN PLACE FOR KIDS.
THEN WHERE'S A FUN PLACE FOR KIDS TO GO!?
UH...

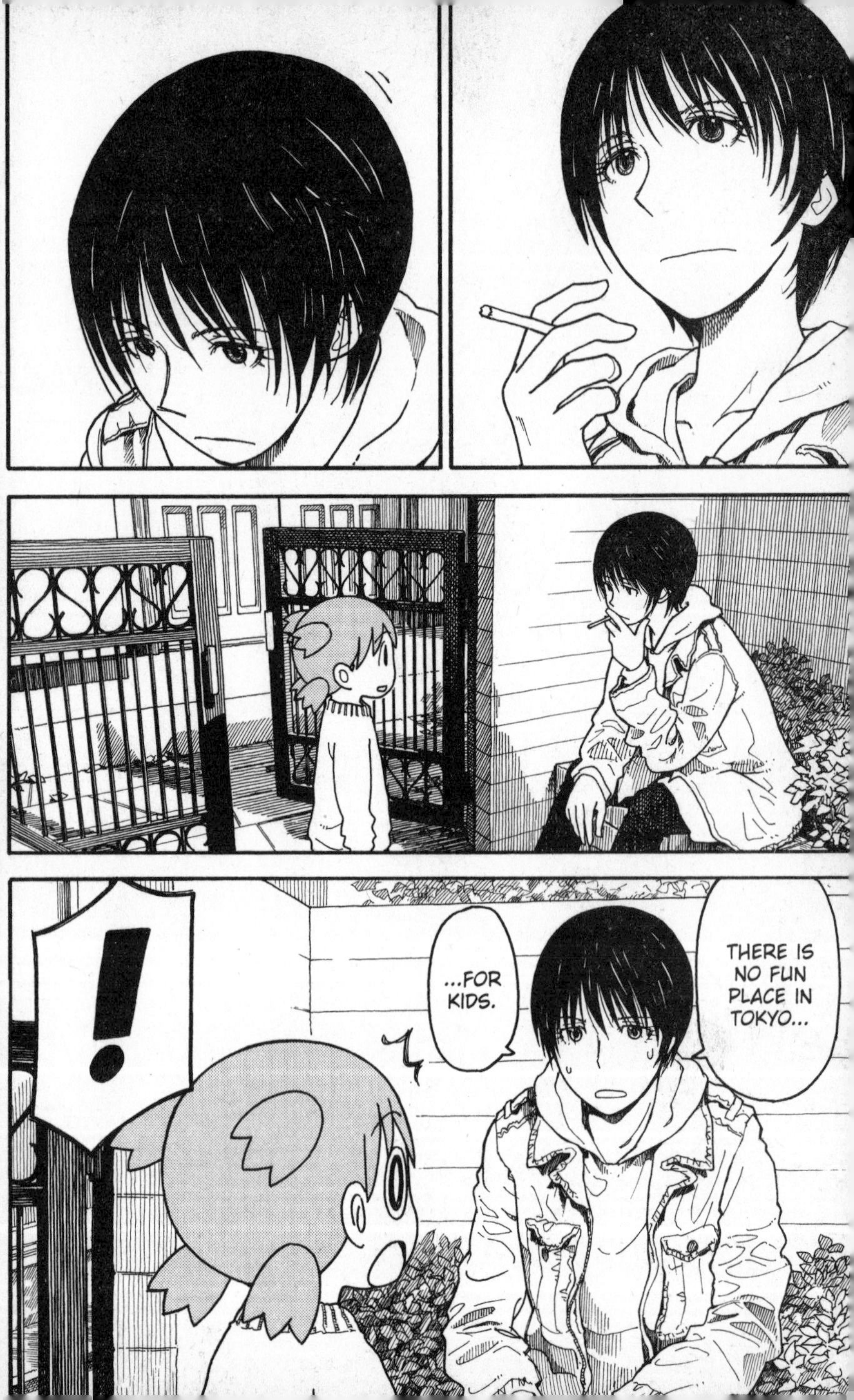
THERE IS NO FUN PLACE IN TOKYO...
...FOR KIDS.
!

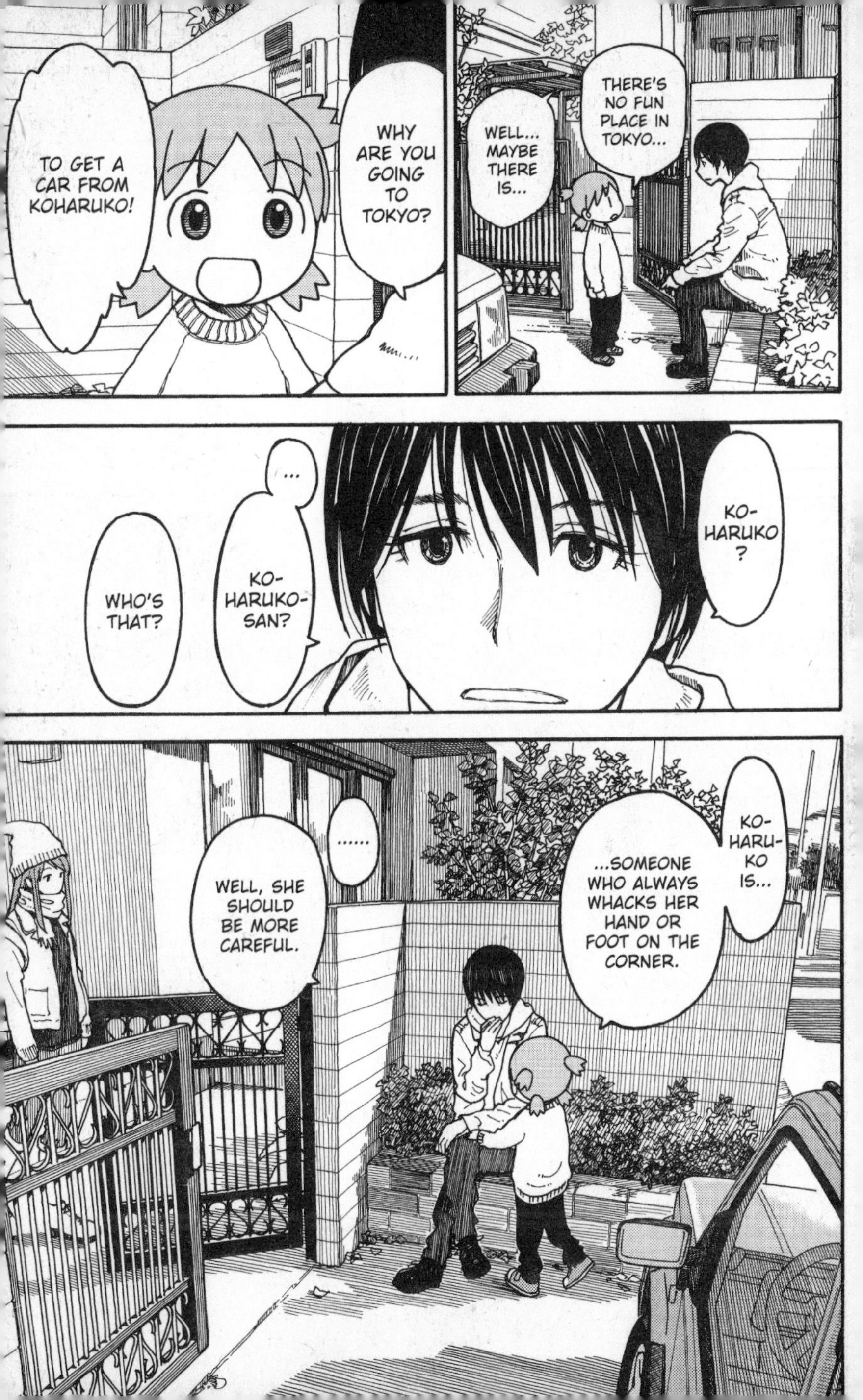
THERE'S NO FUN PLACE IN TOKYO...
WELL... MAYBE THERE IS...
WHY ARE YOU GOING TO TOKYO?
TO GET A CAR FROM KOHARUKO!
KO-HARUKO?
...
KO-HARUKO-SAN?
WHO'S THAT?
KO-HARU-KO IS...
...SOMEONE WHO ALWAYS WHACKS HER HAND OR FOOT ON THE CORNER.
......
WELL, SHE SHOULD BE MORE CAREFUL.

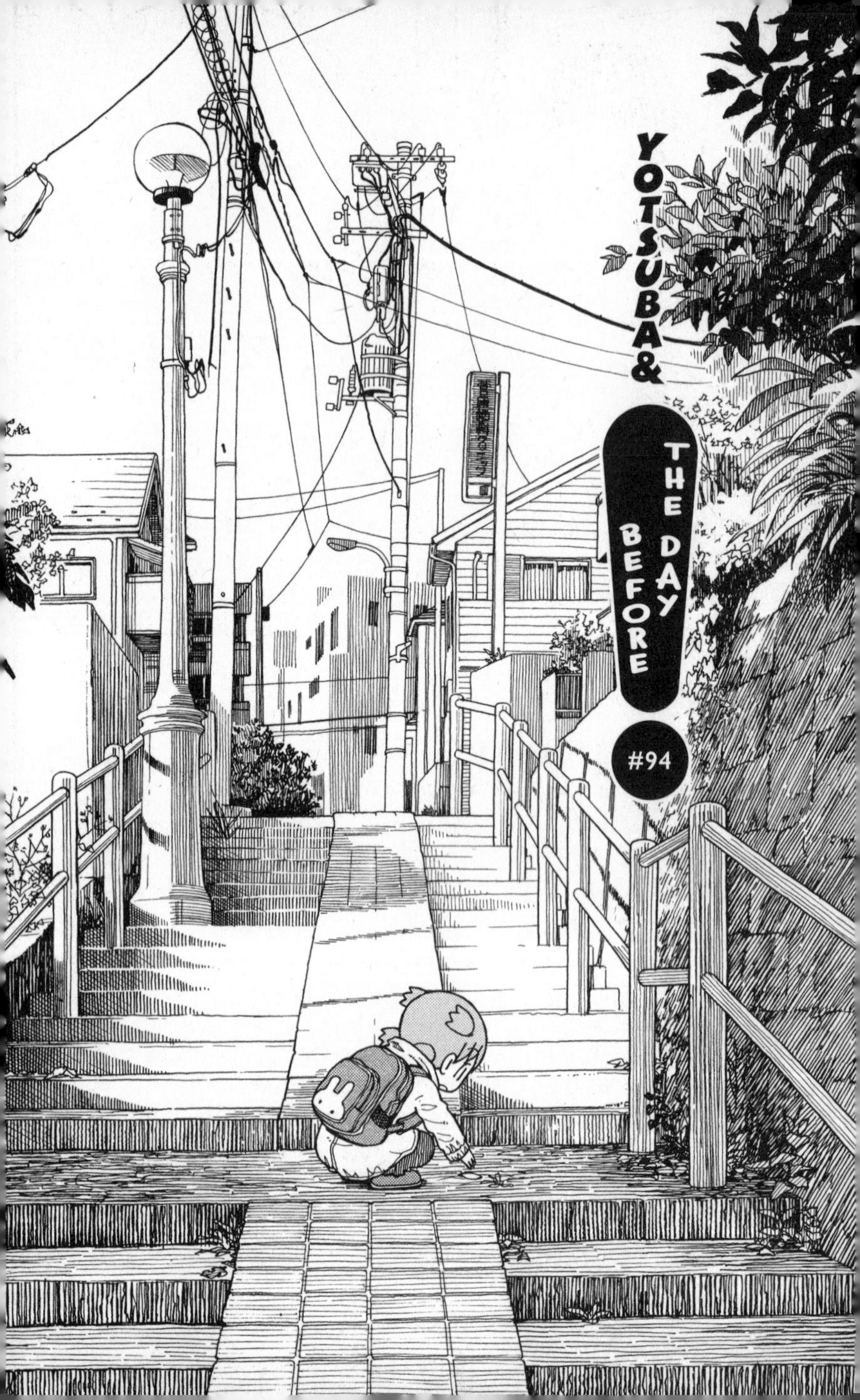
YOTSUBA&
THE DAY BEFORE
#94

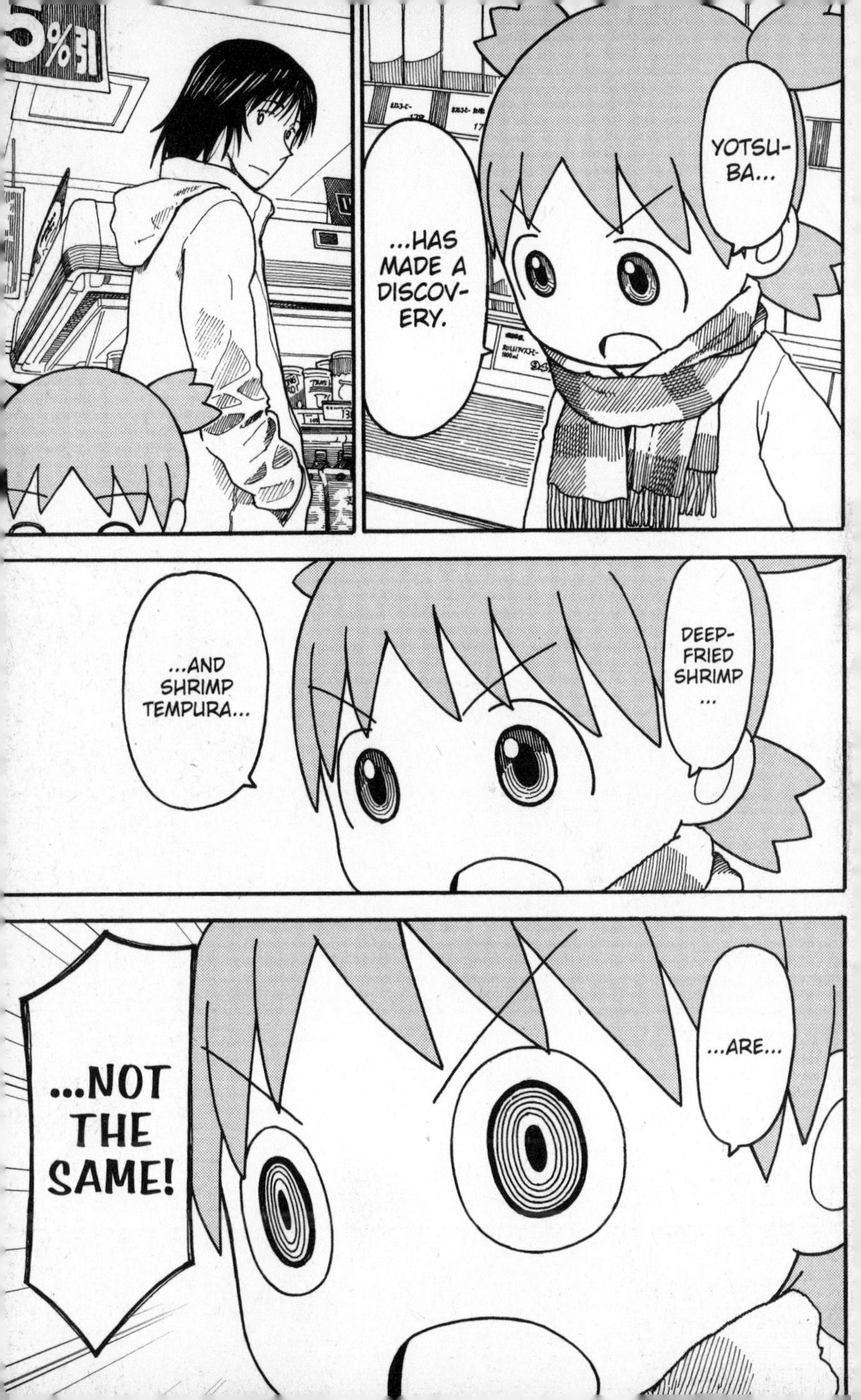
YOTSU-BA...
...HAS MADE A DISCOV-ERY.
DEEP-FRIED SHRIMP ...
...AND SHRIMP TEMPURA...
...ARE...
...NOT THE SAME!

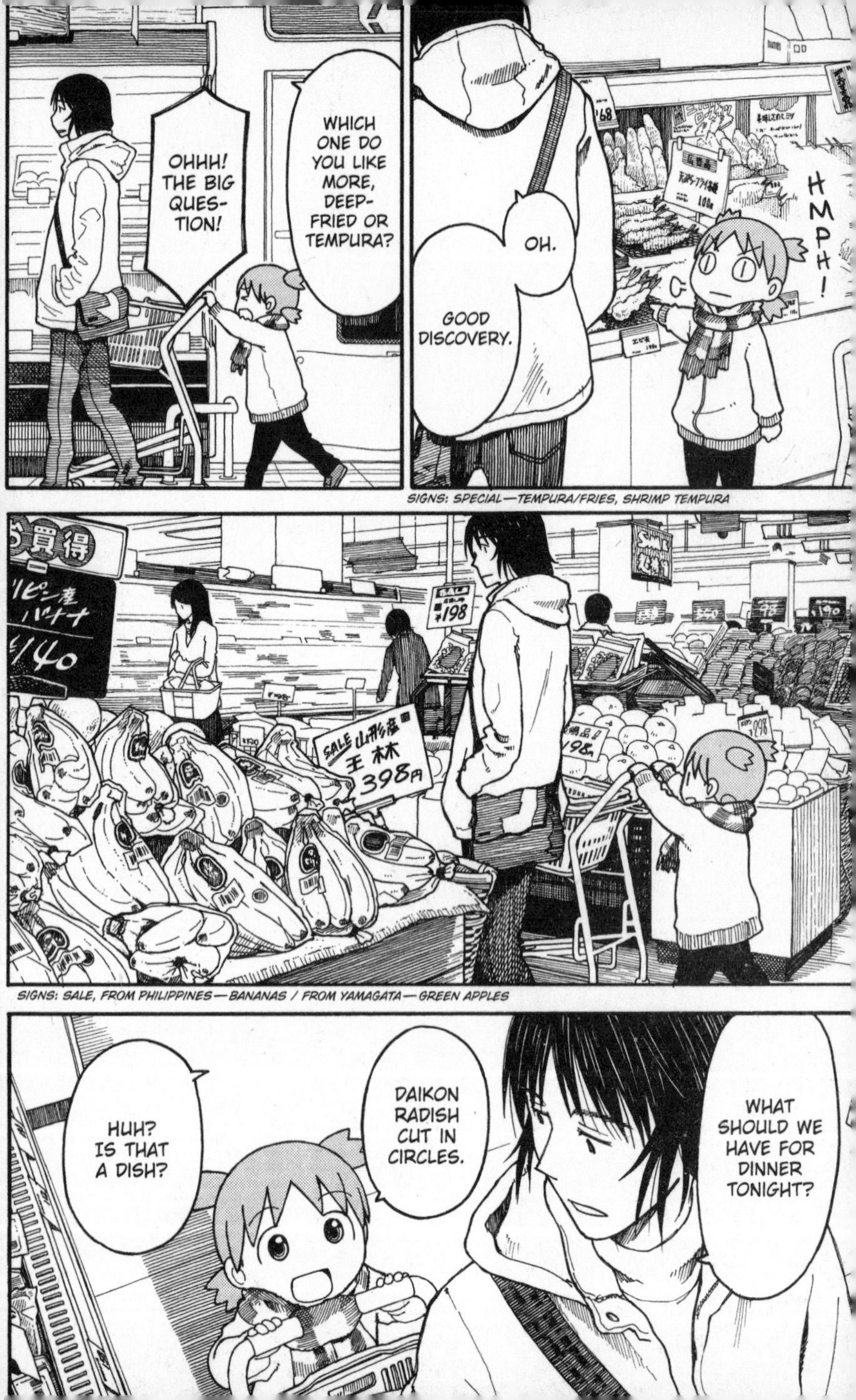
HMPH!
OH.
GOOD DISCOVERY.
WHICH ONE DO YOU LIKE MORE, DEEP-FRIED OR TEMPURA?
OHHH! THE BIG QUESTION!
SIGNS: SPECIAL—TEMPURA/FRIES, SHRIMP TEMPURA
SALE
¥198
SALE 山形産 王林 398円
198円
¥298
SIGNS: SALE, FROM PHILIPPINES—BANANAS / FROM YAMAGATA—GREEN APPLES
WHAT SHOULD WE HAVE FOR DINNER TONIGHT?
DAIKON RADISH CUT IN CIRCLES.
HUH? IS THAT A DISH?

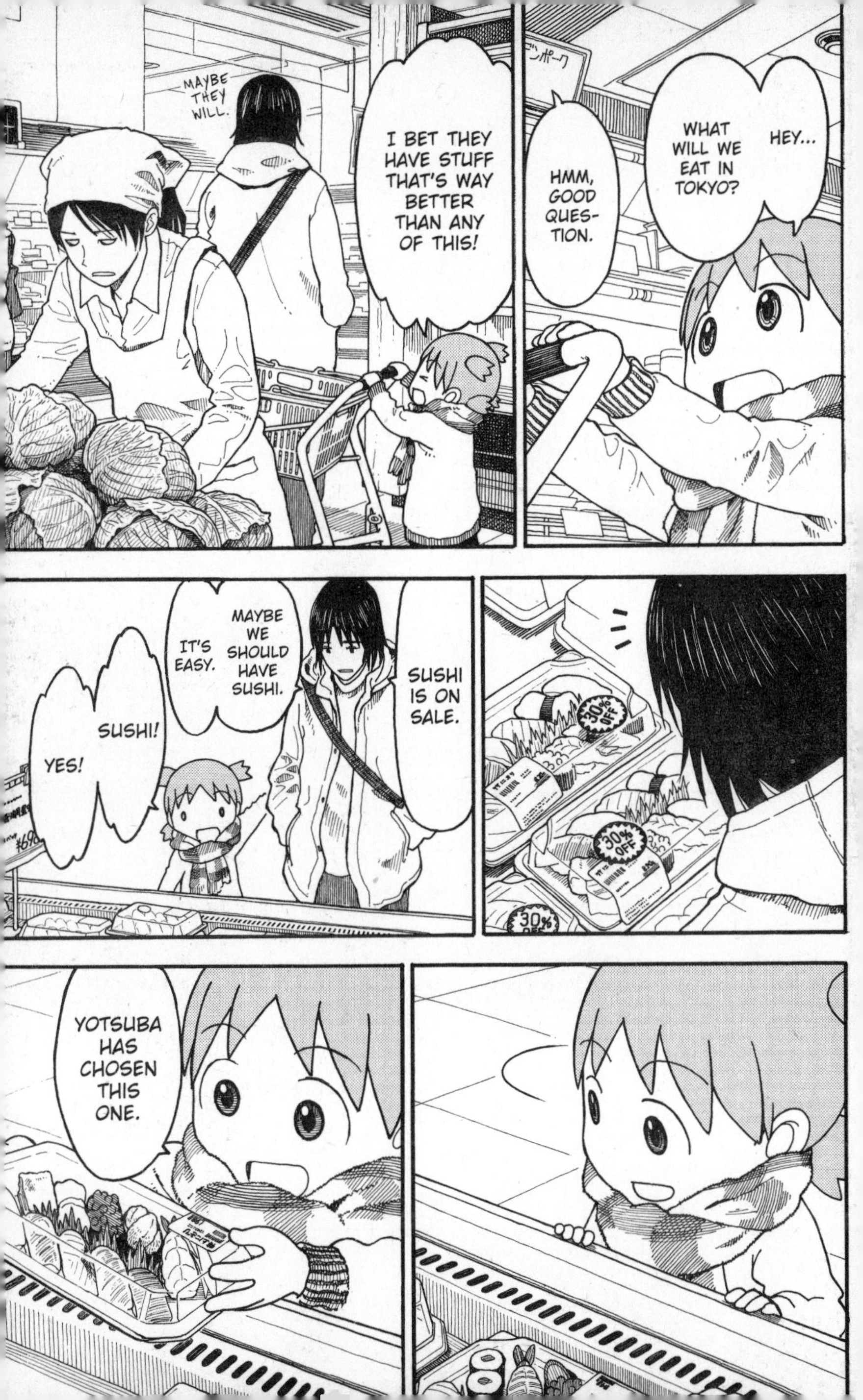
HEY...
WHAT WILL WE EAT IN TOKYO?
HMM, GOOD QUESTION.
I BET THEY HAVE STUFF THAT'S WAY BETTER THAN ANY OF THIS!
MAYBE THEY WILL.
30% OFF
30% OFF
SUSHI IS ON SALE.
MAYBE WE SHOULD HAVE SUSHI.
IT'S EASY.
SUSHI!
YES!
YOTSUBA HAS CHOSEN THIS ONE.

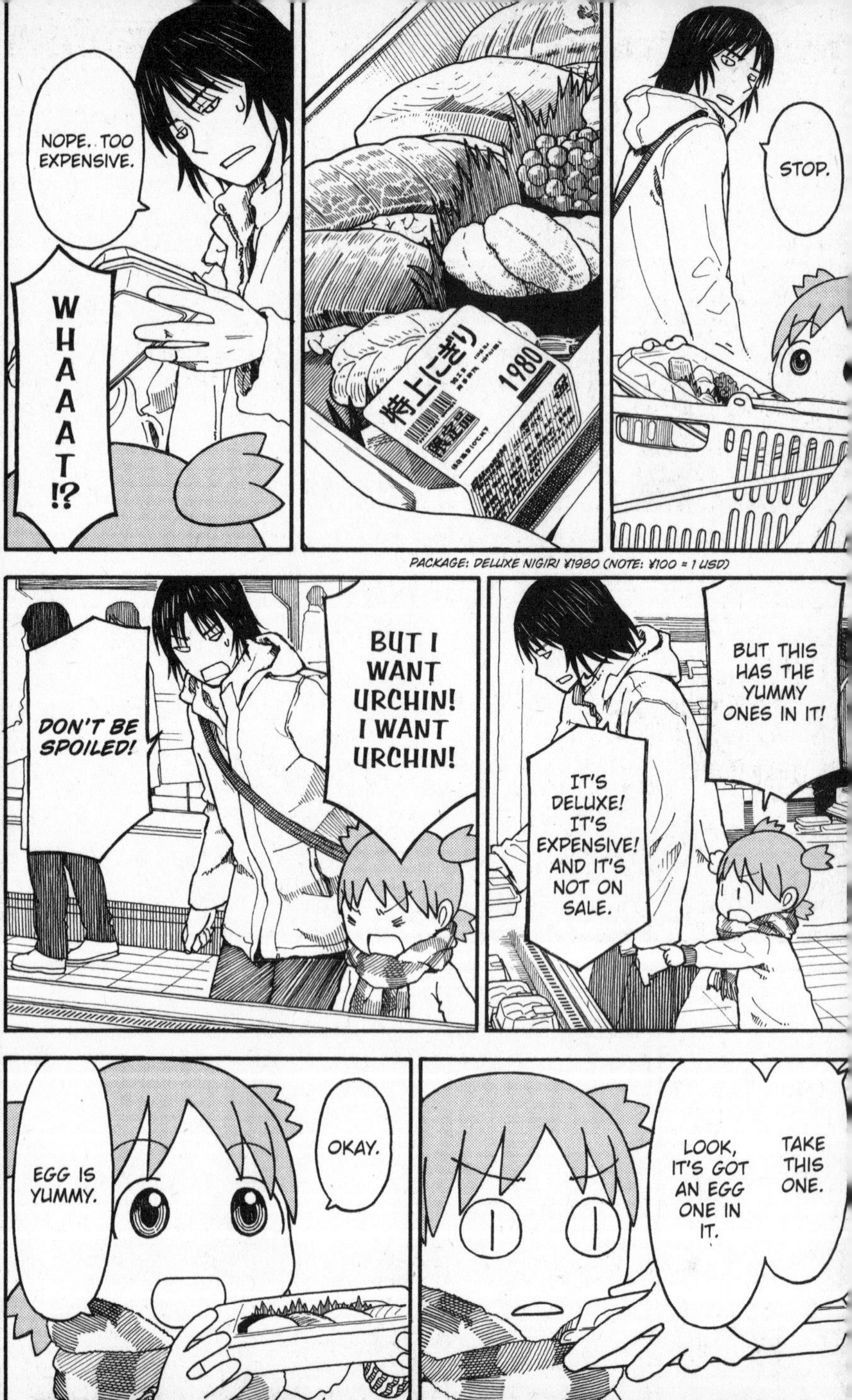
STOP.
特上にぎり
1980
限定品
NOPE. TOO EXPENSIVE.
WHAAAAT!?
PACKAGE: DELUXE NIGIRI ¥1980 (NOTE: ¥100 ≈ 1 USD)
BUT THIS HAS THE YUMMY ONES IN IT!
IT'S DELUXE! IT'S EXPENSIVE! AND IT'S NOT ON SALE.
BUT I WANT URCHIN! I WANT URCHIN!
DON'T BE SPOILED!
TAKE THIS ONE.
LOOK, IT'S GOT AN EGG ONE IN IT.
OKAY.
EGG IS YUMMY.

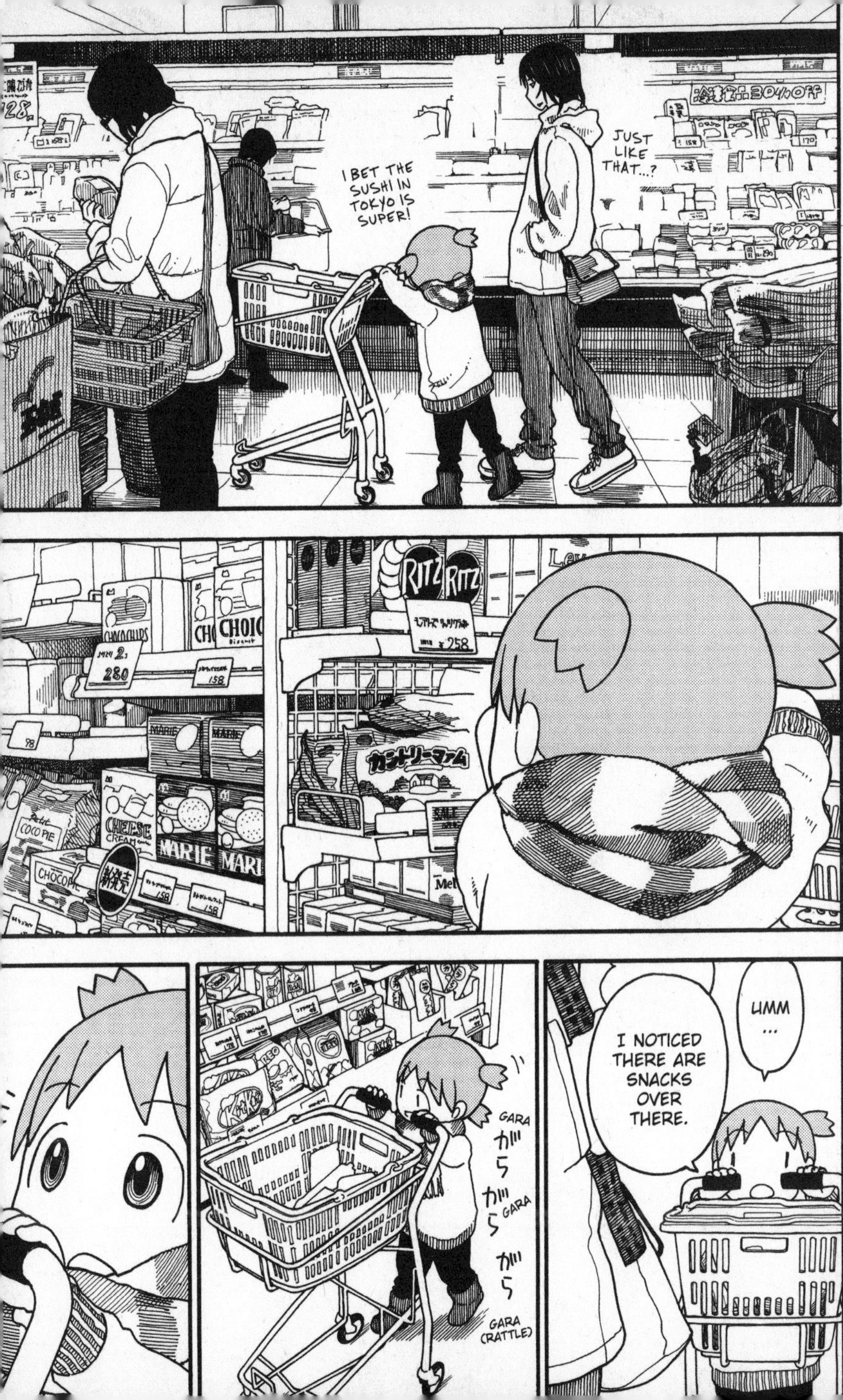

JUST LIKE THAT...?
I BET THE SUSHI IN TOKYO IS SUPER!
UMM ...
I NOTICED THERE ARE SNACKS OVER THERE.
がら GARA
がら GARA
がら GARA (RATTLE)

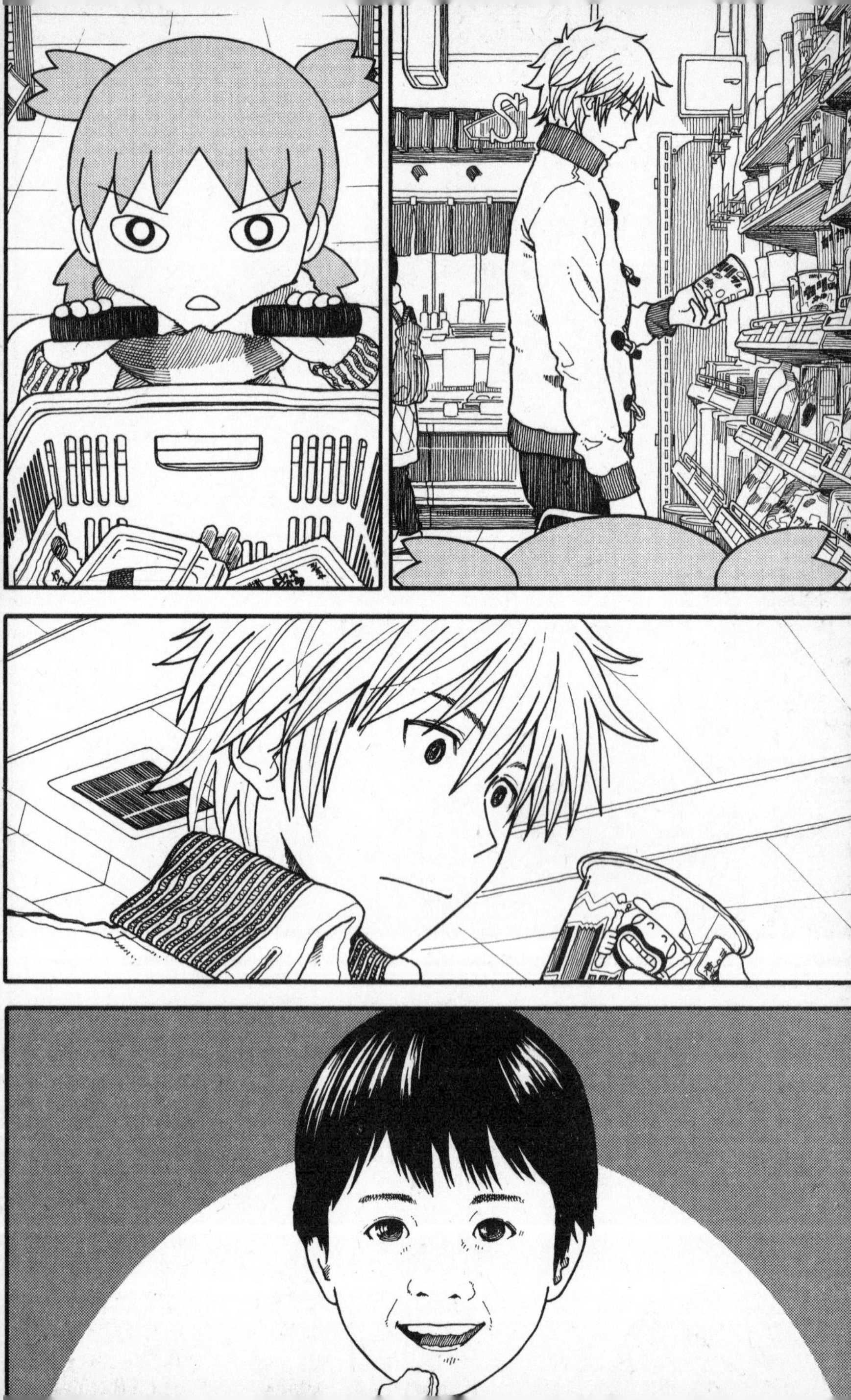

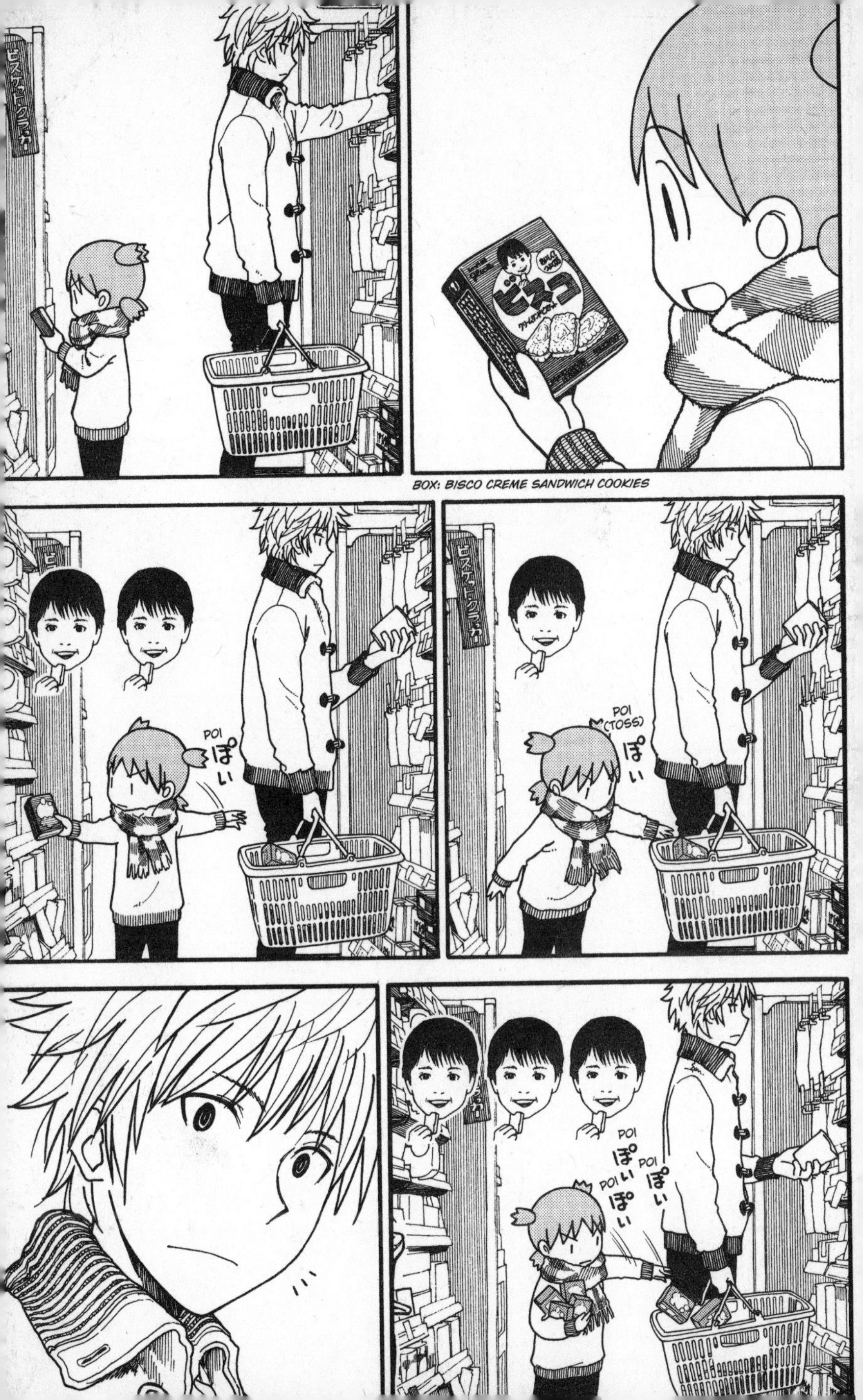
BOX: BISCO CREME SANDWICH COOKIES
ビスケット・クラッカー
POI (TOSS)
ぽい
ビスケット・クラッカー
POI
ぽい
POI
ぽい
POI
ぽい
POI
ぽい

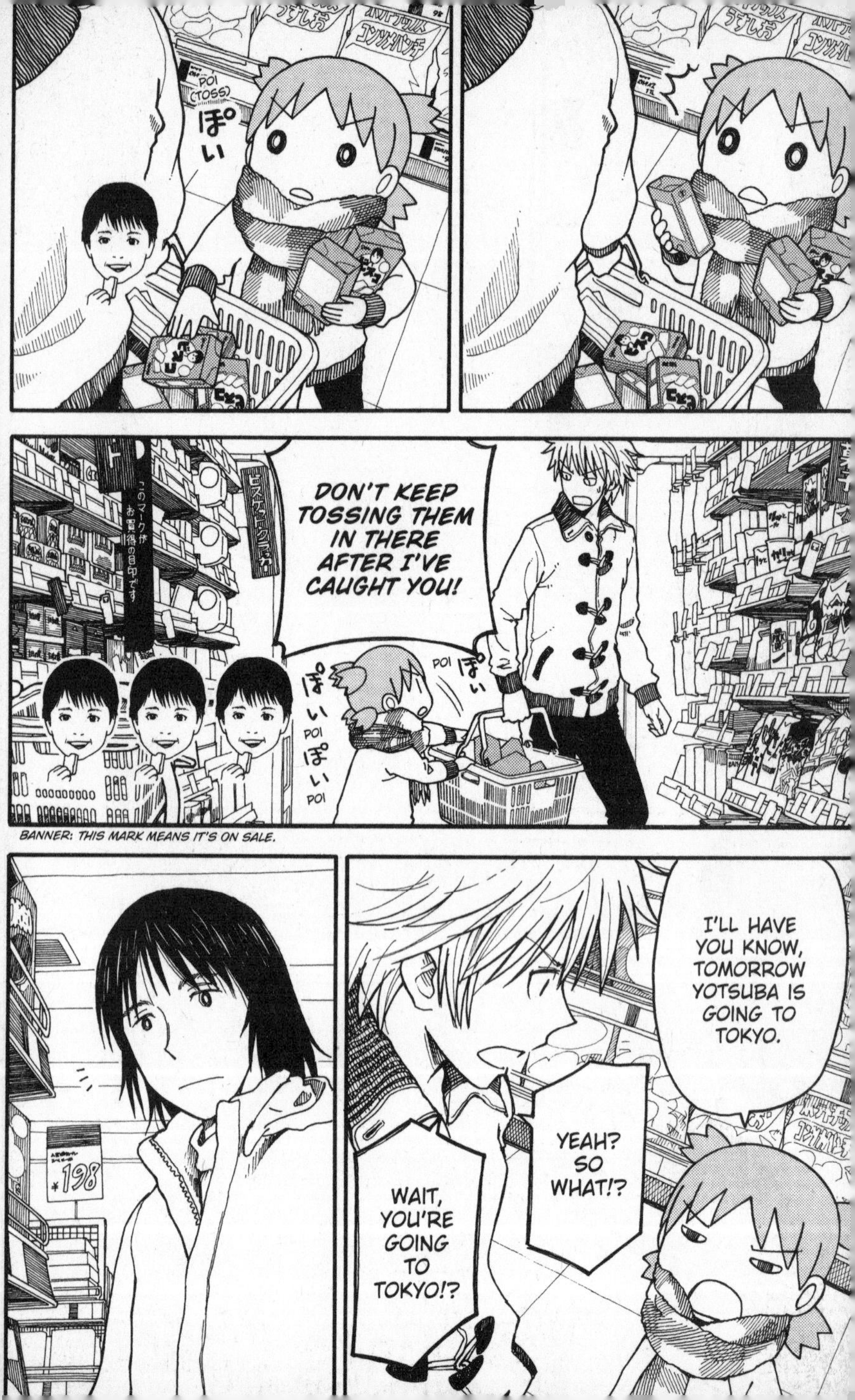
POI (TOSS)
ぽい
このマークが お買得の目印です
DON'T KEEP TOSSING THEM IN THERE AFTER I'VE CAUGHT YOU!
ぽい POI
ぽい POI
ぽい POI
I'LL HAVE YOU KNOW, TOMORROW YOTSUBA IS GOING TO TOKYO.
YEAH? SO WHAT!?
WAIT, YOU'RE GOING TO TOKYO!?
BANNER: THIS MARK MEANS IT'S ON SALE.

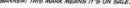

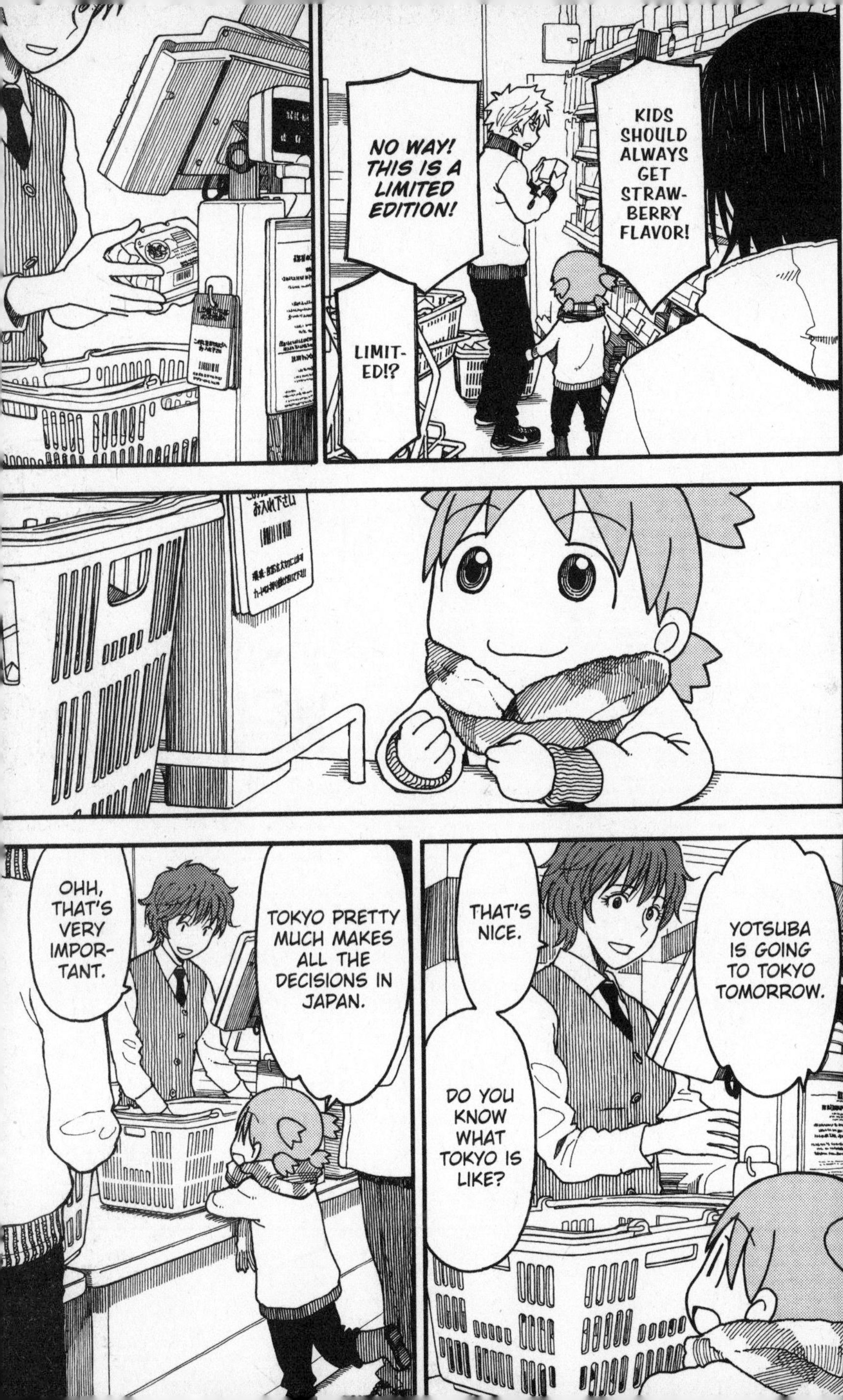
KIDS SHOULD ALWAYS GET STRAWBERRY FLAVOR!
NO WAY! THIS IS A LIMITED EDITION!
LIMITED!?
YOTSUBA IS GOING TO TOKYO TOMORROW.
THAT'S NICE.
DO YOU KNOW WHAT TOKYO IS LIKE?
TOKYO PRETTY MUCH MAKES ALL THE DECISIONS IN JAPAN.
OHH, THAT'S VERY IMPORTANT.

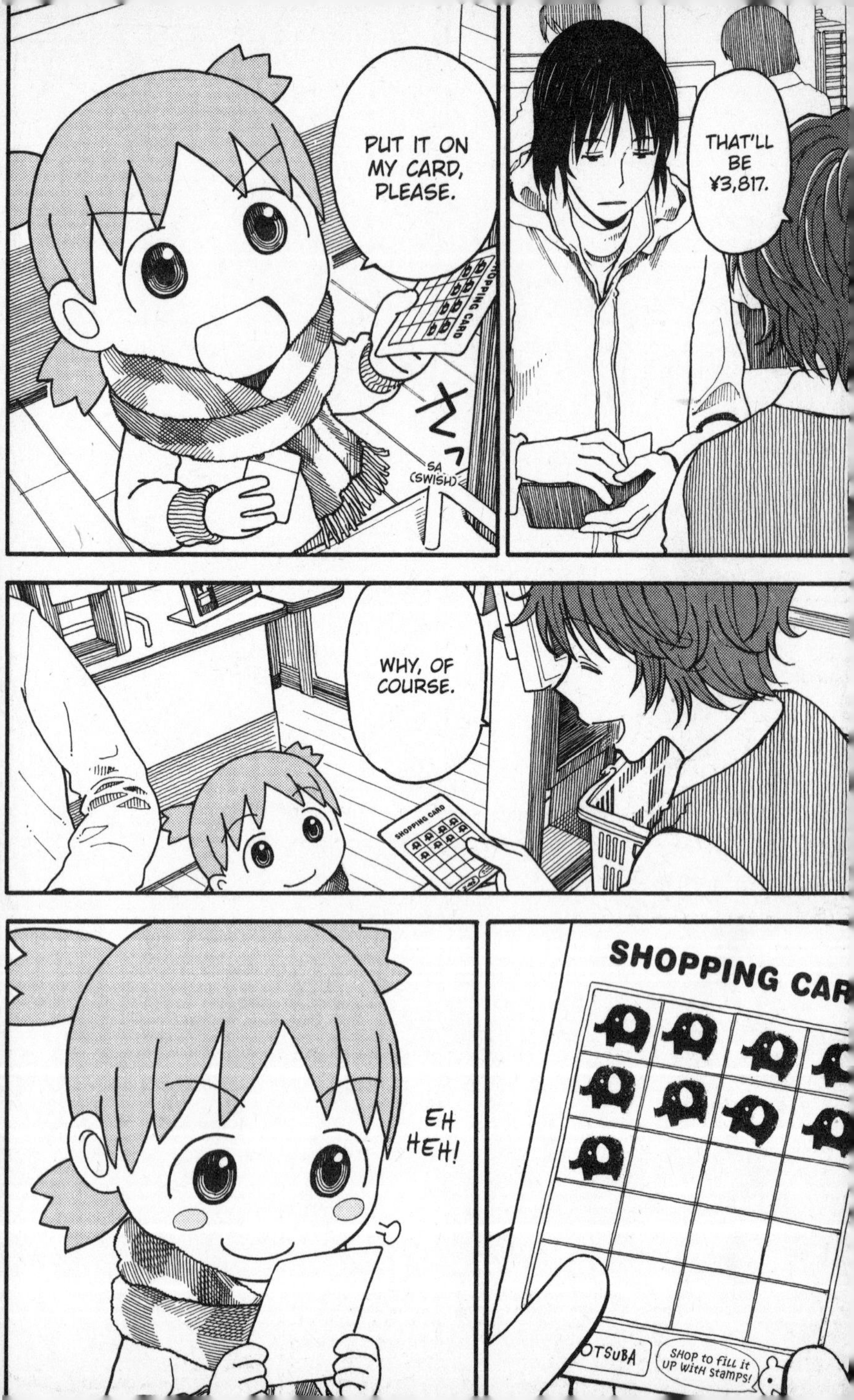
THAT'LL BE ¥3,817.
PUT IT ON MY CARD, PLEASE.
SHOPPING CARD
さっ
SA (SWISH)
WHY, OF COURSE.
SHOPPING CARD
SHOPPING CAR
OTSUBA
SHOP to fill it UP with stamps!
EH HEH!

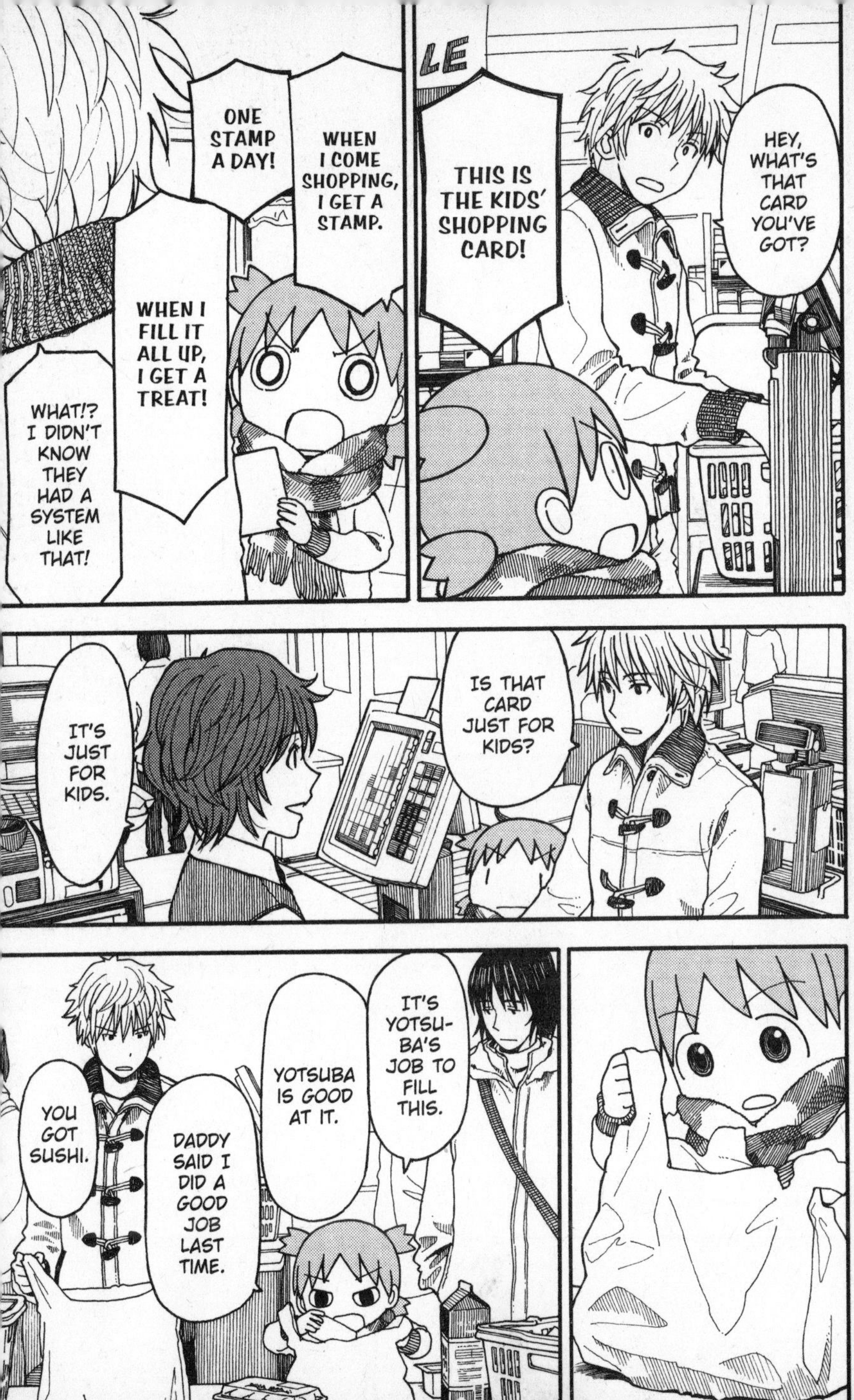
HEY, WHAT'S THAT CARD YOU'VE GOT?
THIS IS THE KIDS' SHOPPING CARD!
WHEN I COME SHOPPING, I GET A STAMP.
ONE STAMP A DAY!
WHEN I FILL IT ALL UP, I GET A TREAT!
WHAT!? I DIDN'T KNOW THEY HAD A SYSTEM LIKE THAT!
IS THAT CARD JUST FOR KIDS?
IT'S JUST FOR KIDS.
IT'S YOTSUBA'S JOB TO FILL THIS.
YOTSUBA IS GOOD AT IT.
DADDY SAID I DID A GOOD JOB LAST TIME.
YOU GOT SUSHI.

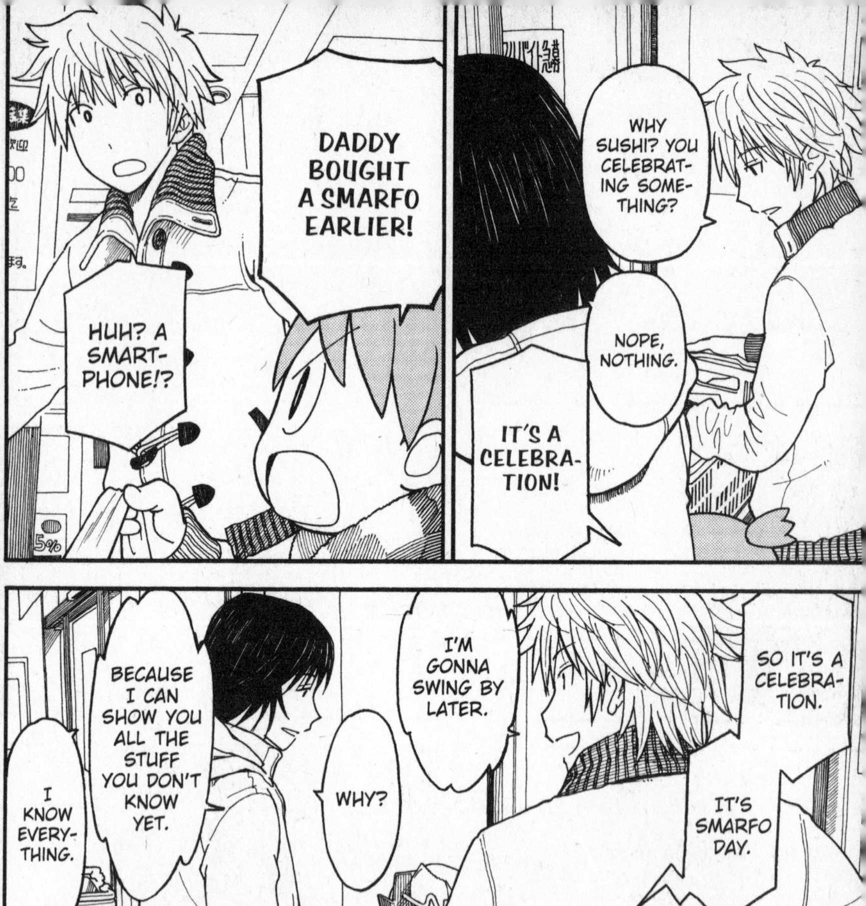
WHY SUSHI? YOU CELEBRATING SOMETHING?
NOPE, NOTHING.
IT'S A CELEBRATION!
DADDY BOUGHT A SMARFO EARLIER!
HUH? A SMARTPHONE!?
SO IT'S A CELEBRATION.
IT'S SMARFO DAY.
I'M GONNA SWING BY LATER.
WHY?
BECAUSE I CAN SHOW YOU ALL THE STUFF YOU DON'T KNOW YET.
I KNOW EVERYTHING.

NOTE: LINE IS THE MOST POPULAR JAPANESE SOCIAL MEDIA NETWORK AND INSTANT MESSAGING APP.

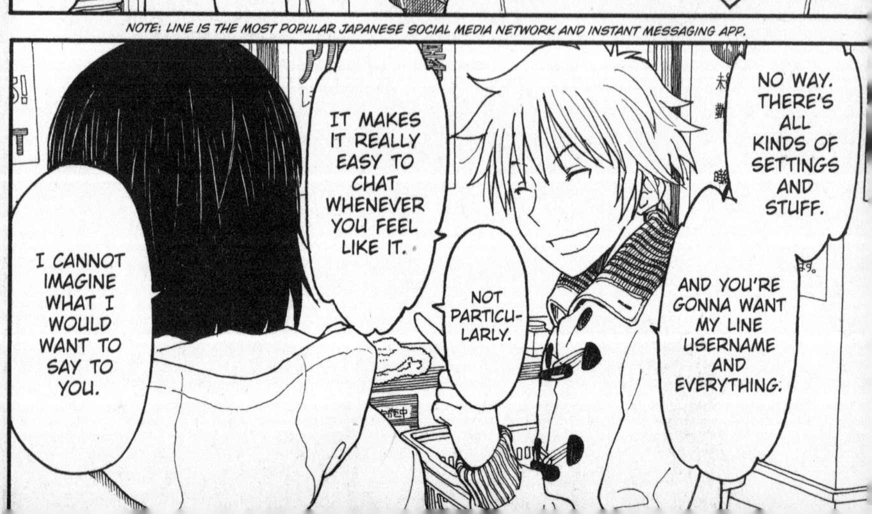
NO WAY. THERE'S ALL KINDS OF SETTINGS AND STUFF.
AND YOU'RE GONNA WANT MY LINE USERNAME AND EVERYTHING.
IT MAKES IT REALLY EASY TO CHAT WHENEVER YOU FEEL LIKE IT.
NOT PARTICULARLY.
I CANNOT IMAGINE WHAT I WOULD WANT TO SAY TO YOU.

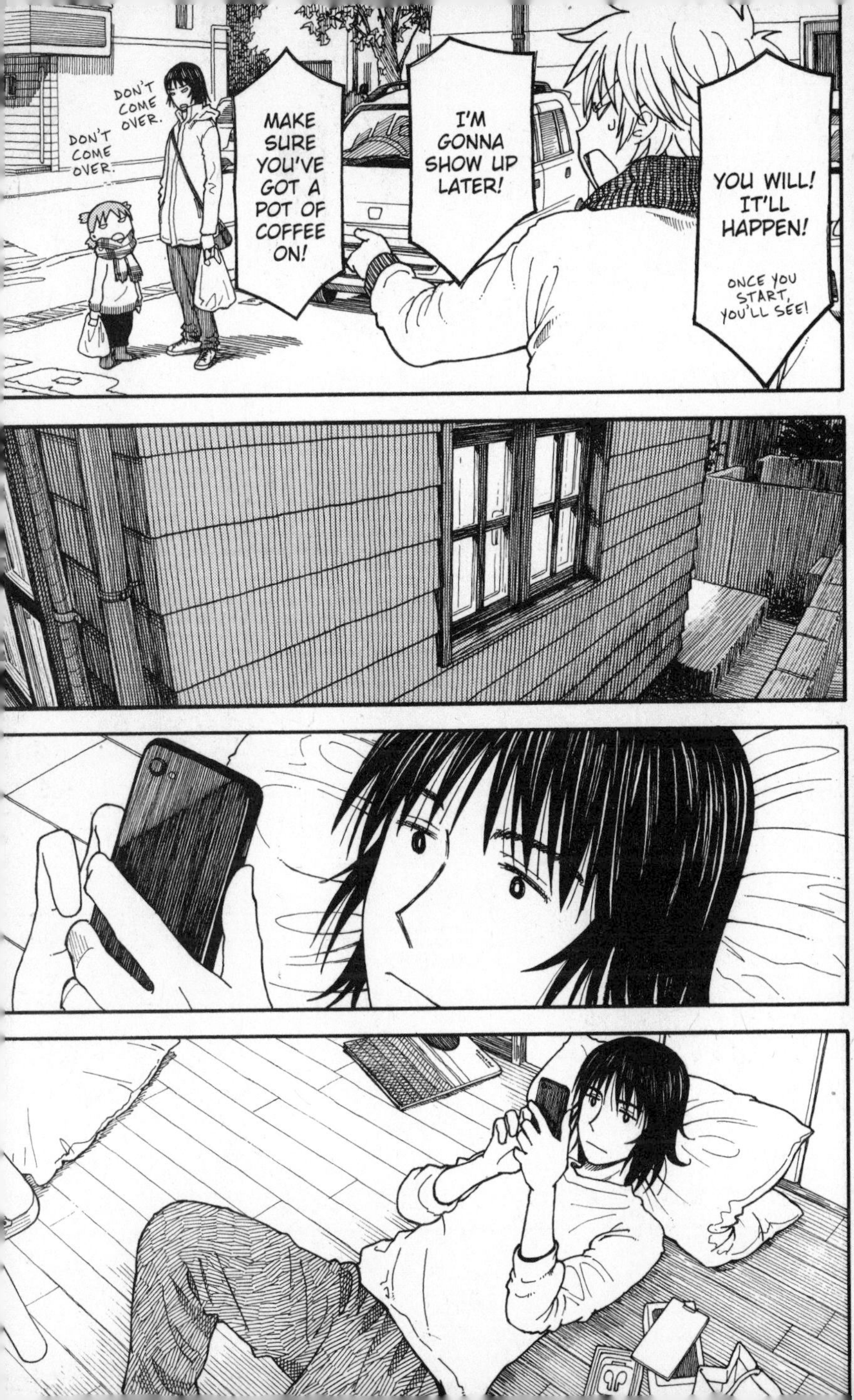
YOU WILL! IT'LL HAPPEN!
ONCE YOU START, YOU'LL SEE!
I'M GONNA SHOW UP LATER!
MAKE SURE YOU'VE GOT A POT OF COFFEE ON!
DON'T COME OVER.
DON'T COME OVER.

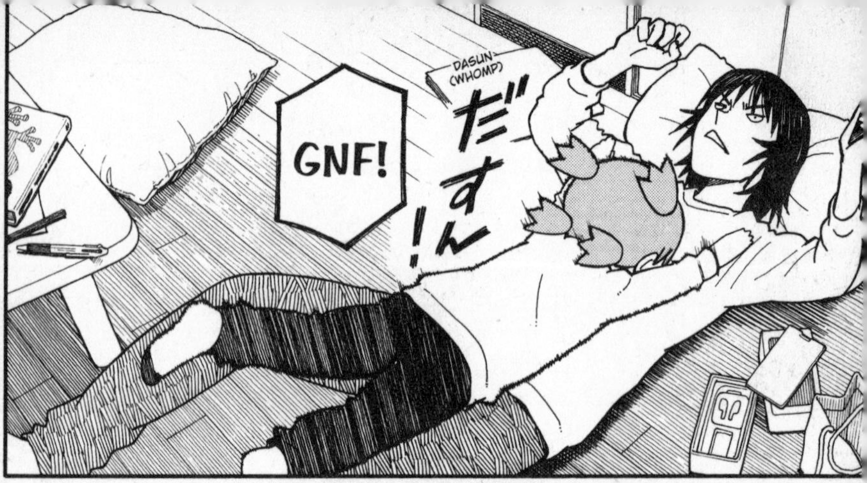
DASUN (WHOMP)
だすん！
GNF!

NOTE: YOTSUBA IS MIMICKING NIGIRI SUSHI, IN WHICH THE PRIMARY INGREDIENT IS PLACED ON AND PRESSED INTO THE RICE BELOW.

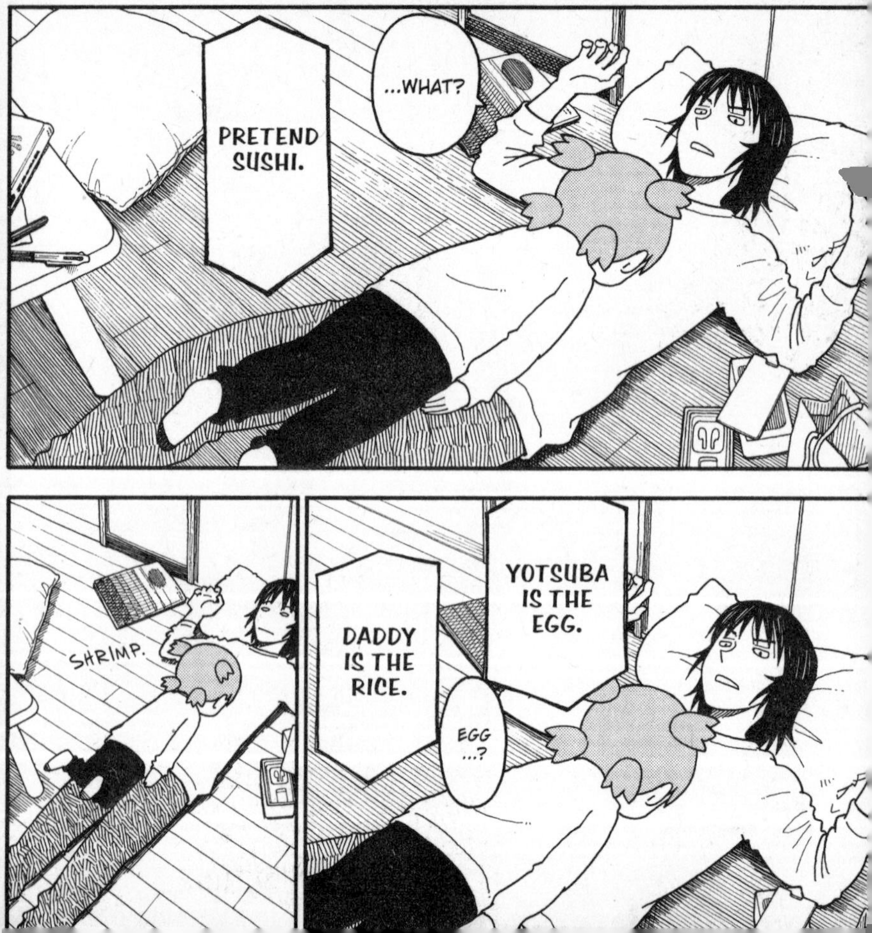
...WHAT?
PRETEND SUSHI.
YOTSUBA IS THE EGG.
DADDY IS THE RICE.
EGG ...?
SHRIMP.

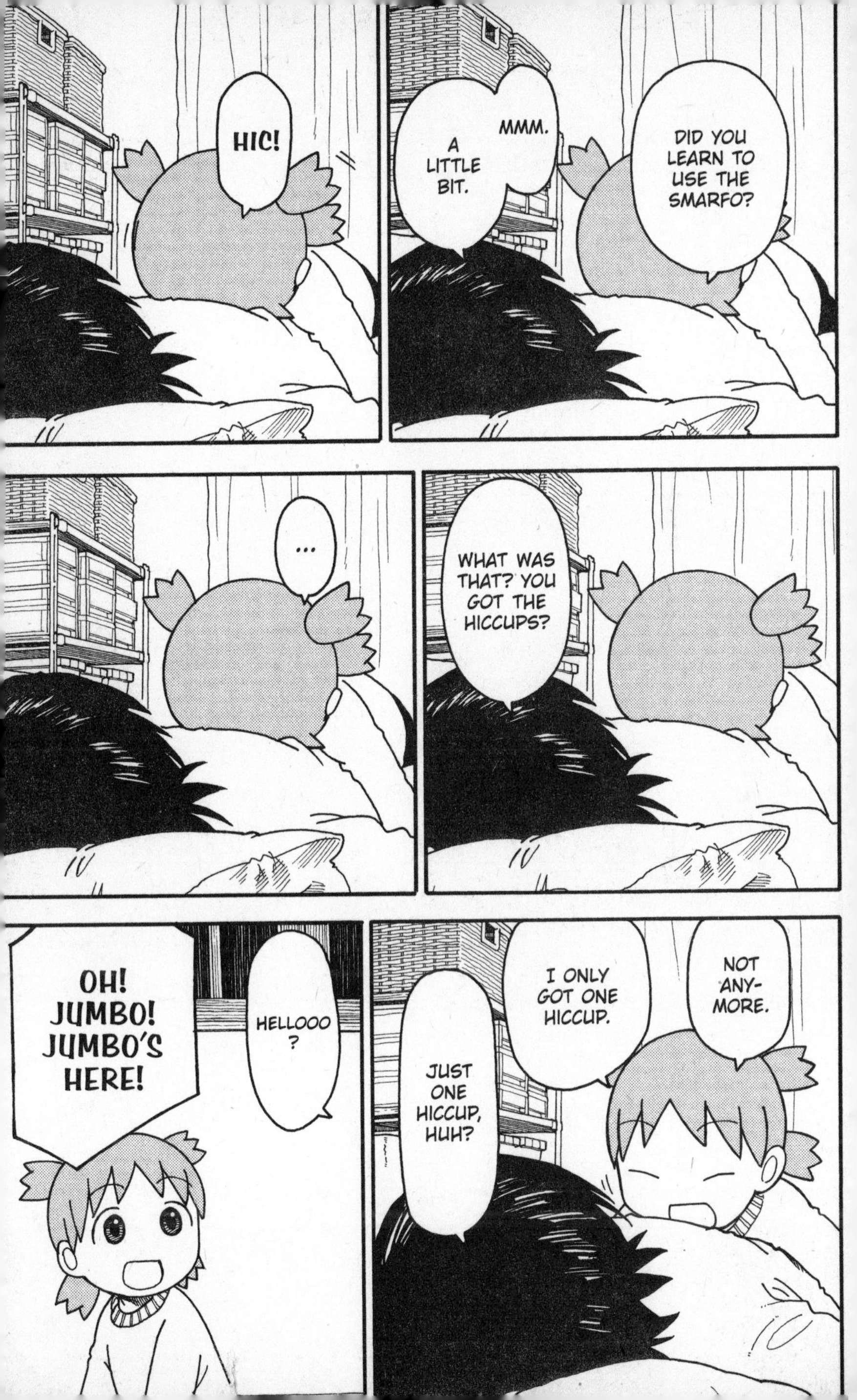
DID YOU LEARN TO USE THE SMARFO?
MMM.
A LITTLE BIT.
HIC!
WHAT WAS THAT? YOU GOT THE HICCUPS?
...
NOT ANY-MORE.
I ONLY GOT ONE HICCUP.
JUST ONE HICCUP, HUH?
HELLOOO?
OH! JUMBO! JUMBO'S HERE!

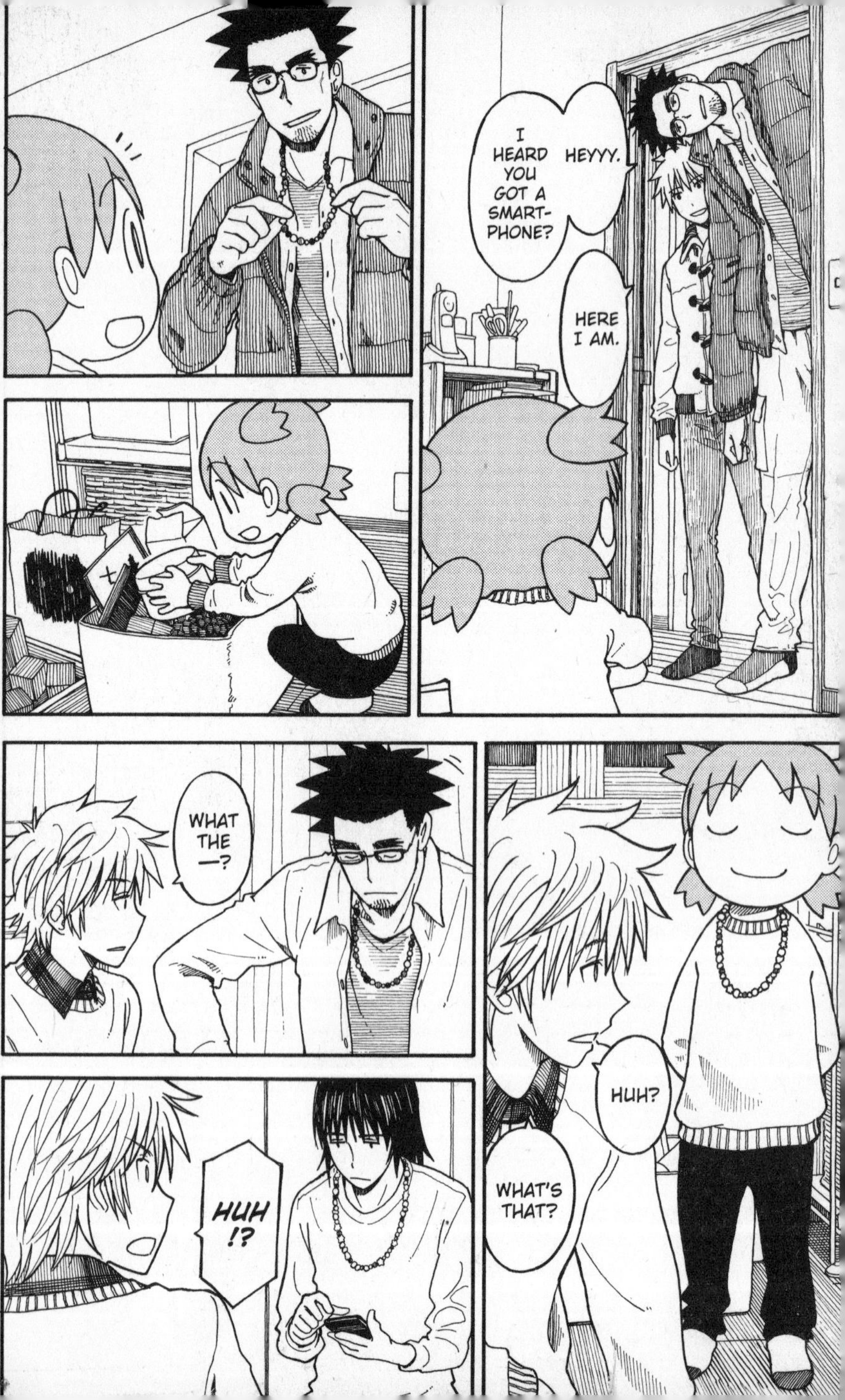
HEYYY.
I HEARD YOU GOT A SMART-PHONE?
HERE I AM.
HUH?
WHAT'S THAT?
WHAT THE —?
HUH !?

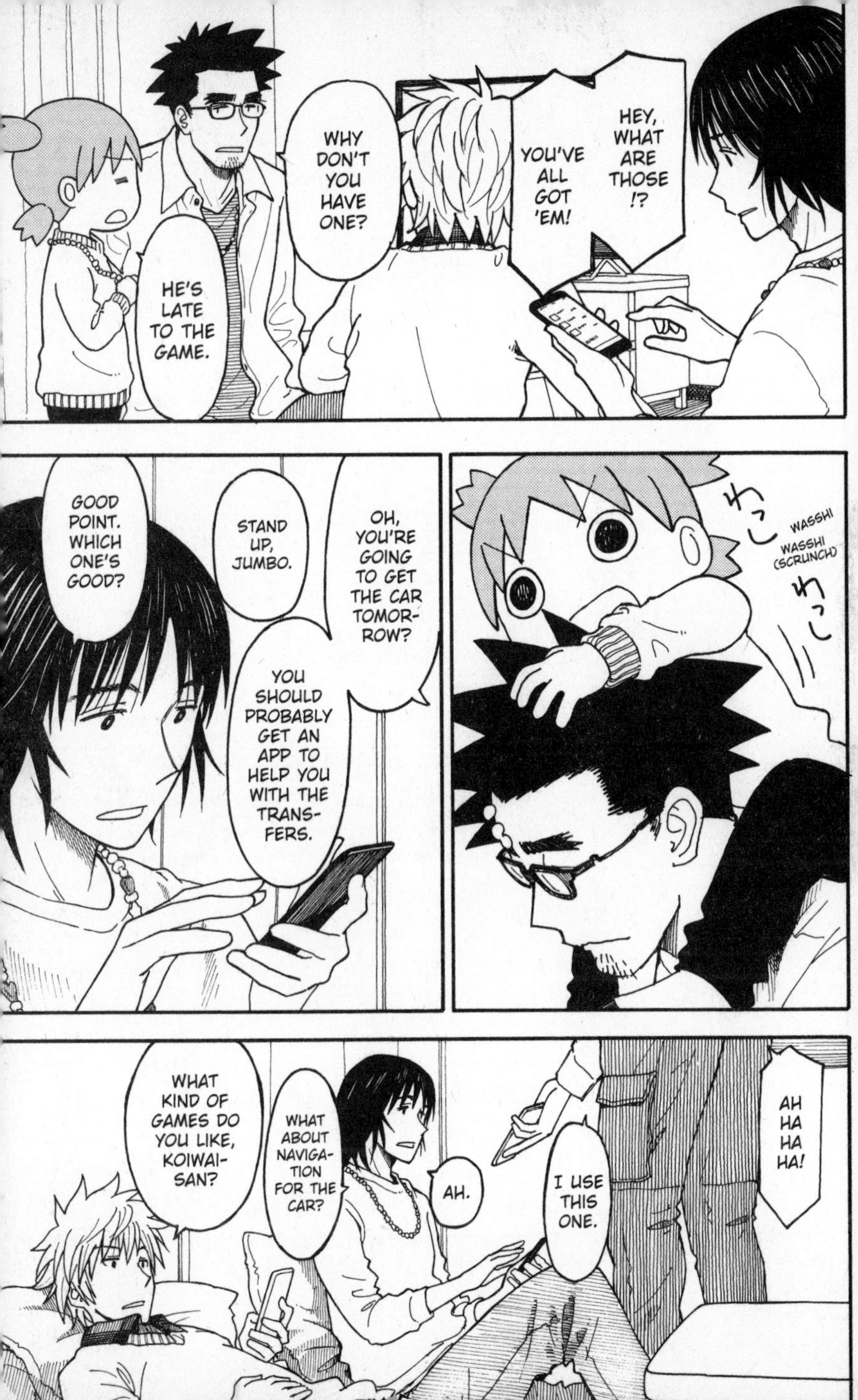
HEY, WHAT ARE THOSE !?
YOU'VE ALL GOT 'EM!
WHY DON'T YOU HAVE ONE?
HE'S LATE TO THE GAME.
わしわし
WASSHI WASSHI (SCRUNCH)
OH, YOU'RE GOING TO GET THE CAR TOMORROW?
YOU SHOULD PROBABLY GET AN APP TO HELP YOU WITH THE TRANSFERS.
STAND UP, JUMBO.
GOOD POINT. WHICH ONE'S GOOD?
AH HA HA HA!
I USE THIS ONE.
AH.
WHAT ABOUT NAVIGATION FOR THE CAR?
WHAT KIND OF GAMES DO YOU LIKE, KOIWAI-SAN?

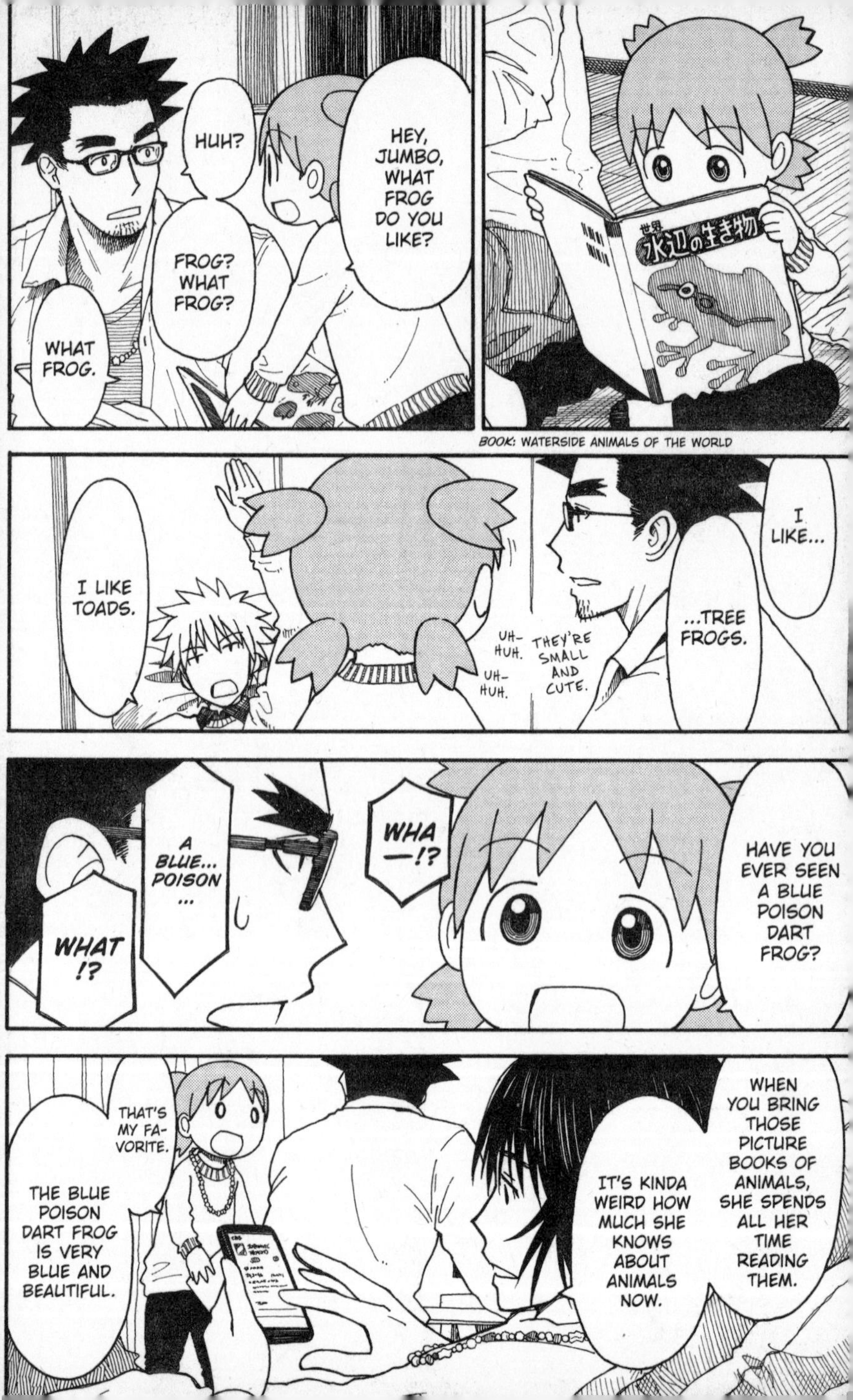
世界
水辺の生き物
BOOK: WATERSIDE ANIMALS OF THE WORLD
HEY, JUMBO, WHAT FROG DO YOU LIKE?
HUH?
FROG? WHAT FROG?
WHAT FROG.
I LIKE...
...TREE FROGS.
THEY'RE SMALL AND CUTE.
UH-HUH.
UH-HUH.
I LIKE TOADS.
HAVE YOU EVER SEEN A BLUE POISON DART FROG?
WHA—!?
A BLUE... POISON...
WHAT!?
WHEN YOU BRING THOSE PICTURE BOOKS OF ANIMALS, SHE SPENDS ALL HER TIME READING THEM.
IT'S KINDA WEIRD HOW MUCH SHE KNOWS ABOUT ANIMALS NOW.
THAT'S MY FA-VORITE.
THE BLUE POISON DART FROG IS VERY BLUE AND BEAUTIFUL.

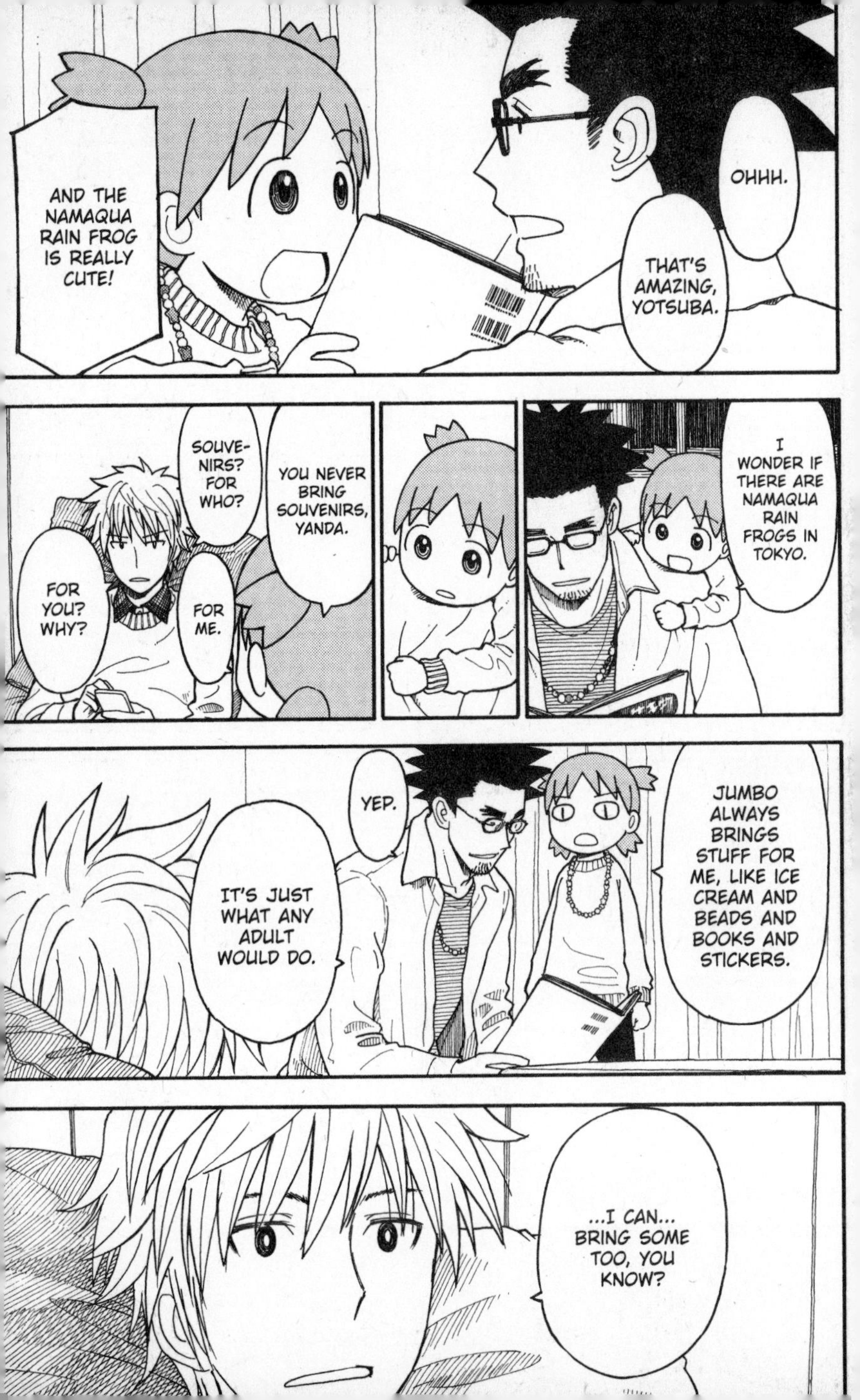
OHHH.
THAT'S AMAZING, YOTSUBA.
AND THE NAMAQUA RAIN FROG IS REALLY CUTE!
I WONDER IF THERE ARE NAMAQUA RAIN FROGS IN TOKYO.
YOU NEVER BRING SOUVENIRS, YANDA.
SOUVE-NIRS? FOR WHO?
FOR ME.
FOR YOU? WHY?
JUMBO ALWAYS BRINGS STUFF FOR ME, LIKE ICE CREAM AND BEADS AND BOOKS AND STICKERS.
YEP.
IT'S JUST WHAT ANY ADULT WOULD DO.
...I CAN... BRING SOME TOO, YOU KNOW?

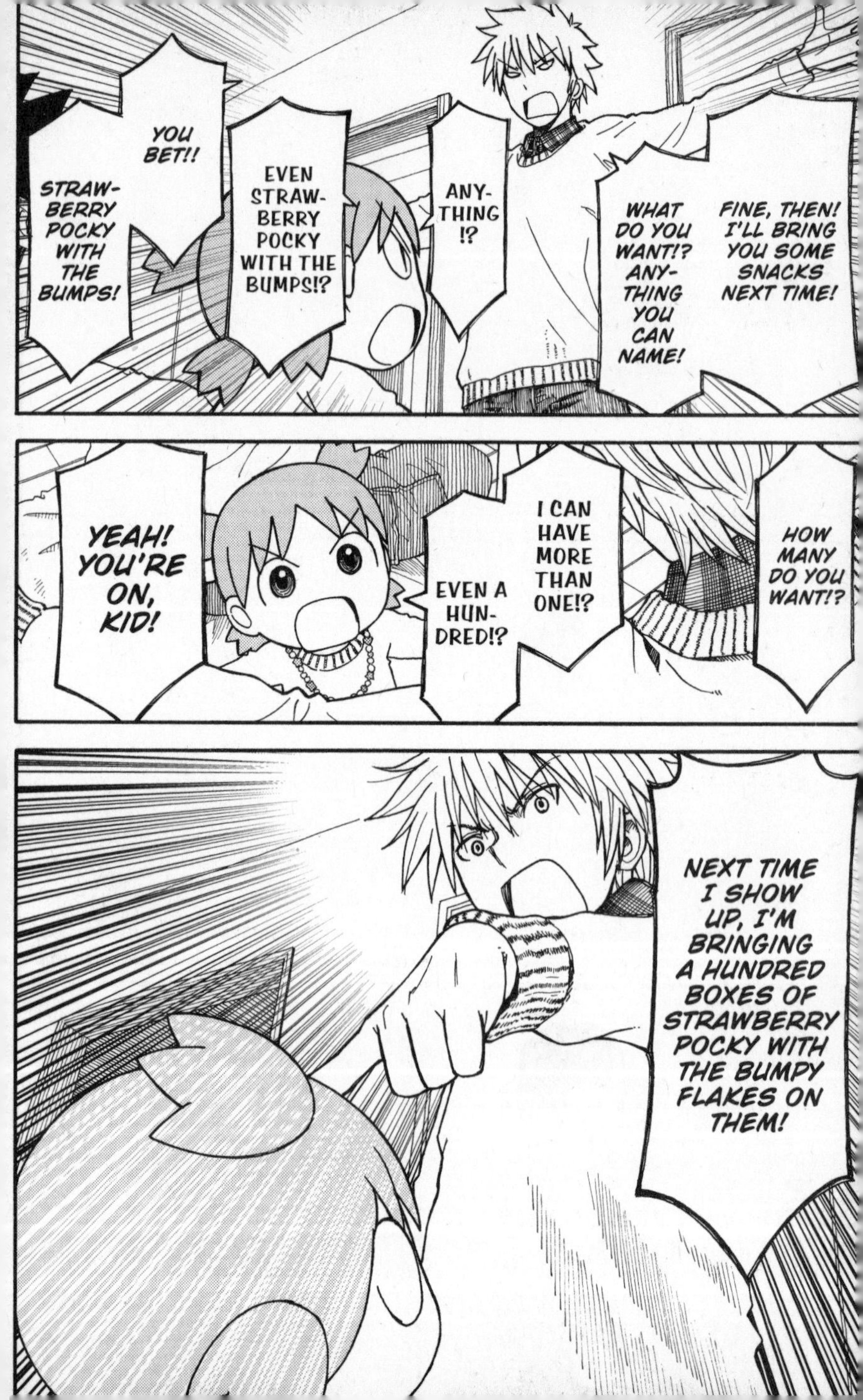
FINE, THEN! I'LL BRING YOU SOME SNACKS NEXT TIME!
WHAT DO YOU WANT!? ANY-THING YOU CAN NAME!
ANY-THING!?
EVEN STRAW-BERRY POCKY WITH THE BUMPS!?
YOU BET!!
STRAW-BERRY POCKY WITH THE BUMPS!
HOW MANY DO YOU WANT!?
I CAN HAVE MORE THAN ONE!?
EVEN A HUN-DRED!?
YEAH! YOU'RE ON, KID!
NEXT TIME I SHOW UP, I'M BRINGING A HUNDRED BOXES OF STRAWBERRY POCKY WITH THE BUMPY FLAKES ON THEM!

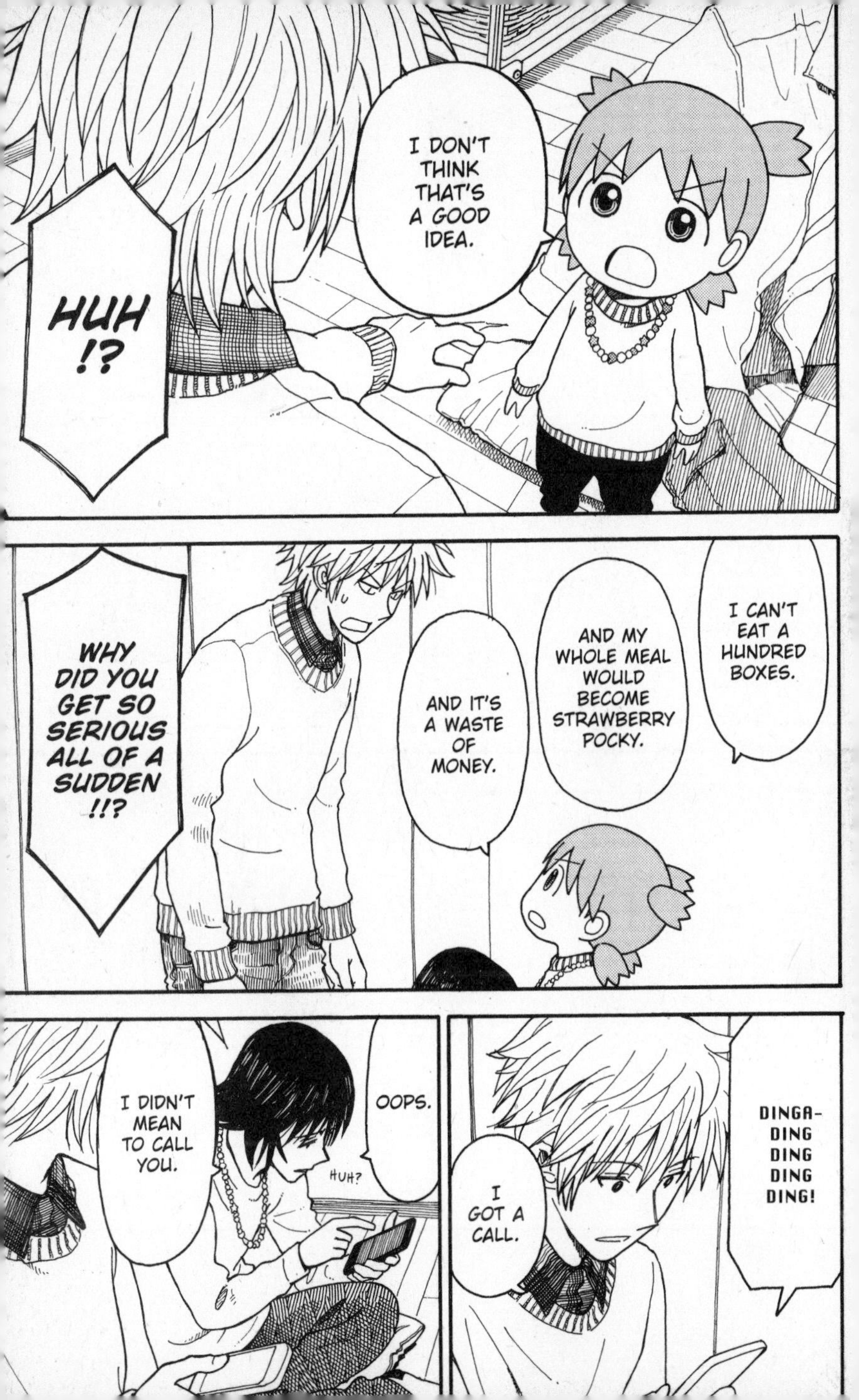
I DON'T THINK THAT'S A GOOD IDEA.
HUH!?
I CAN'T EAT A HUNDRED BOXES.
AND MY WHOLE MEAL WOULD BECOME STRAWBERRY POCKY.
AND IT'S A WASTE OF MONEY.
WHY DID YOU GET SO SERIOUS ALL OF A SUDDEN!!?
DINGA-DING DING DING DING!
I GOT A CALL.
OOPS.
HUH?
I DIDN'T MEAN TO CALL YOU.

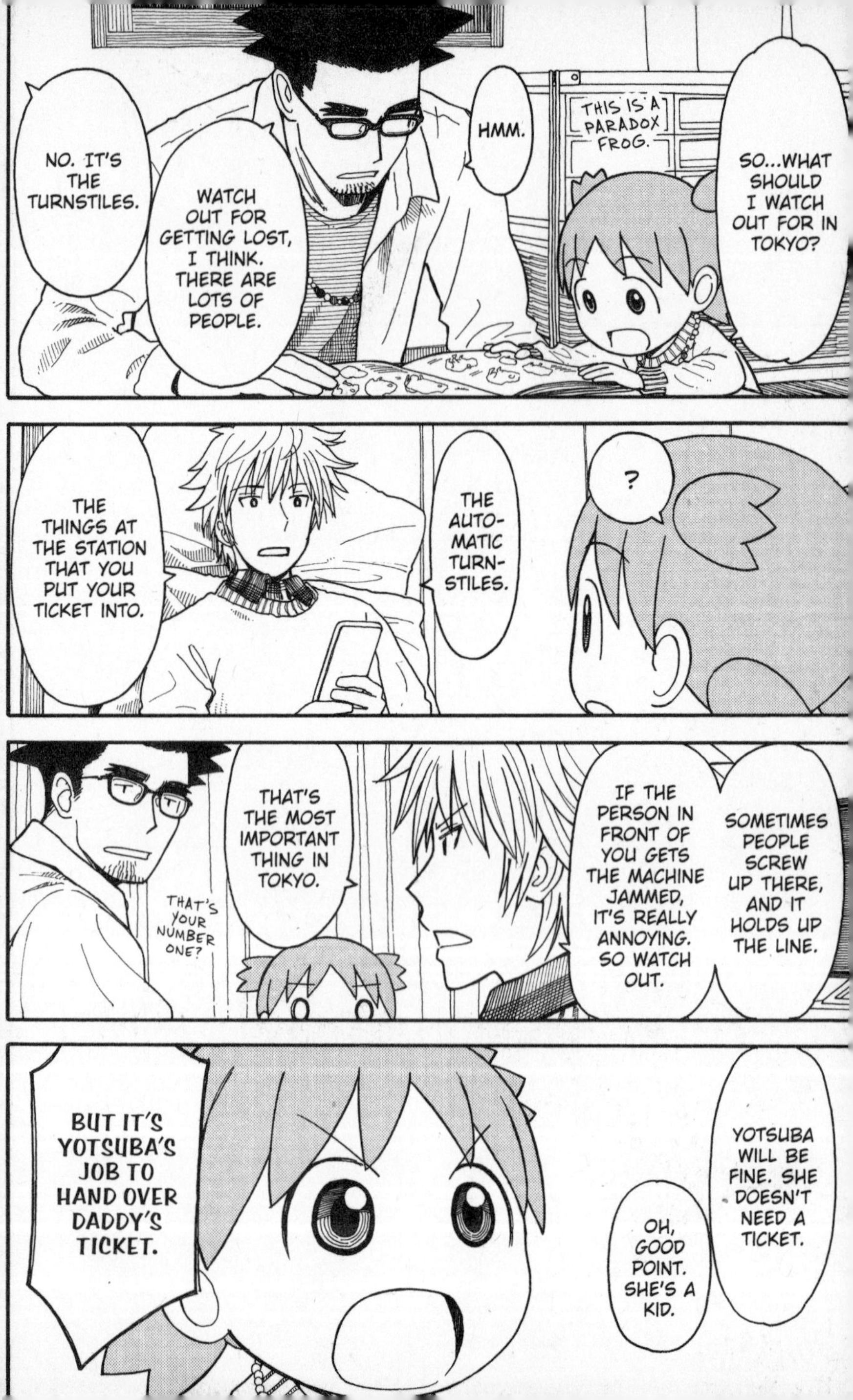
SO...WHAT SHOULD I WATCH OUT FOR IN TOKYO?
THIS IS A PARADOX FROG.
HMM.
WATCH OUT FOR GETTING LOST, I THINK. THERE ARE LOTS OF PEOPLE.
NO. IT'S THE TURNSTILES.
?
THE AUTOMATIC TURNSTILES.
THE THINGS AT THE STATION THAT YOU PUT YOUR TICKET INTO.
SOMETIMES PEOPLE SCREW UP THERE, AND IT HOLDS UP THE LINE.
IF THE PERSON IN FRONT OF YOU GETS THE MACHINE JAMMED, IT'S REALLY ANNOYING. SO WATCH OUT.
THAT'S THE MOST IMPORTANT THING IN TOKYO.
THAT'S YOUR NUMBER ONE?
YOTSUBA WILL BE FINE. SHE DOESN'T NEED A TICKET.
OH, GOOD POINT. SHE'S A KID.
BUT IT'S YOTSUBA'S JOB TO HAND OVER DADDY'S TICKET.

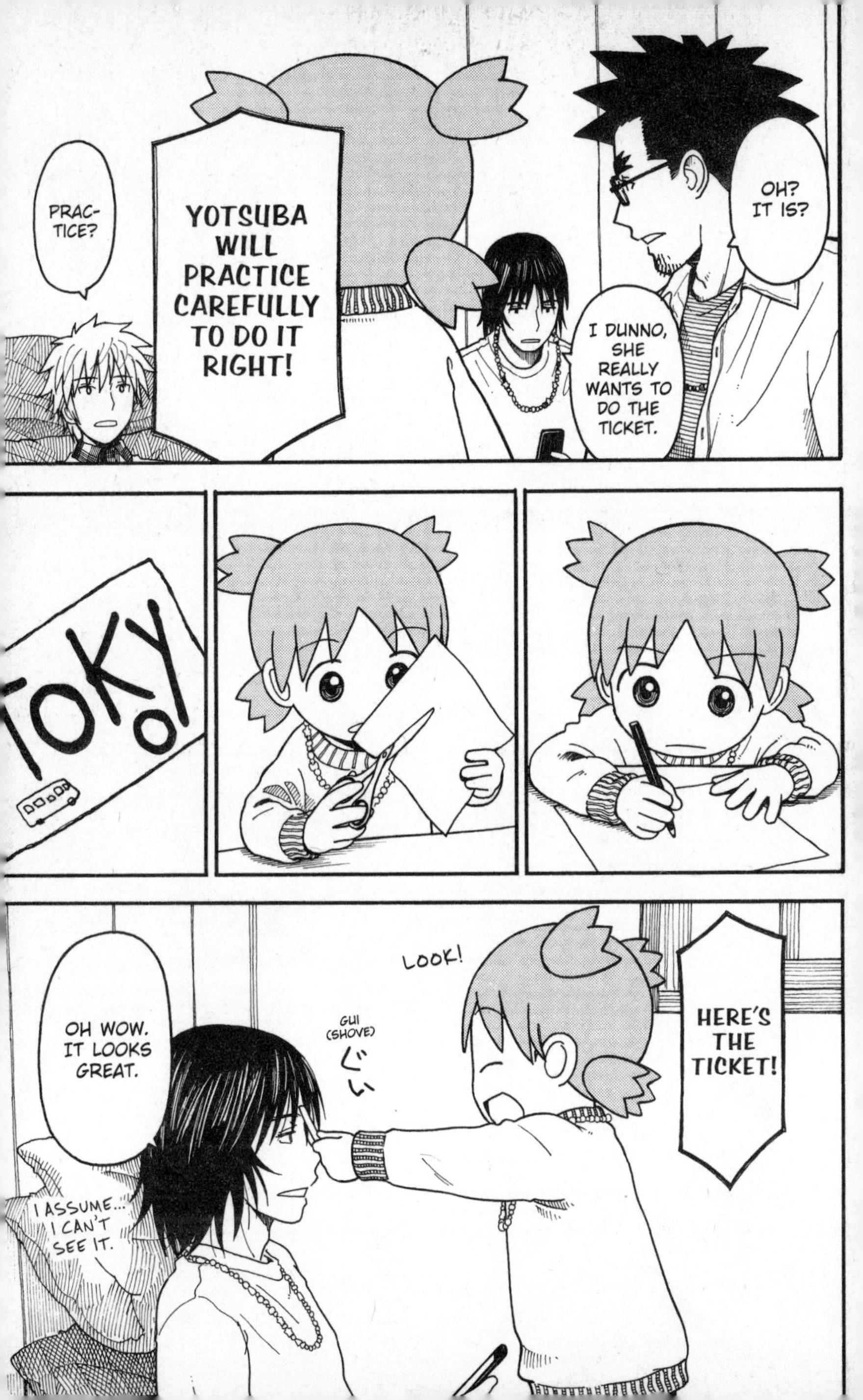
OH? IT IS?
I DUNNO, SHE REALLY WANTS TO DO THE TICKET.
YOTSUBA WILL PRACTICE CAREFULLY TO DO IT RIGHT!
PRAC- TICE?
TOKYO
HERE'S THE TICKET!
LOOK!
GUI (SHOVE)
ぐい
OH WOW. IT LOOKS GREAT.
I ASSUME... I CAN'T SEE IT.

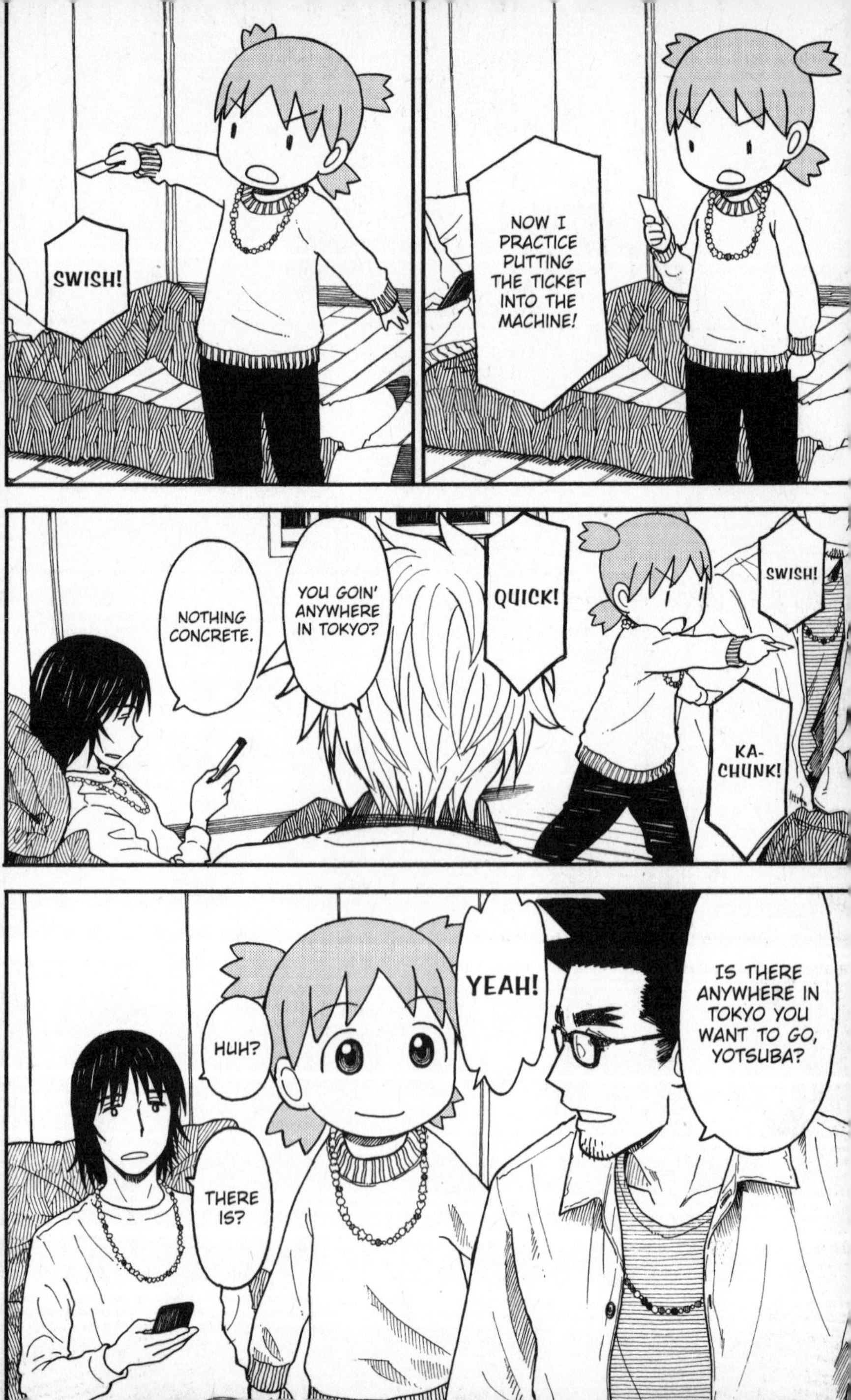
NOW I PRACTICE PUTTING THE TICKET INTO THE MACHINE!
SWISH!
SWISH!
KA-CHUNK!
QUICK!
YOU GOIN' ANYWHERE IN TOKYO?
NOTHING CONCRETE.
IS THERE ANYWHERE IN TOKYO YOU WANT TO GO, YOTSUBA?
YEAH!
HUH?
THERE IS?

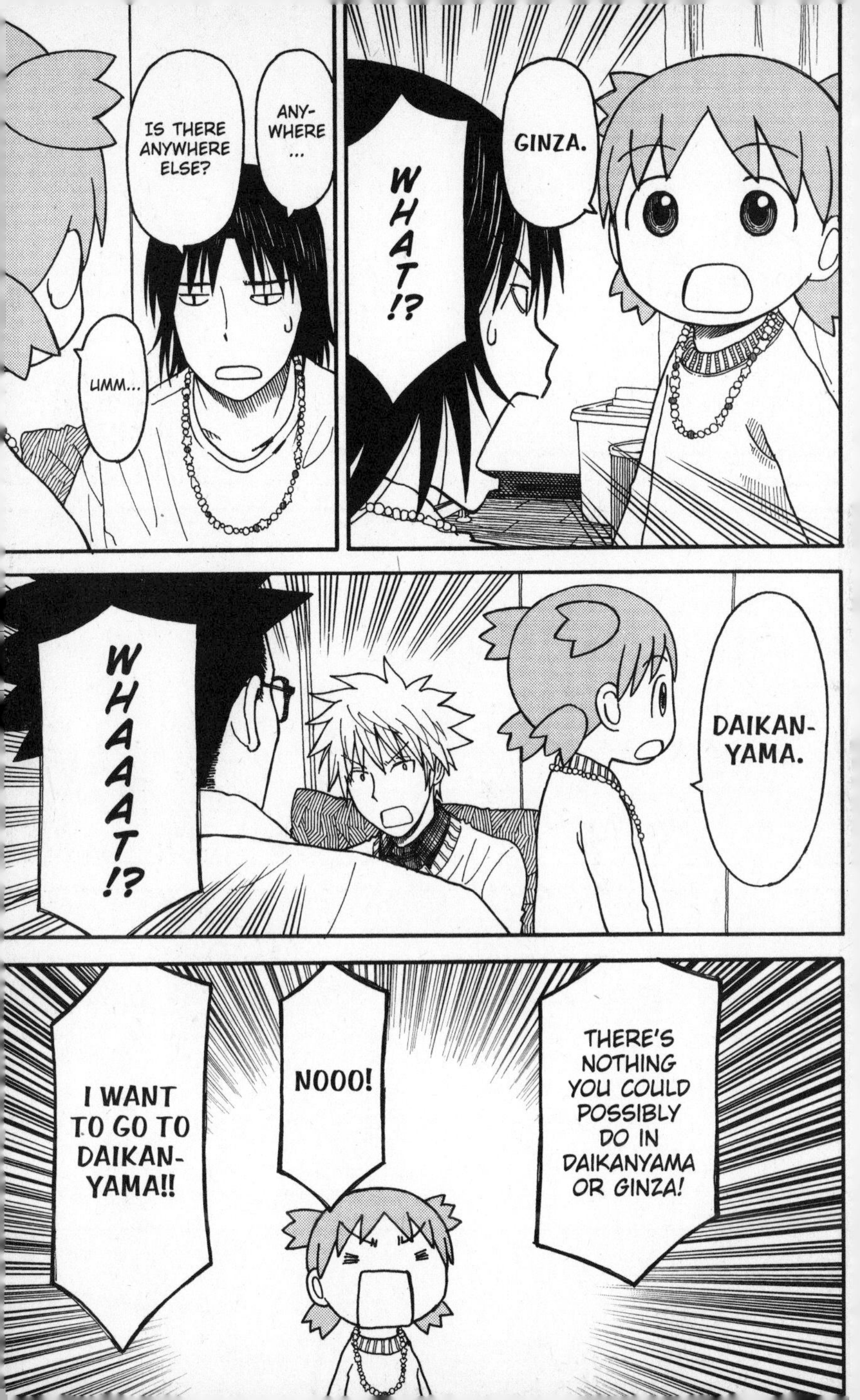
GINZA.
WHAT!?
ANY-WHERE ...
IS THERE ANYWHERE ELSE?
UMM...
DAIKAN-YAMA.
WHAAAAT!?
THERE'S NOTHING YOU COULD POSSIBLY DO IN DAIKANYAMA OR GINZA!
NOOO!
I WANT TO GO TO DAIKAN-YAMA!!

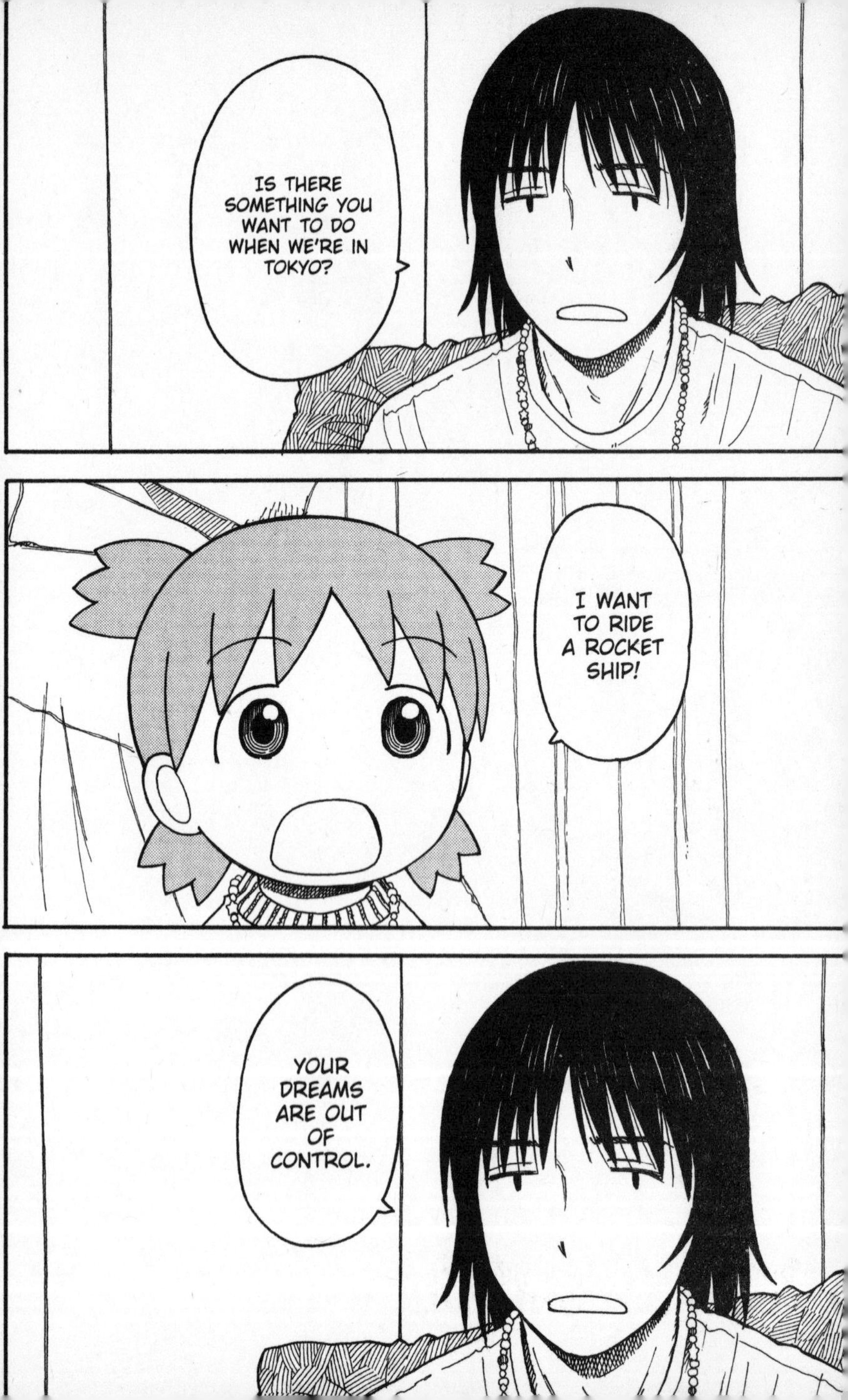
IS THERE SOMETHING YOU WANT TO DO WHEN WE'RE IN TOKYO?
I WANT TO RIDE A ROCKET SHIP!
YOUR DREAMS ARE OUT OF CONTROL.

YOTSUBA&!

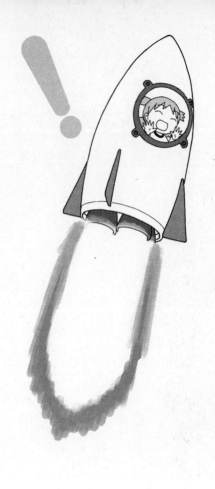

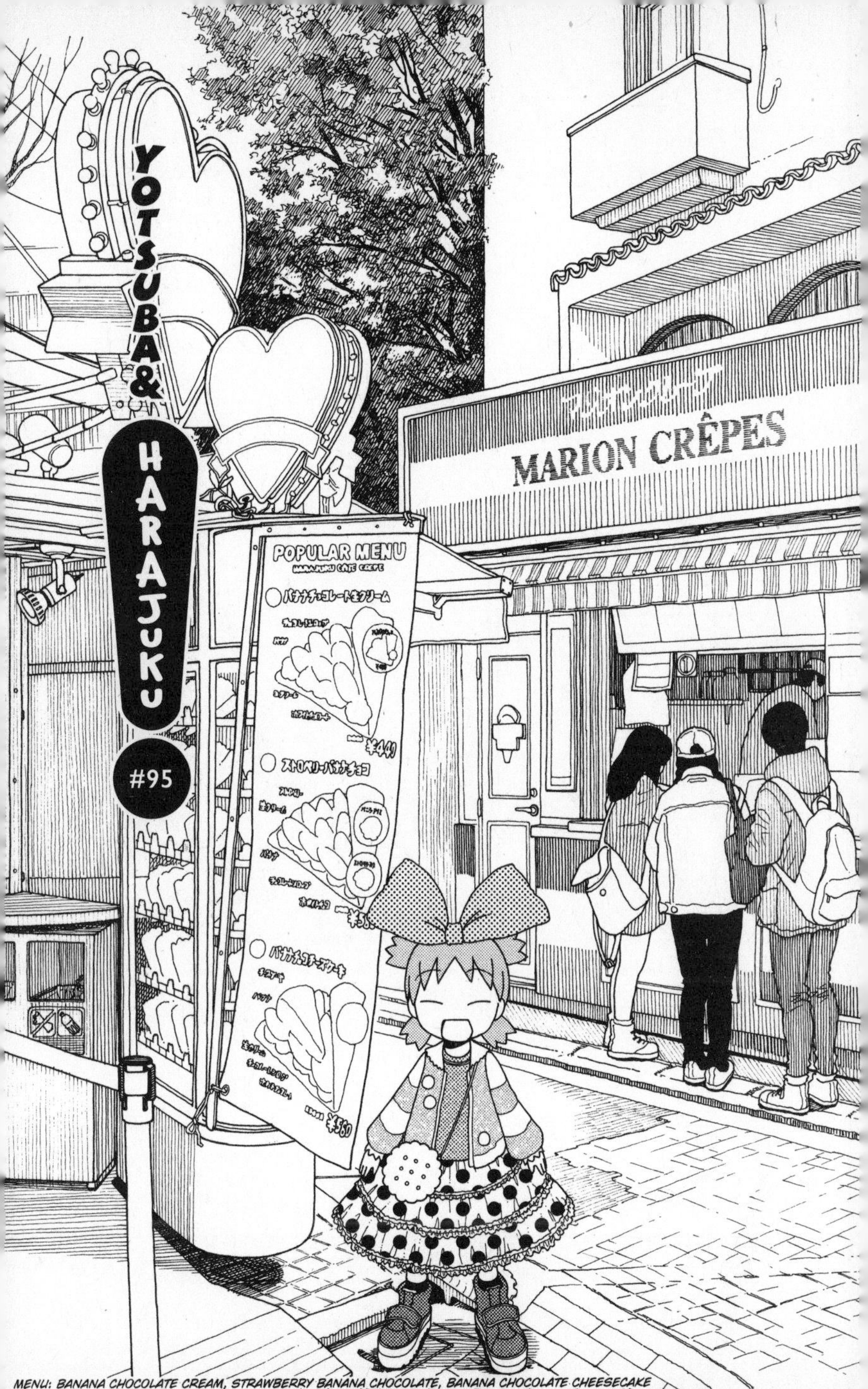
YOTSUBA&
HARAJUKU
#95
MARION CRÊPES
POPULAR MENU
バナナチョコレート生クリーム
ストロベリーバナナチョコ
バナナチョコチーズケーキ
¥560

MENU: BANANA CHOCOLATE CREAM, STRAWBERRY BANANA CHOCOLATE, BANANA CHOCOLATE CHEESECAKE

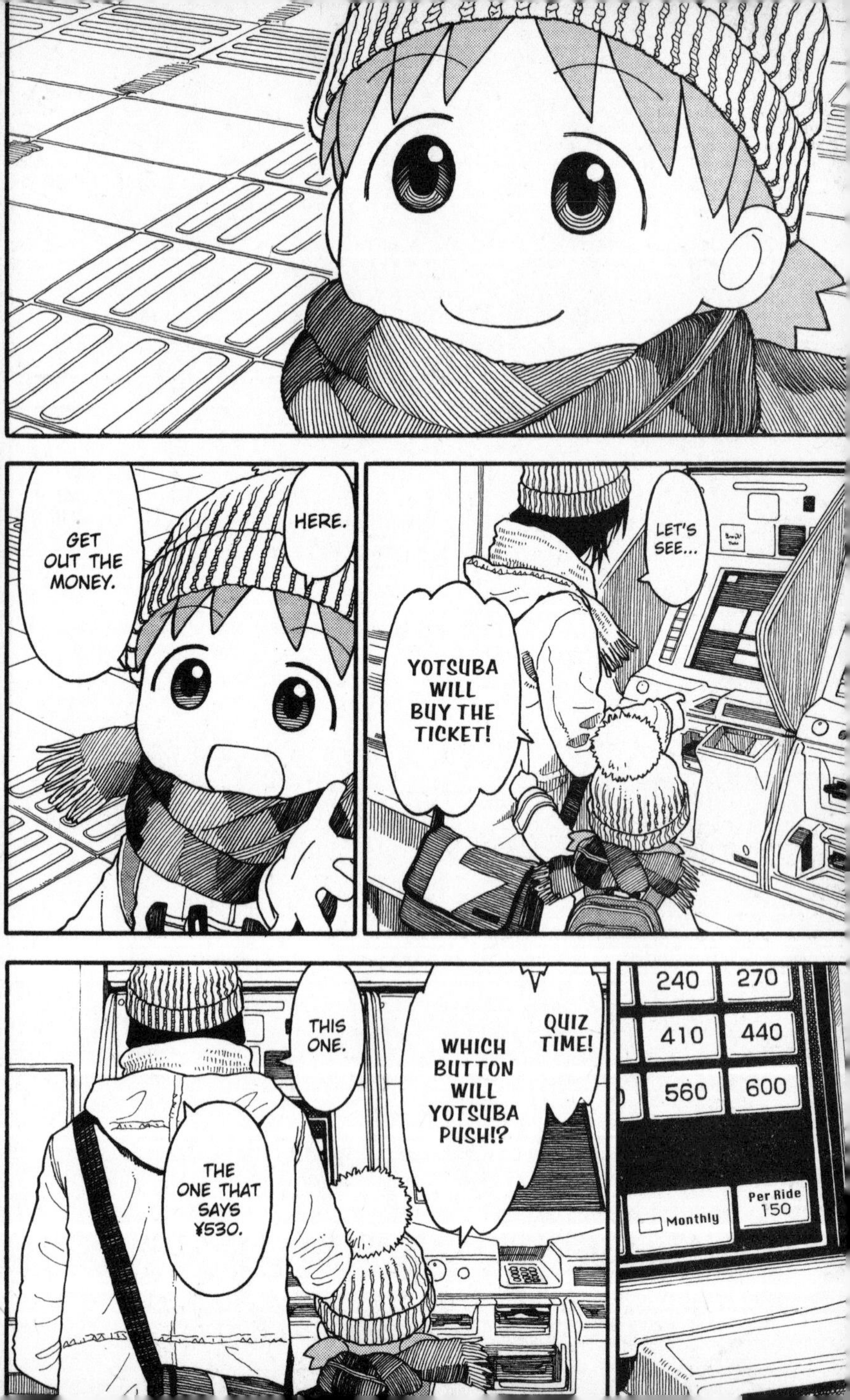
LET'S SEE...
YOTSUBA WILL BUY THE TICKET!
HERE.
GET OUT THE MONEY.
240
270
410
440
560
600
Per Ride 150
Monthly
QUIZ TIME!
WHICH BUTTON WILL YOTSUBA PUSH!?
THIS ONE.
THE ONE THAT SAYS ¥530.

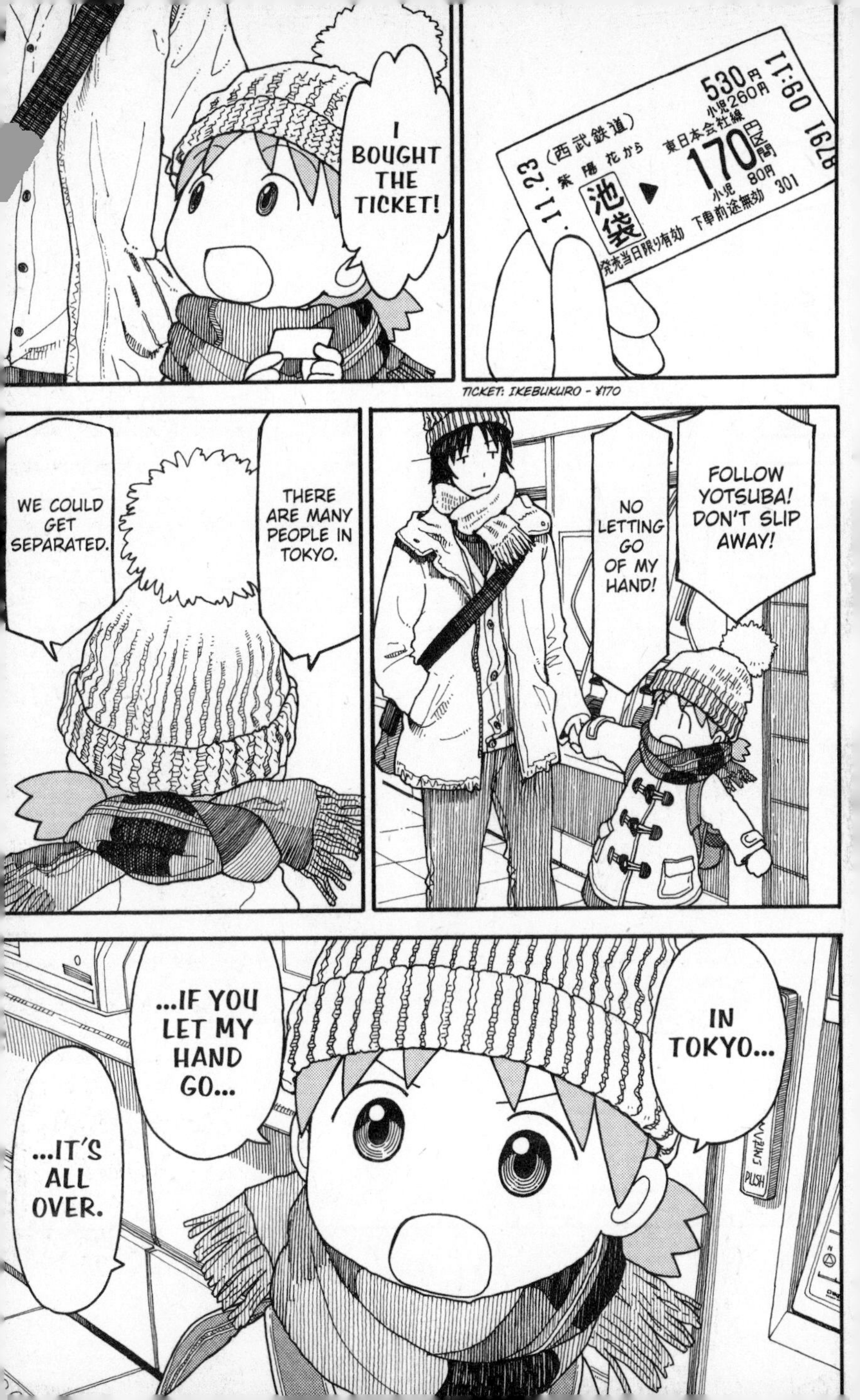
11.23 (西武鉄道)
池袋
170円区間
530円 小児260円
東日本会社線
発売当日限り有効 下車前途無効
TICKET: IKEBUKURO - ¥170
I BOUGHT THE TICKET!
FOLLOW YOTSUBA! DON'T SLIP AWAY!
NO LETTING GO OF MY HAND!
THERE ARE MANY PEOPLE IN TOKYO.
WE COULD GET SEPARATED.
IN TOKYO...
...IF YOU LET MY HAND GO...
...IT'S ALL OVER.
PUSH

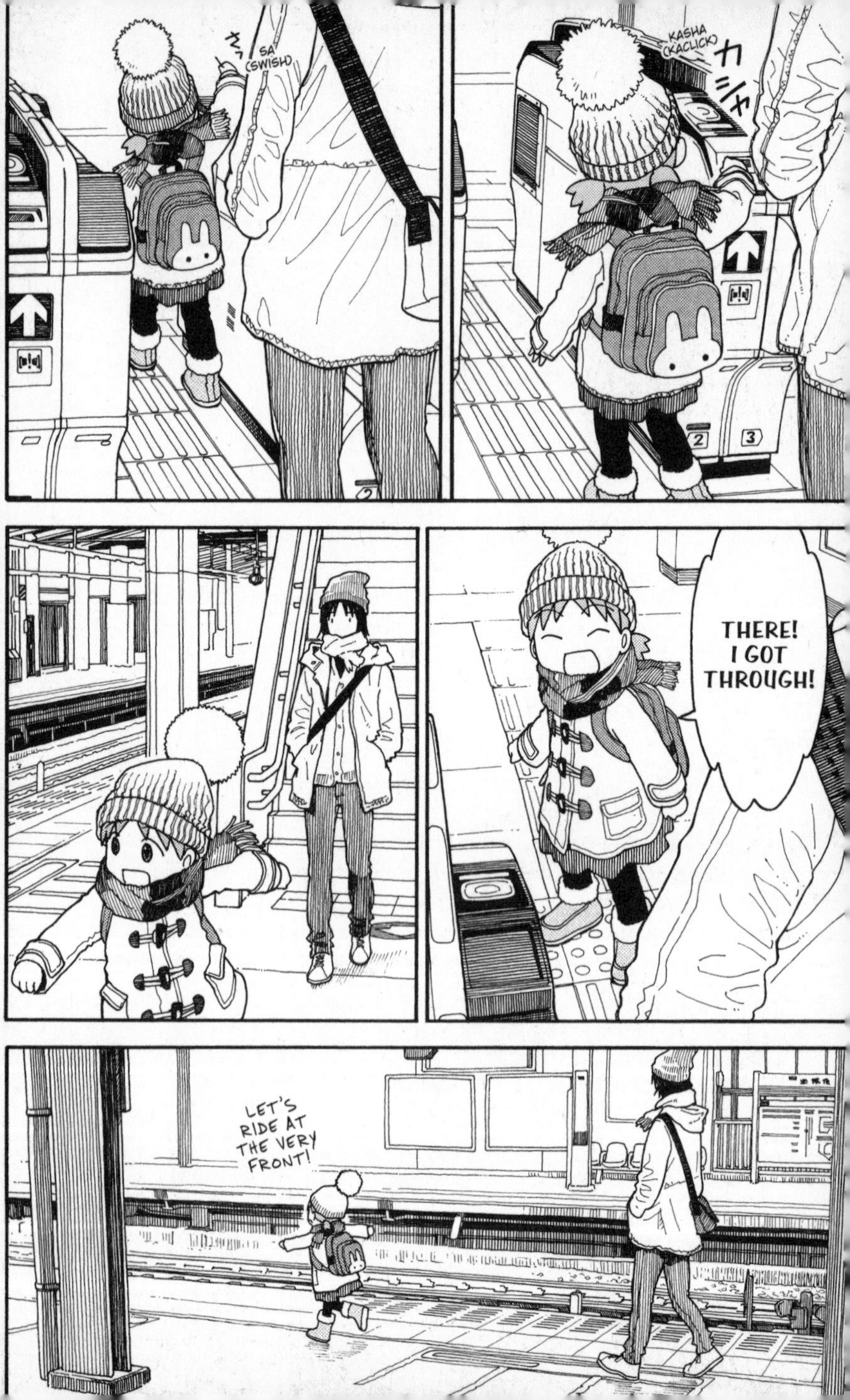
カシャ
KASHA (KACLICK)
さっ
SA (SWISH)
THERE! I GOT THROUGH!
LET'S RIDE AT THE VERY FRONT!

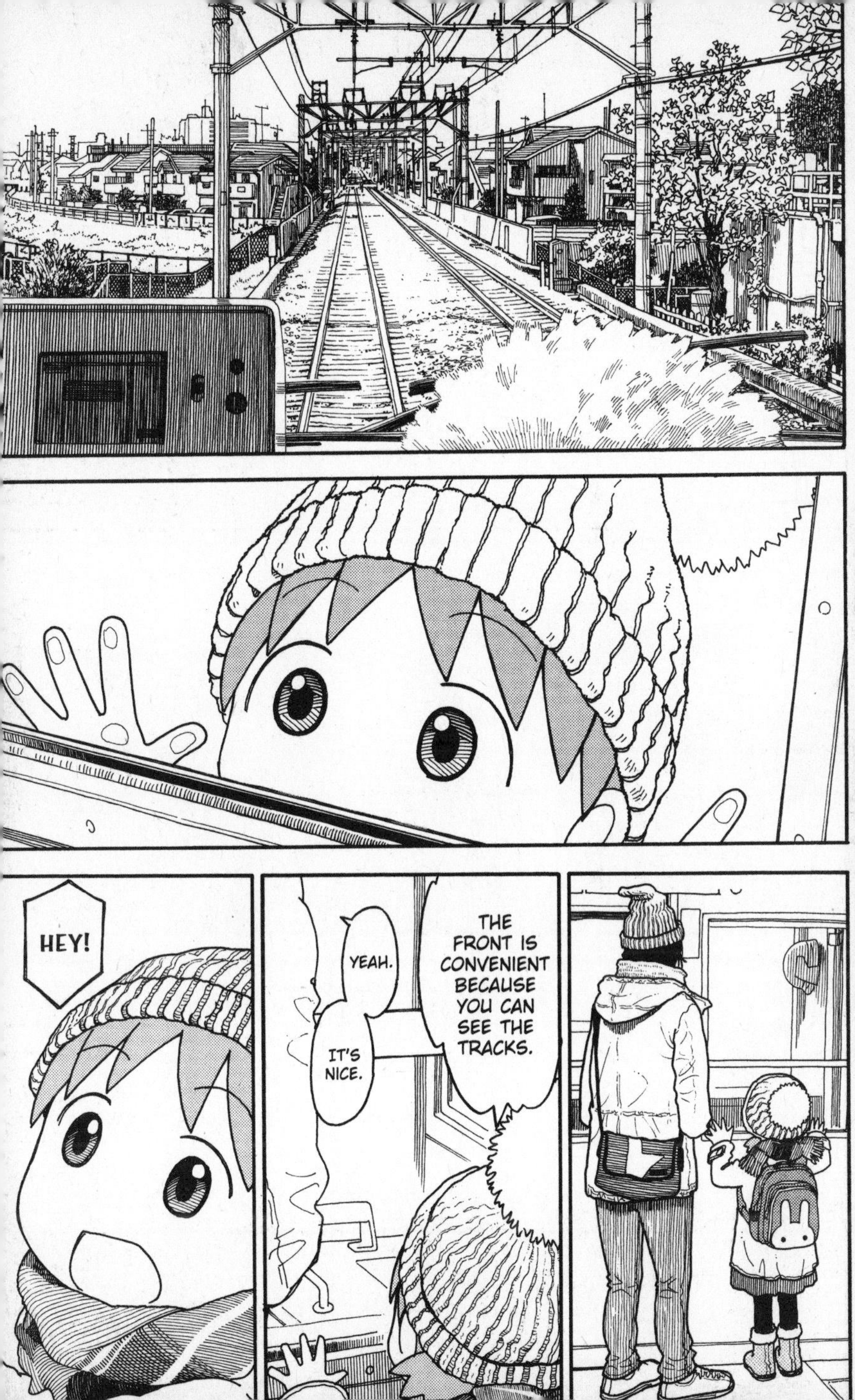
THE FRONT IS CONVENIENT BECAUSE YOU CAN SEE THE TRACKS.
YEAH.
IT'S NICE.
HEY!

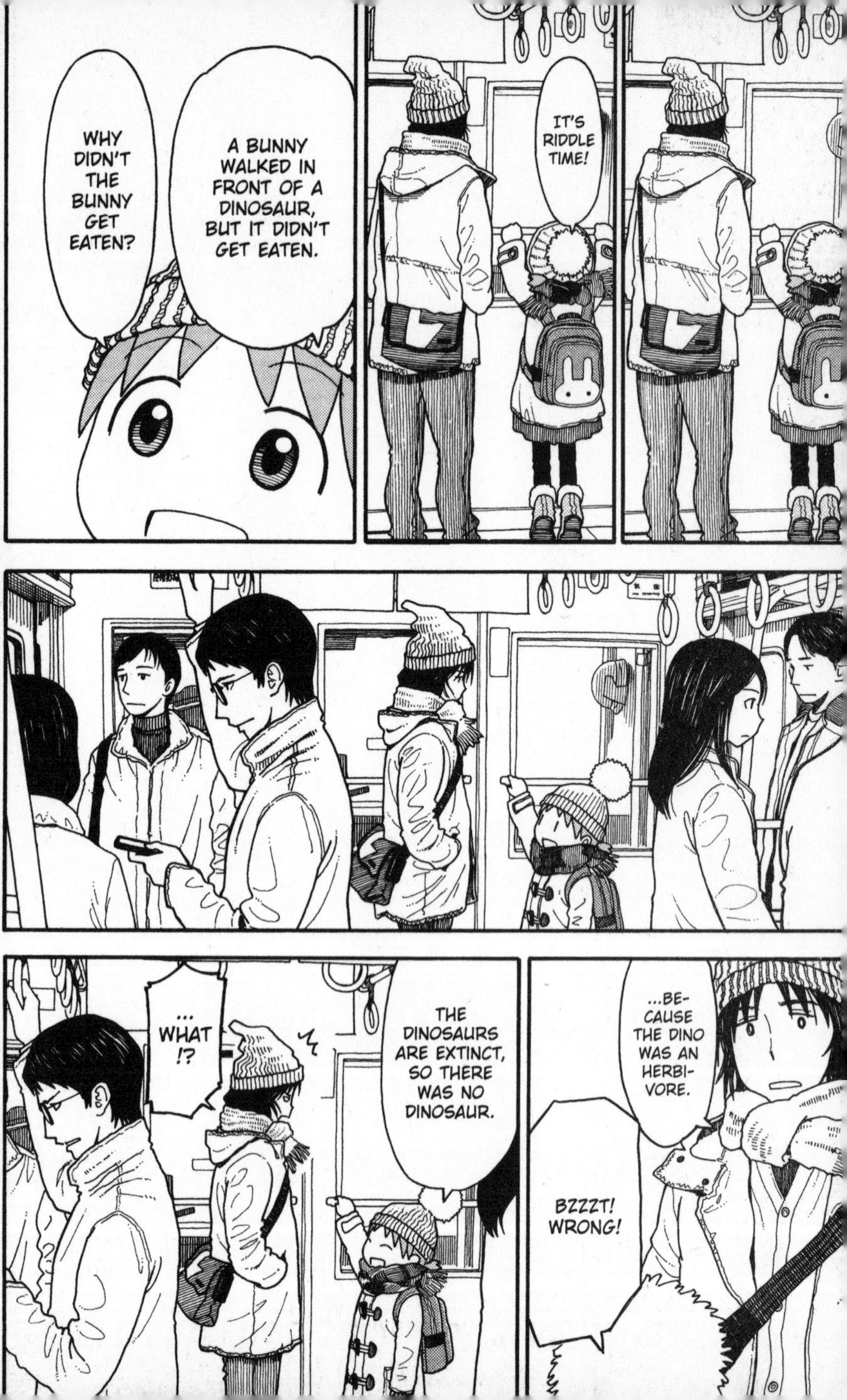
IT'S RIDDLE TIME!
A BUNNY WALKED IN FRONT OF A DINOSAUR, BUT IT DIDN'T GET EATEN.
WHY DIDN'T THE BUNNY GET EATEN?
...BE-CAUSE THE DINO WAS AN HERBI-VORE.
BZZZT! WRONG!
THE DINOSAURS ARE EXTINCT, SO THERE WAS NO DINOSAUR.
... WHAT !?

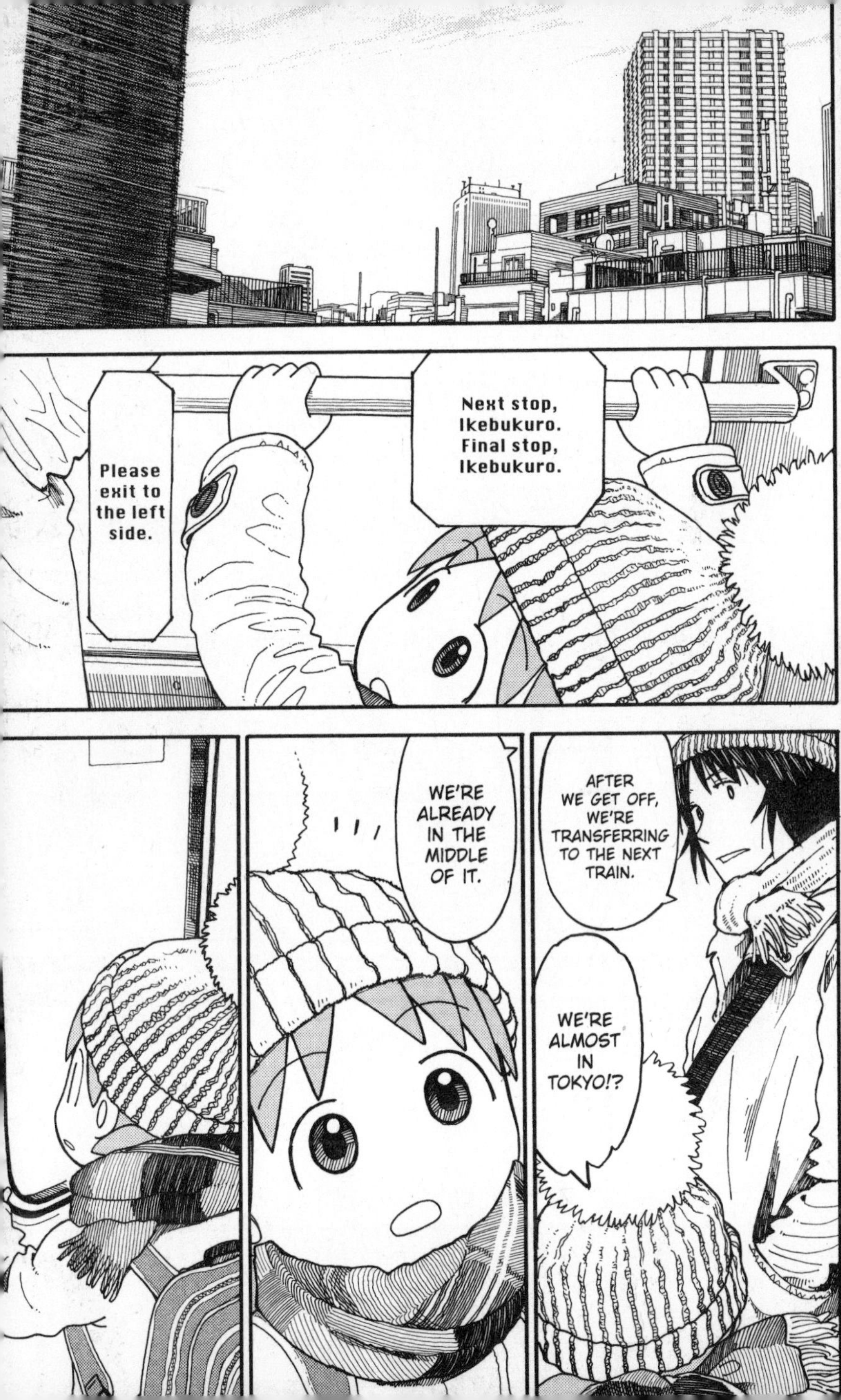
Next stop, Ikebukuro. Final stop, Ikebukuro.
Please exit to the left side.
AFTER WE GET OFF, WE'RE TRANSFERRING TO THE NEXT TRAIN.
WE'RE ALMOST IN TOKYO!?
WE'RE ALREADY IN THE MIDDLE OF IT.

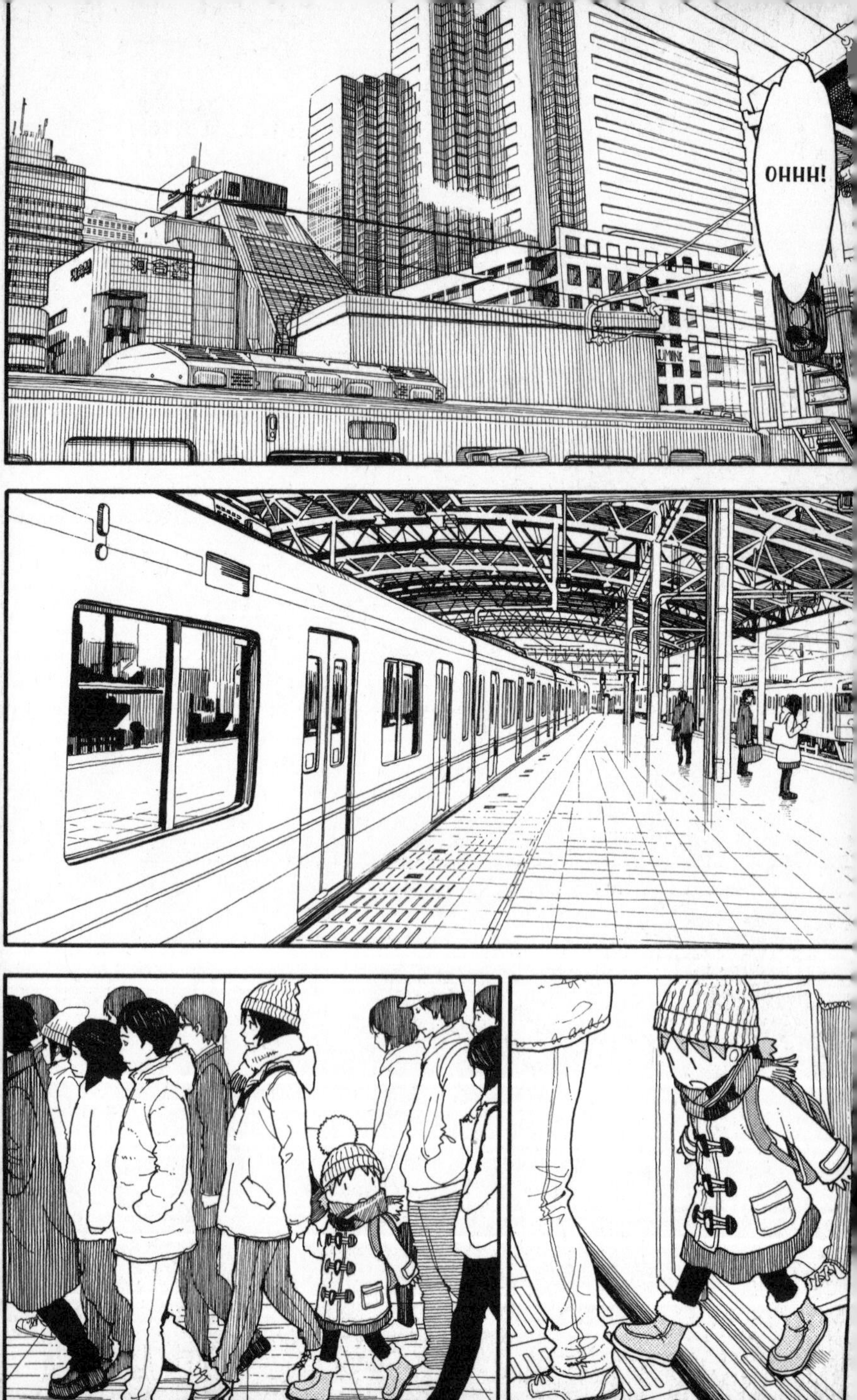
OHHH!

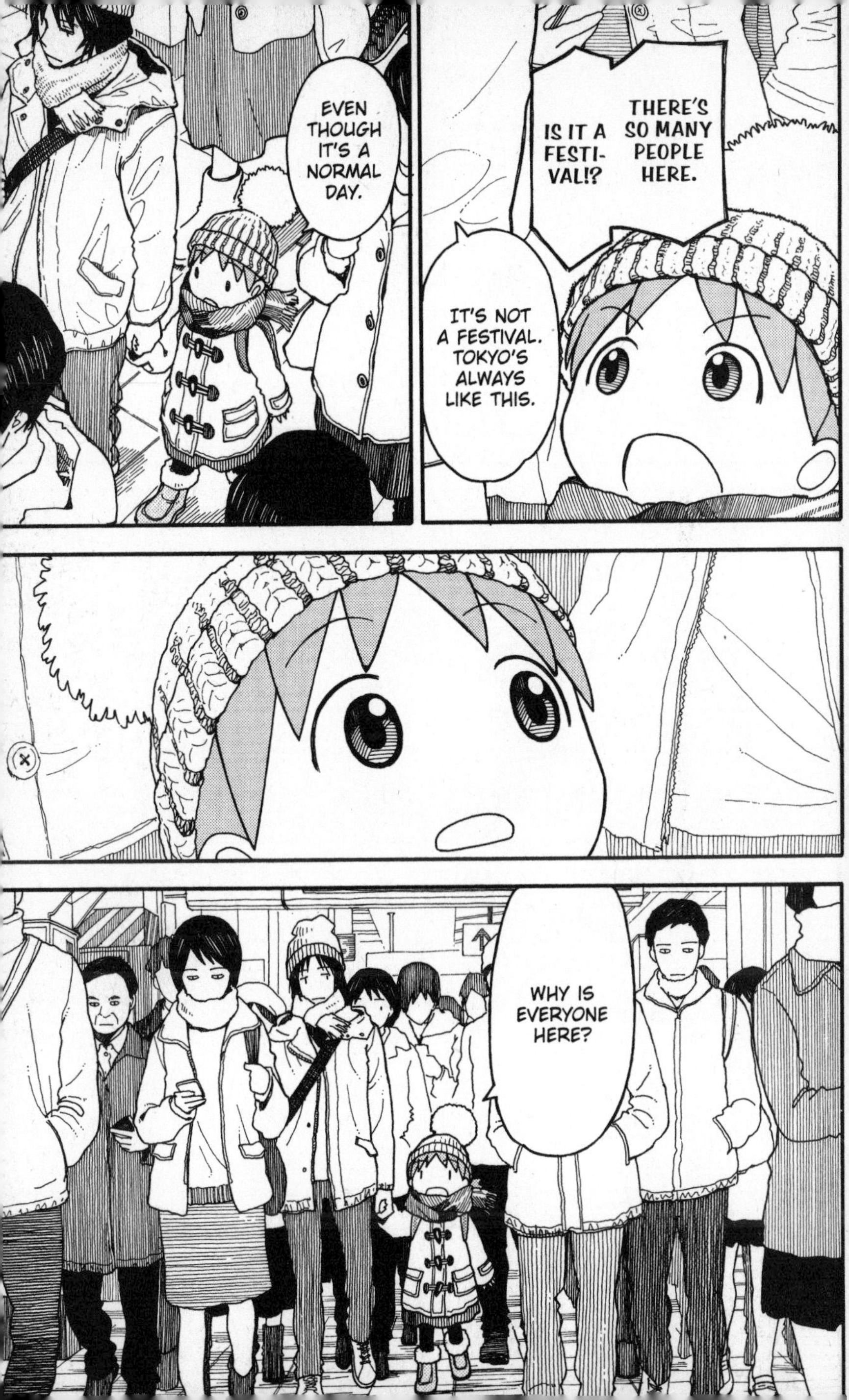
THERE'S SO MANY PEOPLE HERE.
IS IT A FESTI-VAL!?
IT'S NOT A FESTIVAL. TOKYO'S ALWAYS LIKE THIS.
EVEN THOUGH IT'S A NORMAL DAY.
WHY IS EVERYONE HERE?

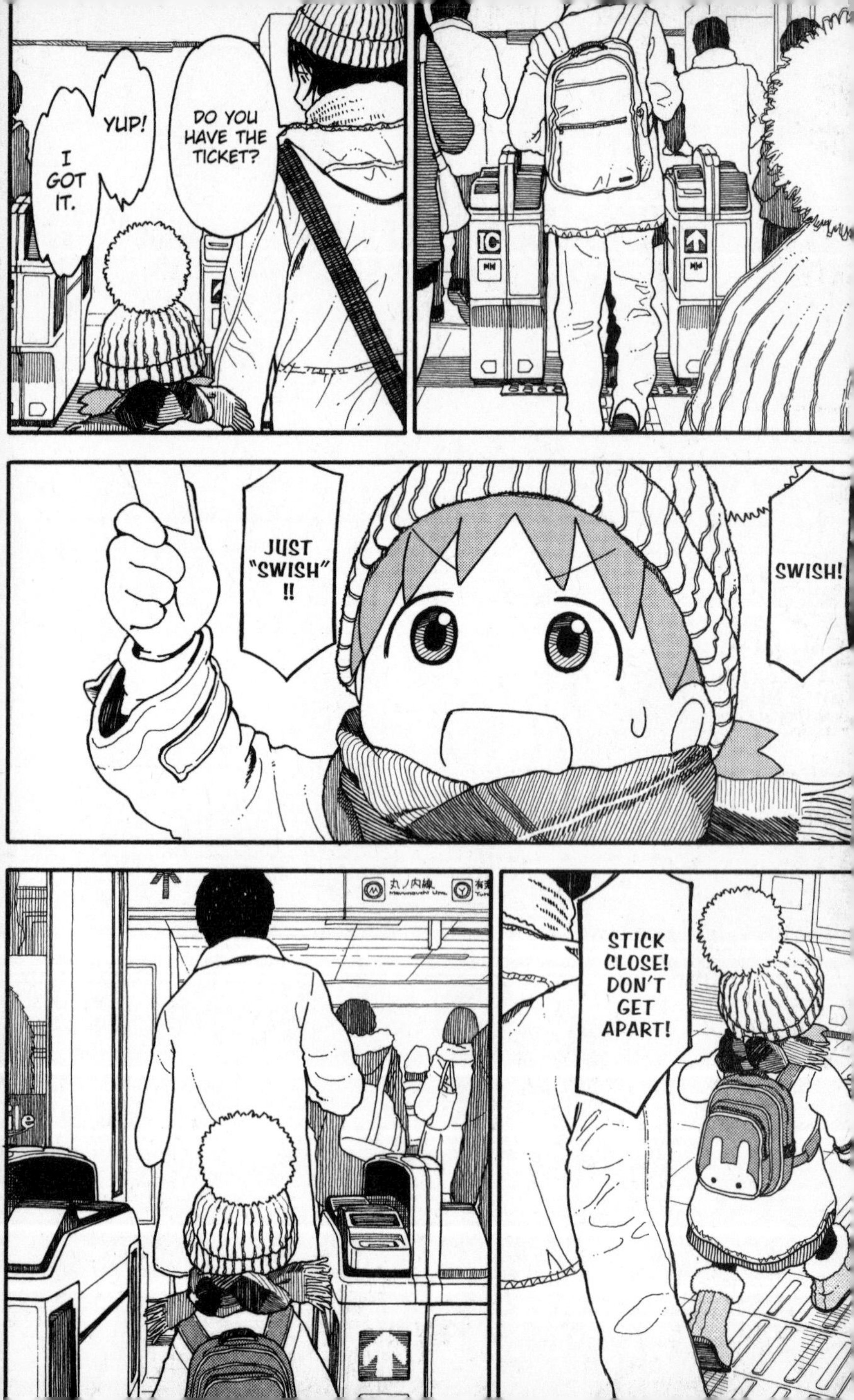
DO YOU HAVE THE TICKET?
YUP! I GOT IT.
SWISH!
JUST "SWISH" !!
STICK CLOSE! DON'T GET APART!

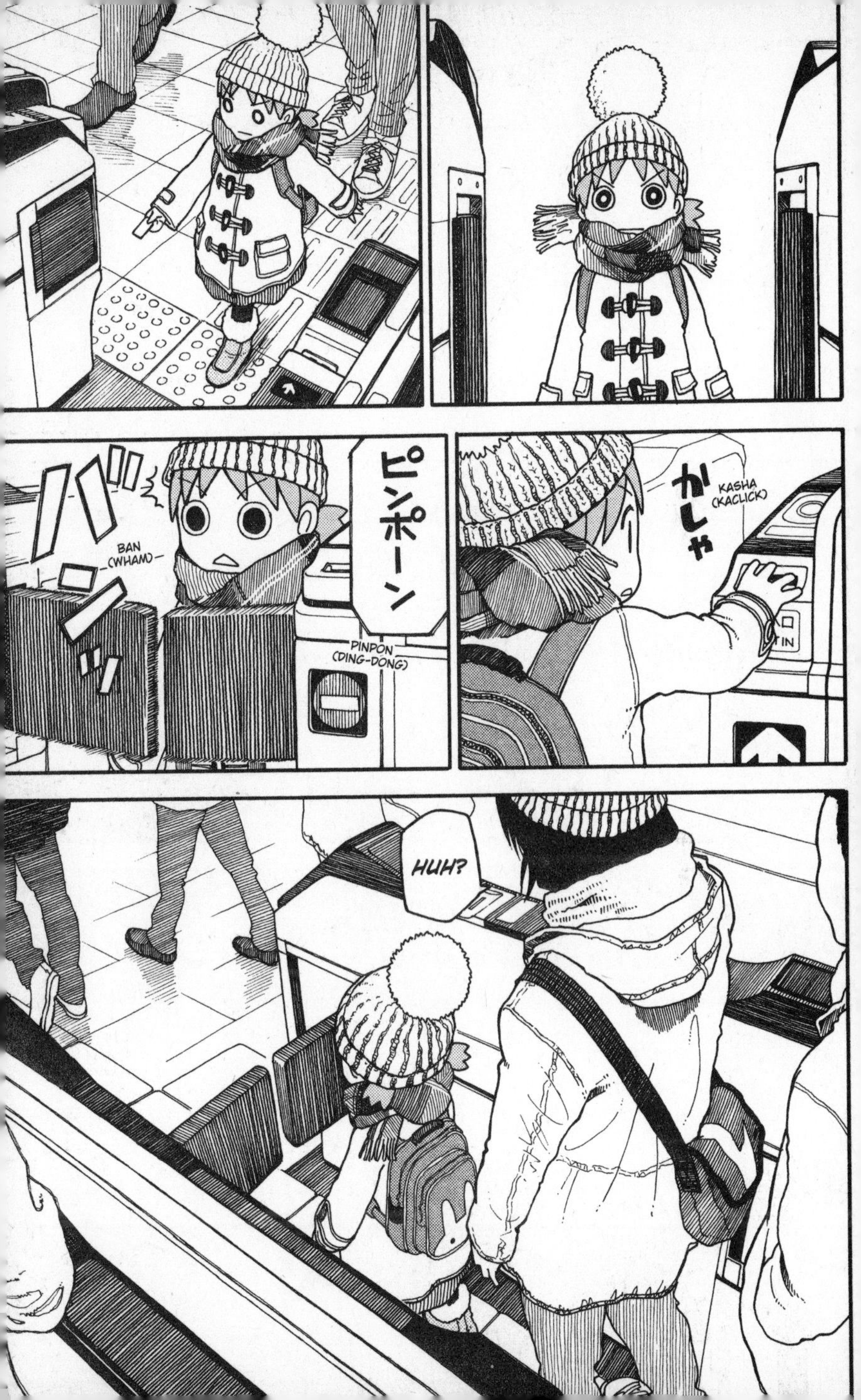

かしゃ
KASHA
(KACLICK)
ピンポーン
PINPON
(DING-DONG)
BAN
(WHAM)
HUH?

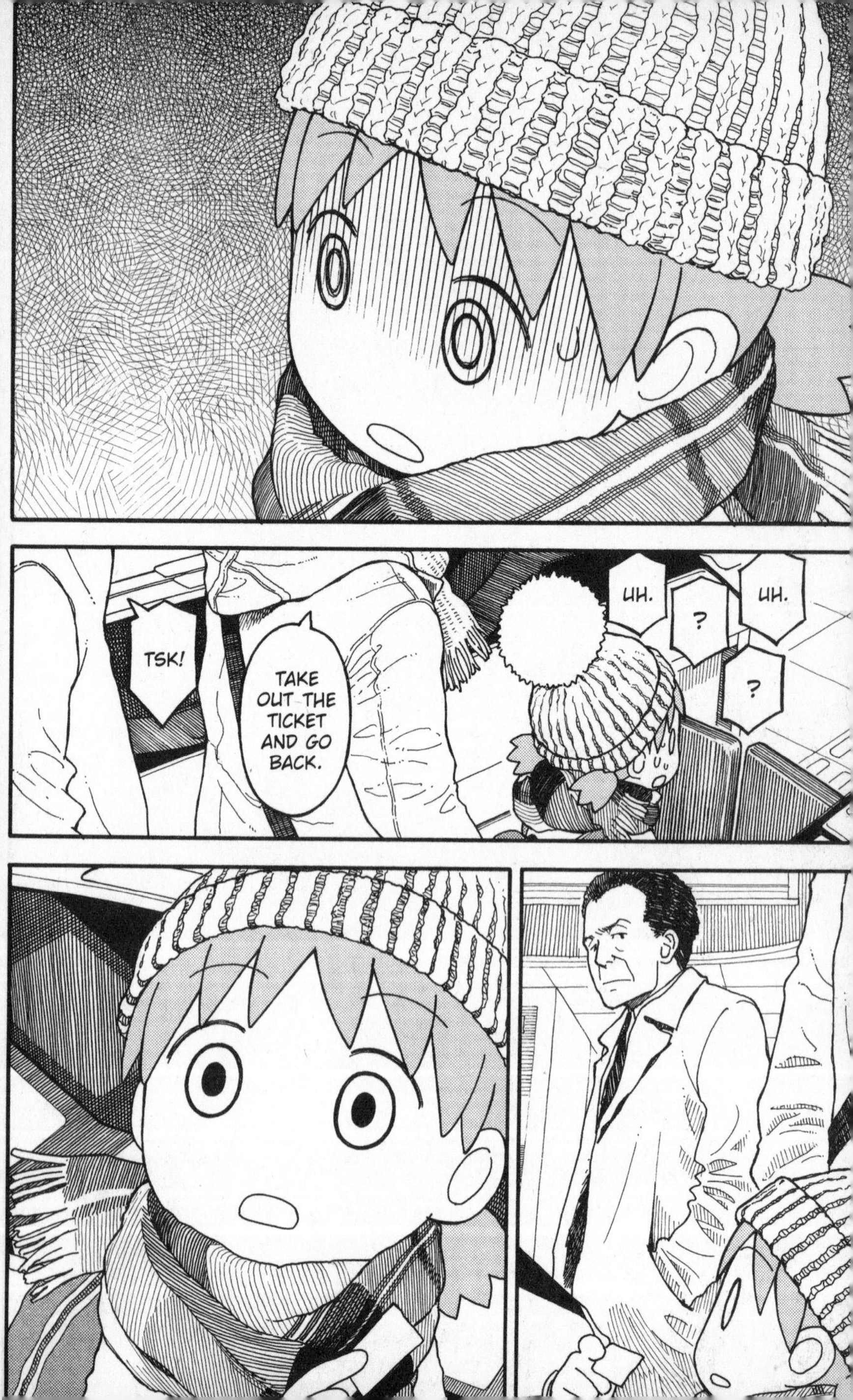
UH.
?
UH.
?
TAKE OUT THE TICKET AND GO BACK.
TSK!

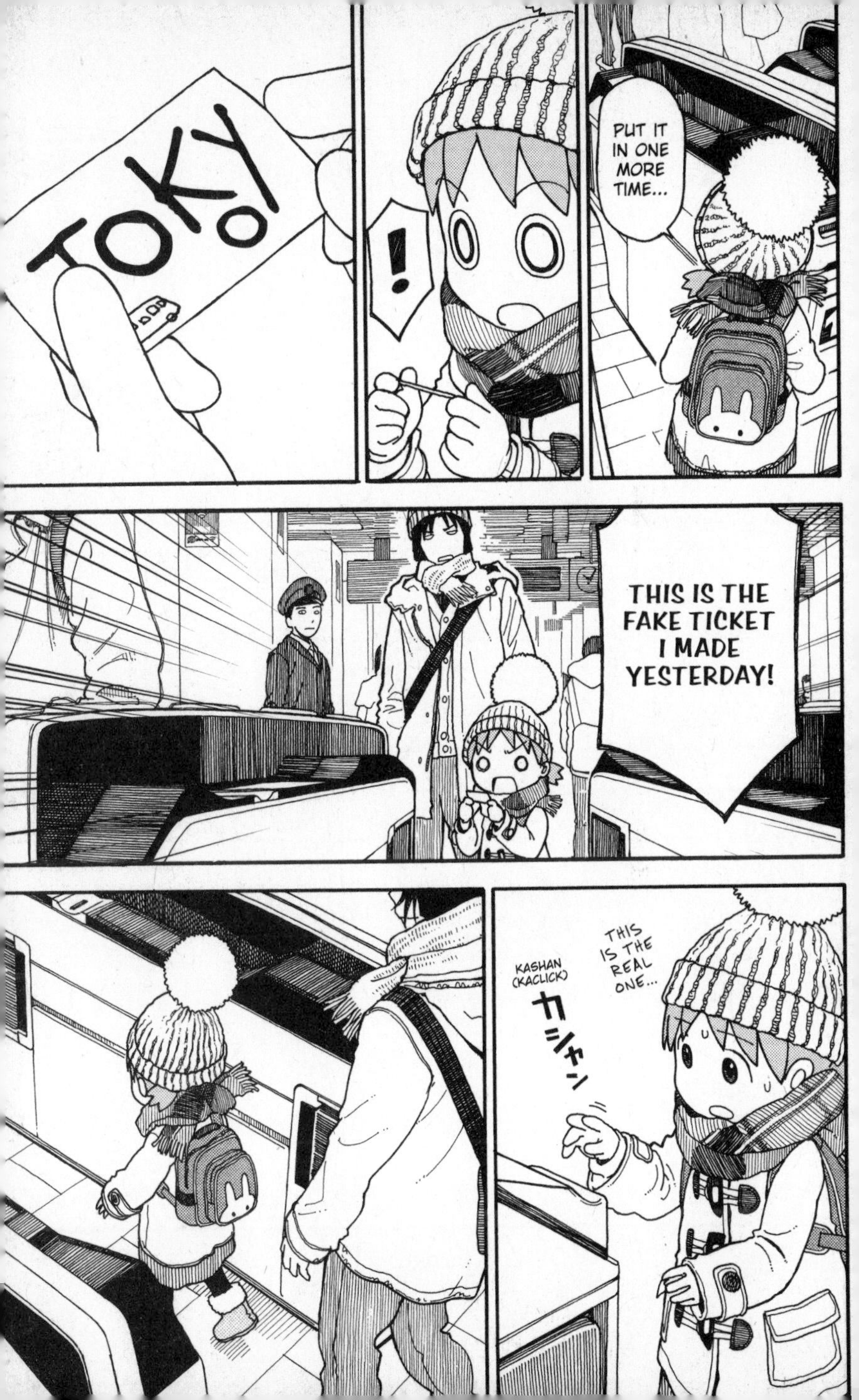
PUT IT IN ONE MORE TIME...
!
TOKYO
THIS IS THE FAKE TICKET I MADE YESTERDAY!
THIS IS THE REAL ONE...
KASHAN (KACLICK)
カシャン

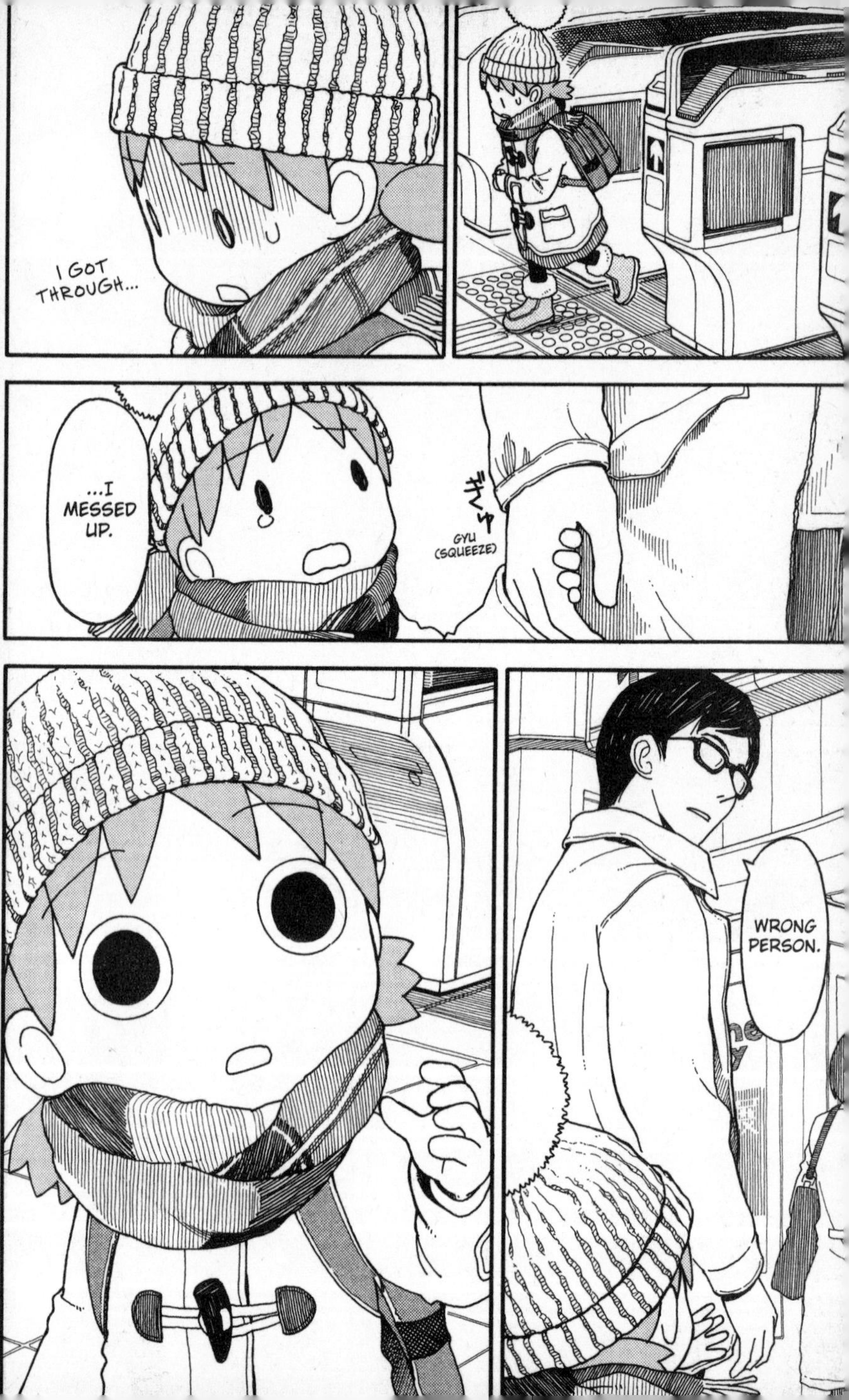
I GOT THROUGH...
ぎゅ
GYU (SQUEEZE)
...I MESSED UP.
WRONG PERSON.

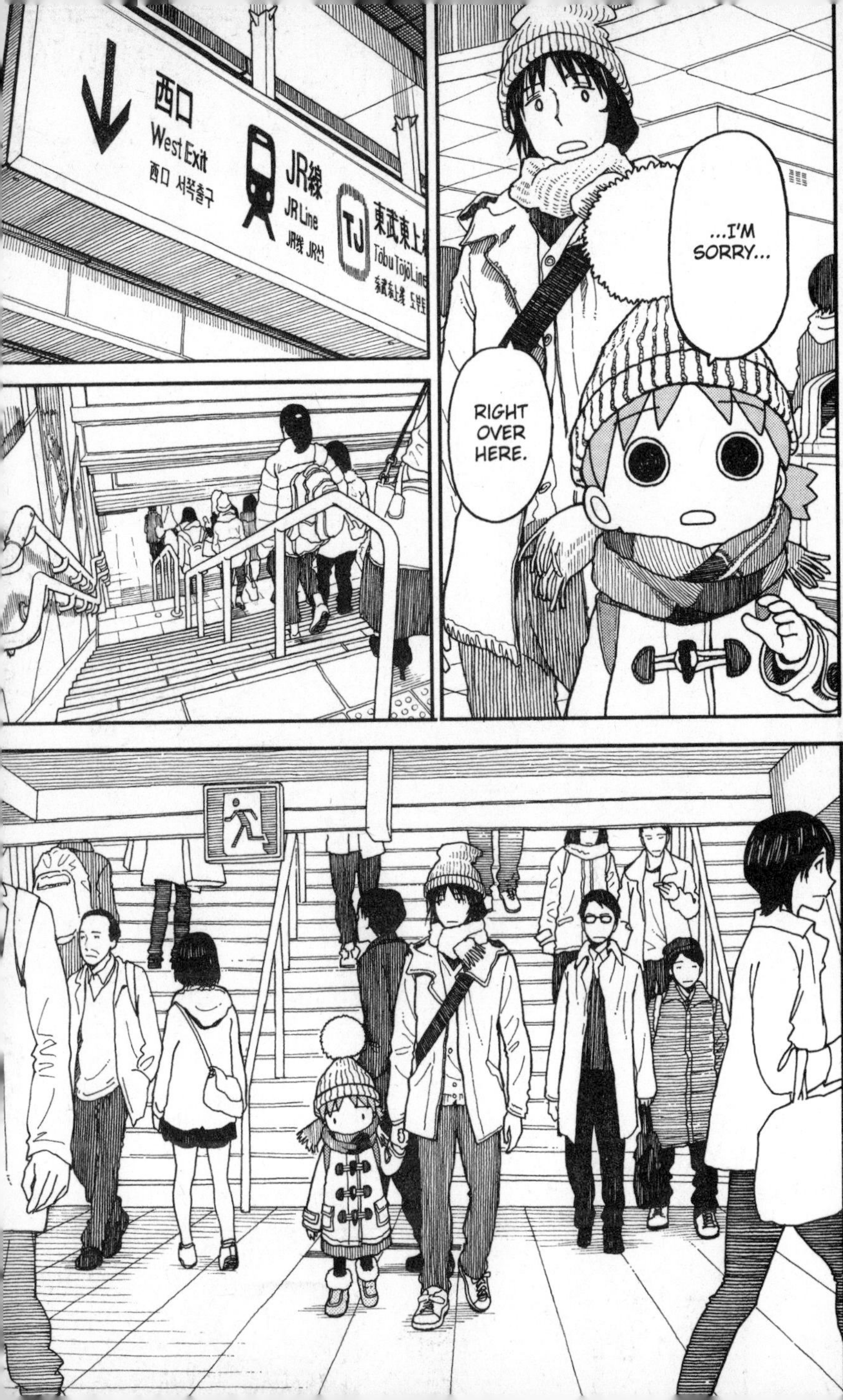
...I'M SORRY...
RIGHT OVER HERE.
西口
West Exit
西口 서쪽출구
JR線
JR Line
JR线 JR선
TJ
東武東上
Tōbu Tōjō Line

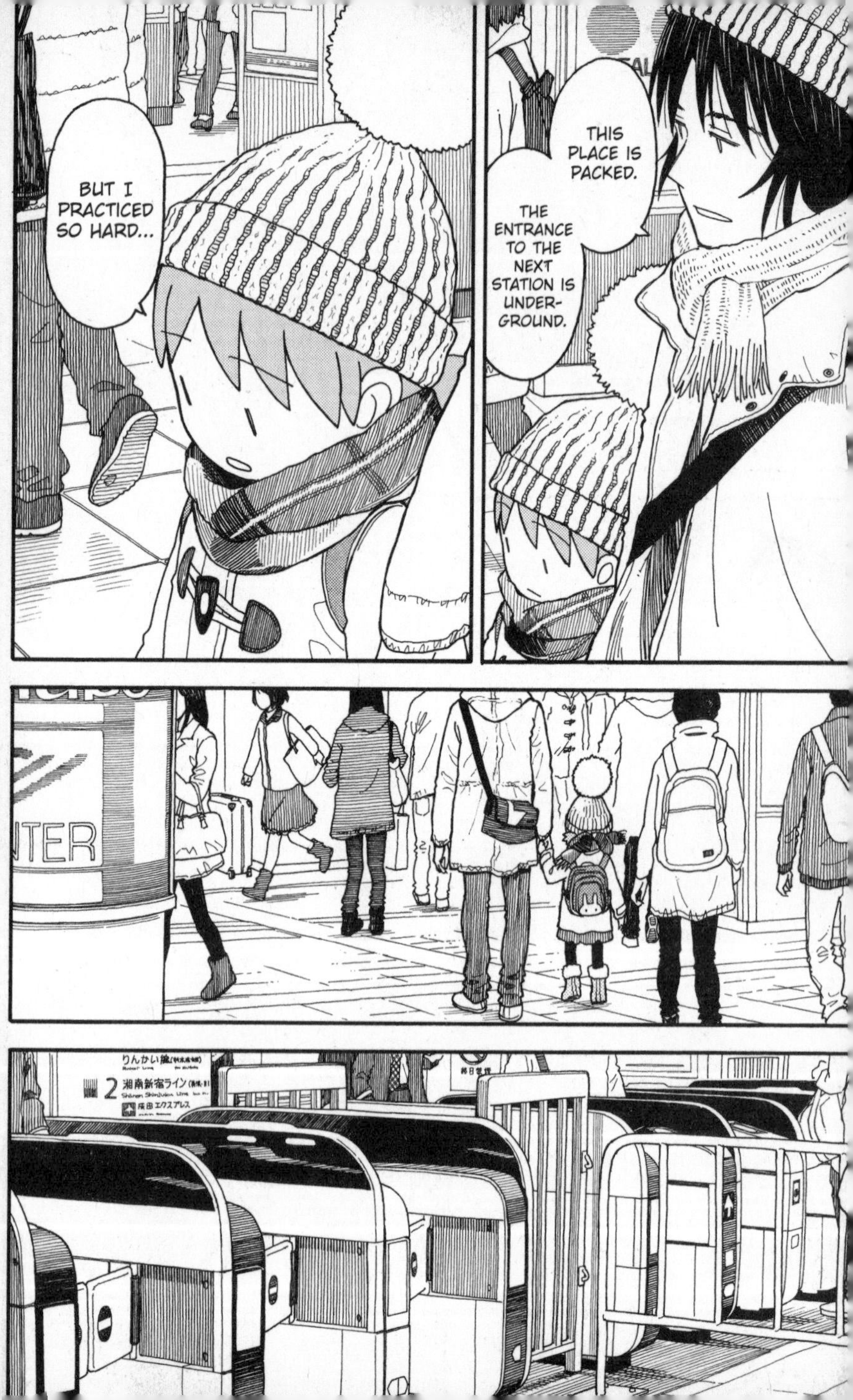
THIS PLACE IS PACKED.
THE ENTRANCE TO THE NEXT STATION IS UNDERGROUND.
BUT I PRACTICED SO HARD...
りんかい線
2 湘南新宿ライン
成田エクスプレス

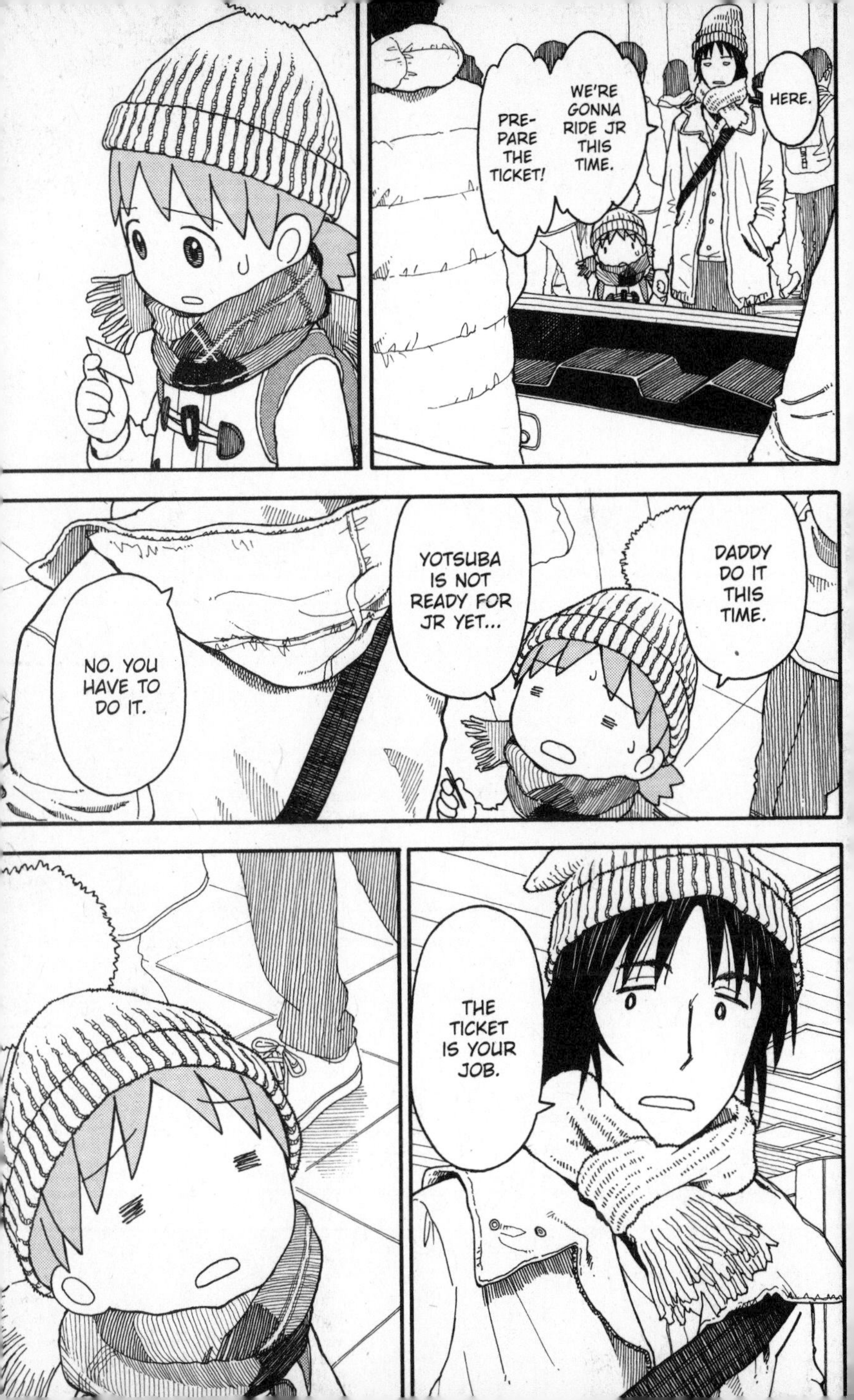
HERE.
WE'RE GONNA RIDE JR THIS TIME.
PRE-PARE THE TICKET!
DADDY DO IT THIS TIME.
YOTSUBA IS NOT READY FOR JR YET...
NO. YOU HAVE TO DO IT.
THE TICKET IS YOUR JOB.

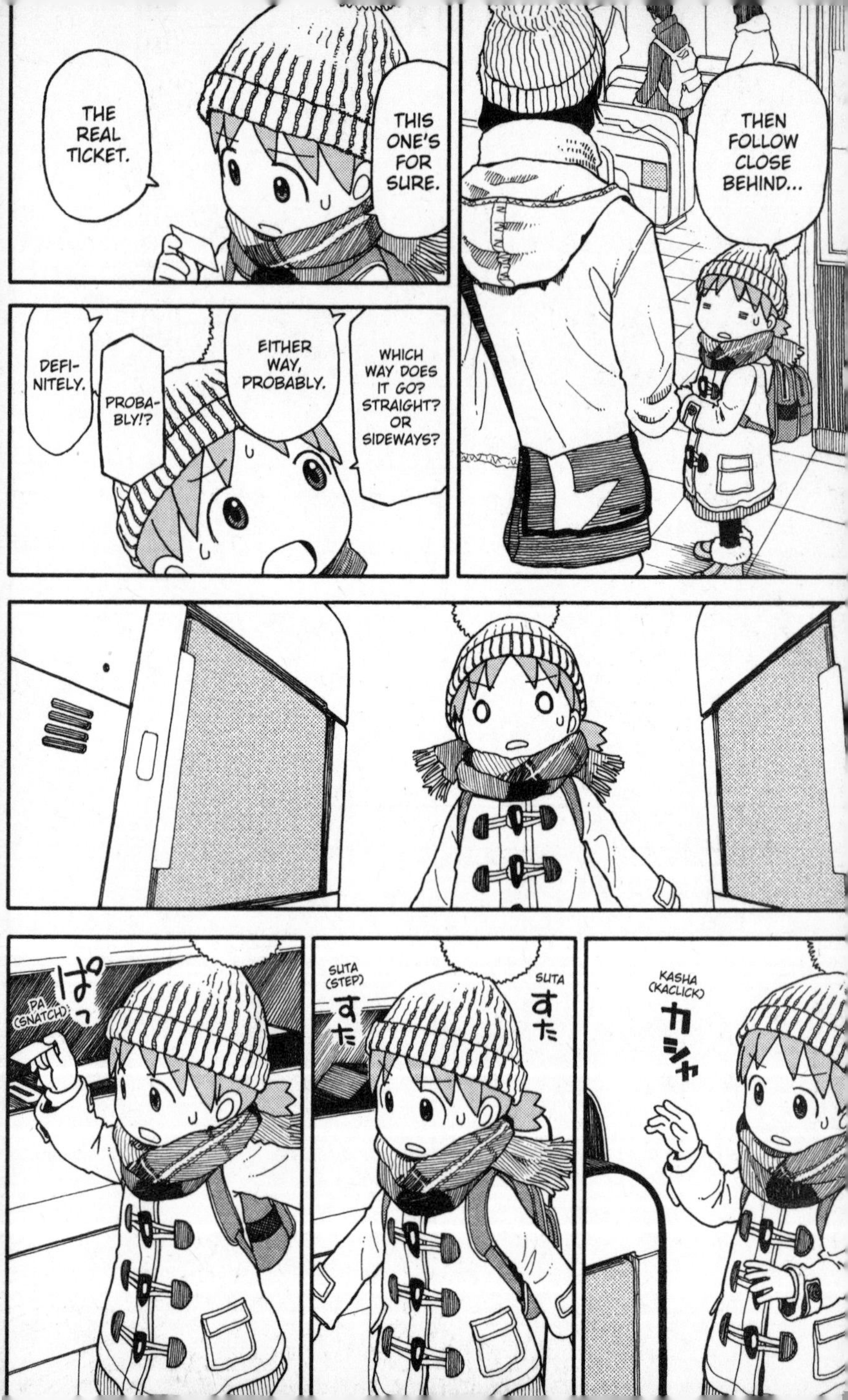
THEN FOLLOW CLOSE BEHIND...
THIS ONE'S FOR SURE.
THE REAL TICKET.
WHICH WAY DOES IT GO? STRAIGHT? OR SIDEWAYS?
EITHER WAY, PROBABLY.
PROBABLY!?
DEFINITELY.
KASHA (KACLICK)
カシャ
SUTA
すた
SUTA (STEP)
すた
ぱっ
PA (SNATCH)

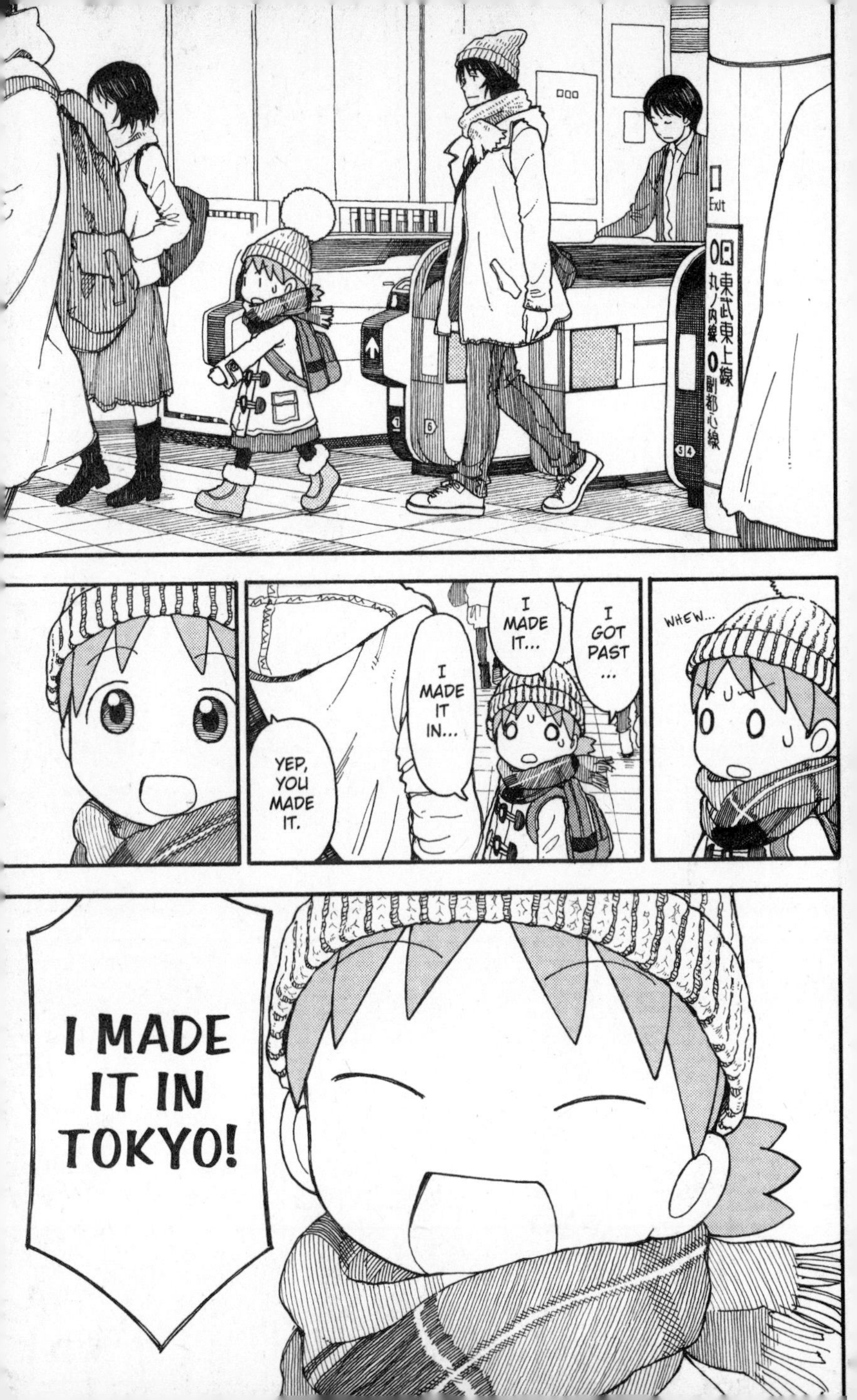
Exit
東武東上線
丸ノ内線
副都心線
WHEW...
I GOT PAST...
I MADE IT...
I MADE IT IN...
YEP, YOU MADE IT.
I MADE IT IN TOKYO!

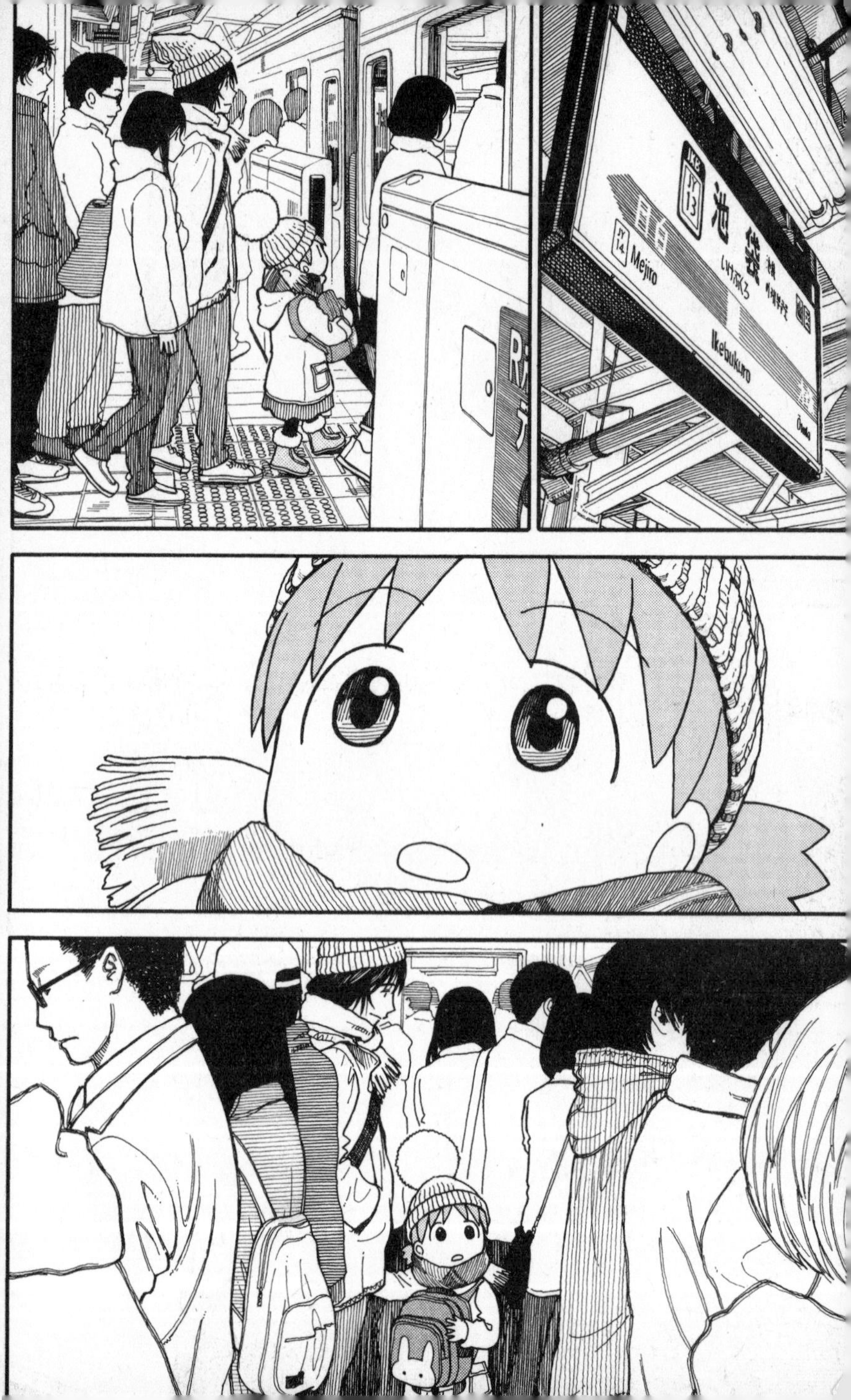
JY 13
池袋
いけぶくろ
Ikebukuro
目白
JY 14
Mejiro
Ōtsuka

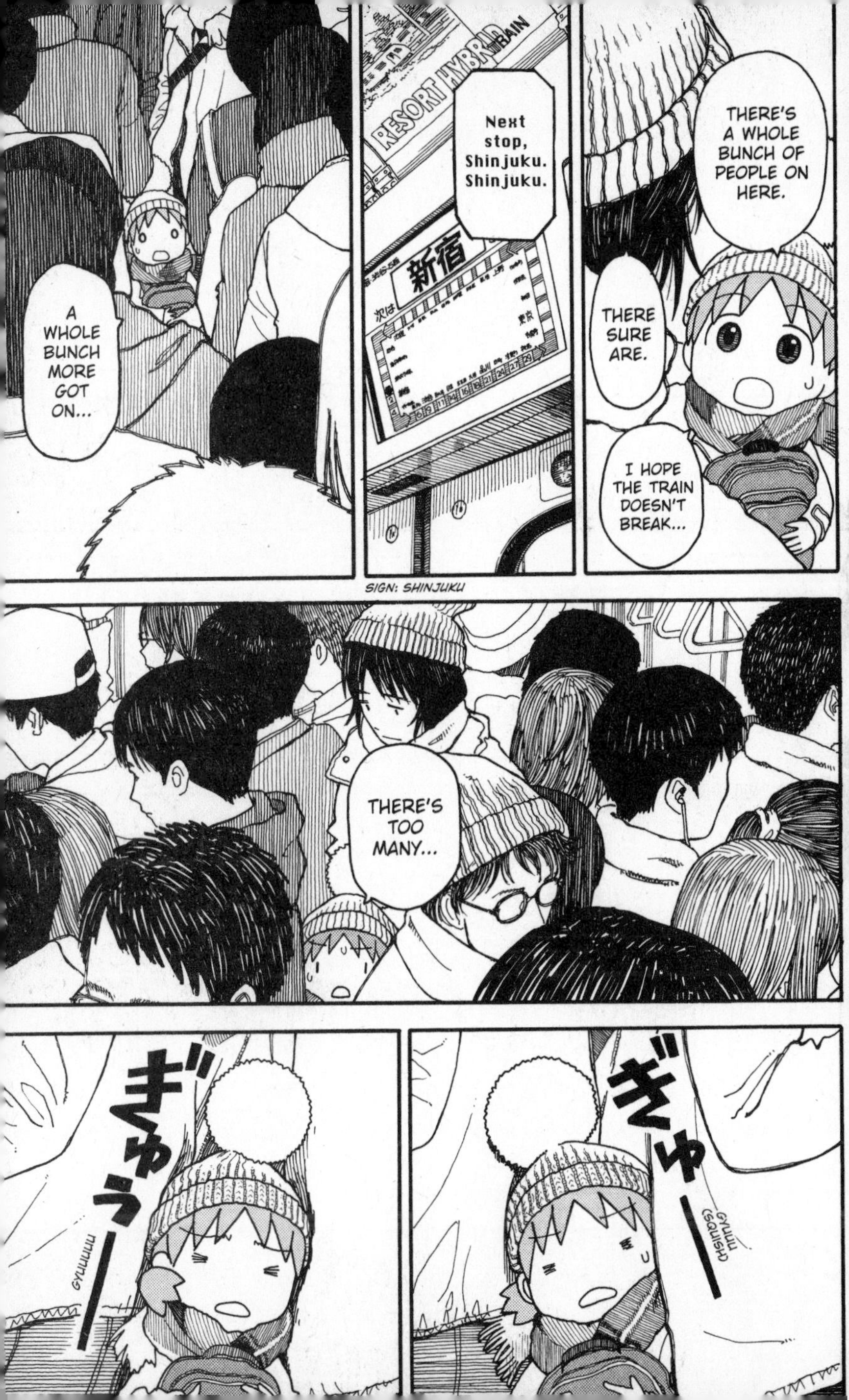
THERE'S A WHOLE BUNCH OF PEOPLE ON HERE.
THERE SURE ARE.
I HOPE THE TRAIN DOESN'T BREAK...
RESORT HYBRID TRAIN
Next stop, Shinjuku. Shinjuku.
次は
新宿
A WHOLE BUNCH MORE GOT ON...
SIGN: SHINJUKU
THERE'S TOO MANY...
ぎゅー
GYUUU (SQUISH)
ぎゅうー
GYUUUUU

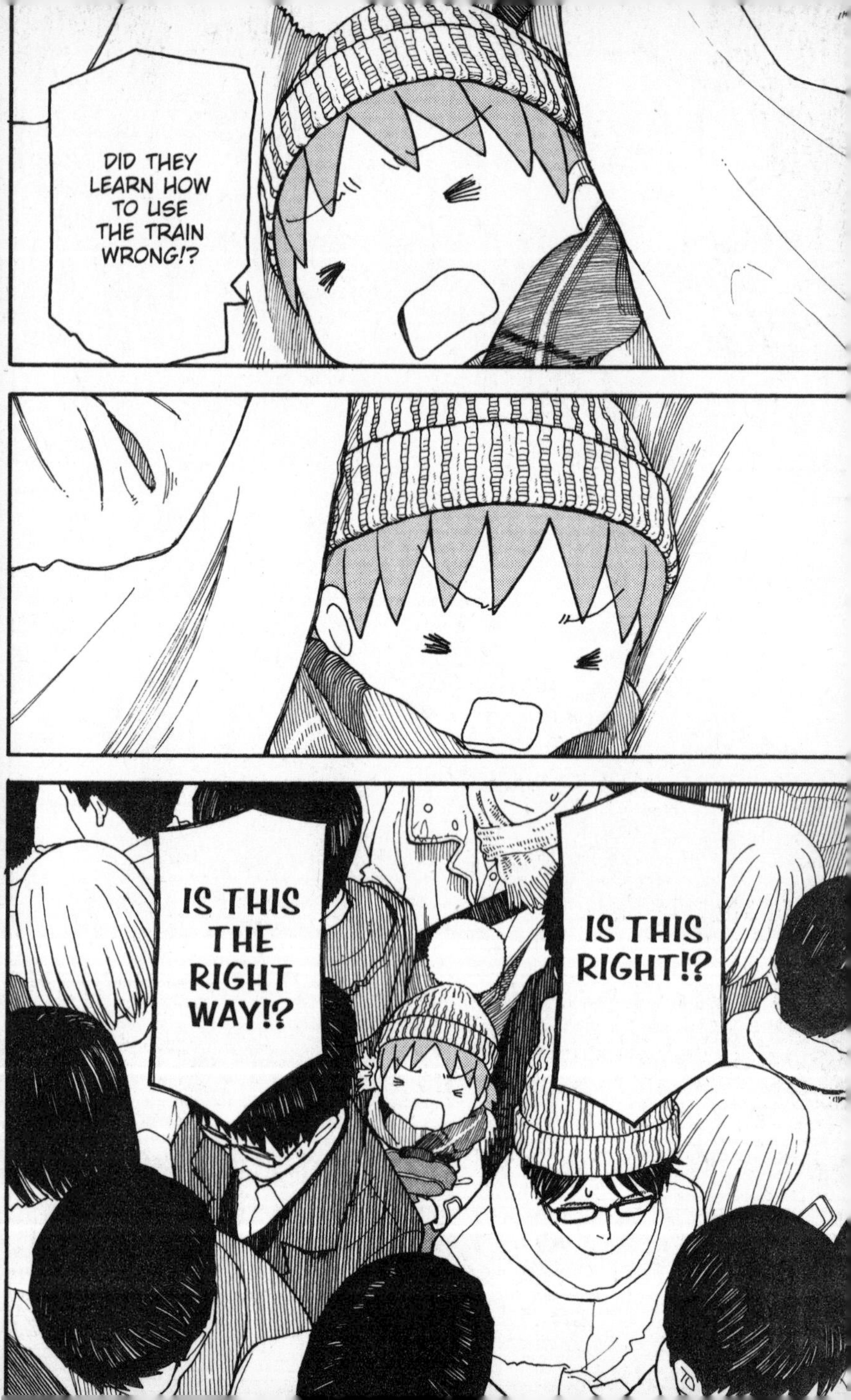
DID THEY LEARN HOW TO USE THE TRAIN WRONG!?
IS THIS RIGHT!?
IS THIS THE RIGHT WAY!?

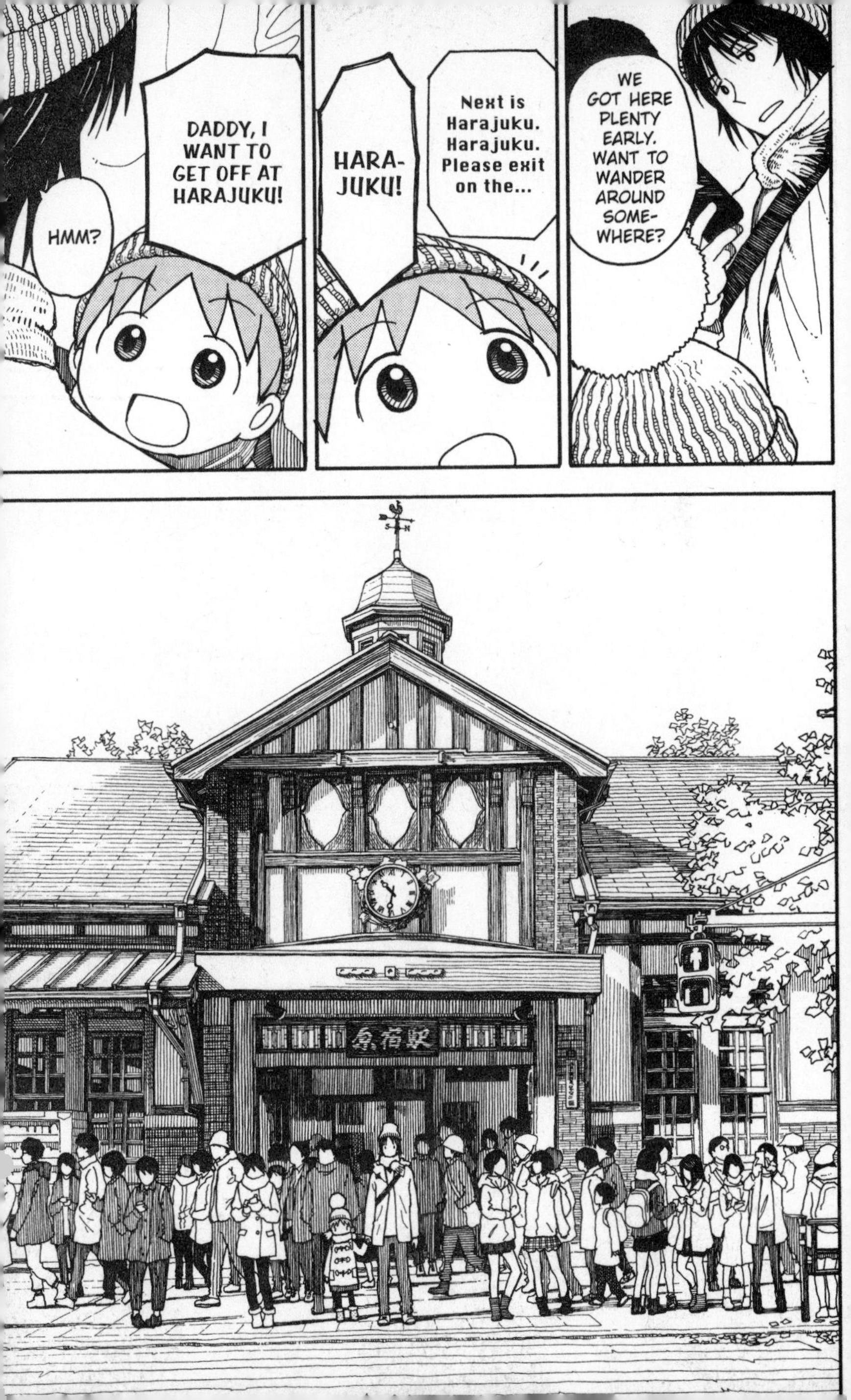
WE GOT HERE PLENTY EARLY. WANT TO WANDER AROUND SOME-WHERE?
Next is Harajuku. Harajuku. Please exit on the...
HARA-JUKU!
DADDY, I WANT TO GET OFF AT HARAJUKU!
HMM?
原宿駅

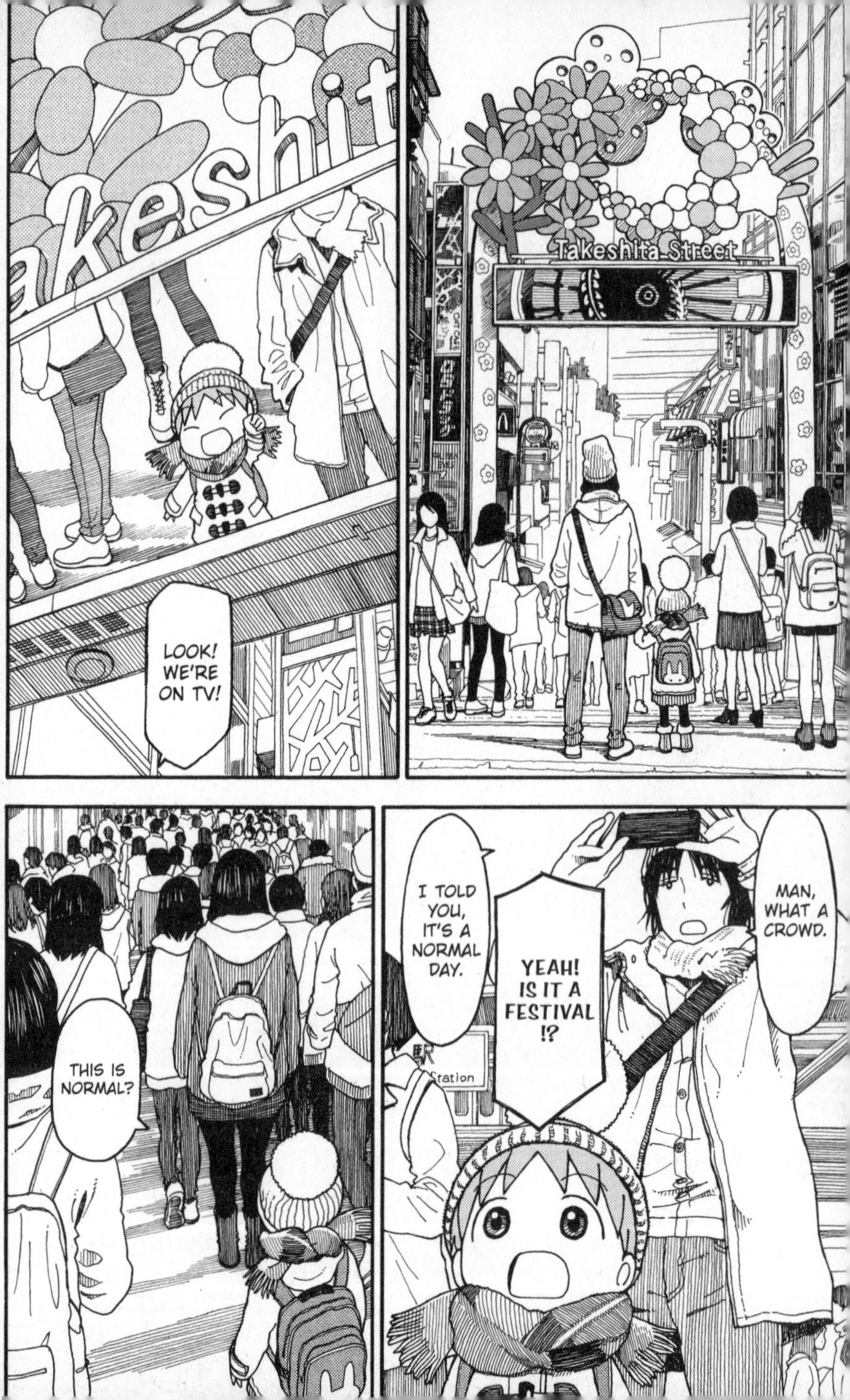
Takeshita Street
akeshit
LOOK! WE'RE ON TV!
MAN, WHAT A CROWD.
YEAH! IS IT A FESTIVAL !?
I TOLD YOU, IT'S A NORMAL DAY.
Station
THIS IS NORMAL?

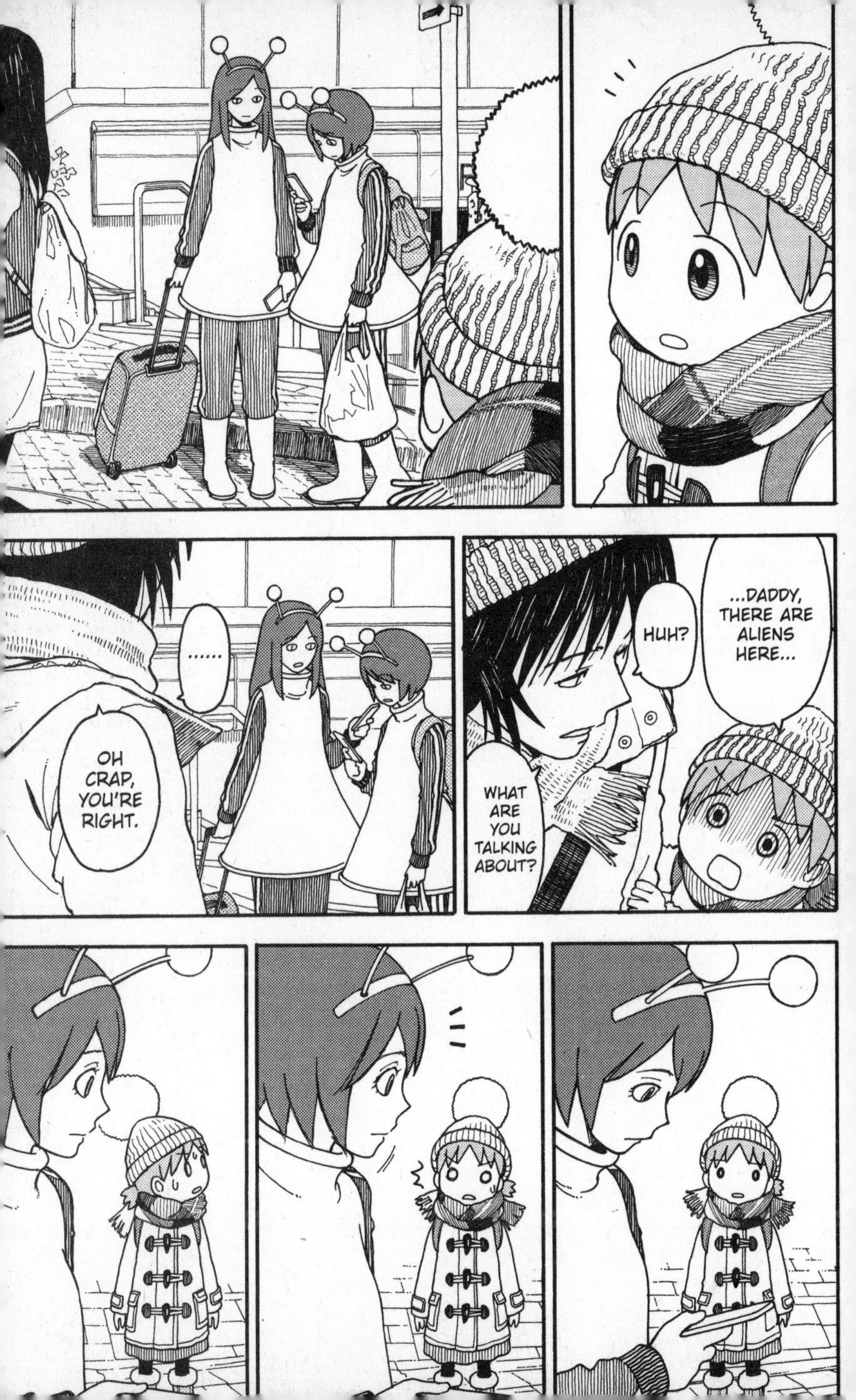
...DADDY, THERE ARE ALIENS HERE...
HUH?
WHAT ARE YOU TALKING ABOUT?
......
OH CRAP, YOU'RE RIGHT.

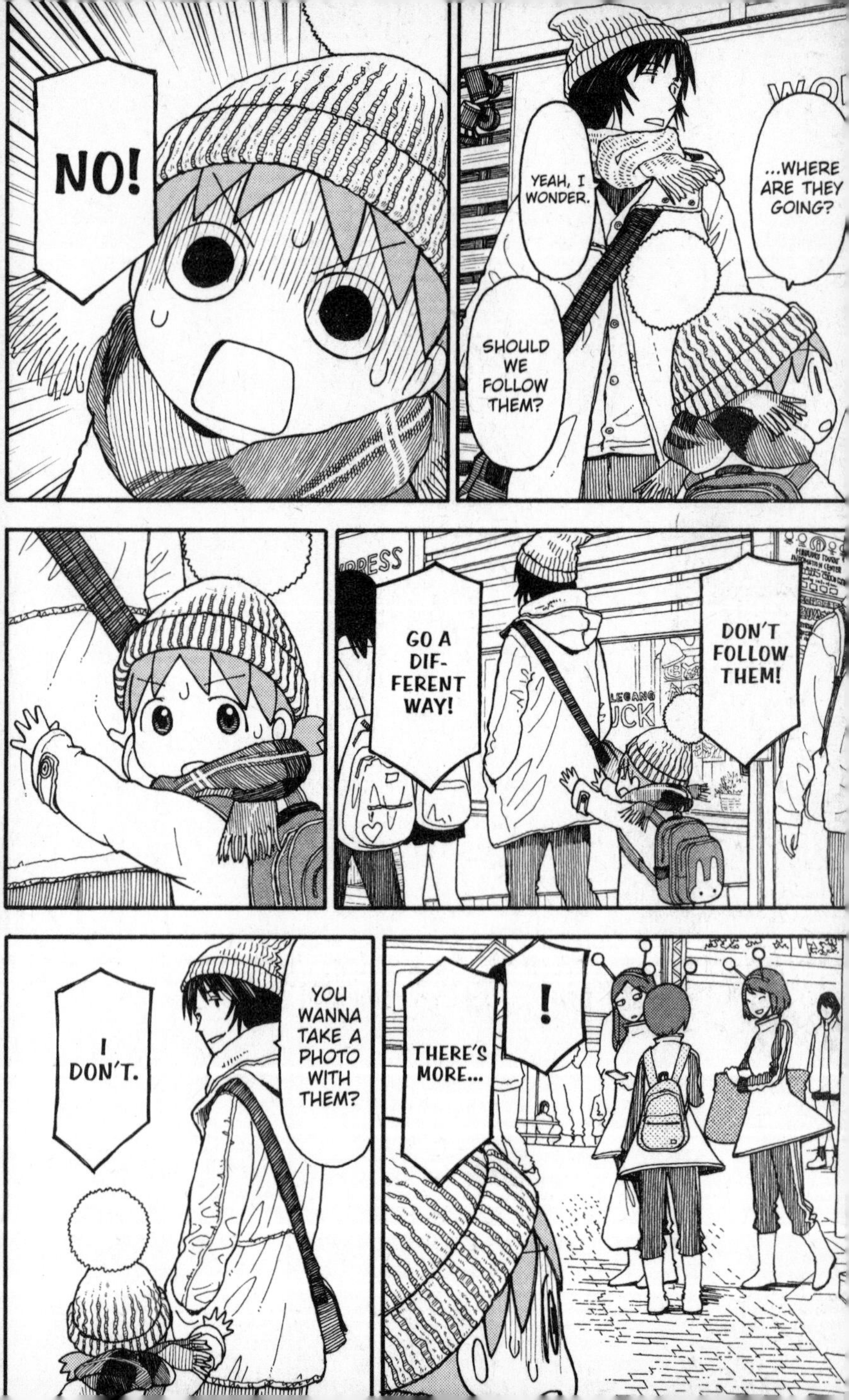
...WHERE ARE THEY GOING?
YEAH, I WONDER.
SHOULD WE FOLLOW THEM?
NO!
DON'T FOLLOW THEM!
GO A DIF-FERENT WAY!
!
THERE'S MORE...
YOU WANNA TAKE A PHOTO WITH THEM?
I DON'T.

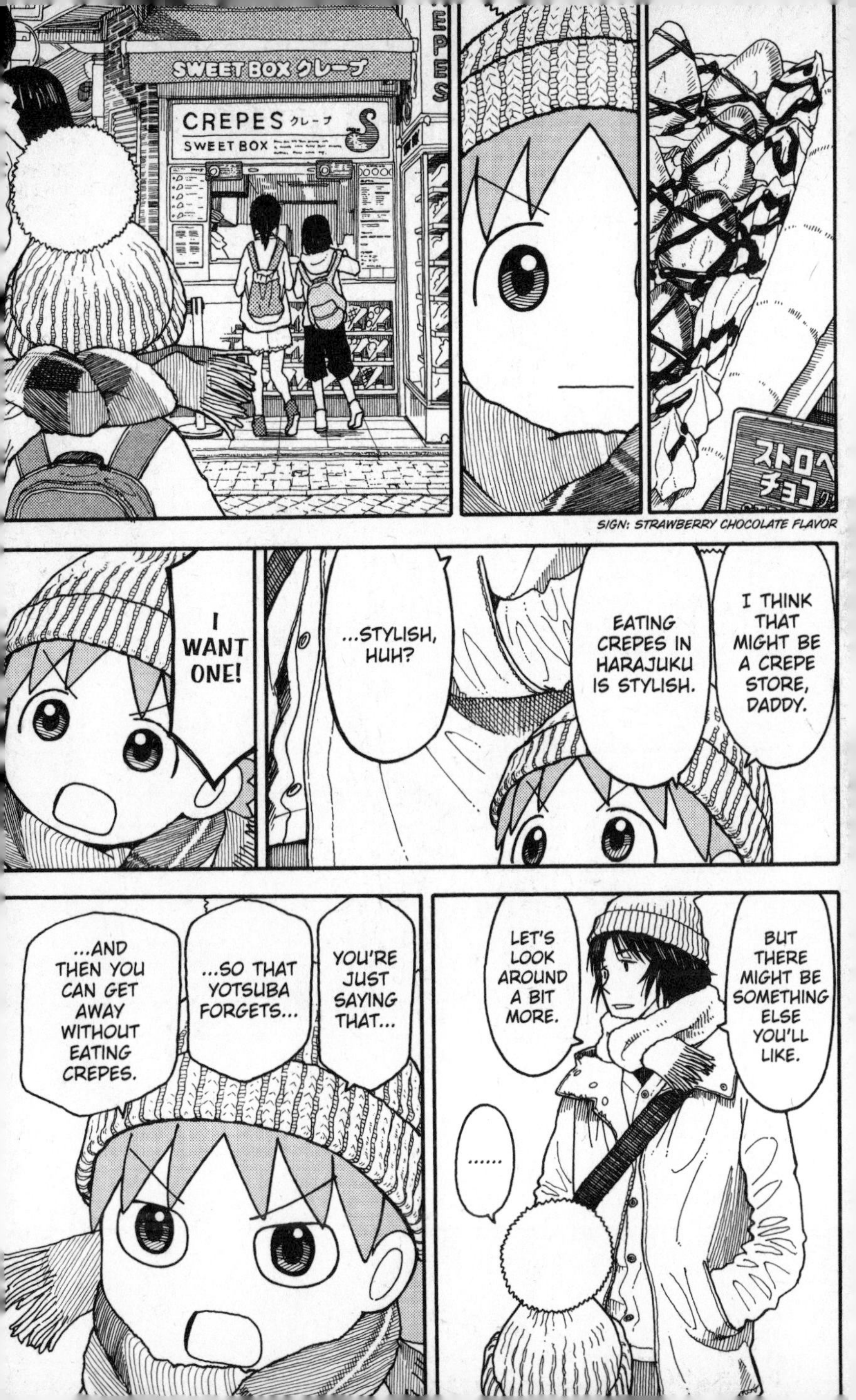
ストロベ チョコ
SIGN: STRAWBERRY CHOCOLATE FLAVOR
SWEET BOX クレープ
CREPES クレープ
SWEET BOX
I THINK THAT MIGHT BE A CREPE STORE, DADDY.
EATING CREPES IN HARAJUKU IS STYLISH.
...STYLISH, HUH?
I WANT ONE!
BUT THERE MIGHT BE SOMETHING ELSE YOU'LL LIKE.
LET'S LOOK AROUND A BIT MORE.
......
YOU'RE JUST SAYING THAT...
...SO THAT YOTSUBA FORGETS...
...AND THEN YOU CAN GET AWAY WITHOUT EATING CREPES.

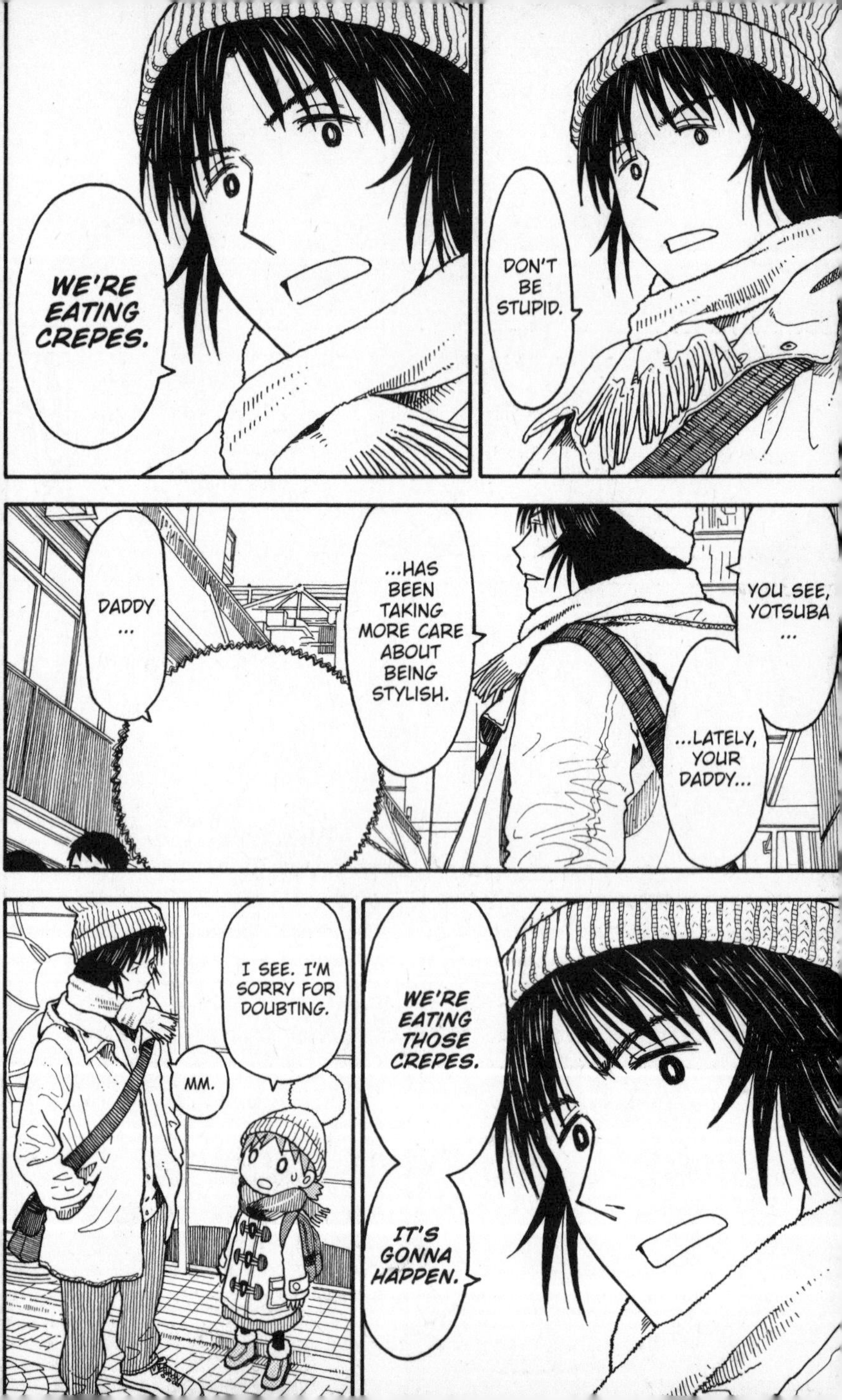
DON'T BE STUPID.
WE'RE EATING CREPES.
YOU SEE, YOTSUBA ...
...LATELY, YOUR DADDY...
...HAS BEEN TAKING MORE CARE ABOUT BEING STYLISH.
DADDY ...
WE'RE EATING THOSE CREPES.
IT'S GONNA HAPPEN.
I SEE. I'M SORRY FOR DOUBTING.
MM.

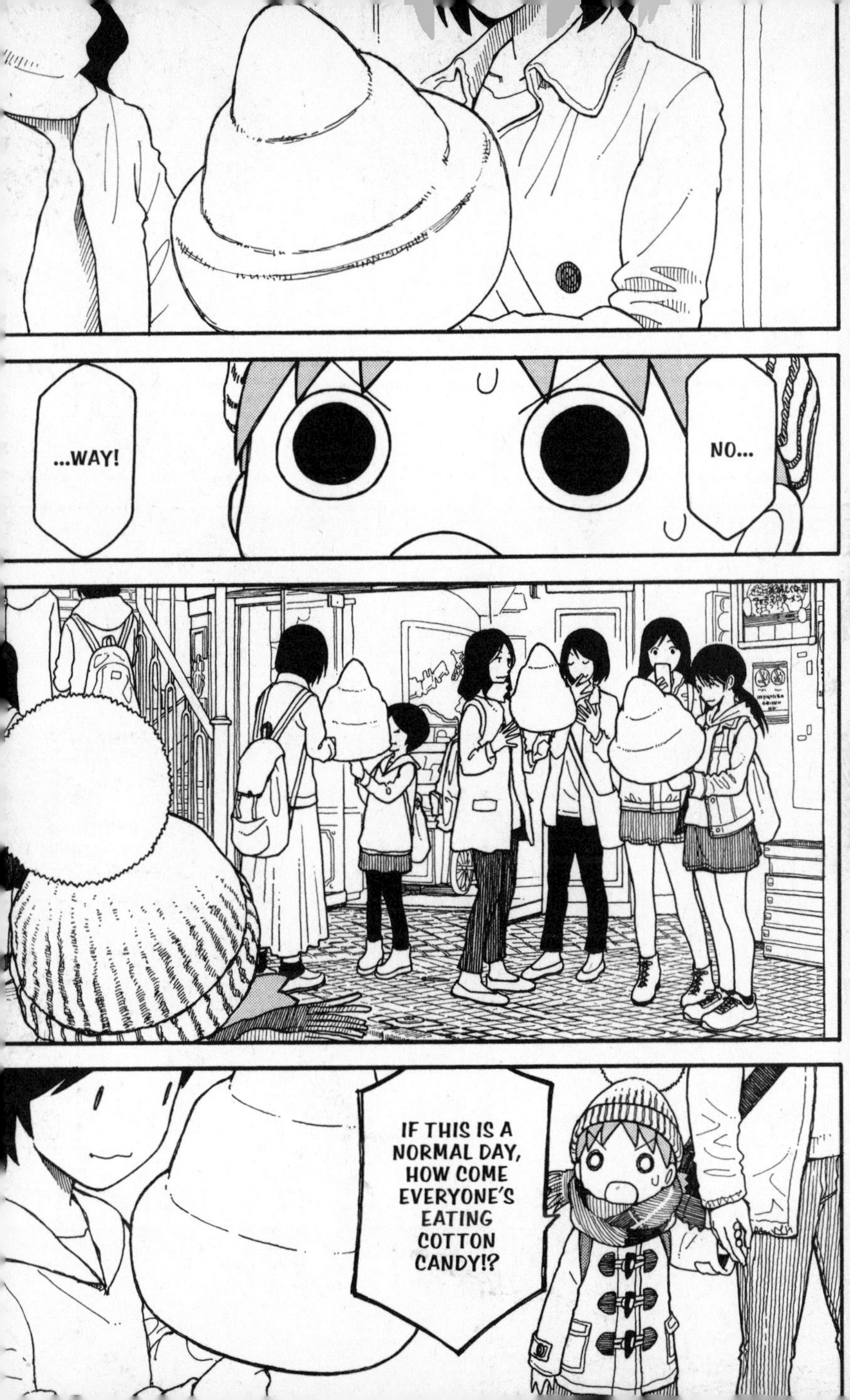
NO...
...WAY!
IF THIS IS A NORMAL DAY, HOW COME EVERYONE'S EATING COTTON CANDY!?

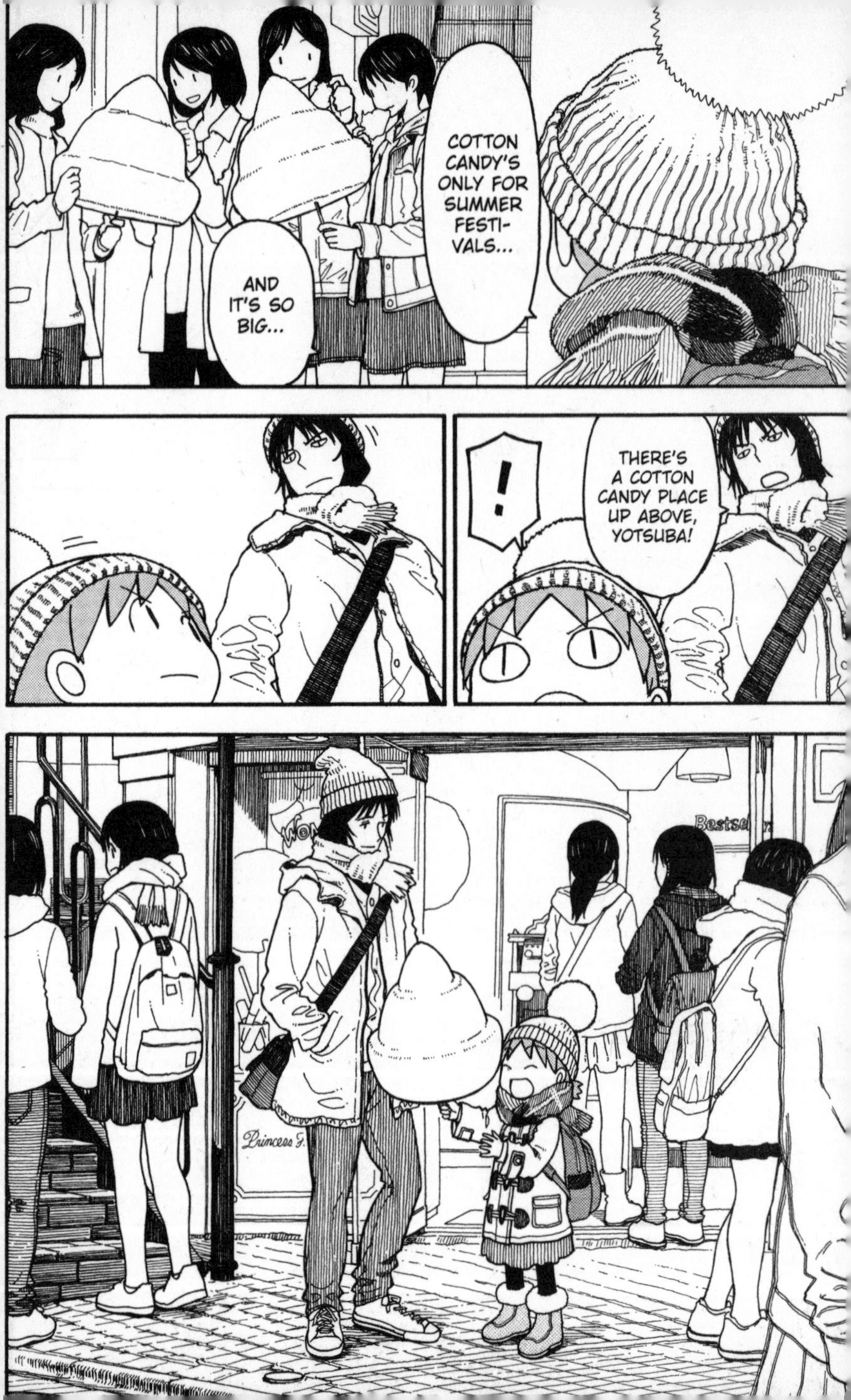
COTTON CANDY'S ONLY FOR SUMMER FESTI- VALS...
AND IT'S SO BIG...
THERE'S A COTTON CANDY PLACE UP ABOVE, YOTSUBA!
!
Princess F.

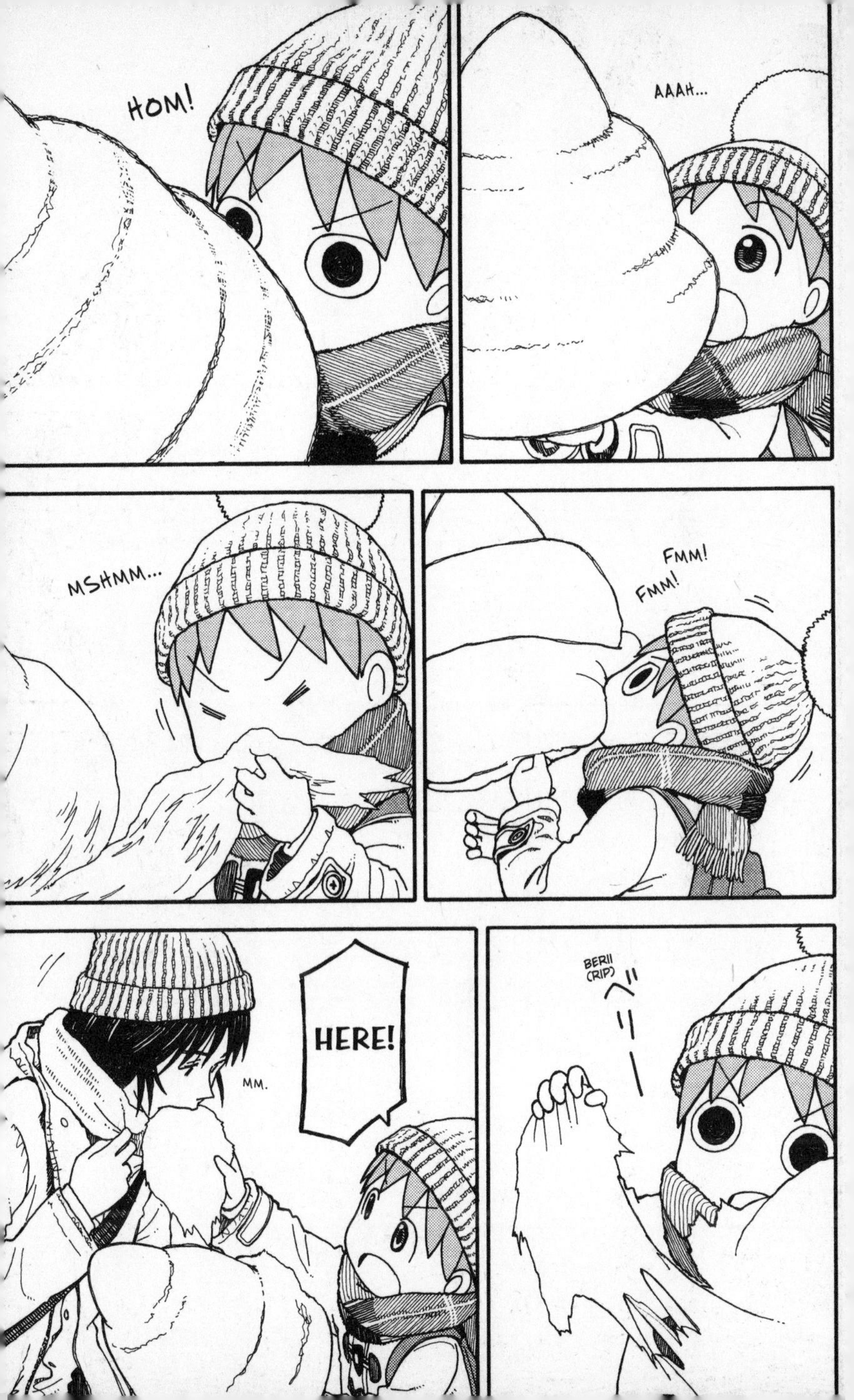
AAAH...
HOM!
FMM!
FMM!
MSHMM...
BERII (RIP)
HERE!
MM.

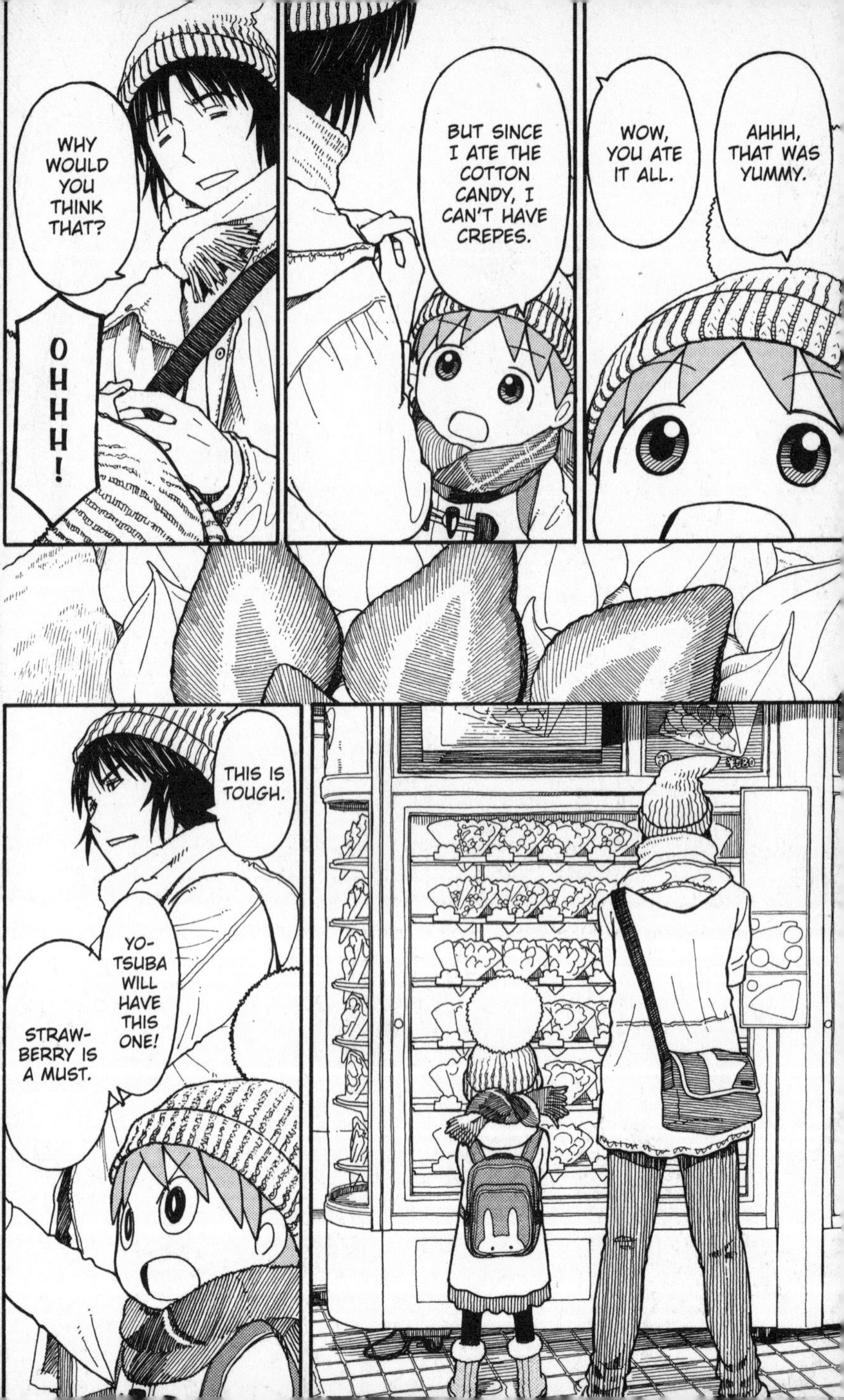
AHHH, THAT WAS YUMMY.
WOW, YOU ATE IT ALL.
BUT SINCE I ATE THE COTTON CANDY, I CAN'T HAVE CREPES.
WHY WOULD YOU THINK THAT?
OHHHH!
THIS IS TOUGH.
YO-TSUBA WILL HAVE THIS ONE!
STRAW-BERRY IS A MUST.

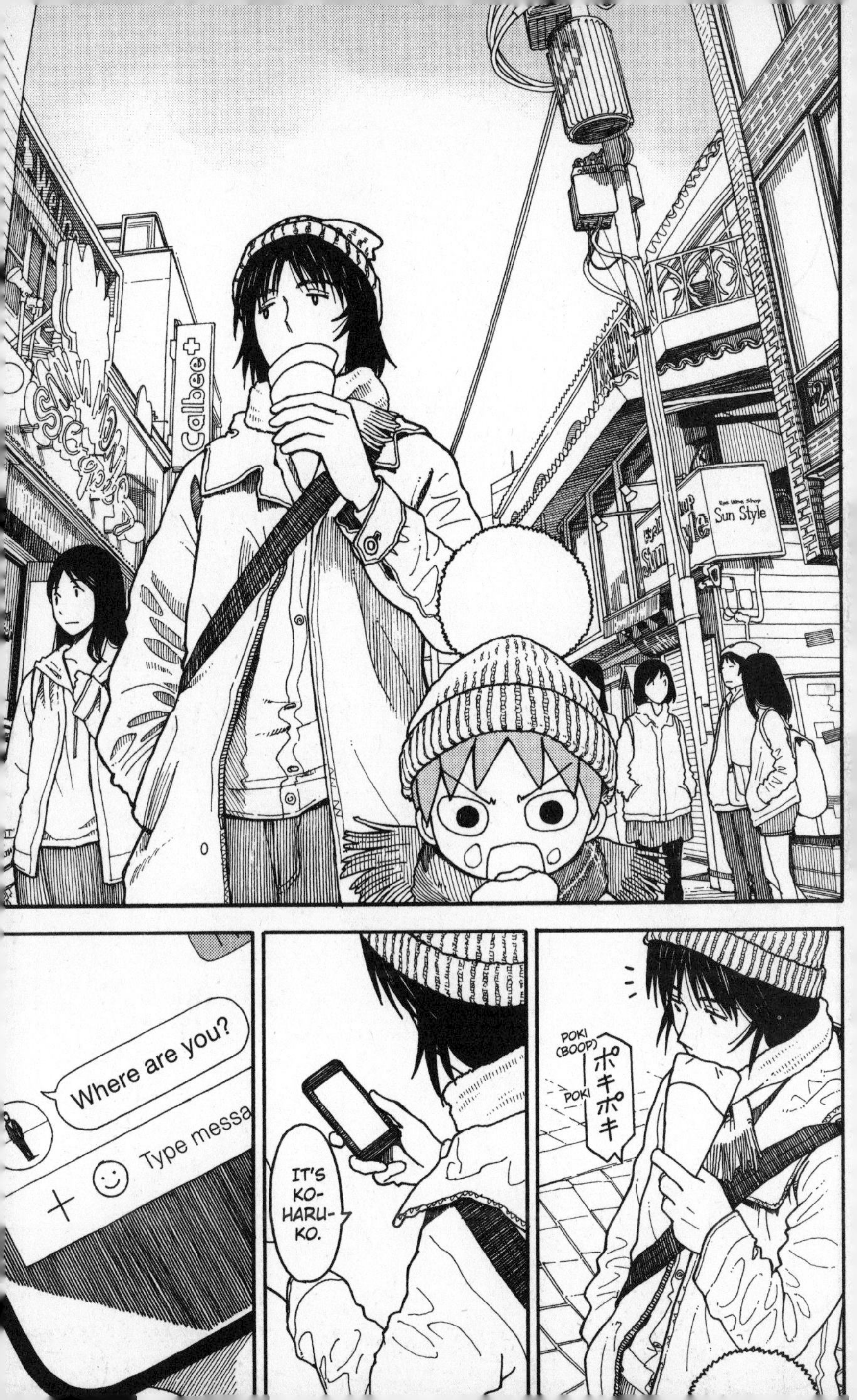
Calbee
Sun Style
POKI (BOOP)
ポキポキ
POKI
IT'S KO-HARU-KO.
Where are you?
Type messa

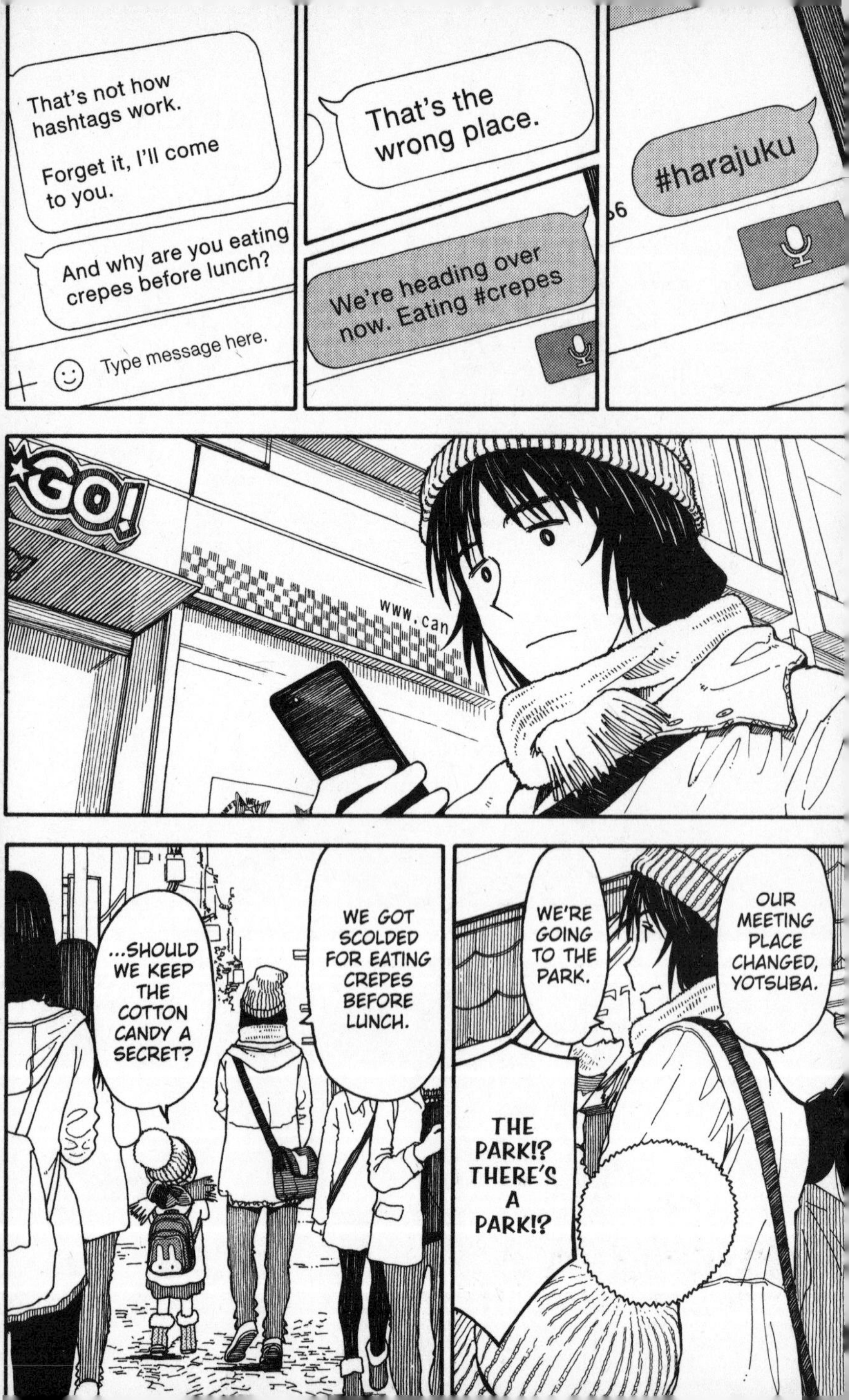

#harajuku
That's the wrong place.
We're heading over now. Eating #crepes
That's not how hashtags work.
Forget it, I'll come to you.
And why are you eating crepes before lunch?
Type message here.
GO!
www.can
OUR MEETING PLACE CHANGED, YOTSUBA.
WE'RE GOING TO THE PARK.
THE PARK!? THERE'S A PARK!?
WE GOT SCOLDED FOR EATING CREPES BEFORE LUNCH.
...SHOULD WE KEEP THE COTTON CANDY A SECRET?

YOTSUBA&!

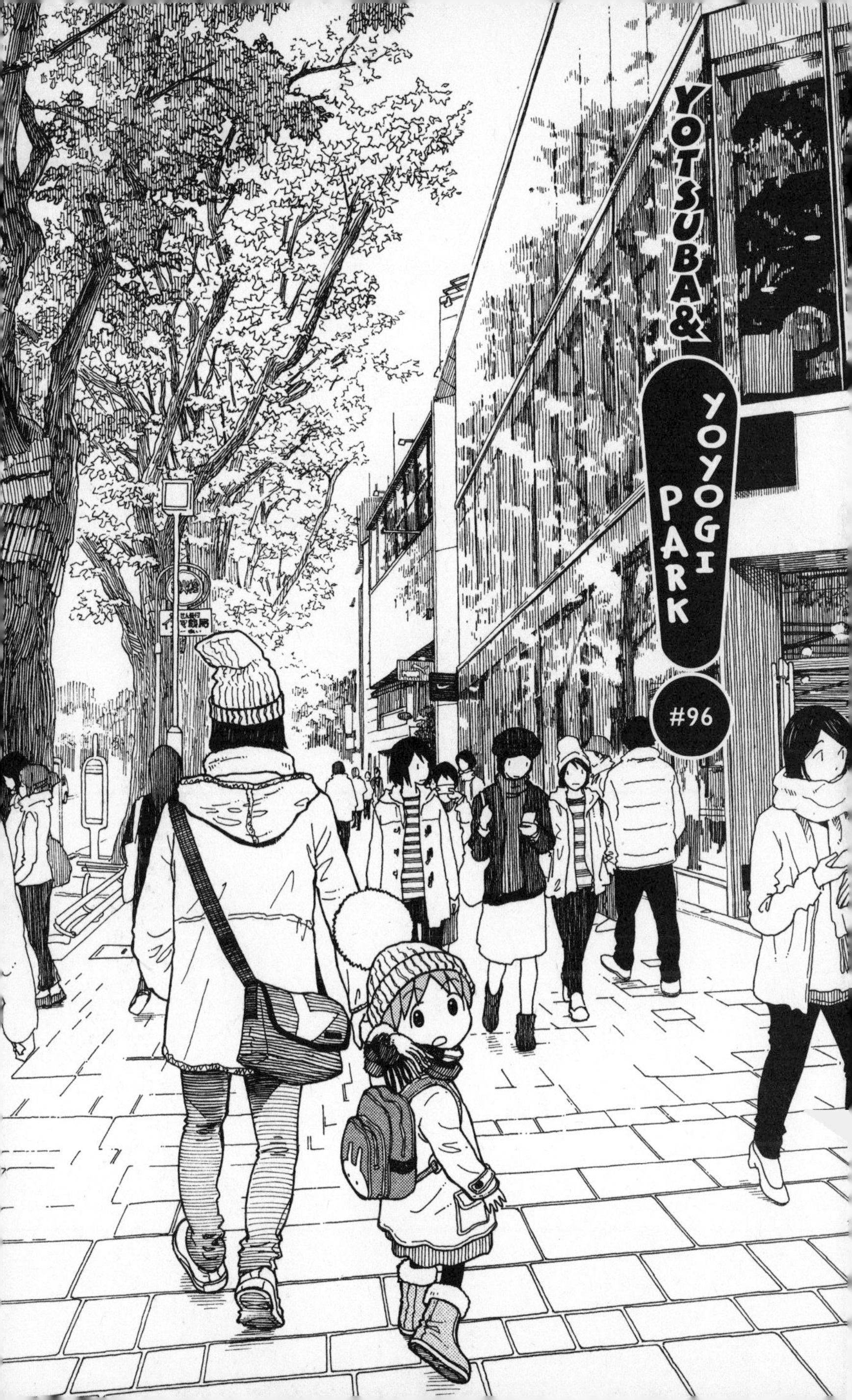
YOTSUBA&
YOYOGI PARK
#96

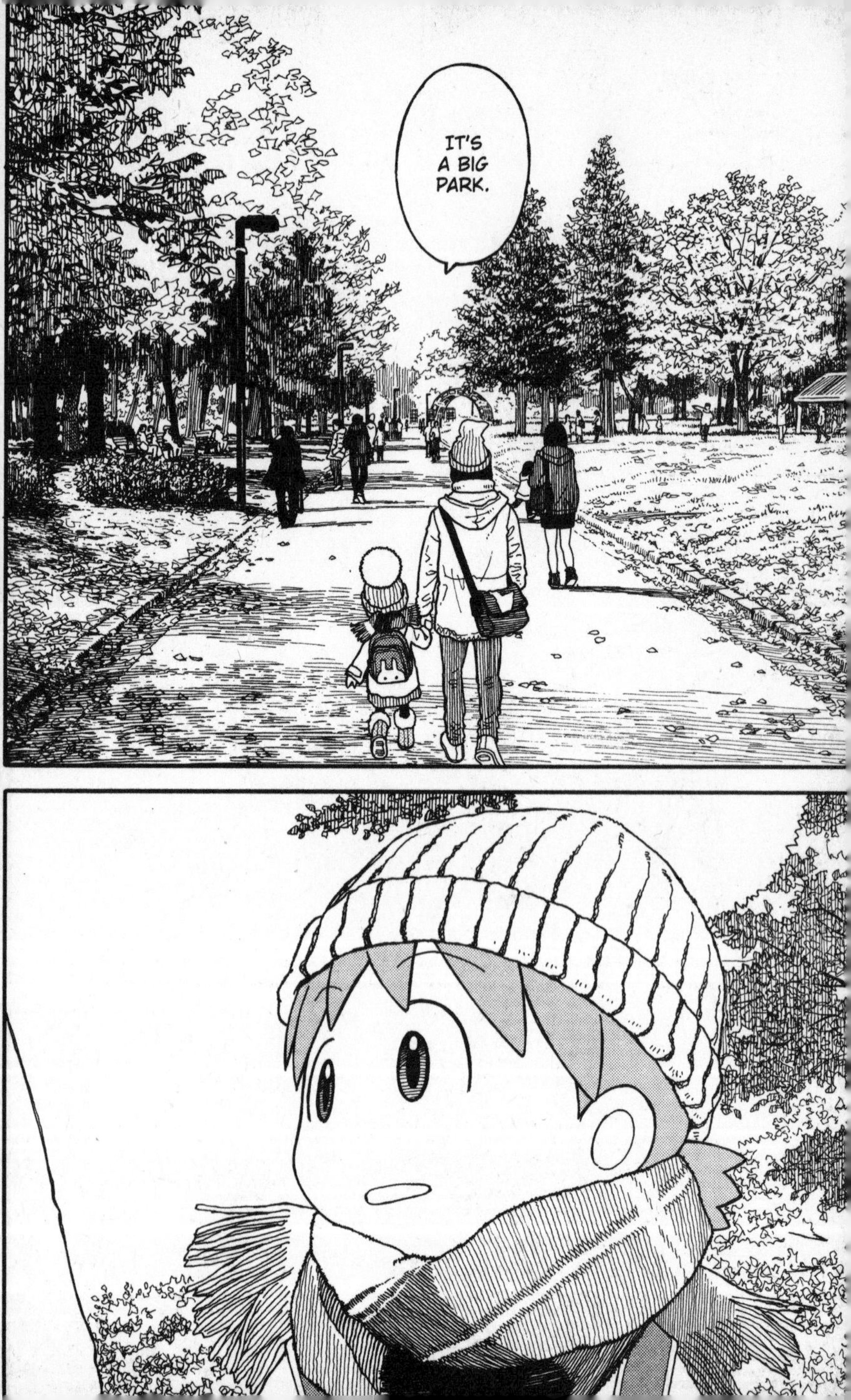
IT'S A BIG PARK.

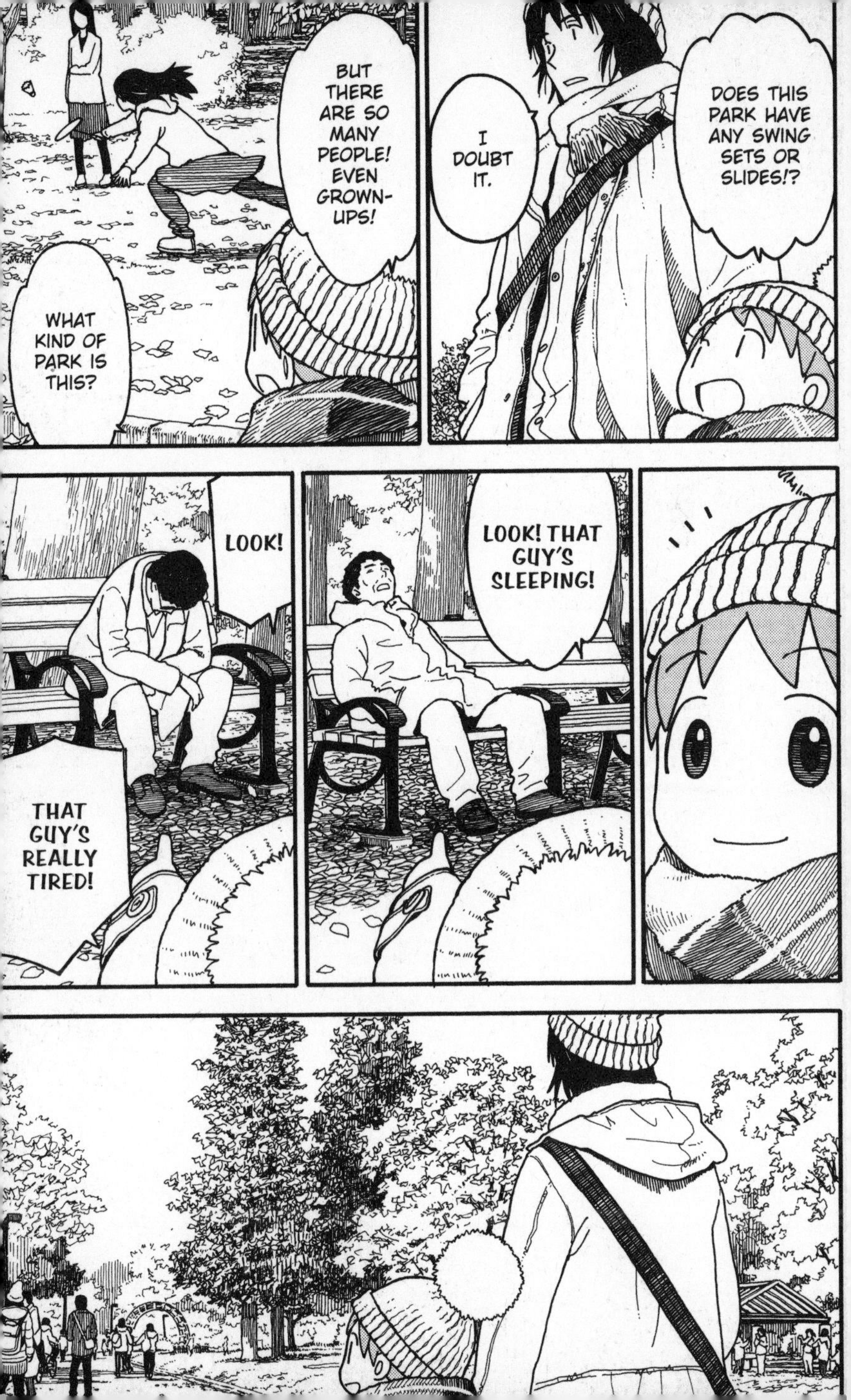
DOES THIS PARK HAVE ANY SWING SETS OR SLIDES!?
I DOUBT IT.
BUT THERE ARE SO MANY PEOPLE! EVEN GROWN-UPS!
WHAT KIND OF PARK IS THIS?
LOOK! THAT GUY'S SLEEPING!
LOOK!
THAT GUY'S REALLY TIRED!

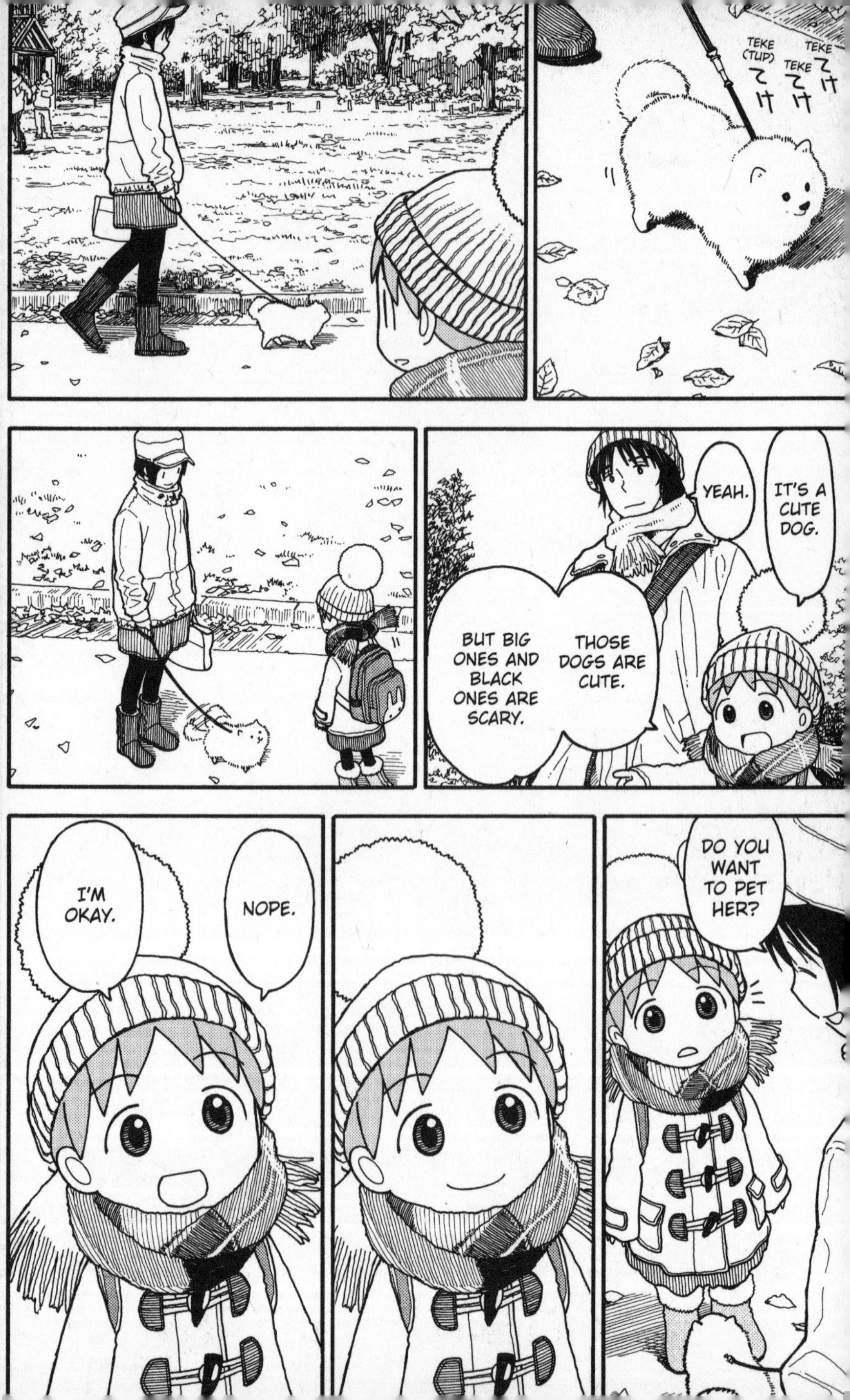
TEKE
てけ
TEKE
てけ
TEKE (TUP)
てけ
IT'S A CUTE DOG.
YEAH.
THOSE DOGS ARE CUTE.
BUT BIG ONES AND BLACK ONES ARE SCARY.
DO YOU WANT TO PET HER?
NOPE.
I'M OKAY.

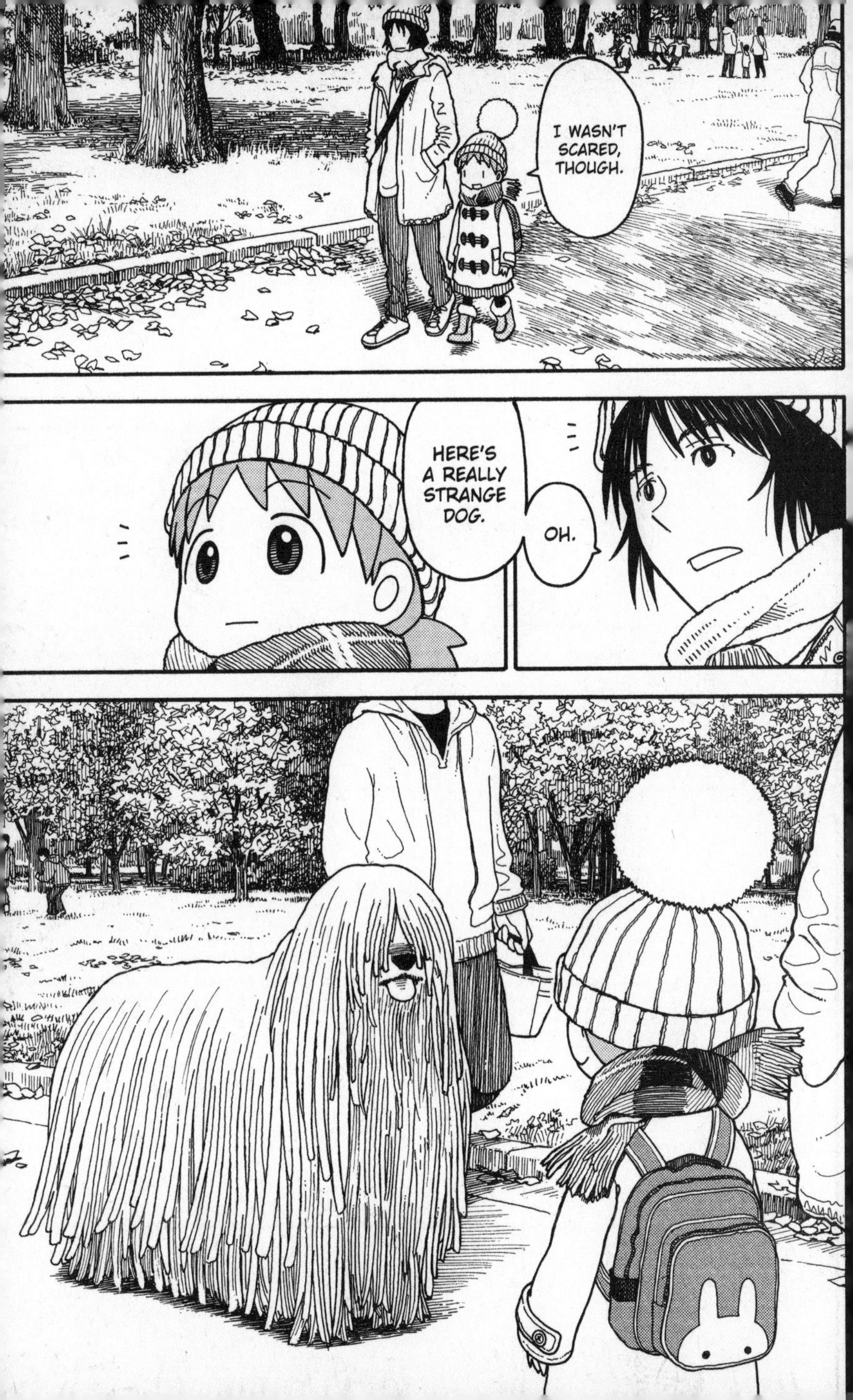
I WASN'T SCARED, THOUGH.
OH.
HERE'S A REALLY STRANGE DOG.

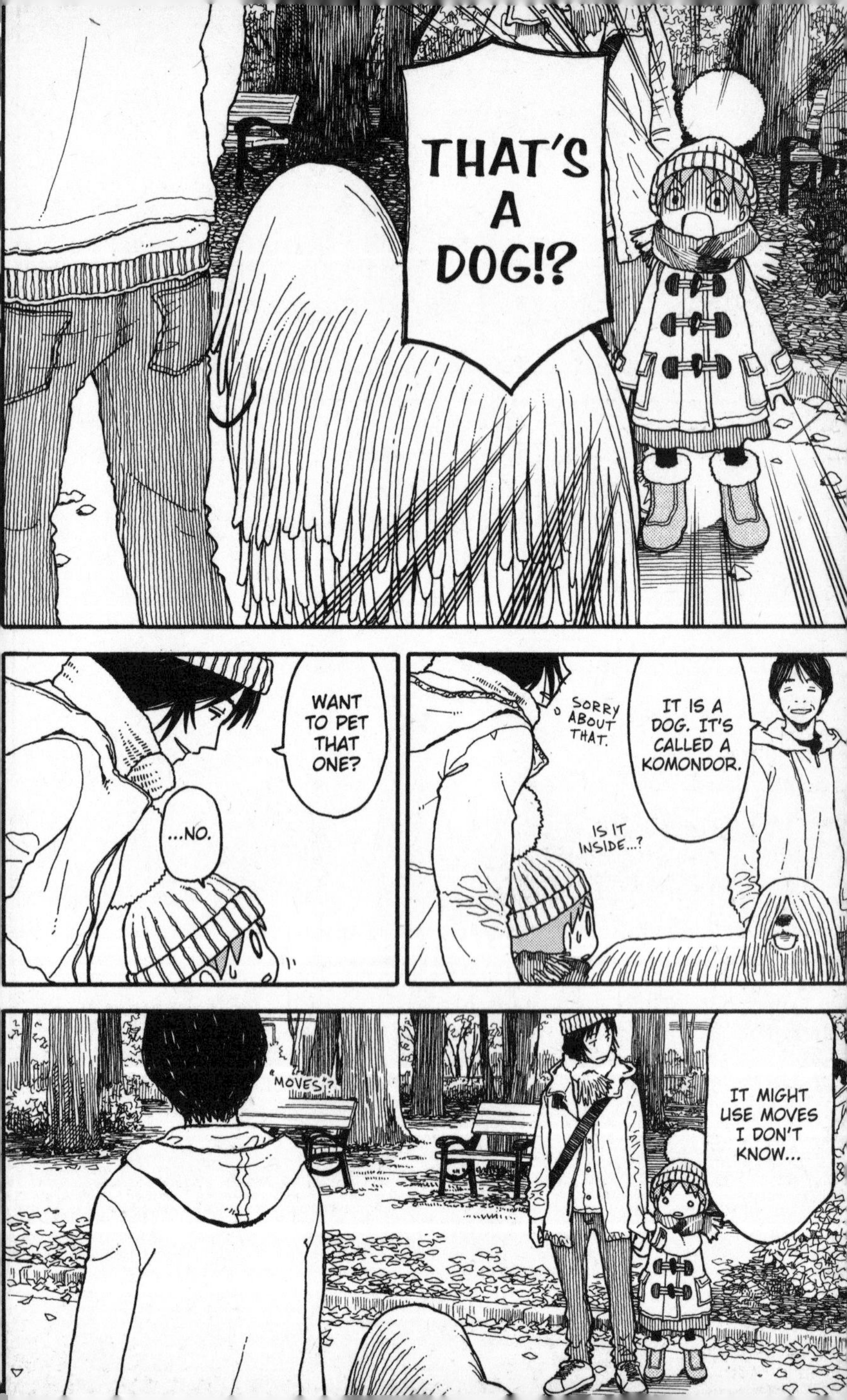
THAT'S A DOG!?
IT IS A DOG. IT'S CALLED A KOMONDOR.
SORRY ABOUT THAT.
IS IT INSIDE...?
WANT TO PET THAT ONE?
...NO.
IT MIGHT USE MOVES I DON'T KNOW...
"MOVES"?

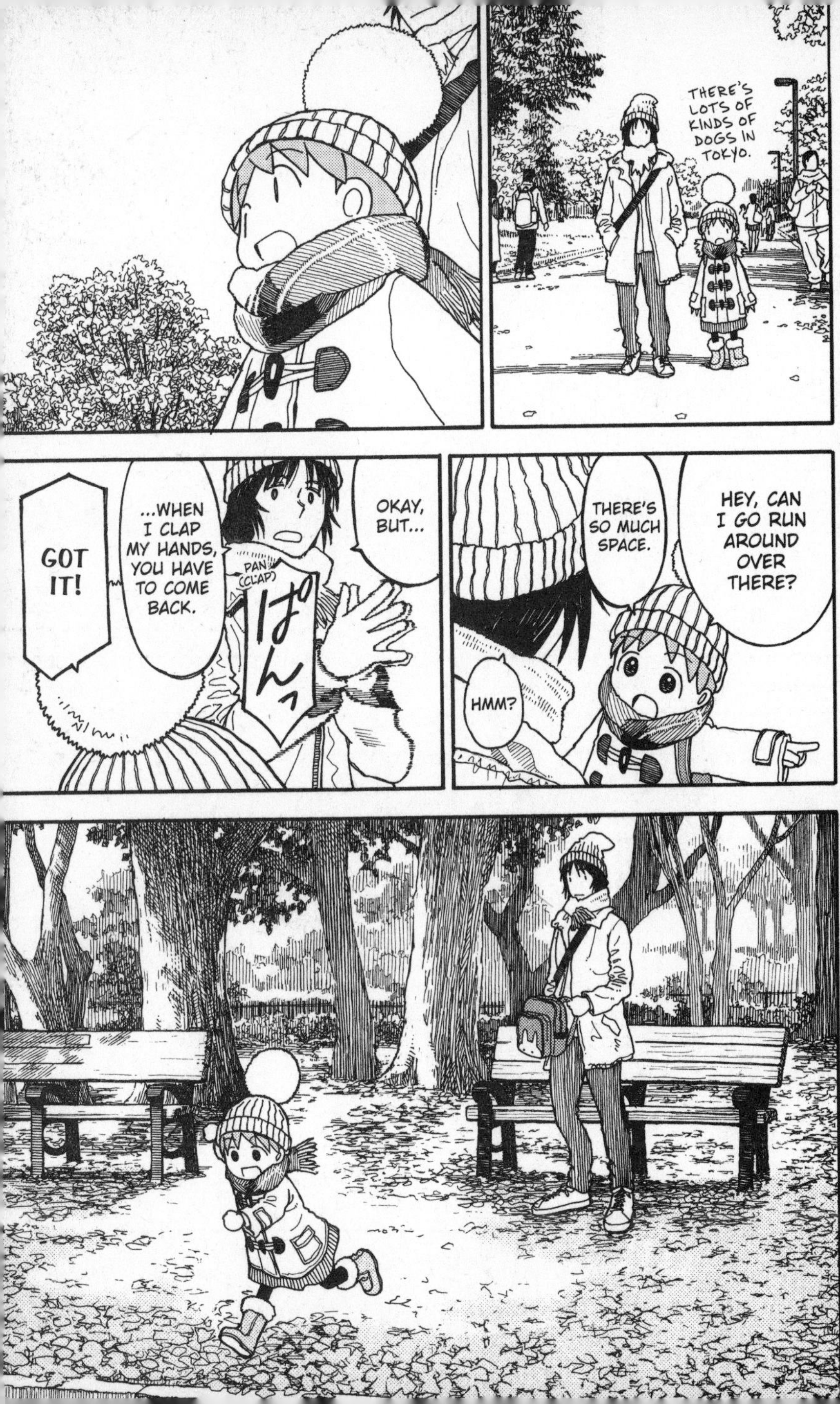
THERE'S LOTS OF KINDS OF DOGS IN TOKYO.
HEY, CAN I GO RUN AROUND OVER THERE?
THERE'S SO MUCH SPACE.
HMM?
OKAY, BUT...
PAN (CLAP)
ぱんっ
...WHEN I CLAP MY HANDS, YOU HAVE TO COME BACK.
GOT IT!

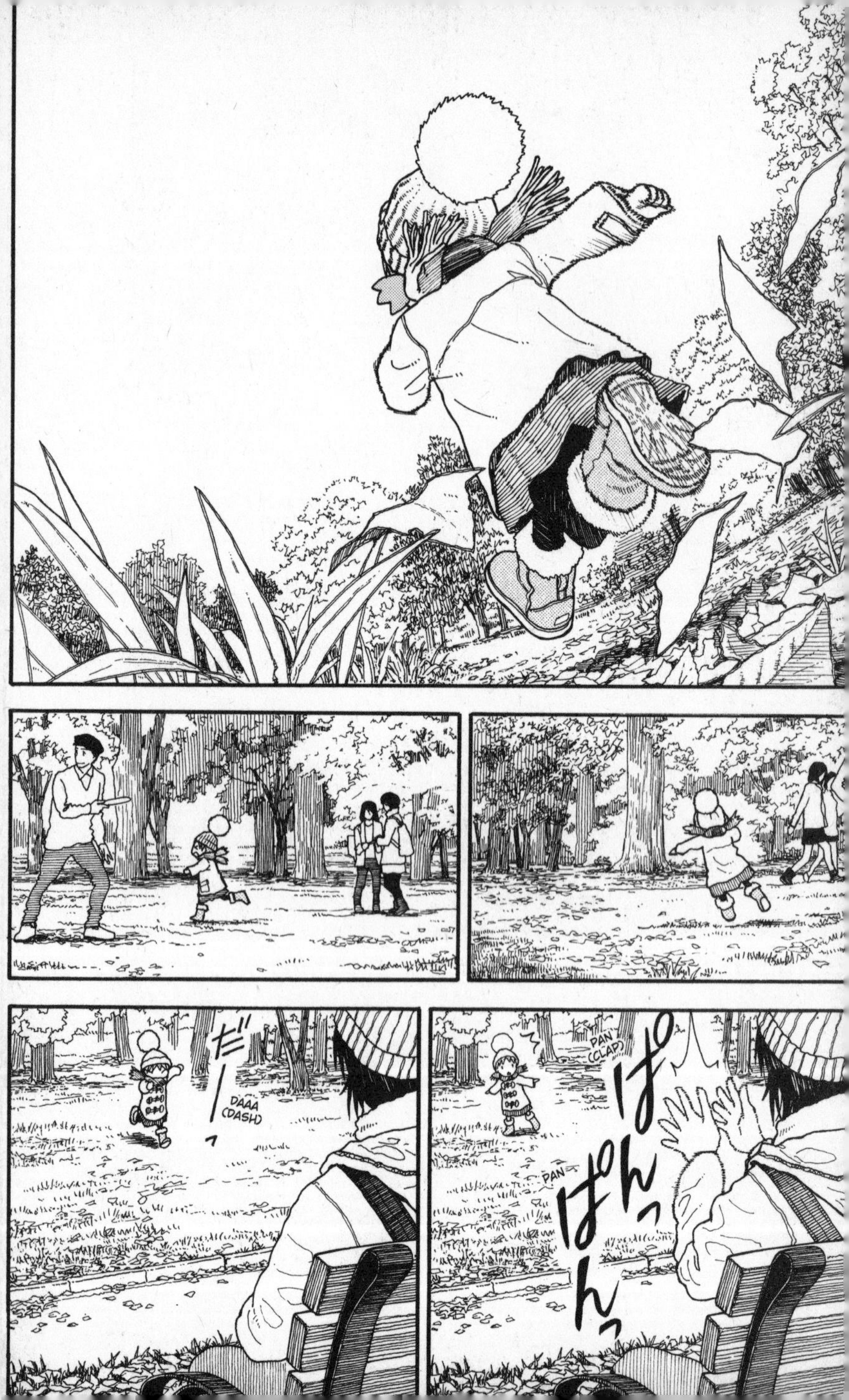
ぱんっ
PAN (CLAP)
ぱんっ
PAN
だーっ
DAAA (DASH)

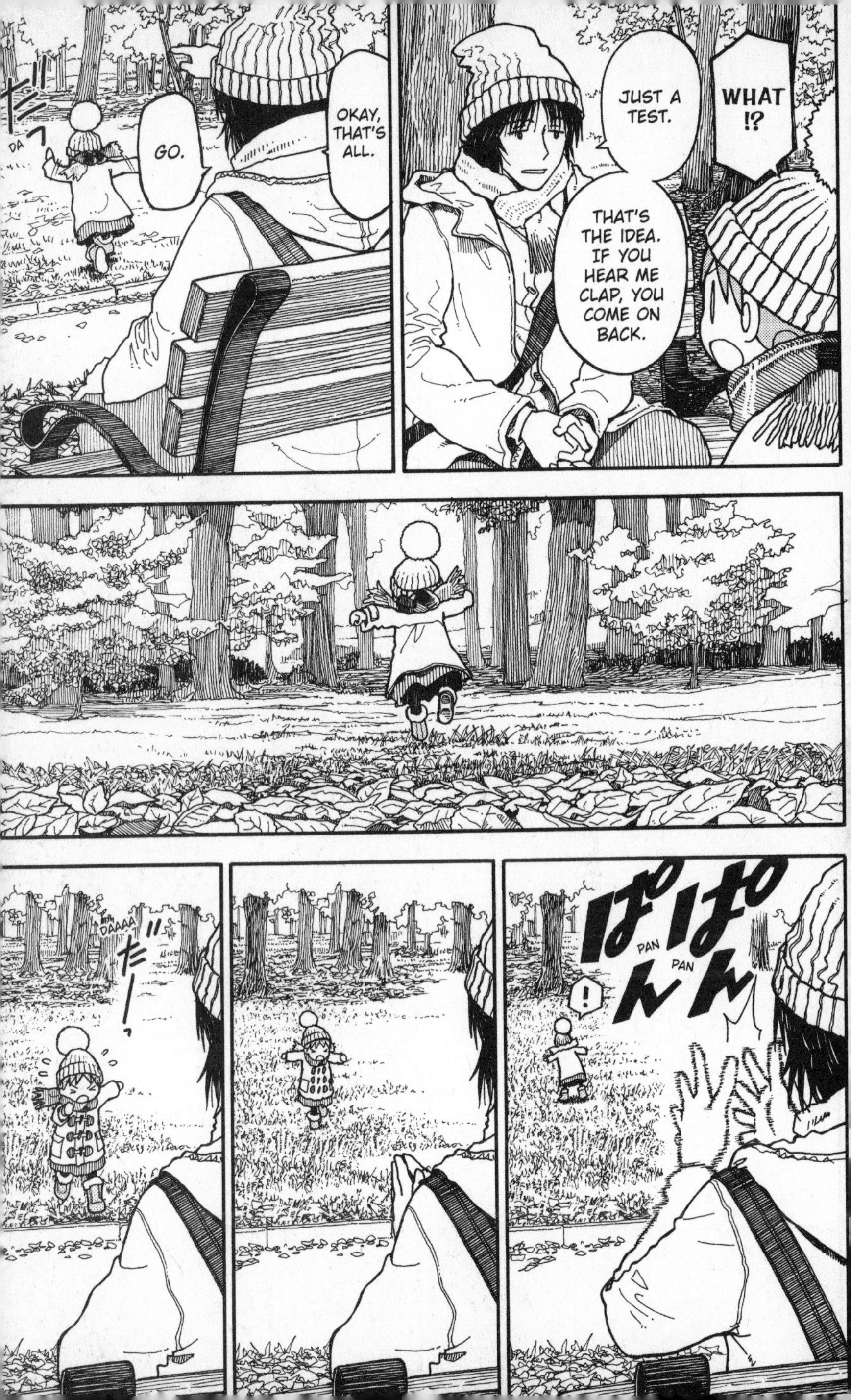
WHAT!?
JUST A TEST.
THAT'S THE IDEA. IF YOU HEAR ME CLAP, YOU COME ON BACK.
OKAY, THAT'S ALL.
GO.
DA
ぱんぱん
PAN PAN
!
DAAAA
たー!

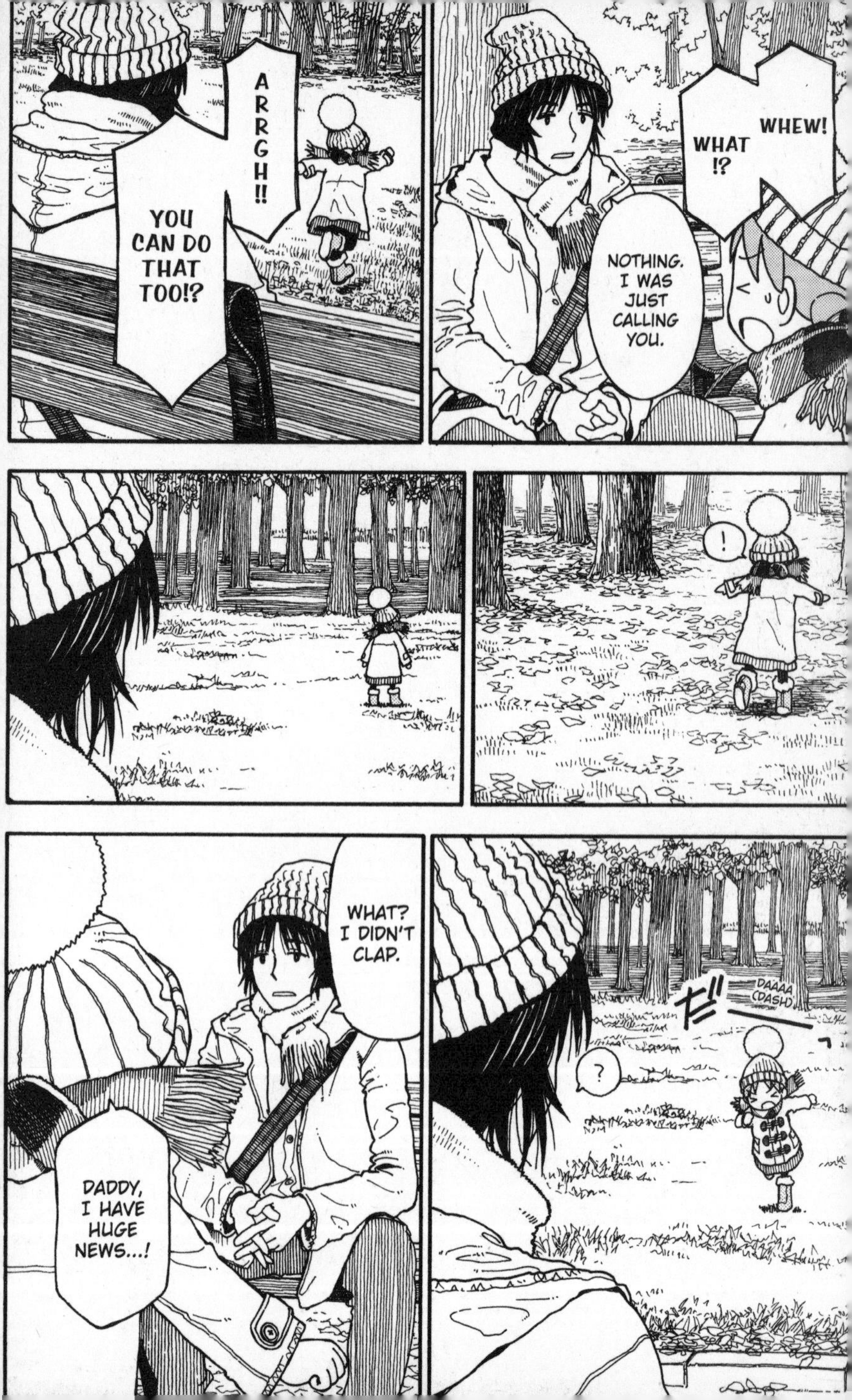

WHEW!
WHAT !?
NOTHING. I WAS JUST CALLING YOU.
ARRGH!!
YOU CAN DO THAT TOO!?
!
DAAAA (DASH)
?
WHAT? I DIDN'T CLAP.
DADDY, I HAVE HUGE NEWS...!

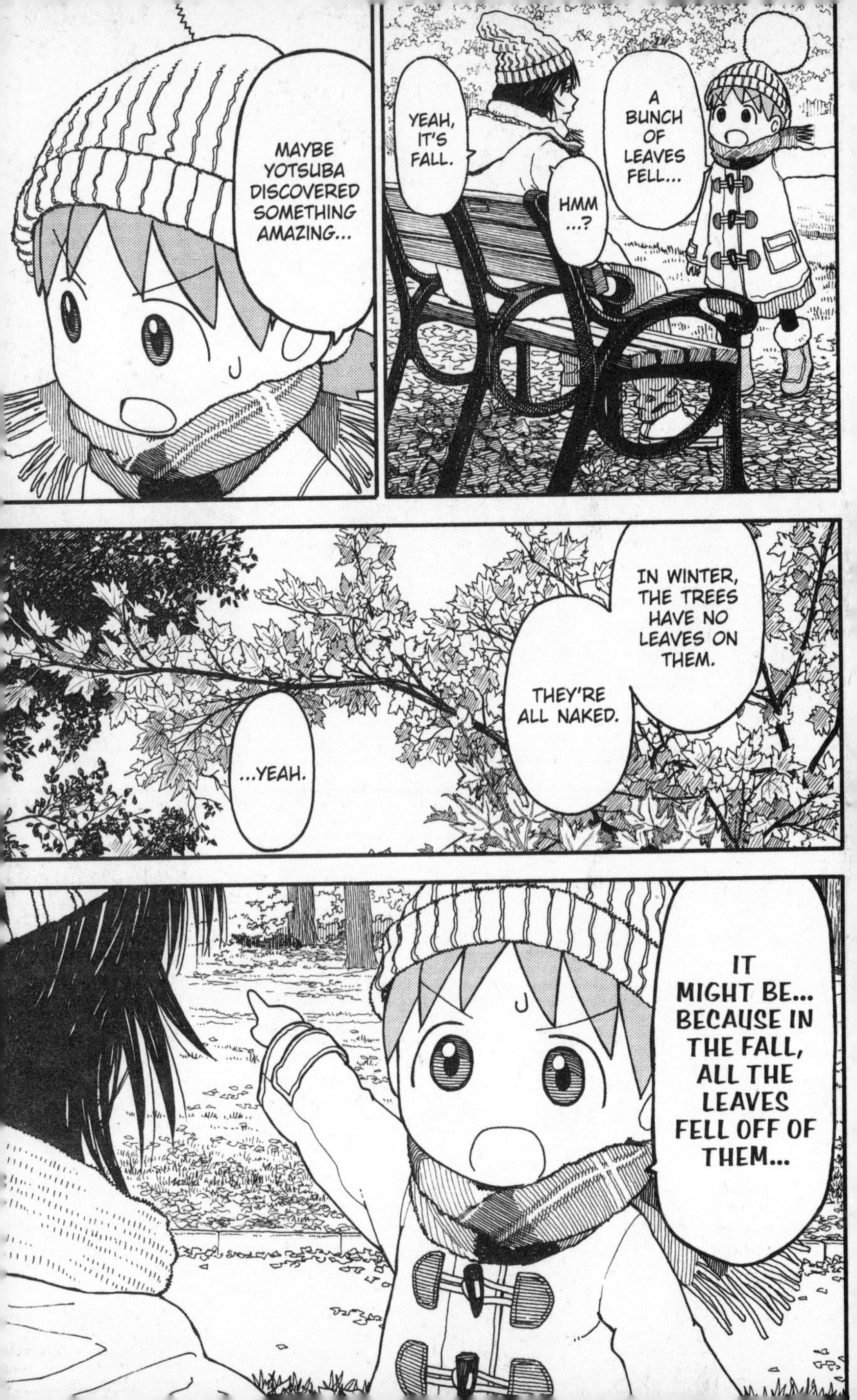
A BUNCH OF LEAVES FELL...
HMM ...?
YEAH, IT'S FALL.
MAYBE YOTSUBA DISCOVERED SOMETHING AMAZING...
IN WINTER, THE TREES HAVE NO LEAVES ON THEM.
THEY'RE ALL NAKED.
...YEAH.
IT MIGHT BE... BECAUSE IN THE FALL, ALL THE LEAVES FELL OFF OF THEM...

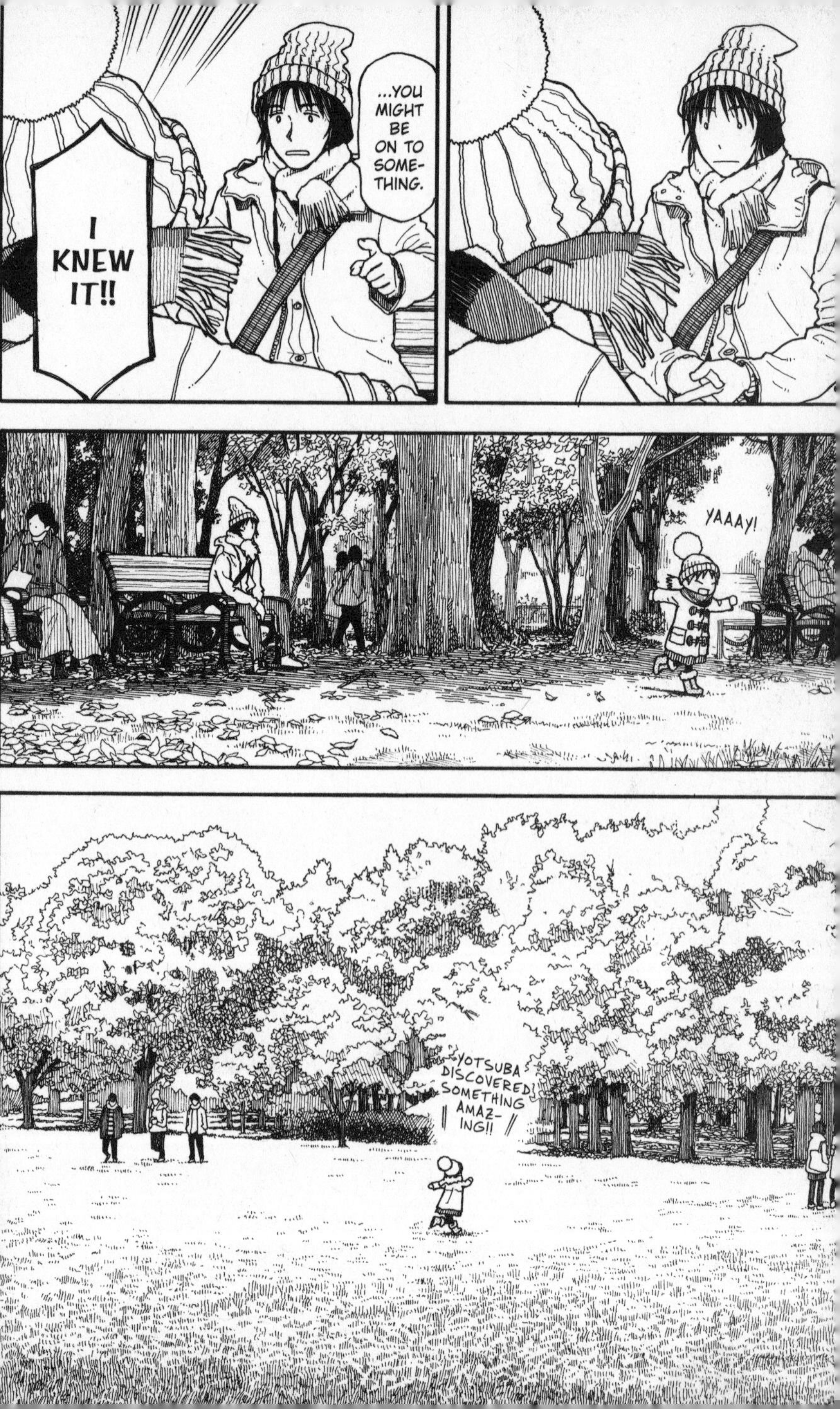
...YOU MIGHT BE ON TO SOME-THING.
I KNEW IT!!
YAAAY!
YOTSUBA DISCOVERED SOMETHING AMAZ-ING!!

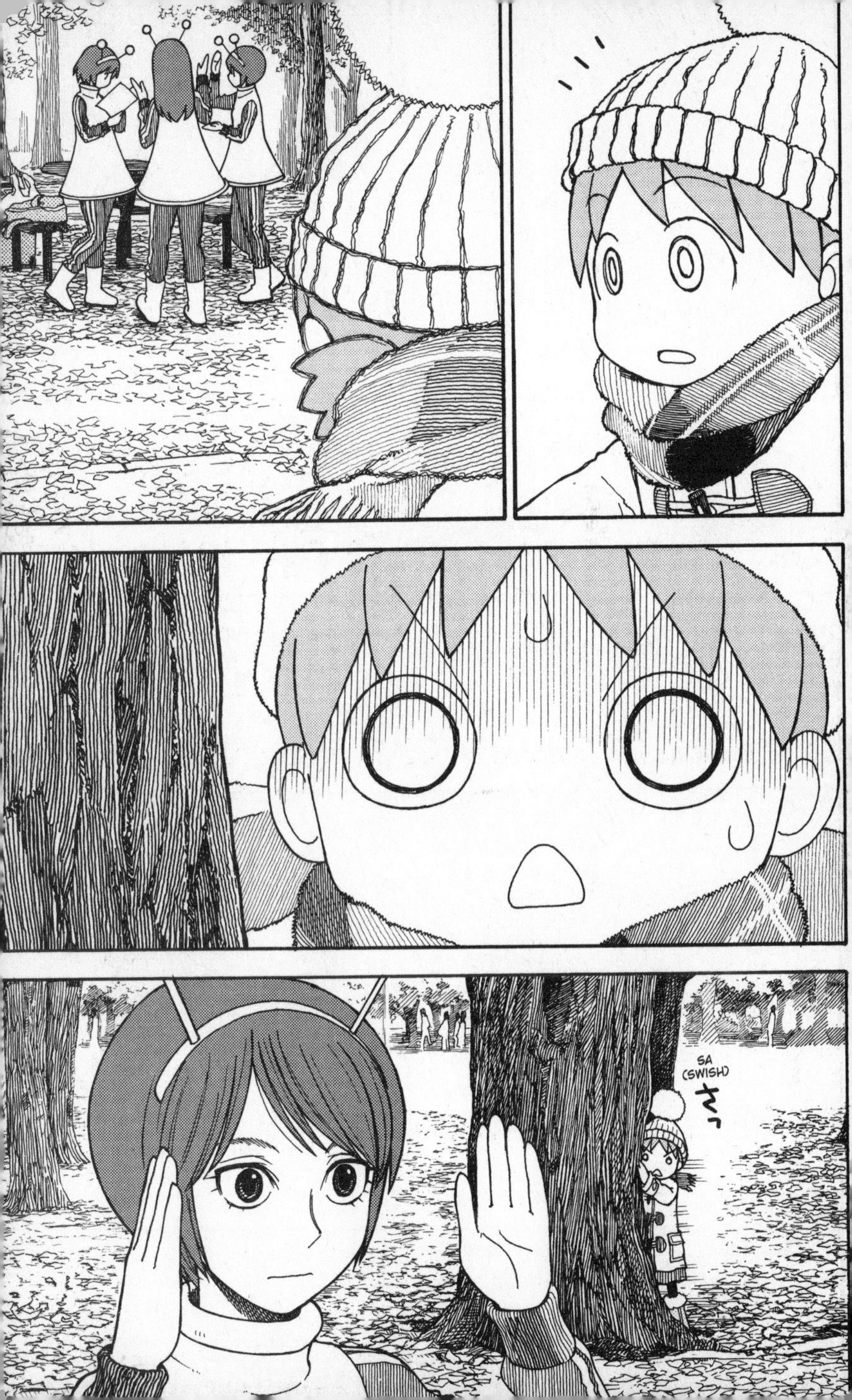
SA (SWISH)
サッ

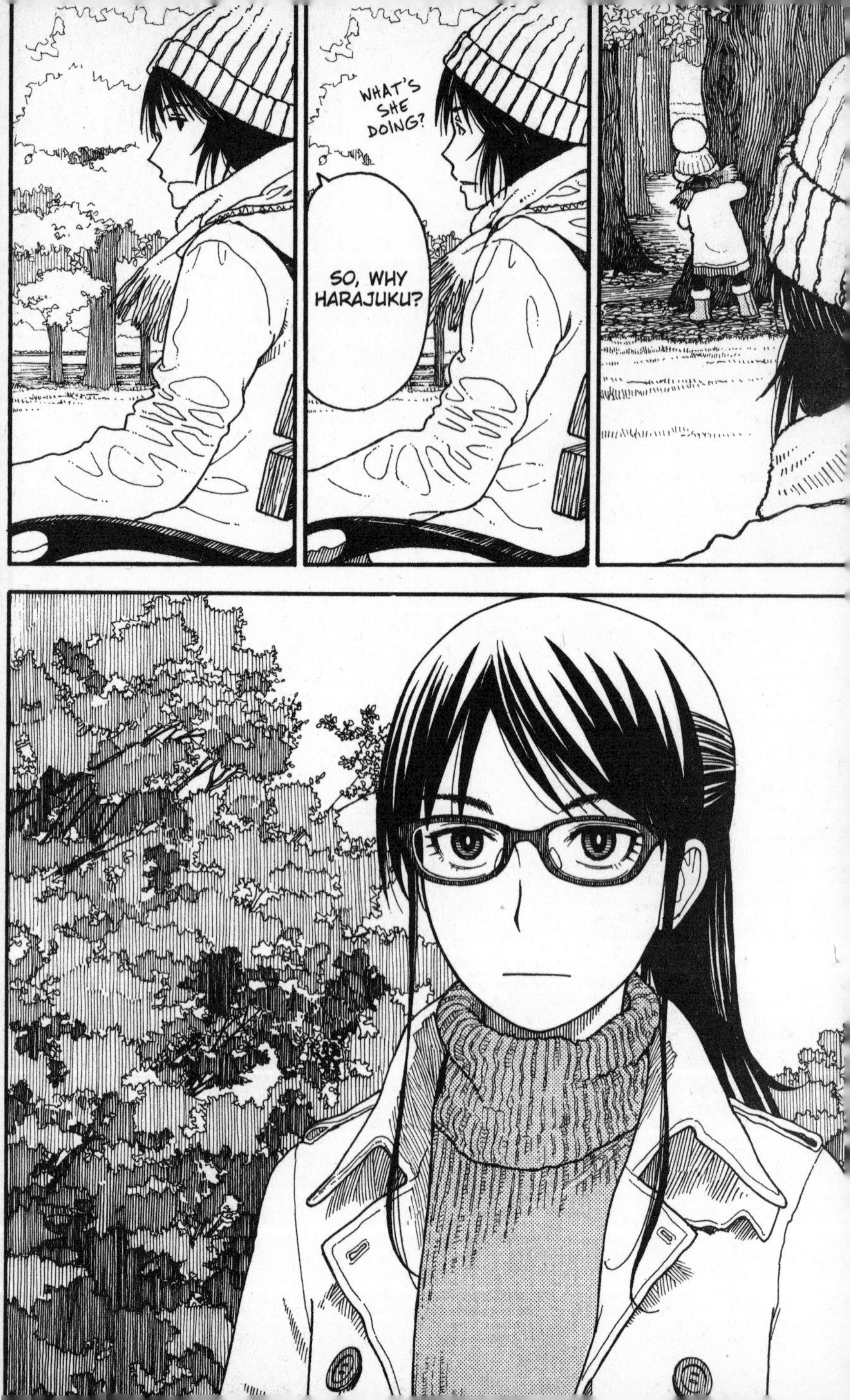
WHAT'S SHE DOING?
SO, WHY HARAJUKU?

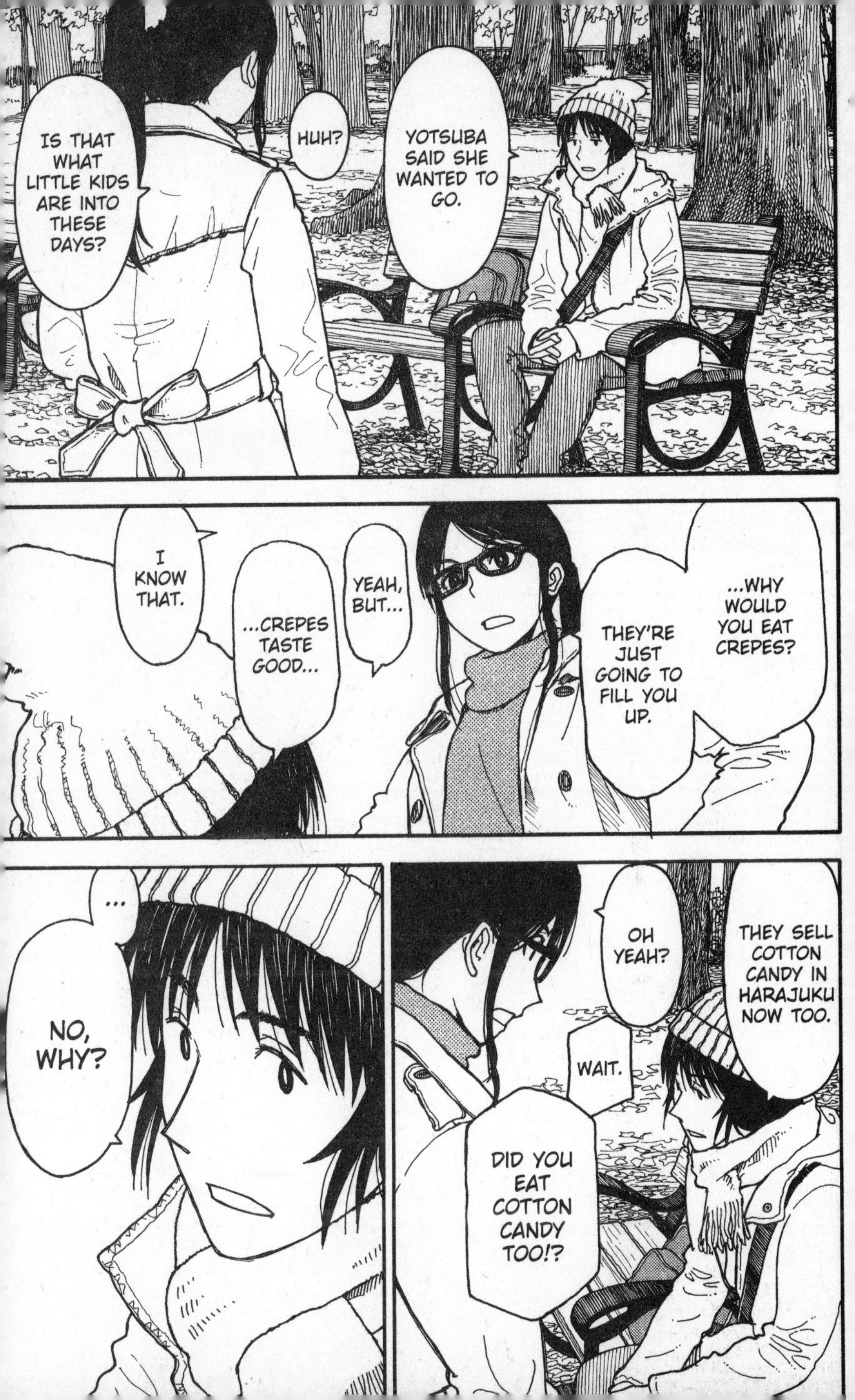
YOTSUBA SAID SHE WANTED TO GO.
HUH?
IS THAT WHAT LITTLE KIDS ARE INTO THESE DAYS?
...WHY WOULD YOU EAT CREPES?
THEY'RE JUST GOING TO FILL YOU UP.
YEAH, BUT...
...CREPES TASTE GOOD...
I KNOW THAT.
THEY SELL COTTON CANDY IN HARAJUKU NOW TOO.
OH YEAH?
WAIT.
DID YOU EAT COTTON CANDY TOO!?
...
NO, WHY?

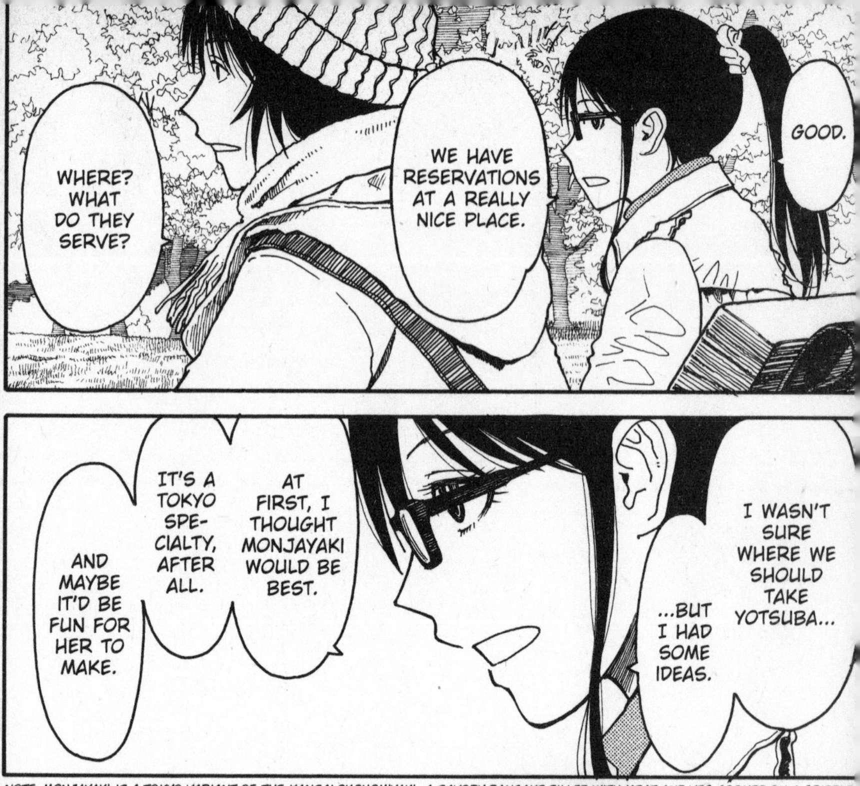
GOOD.
WE HAVE RESERVATIONS AT A REALLY NICE PLACE.
WHERE? WHAT DO THEY SERVE?
I WASN'T SURE WHERE WE SHOULD TAKE YOTSUBA...
...BUT I HAD SOME IDEAS.
AT FIRST, I THOUGHT MONJAYAKI WOULD BE BEST.
IT'S A TOKYO SPECIALTY, AFTER ALL.
AND MAYBE IT'D BE FUN FOR HER TO MAKE.

NOTE: MONJAYAKI IS A TOKYO VARIANT OF THE KANSAI OKONOMIYAKI, A SAVORY PANCAKE FILLED WITH MEAT AND VEG COOKED ON A GRIDDLE.

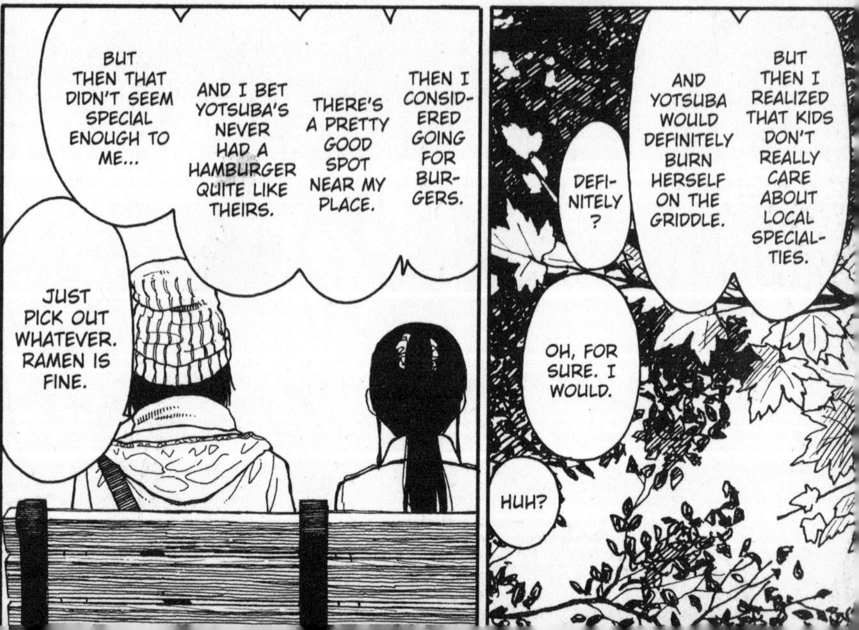
BUT THEN I REALIZED THAT KIDS DON'T REALLY CARE ABOUT LOCAL SPECIALTIES.
AND YOTSUBA WOULD DEFINITELY BURN HERSELF ON THE GRIDDLE.
DEFINITELY?
OH, FOR SURE. I WOULD.
HUH?
THEN I CONSIDERED GOING FOR BURGERS.
THERE'S A PRETTY GOOD SPOT NEAR MY PLACE.
AND I BET YOTSUBA'S NEVER HAD A HAMBURGER QUITE LIKE THEIRS.
BUT THEN THAT DIDN'T SEEM SPECIAL ENOUGH TO ME...
JUST PICK OUT WHATEVER. RAMEN IS FINE.

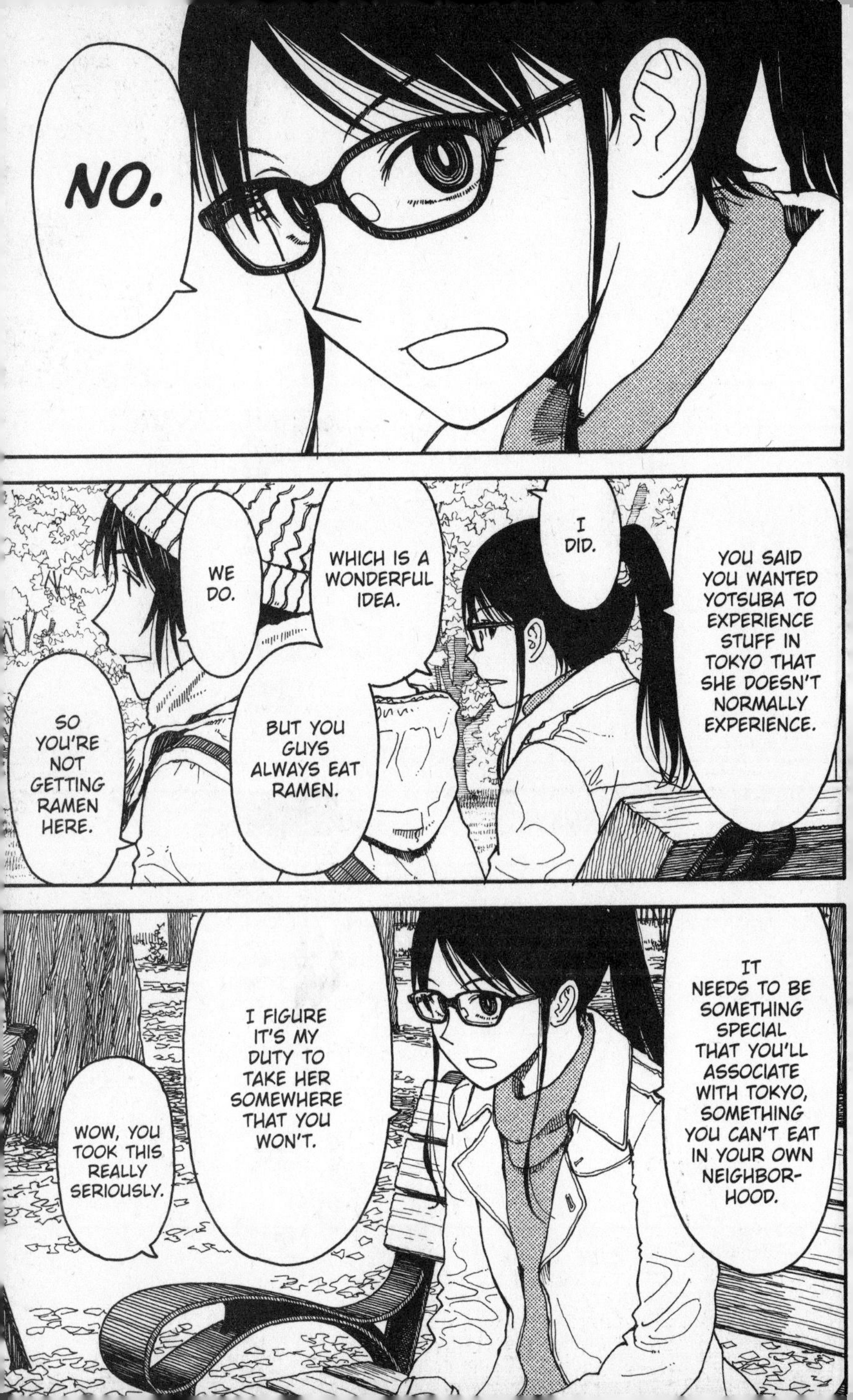
NO.
YOU SAID YOU WANTED YOTSUBA TO EXPERIENCE STUFF IN TOKYO THAT SHE DOESN'T NORMALLY EXPERIENCE.
I DID.
WHICH IS A WONDERFUL IDEA.
BUT YOU GUYS ALWAYS EAT RAMEN.
WE DO.
SO YOU'RE NOT GETTING RAMEN HERE.
IT NEEDS TO BE SOMETHING SPECIAL THAT YOU'LL ASSOCIATE WITH TOKYO, SOMETHING YOU CAN'T EAT IN YOUR OWN NEIGHBOR-HOOD.
I FIGURE IT'S MY DUTY TO TAKE HER SOMEWHERE THAT YOU WON'T.
WOW, YOU TOOK THIS REALLY SERIOUSLY.

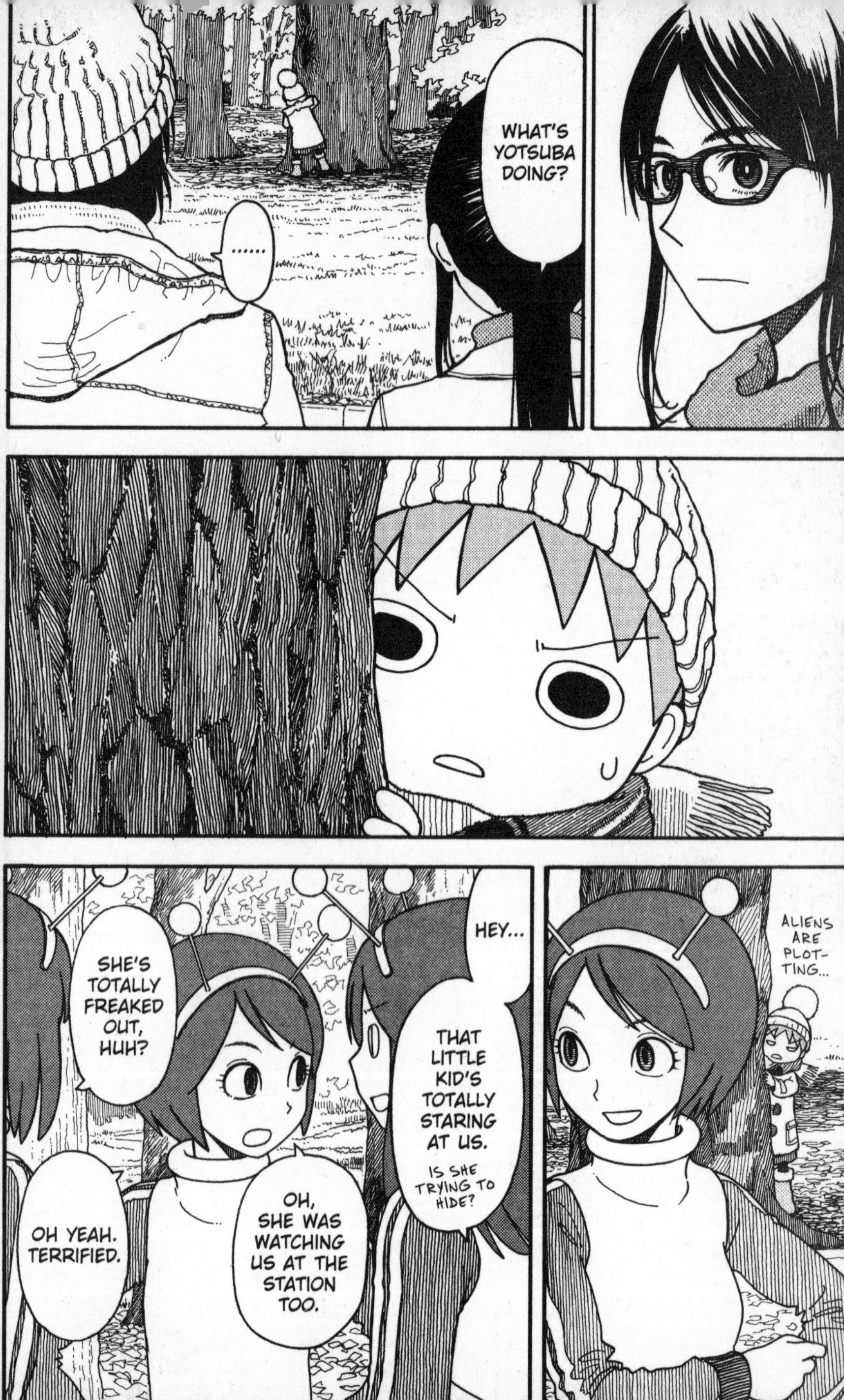
WHAT'S YOTSUBA DOING?
......
ALIENS ARE PLOT-TING...
HEY...
THAT LITTLE KID'S TOTALLY STARING AT US.
IS SHE TRYING TO HIDE?
SHE'S TOTALLY FREAKED OUT, HUH?
OH, SHE WAS WATCHING US AT THE STATION TOO.
OH YEAH. TERRIFIED.

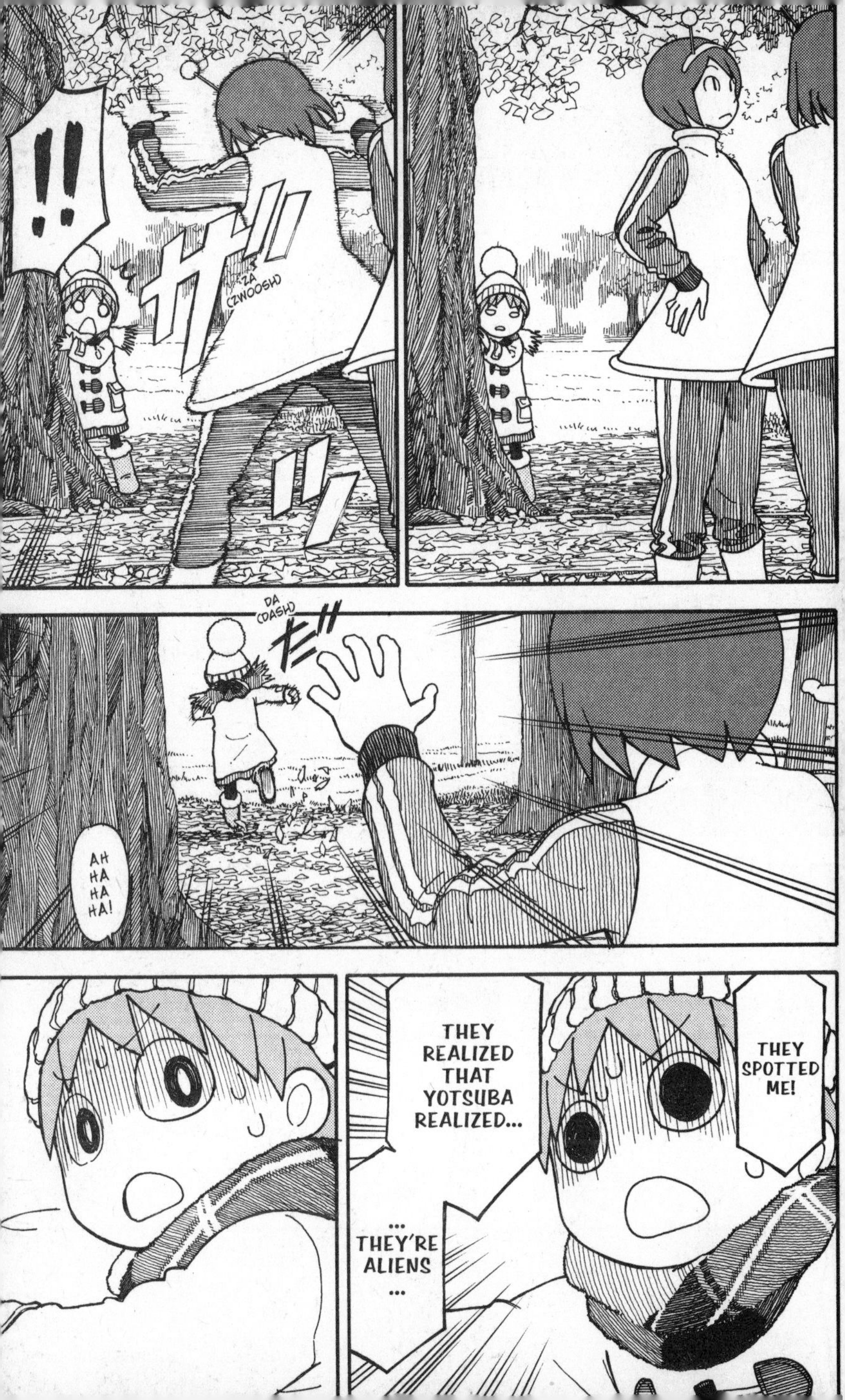
!!
ZA (ZWOOSH)
DA (DASH)
AH HA HA HA!
THEY SPOTTED ME!
THEY REALIZED THAT YOTSUBA REALIZED...
...THEY'RE ALIENS...

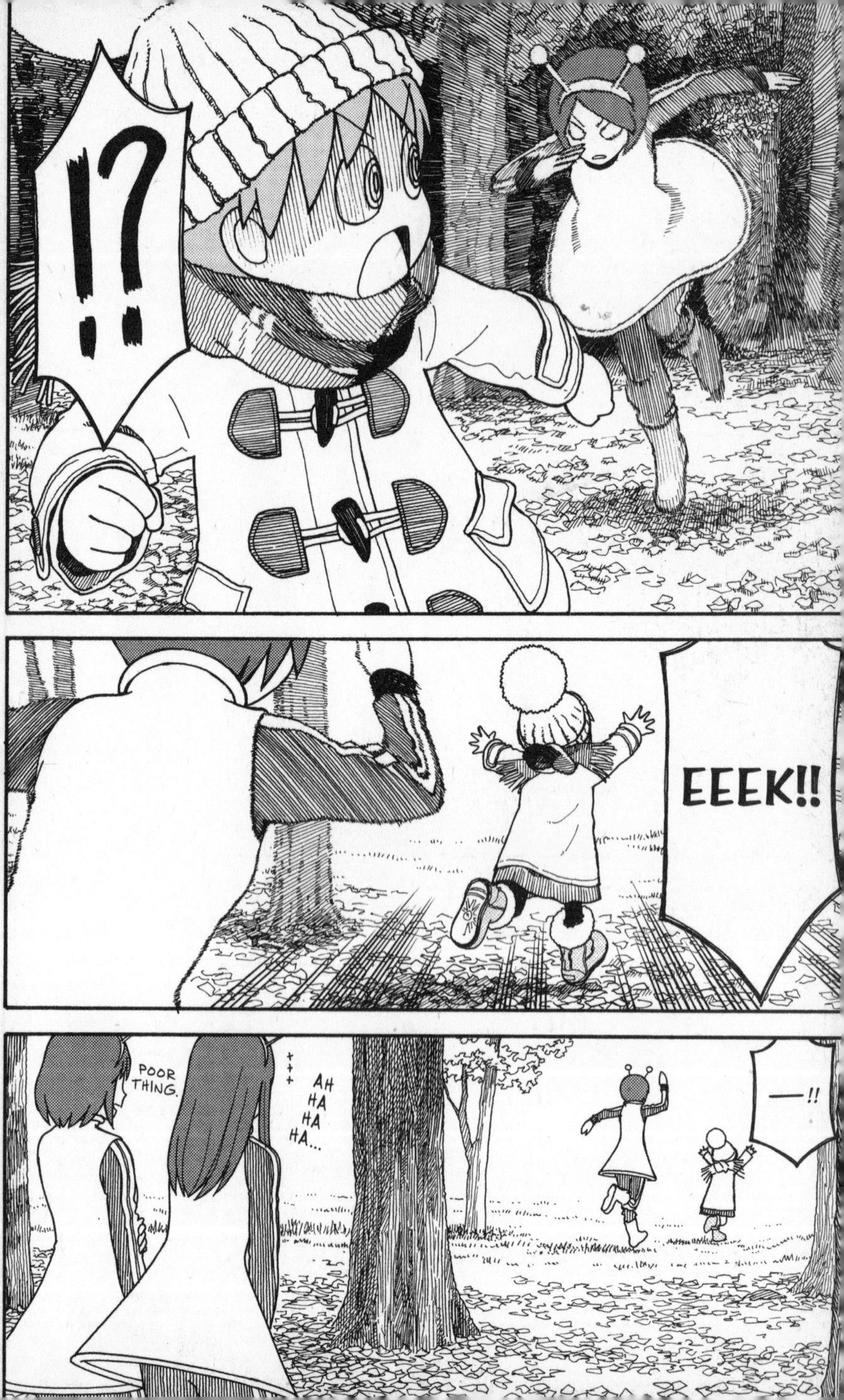
!?
EEEK!!
—!!
AH HA HA HA...
POOR THING.

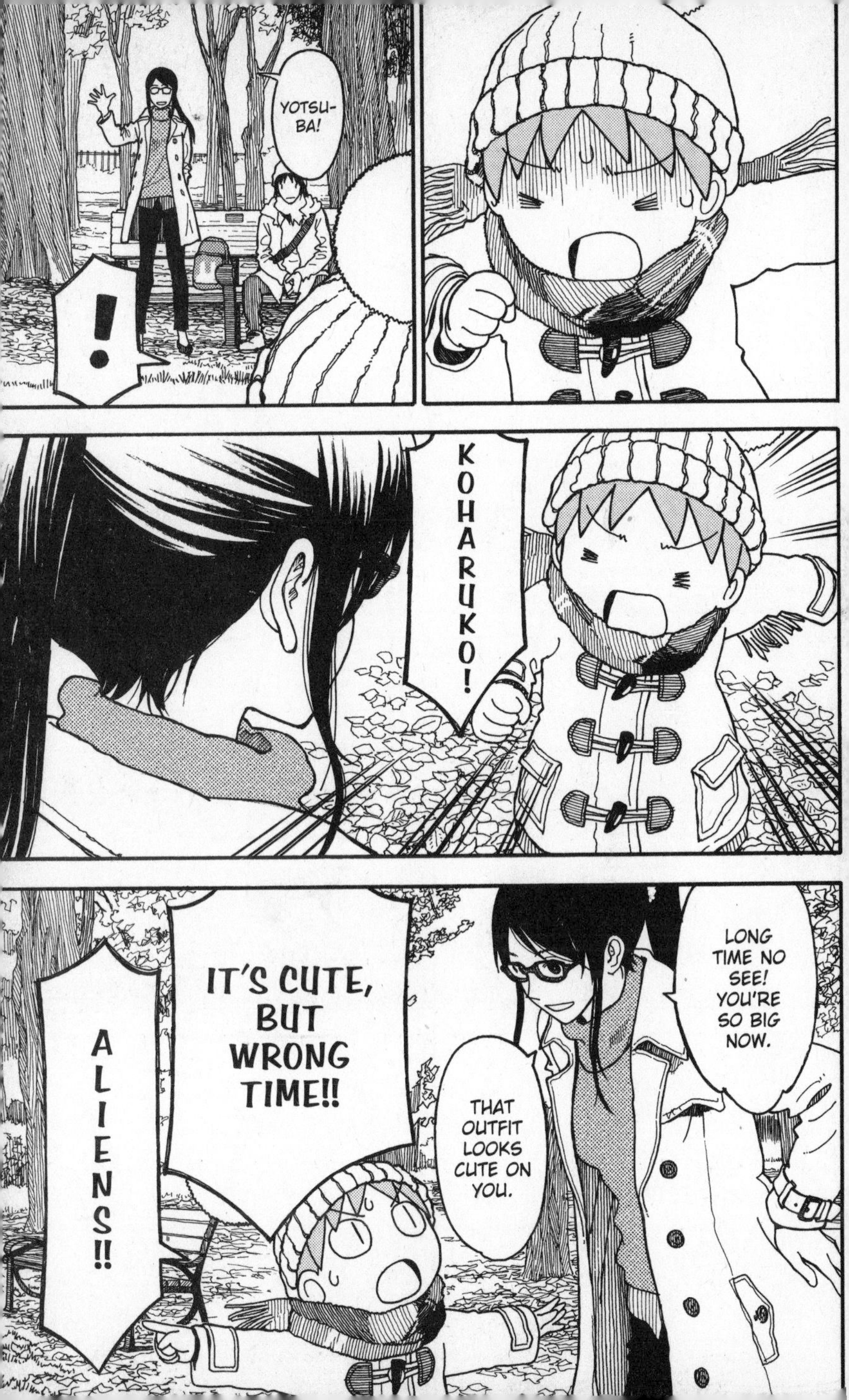
YOTSU-BA!
!
KOHARUKO!
LONG TIME NO SEE! YOU'RE SO BIG NOW.
THAT OUTFIT LOOKS CUTE ON YOU.
IT'S CUTE, BUT WRONG TIME!!
ALIENS!!

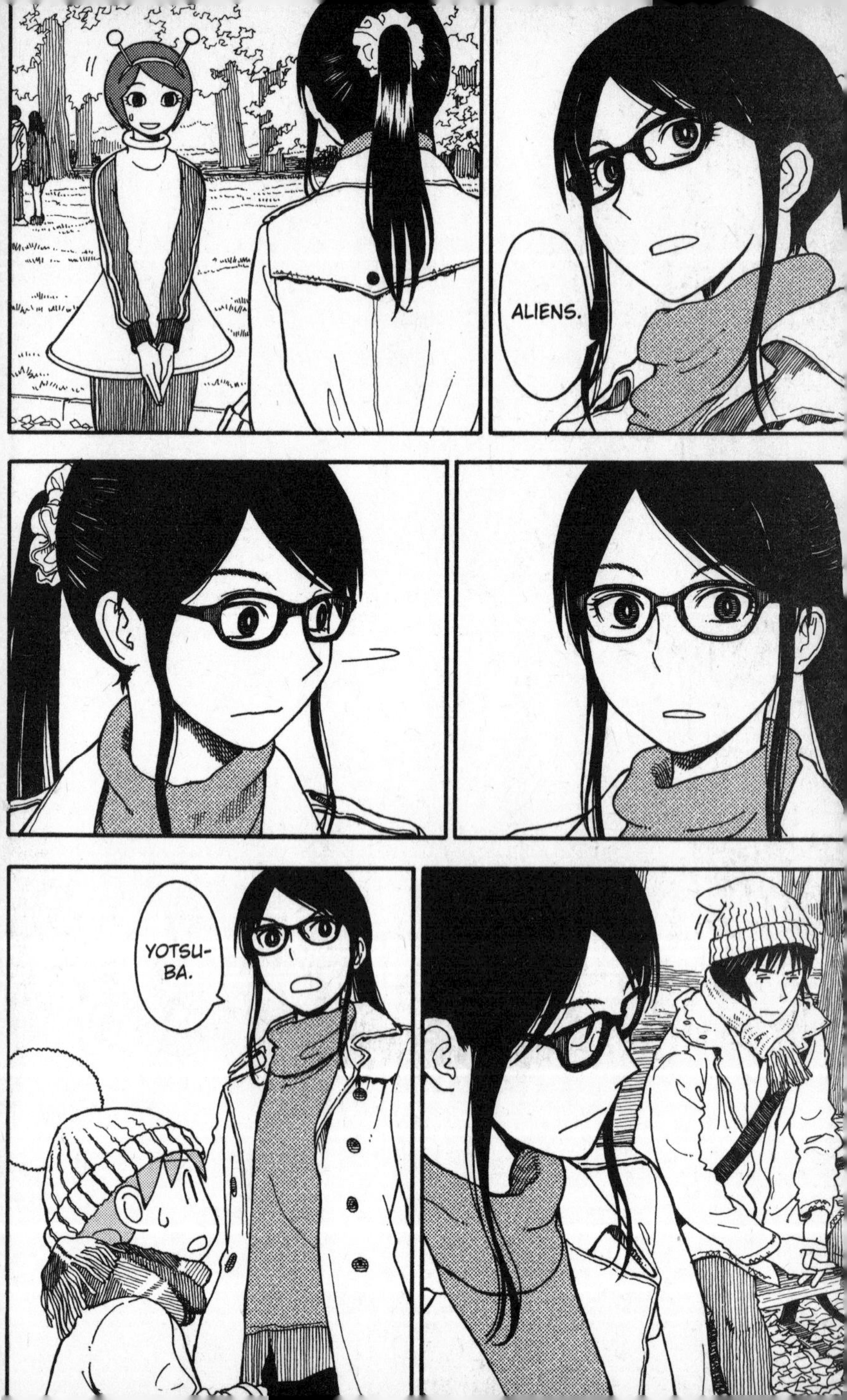
ALIENS.
YOTSU-BA.

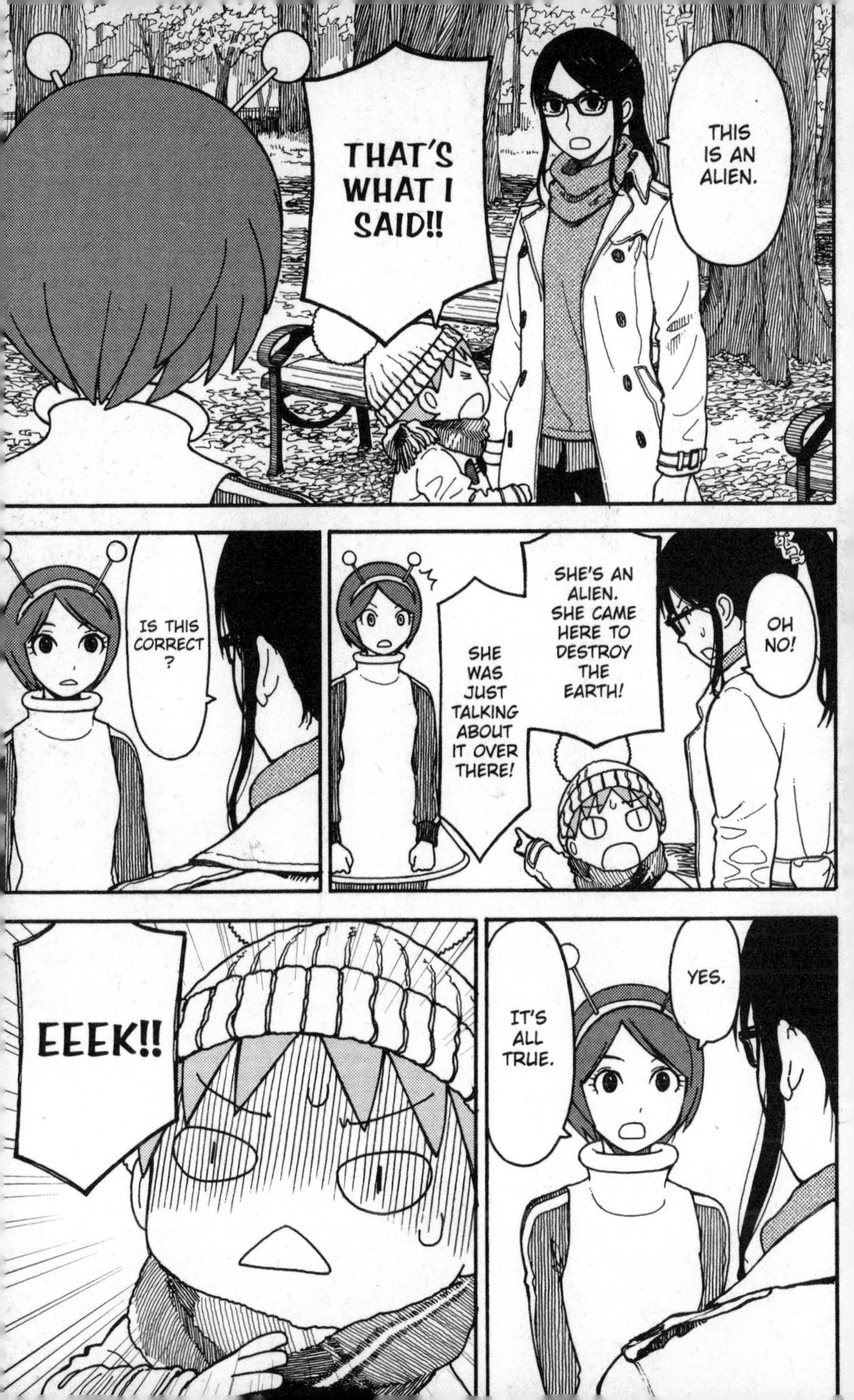
THIS IS AN ALIEN.
THAT'S WHAT I SAID!!
OH NO!
SHE'S AN ALIEN. SHE CAME HERE TO DESTROY THE EARTH!
SHE WAS JUST TALKING ABOUT IT OVER THERE!
IS THIS CORRECT?
YES.
IT'S ALL TRUE.
EEEK!!

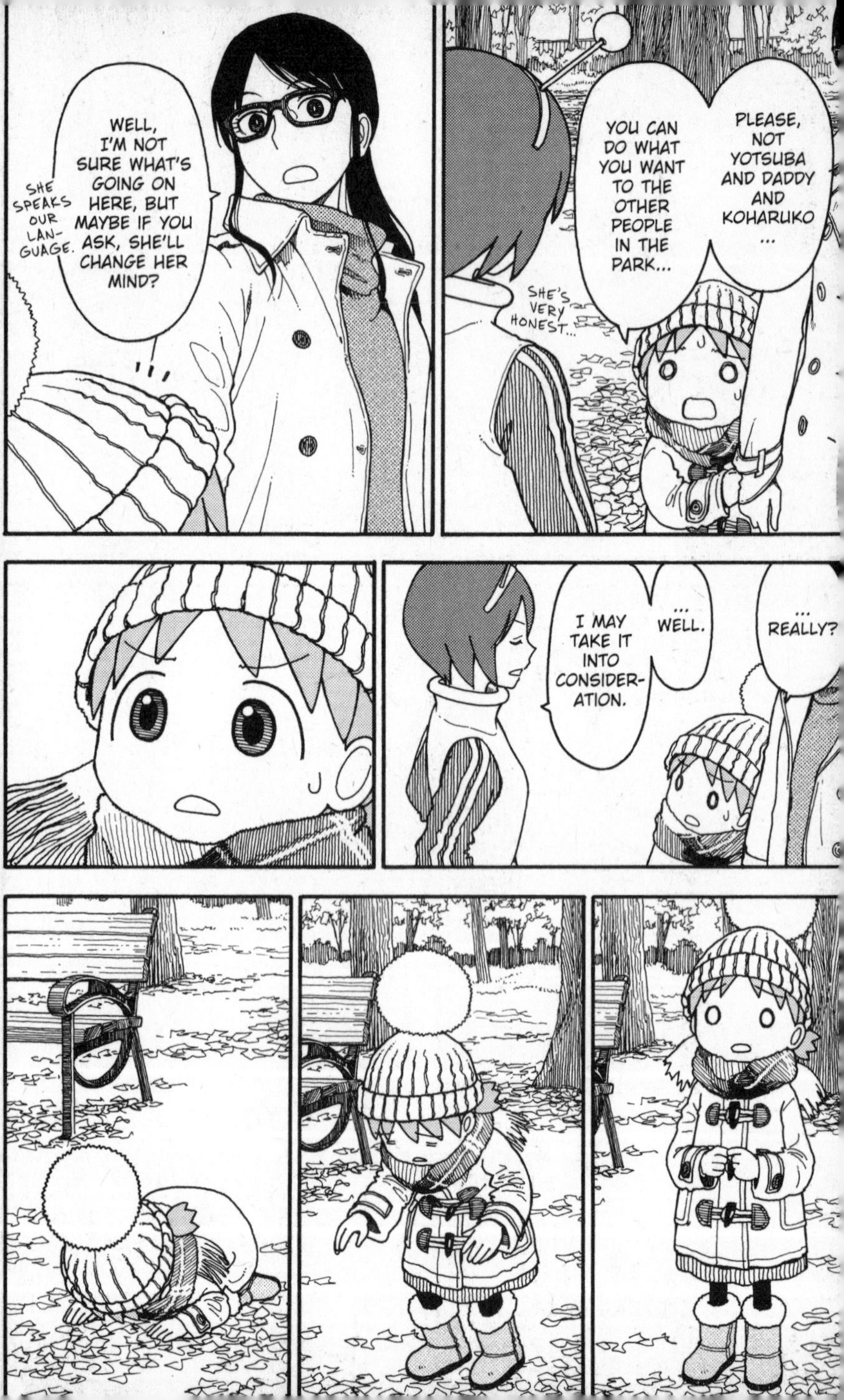
PLEASE, NOT YOTSUBA AND DADDY AND KOHARUKO ...
YOU CAN DO WHAT YOU WANT TO THE OTHER PEOPLE IN THE PARK...
SHE'S VERY HONEST...
WELL, I'M NOT SURE WHAT'S GOING ON HERE, BUT MAYBE IF YOU ASK, SHE'LL CHANGE HER MIND?
SHE SPEAKS OUR LAN-GUAGE.
... REALLY?
... WELL.
I MAY TAKE IT INTO CONSIDER-ATION.

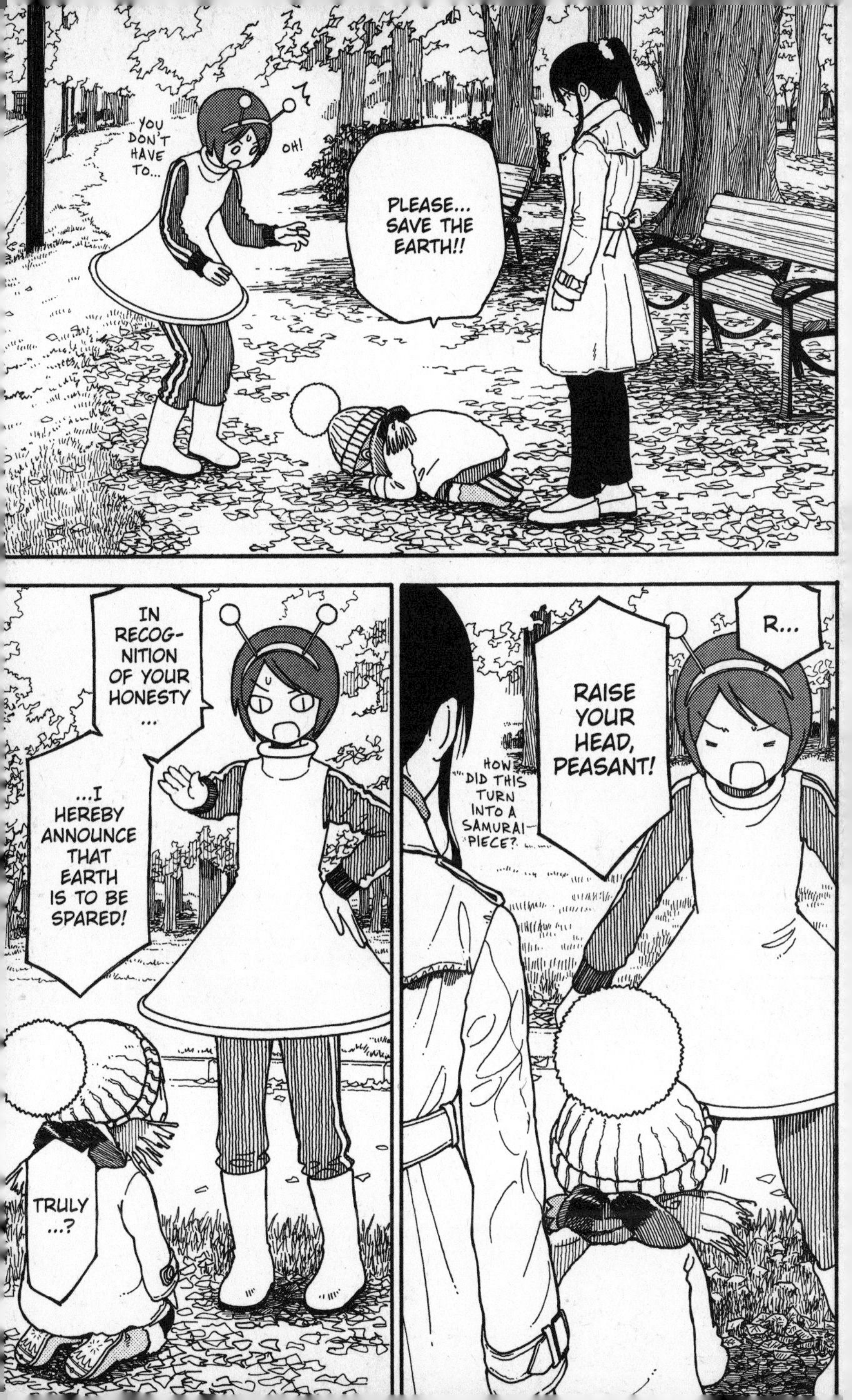
PLEASE... SAVE THE EARTH!!
OH!
YOU DON'T HAVE TO...
R...
RAISE YOUR HEAD, PEASANT!
HOW DID THIS TURN INTO A SAMURAI PIECE?
IN RECOG-NITION OF YOUR HONESTY...
...I HEREBY ANNOUNCE THAT EARTH IS TO BE SPARED!
TRULY...?

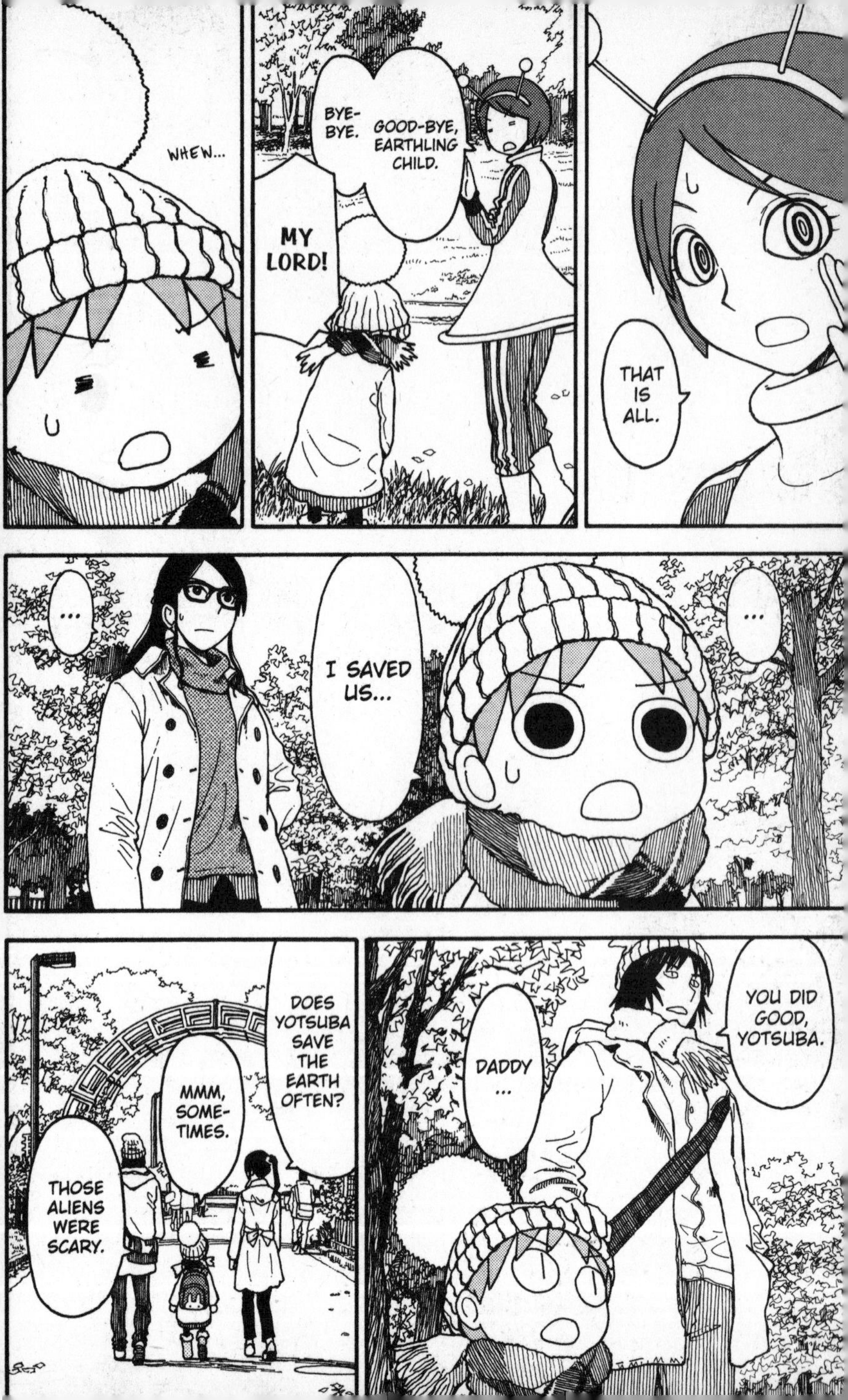
THAT IS ALL.
GOOD-BYE, EARTHLING CHILD.
BYE-BYE.
MY LORD!
WHEW...
...
I SAVED US...
...
YOU DID GOOD, YOTSUBA.
DADDY ...
DOES YOTSUBA SAVE THE EARTH OFTEN?
MMM, SOME-TIMES.
THOSE ALIENS WERE SCARY.

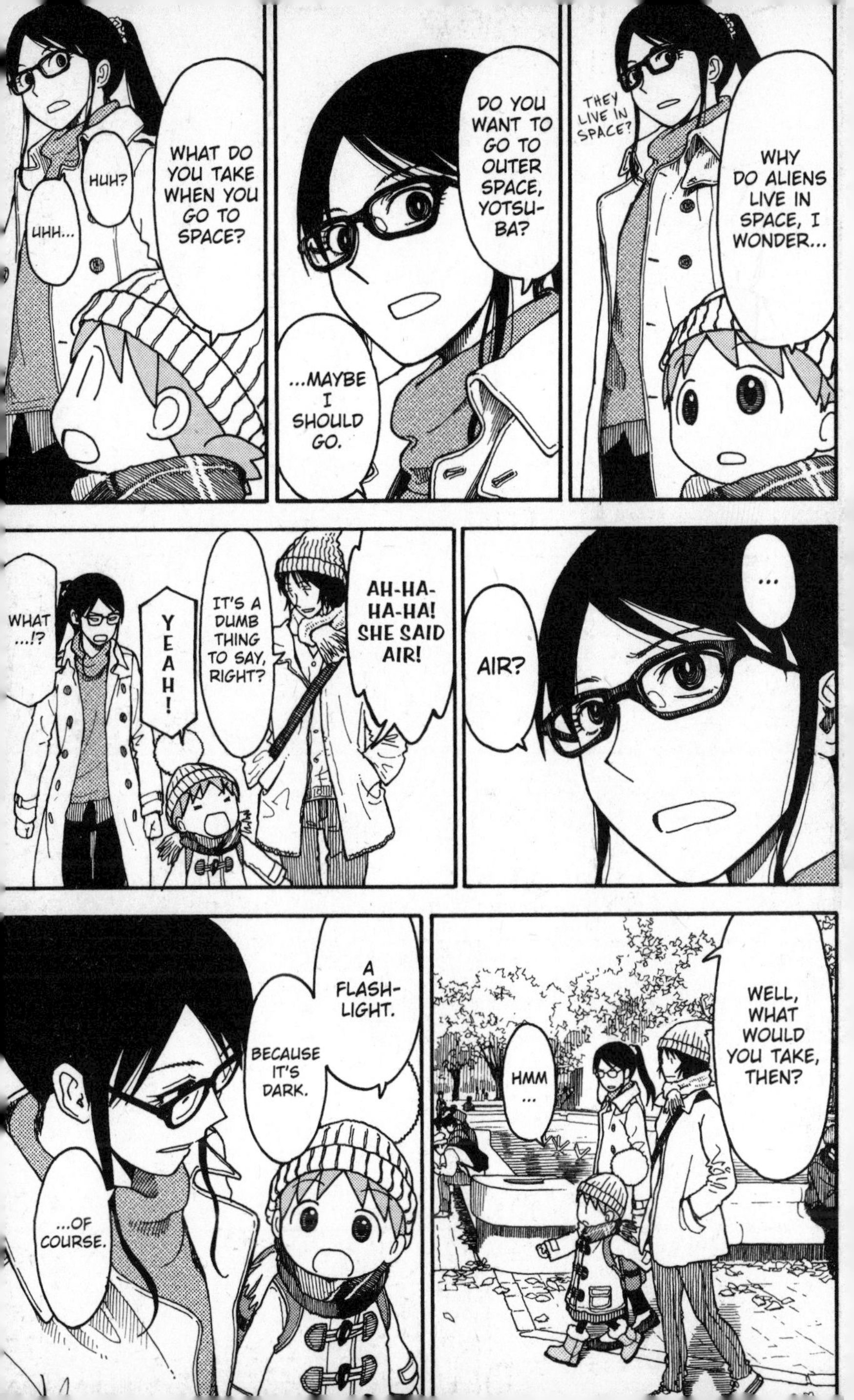
WHY DO ALIENS LIVE IN SPACE, I WONDER...
THEY LIVE IN SPACE?
DO YOU WANT TO GO TO OUTER SPACE, YOTSUBA?
...MAYBE I SHOULD GO.
WHAT DO YOU TAKE WHEN YOU GO TO SPACE?
HUH?
UHH...
...
AIR?
AH-HA-HA-HA! SHE SAID AIR!
IT'S A DUMB THING TO SAY, RIGHT?
YEAH!
WHAT ...!?
WELL, WHAT WOULD YOU TAKE, THEN?
HMM ...
A FLASHLIGHT.
BECAUSE IT'S DARK.
...OF COURSE.

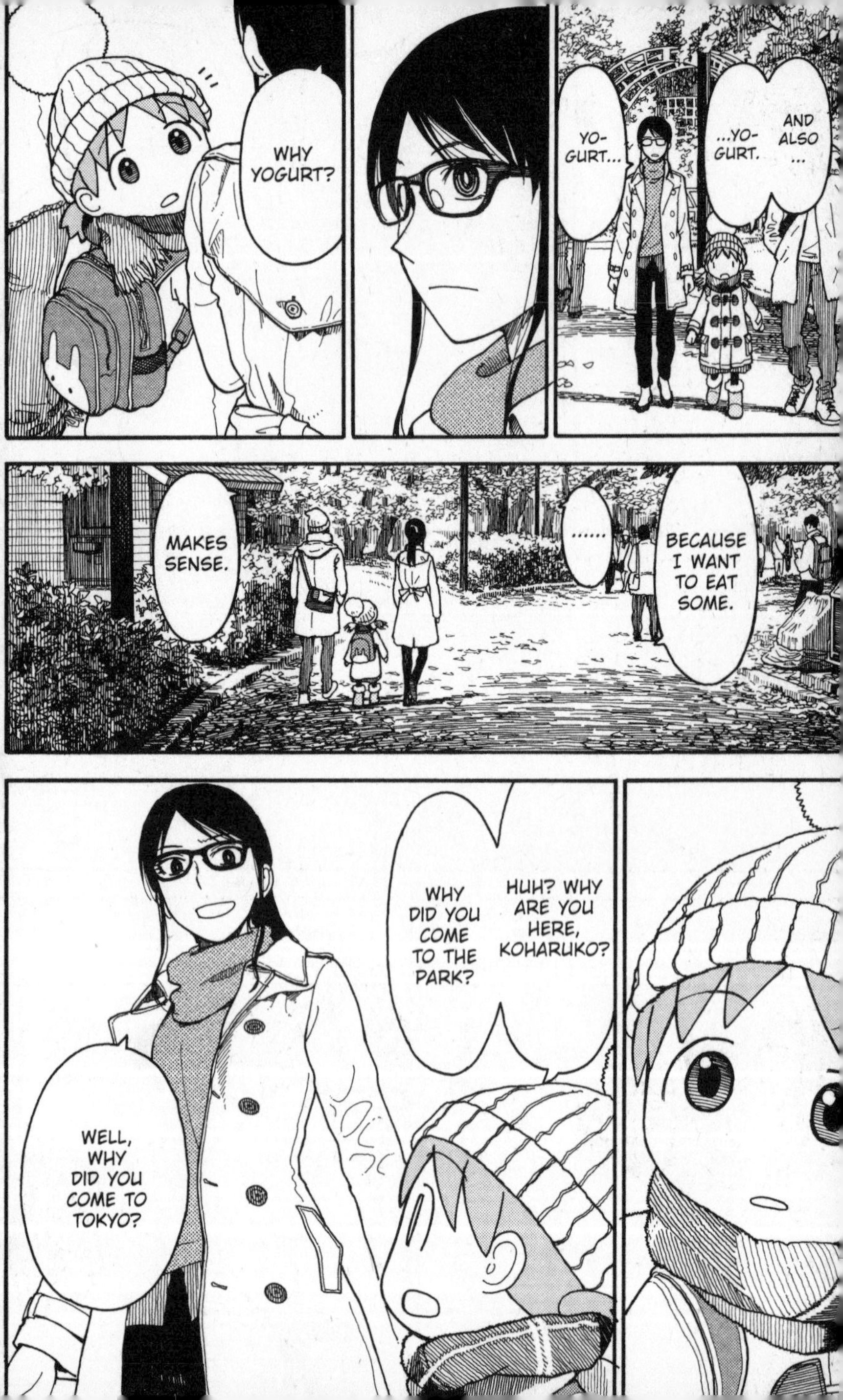
AND ALSO ...
...YO-GURT.
YO-GURT...
WHY YOGURT?
BECAUSE I WANT TO EAT SOME.
......
MAKES SENSE.
HUH? WHY ARE YOU HERE, KOHARUKO?
WHY DID YOU COME TO THE PARK?
WELL, WHY DID YOU COME TO TOKYO?

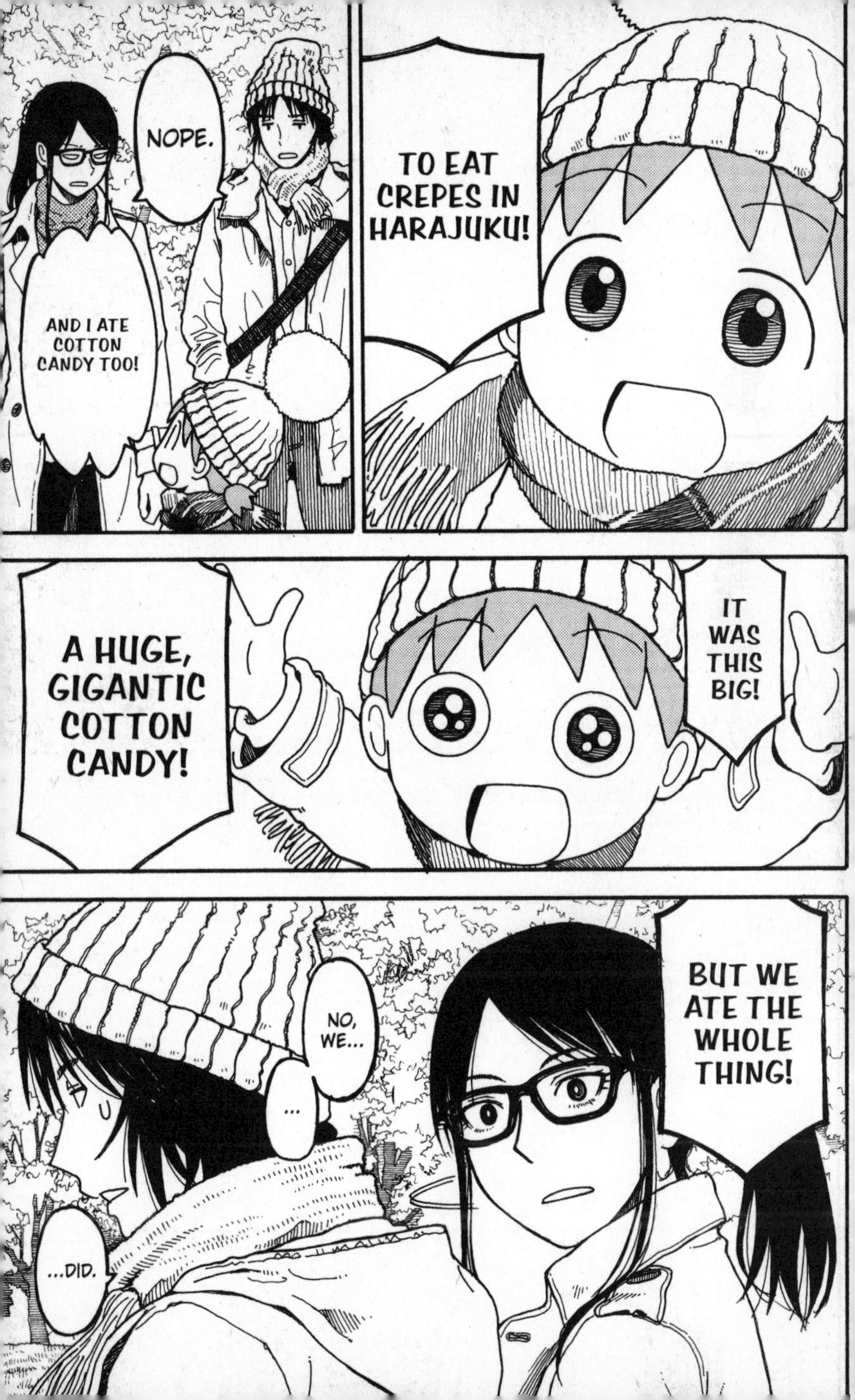
TO EAT CREPES IN HARAJUKU!
NOPE.
AND I ATE COTTON CANDY TOO!
IT WAS THIS BIG!
A HUGE, GIGANTIC COTTON CANDY!
BUT WE ATE THE WHOLE THING!
NO, WE...
...
...DID.

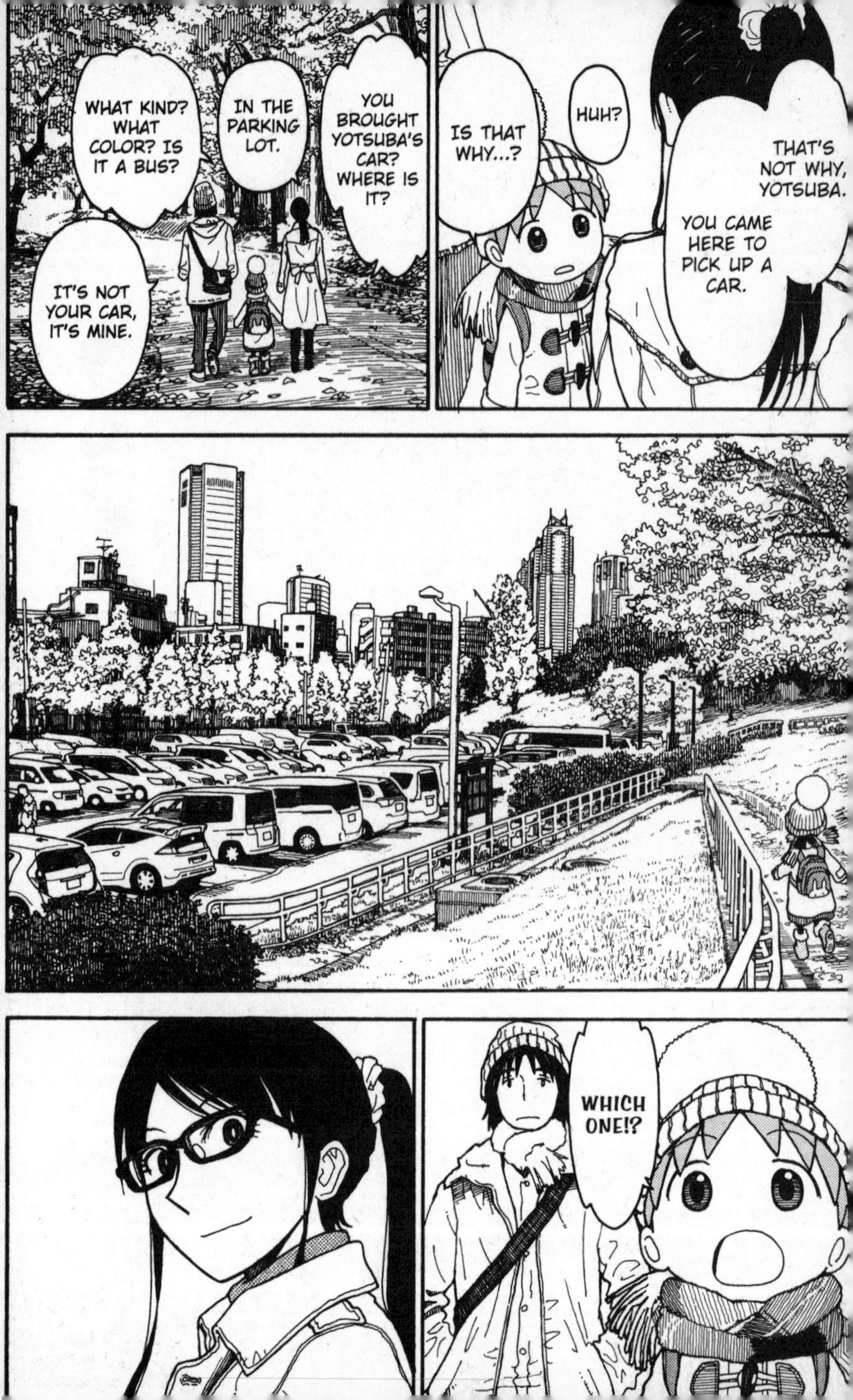
THAT'S NOT WHY, YOTSUBA.
YOU CAME HERE TO PICK UP A CAR.
HUH?
IS THAT WHY...?
YOU BROUGHT YOTSUBA'S CAR? WHERE IS IT?
IN THE PARKING LOT.
WHAT KIND? WHAT COLOR? IS IT A BUS?
IT'S NOT YOUR CAR, IT'S MINE.
WHICH ONE!?

THIS IS IT.

SO THIS IS IT!

OHH!

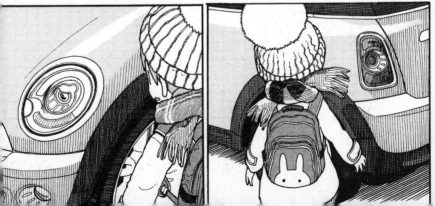

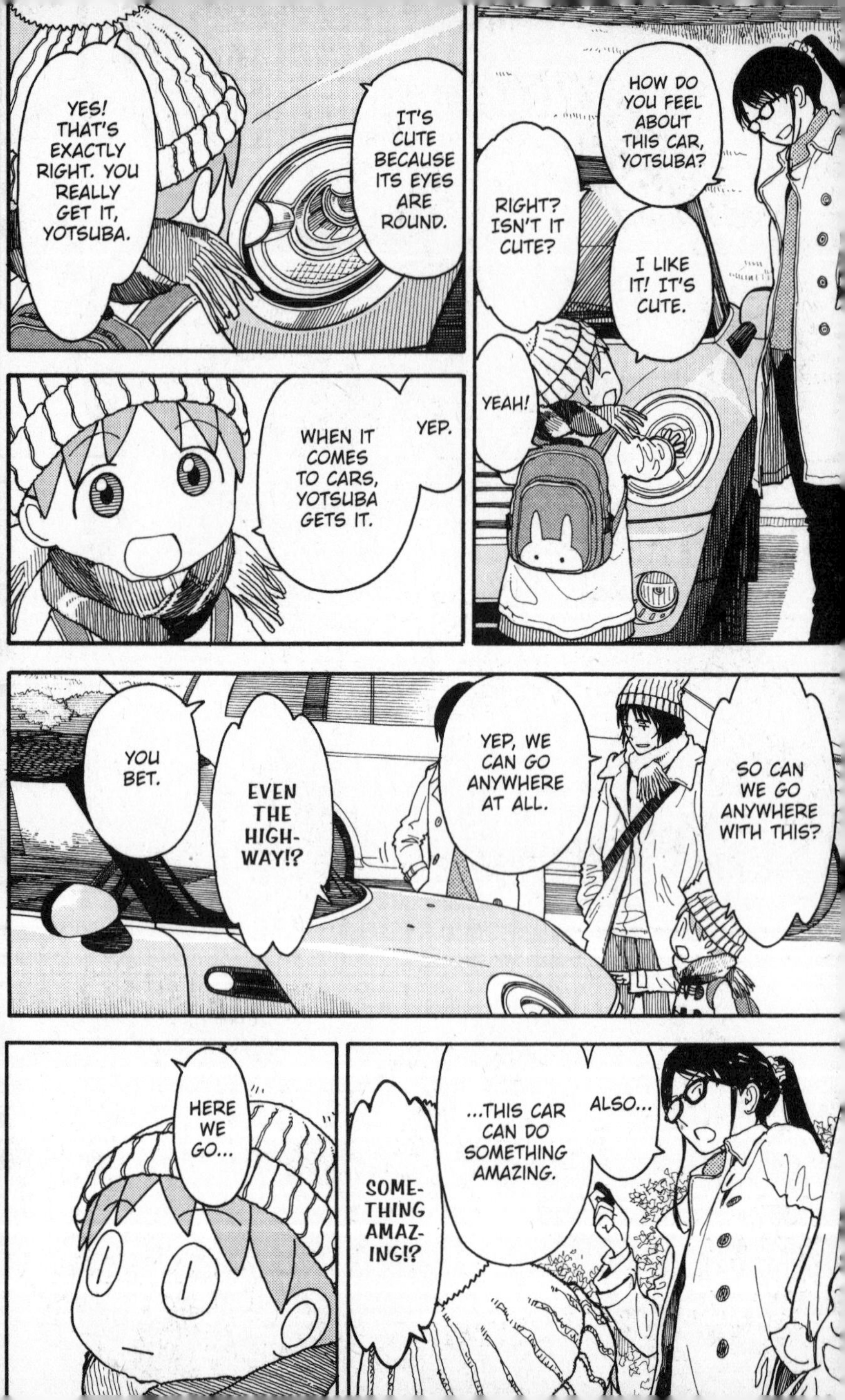
HOW DO YOU FEEL ABOUT THIS CAR, YOTSUBA?
I LIKE IT! IT'S CUTE.
RIGHT? ISN'T IT CUTE?
YEAH!
IT'S CUTE BECAUSE ITS EYES ARE ROUND.
YES! THAT'S EXACTLY RIGHT. YOU REALLY GET IT, YOTSUBA.
YEP.
WHEN IT COMES TO CARS, YOTSUBA GETS IT.
SO CAN WE GO ANYWHERE WITH THIS?
YEP, WE CAN GO ANYWHERE AT ALL.
EVEN THE HIGH-WAY!?
YOU BET.
ALSO...
...THIS CAR CAN DO SOMETHING AMAZING.
SOME-THING AMAZ-ING!?
HERE WE GO...

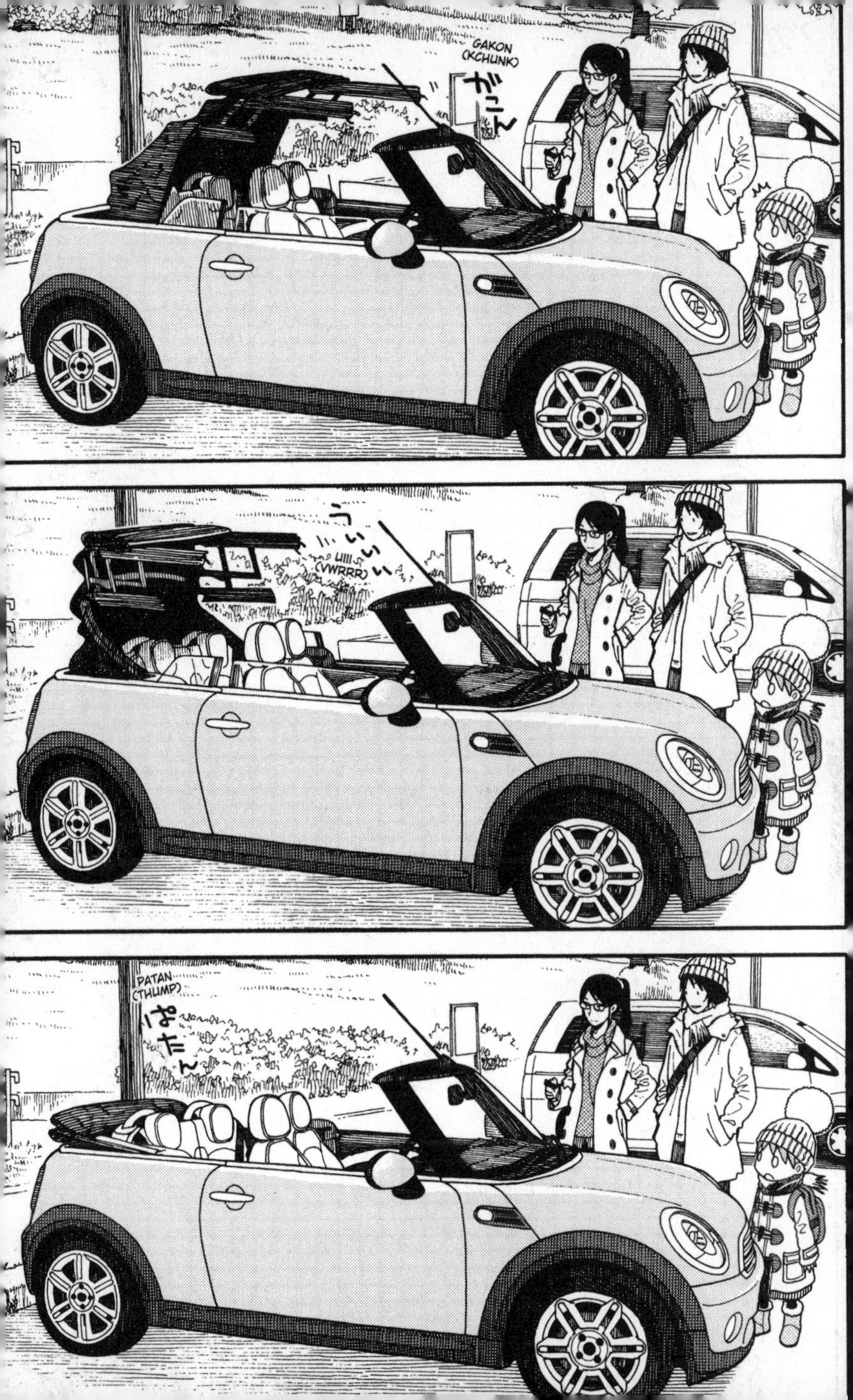
GAKON (KCHUNK)
がこん
ういいい
UIIII (VWRRR)
PATAN (THUMP)
ぱたん

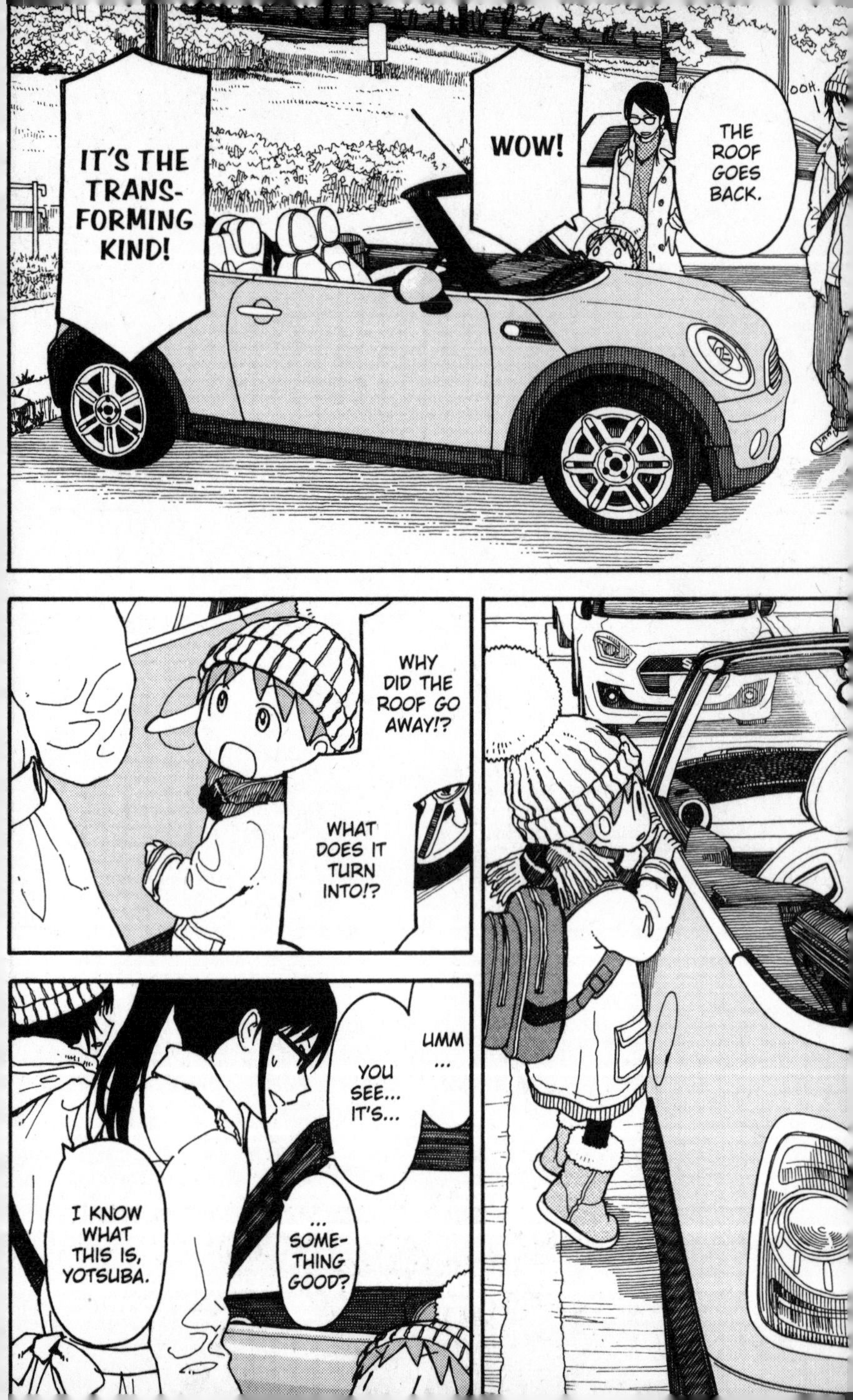
OOH.
THE ROOF GOES BACK.
WOW!
IT'S THE TRANS-FORMING KIND!
WHY DID THE ROOF GO AWAY!?
WHAT DOES IT TURN INTO!?
UMM ...
YOU SEE... IT'S...
... SOME-THING GOOD?
I KNOW WHAT THIS IS, YOTSUBA.

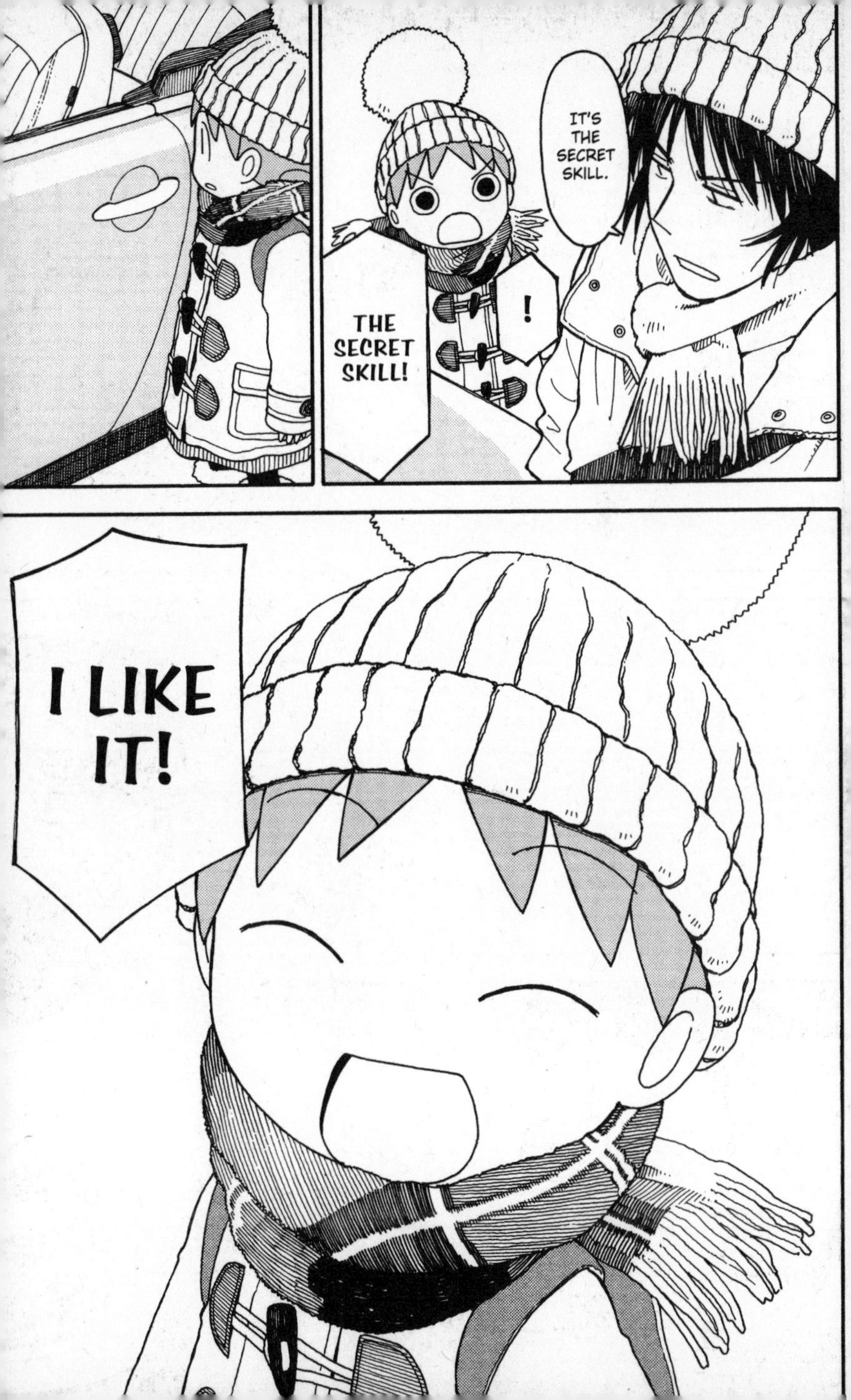
IT'S THE SECRET SKILL.
!
THE SECRET SKILL!
I LIKE IT!

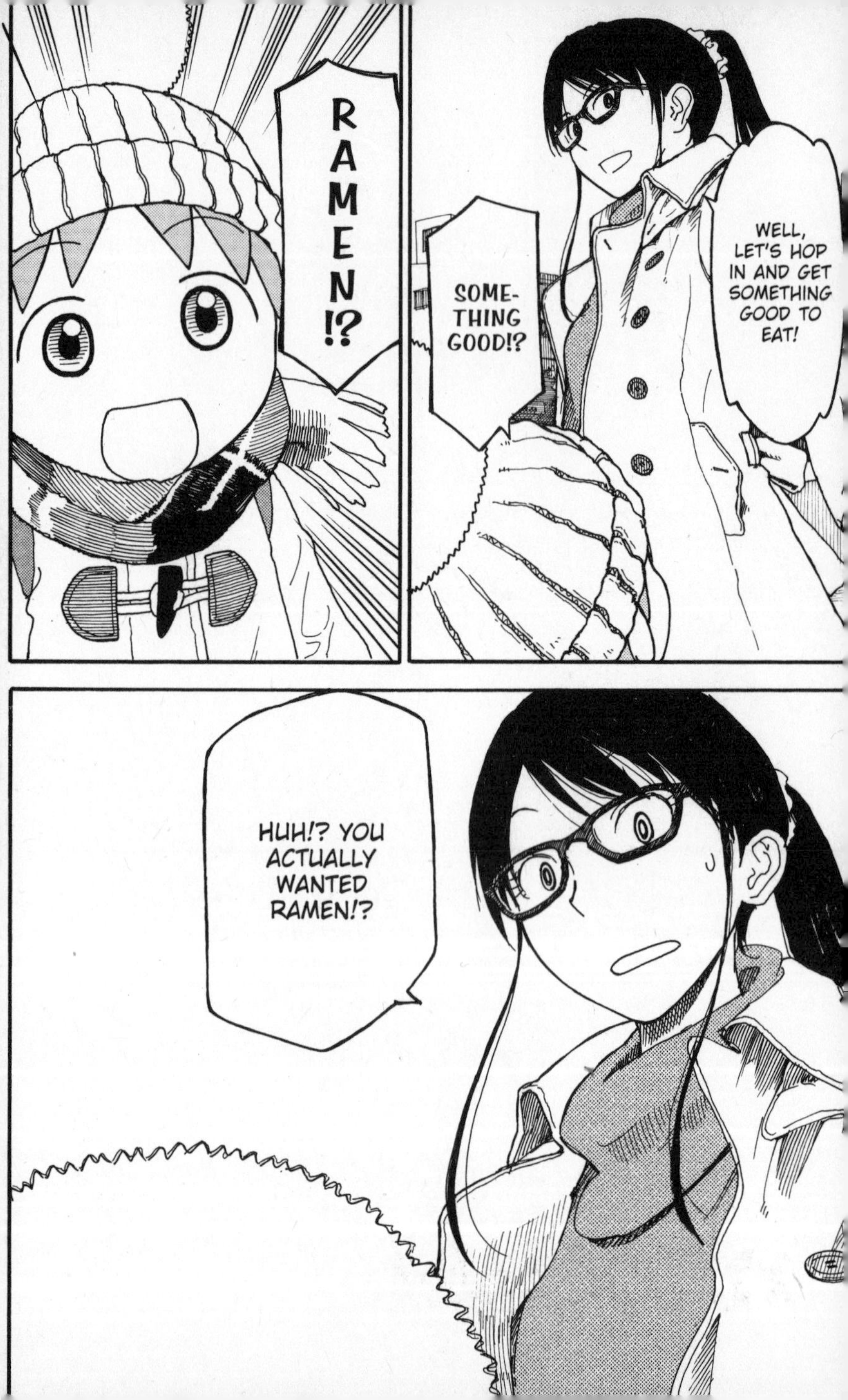
WELL, LET'S HOP IN AND GET SOMETHING GOOD TO EAT!
SOME-THING GOOD!?
RAMEN!?
HUH!? YOU ACTUALLY WANTED RAMEN!?

YOTSUBA&!

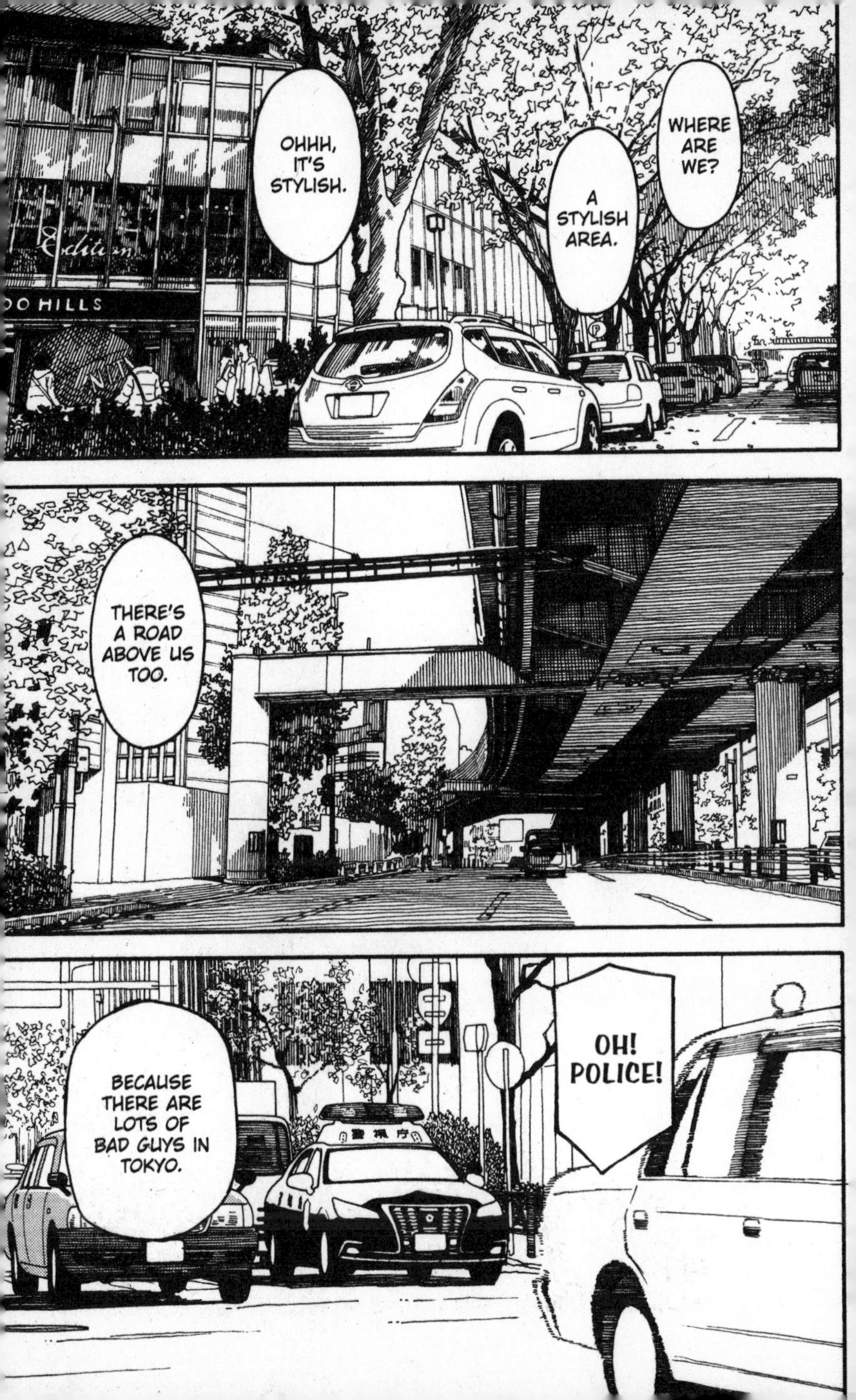
WHERE ARE WE?
A STYLISH AREA.
OHHH, IT'S STYLISH.
THERE'S A ROAD ABOVE US TOO.
OH! POLICE!
BECAUSE THERE ARE LOTS OF BAD GUYS IN TOKYO.

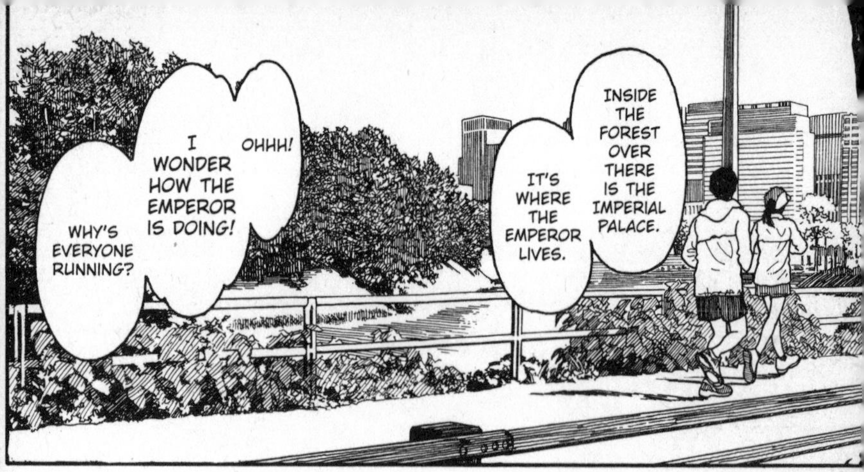
INSIDE THE FOREST OVER THERE IS THE IMPERIAL PALACE.
IT'S WHERE THE EMPEROR LIVES.
OHHH!
I WONDER HOW THE EMPEROR IS DOING!
WHY'S EVERYONE RUNNING?

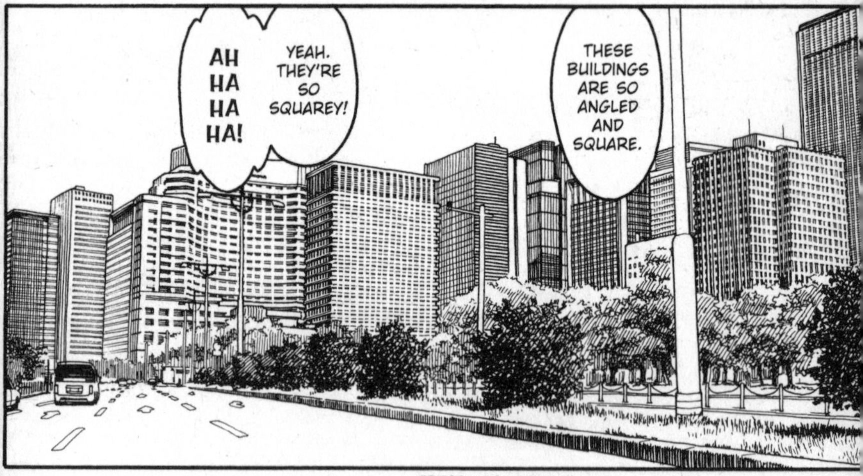
THESE BUILDINGS ARE SO ANGLED AND SQUARE.
YEAH. THEY'RE SO SQUAREY!
AH HA HA HA!

BRIDGE: HEIGHT LIMIT 4M

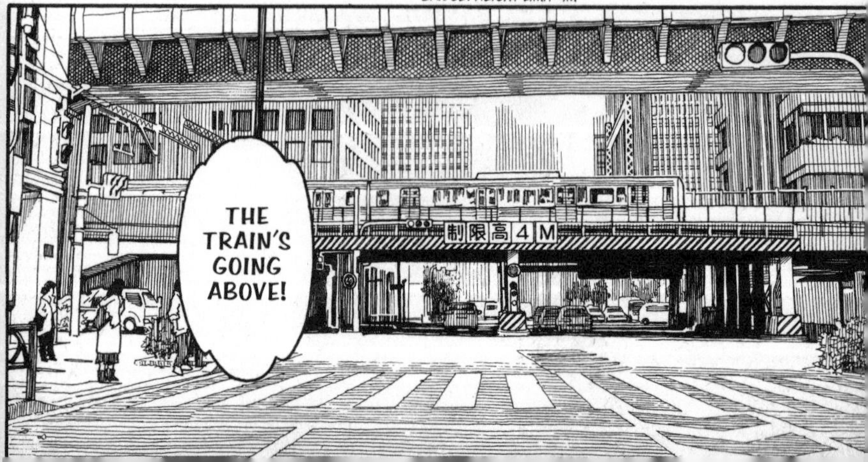
制限高4M
THE TRAIN'S GOING ABOVE!

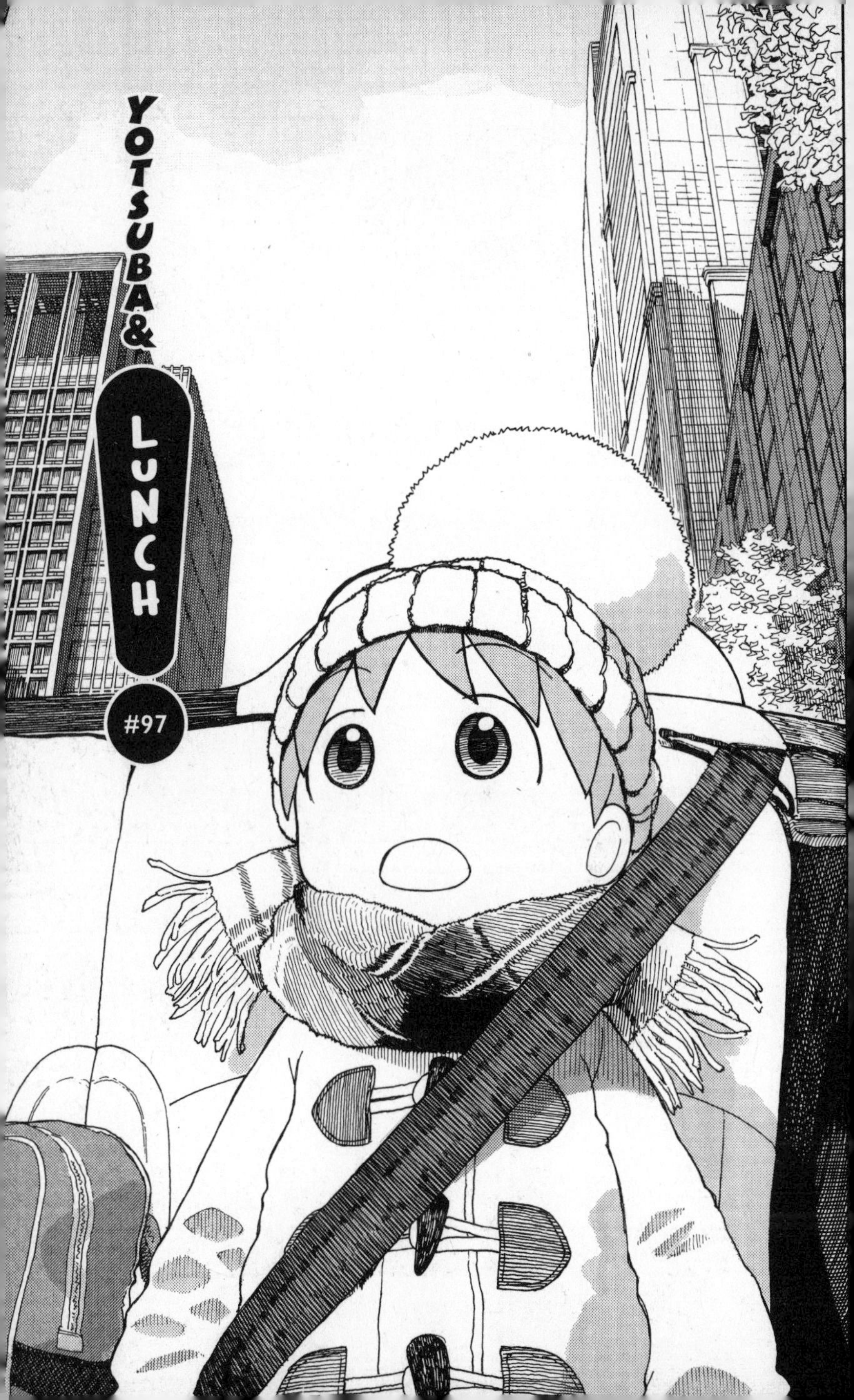
YOTSUBA&
LUNCH
#97

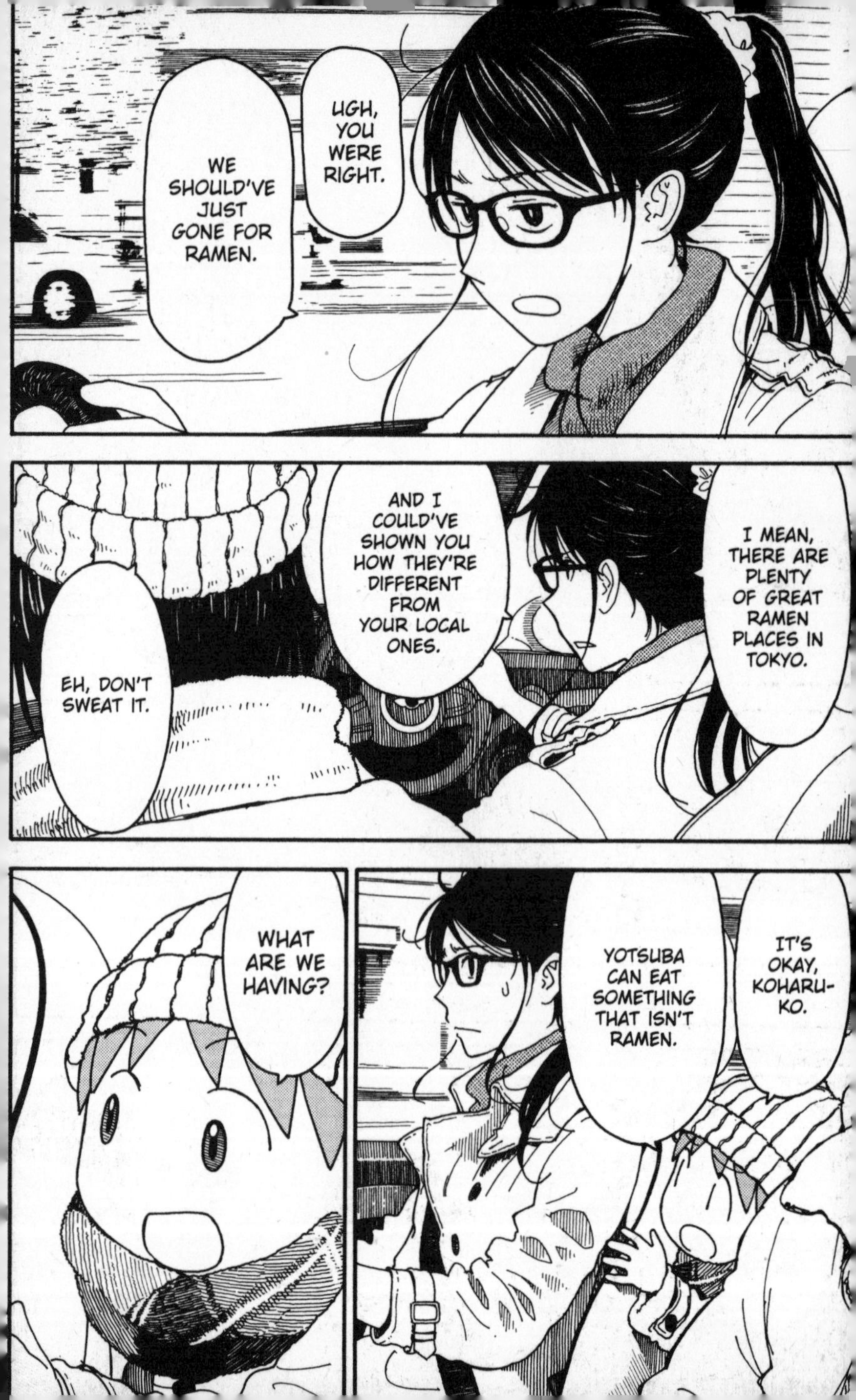
UGH, YOU WERE RIGHT.
WE SHOULD'VE JUST GONE FOR RAMEN.
I MEAN, THERE ARE PLENTY OF GREAT RAMEN PLACES IN TOKYO.
AND I COULD'VE SHOWN YOU HOW THEY'RE DIFFERENT FROM YOUR LOCAL ONES.
EH, DON'T SWEAT IT.
IT'S OKAY, KOHARU-KO.
YOTSUBA CAN EAT SOMETHING THAT ISN'T RAMEN.
WHAT ARE WE HAVING?

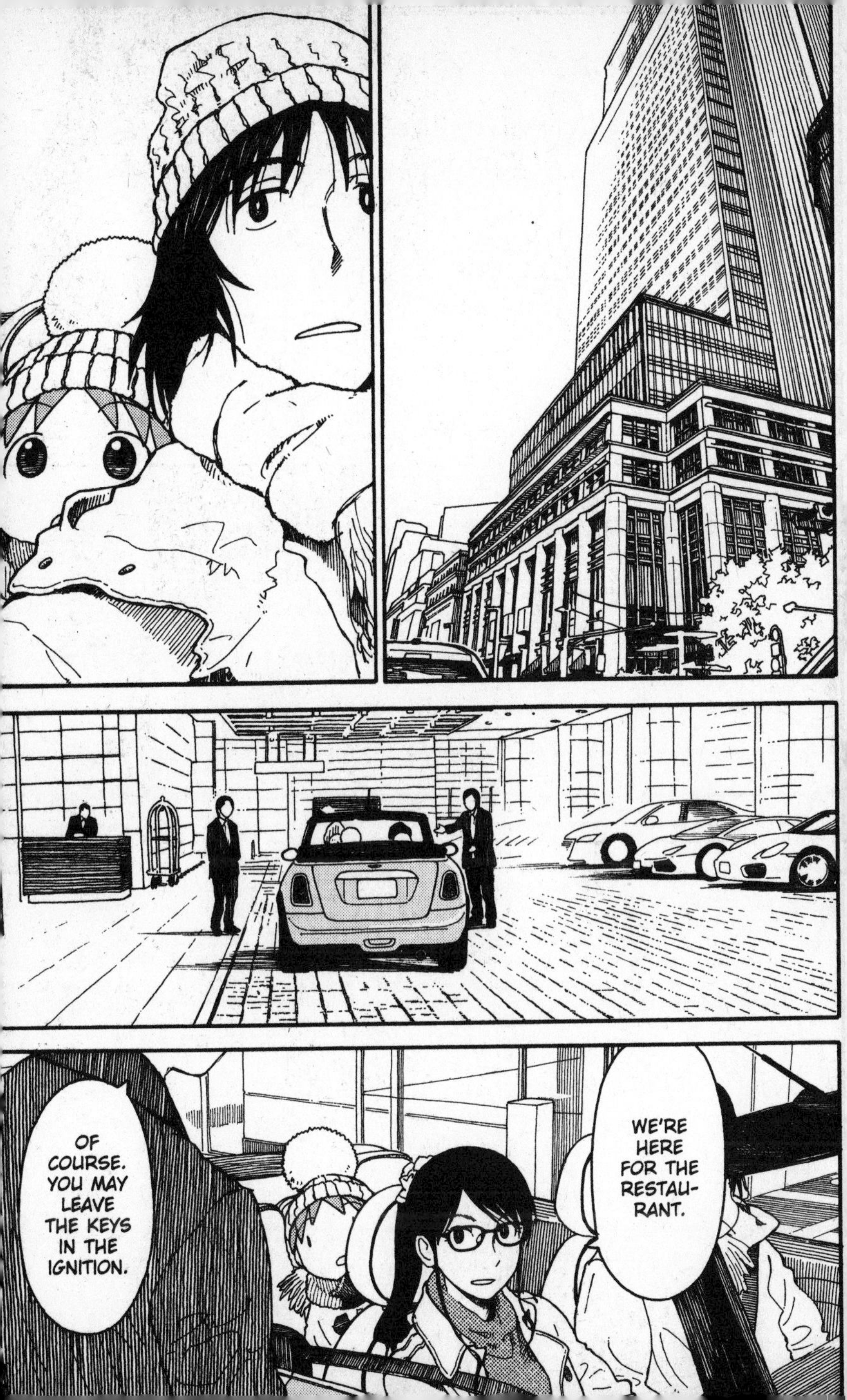
WE'RE HERE FOR THE RESTAU-RANT.
OF COURSE. YOU MAY LEAVE THE KEYS IN THE IGNITION.

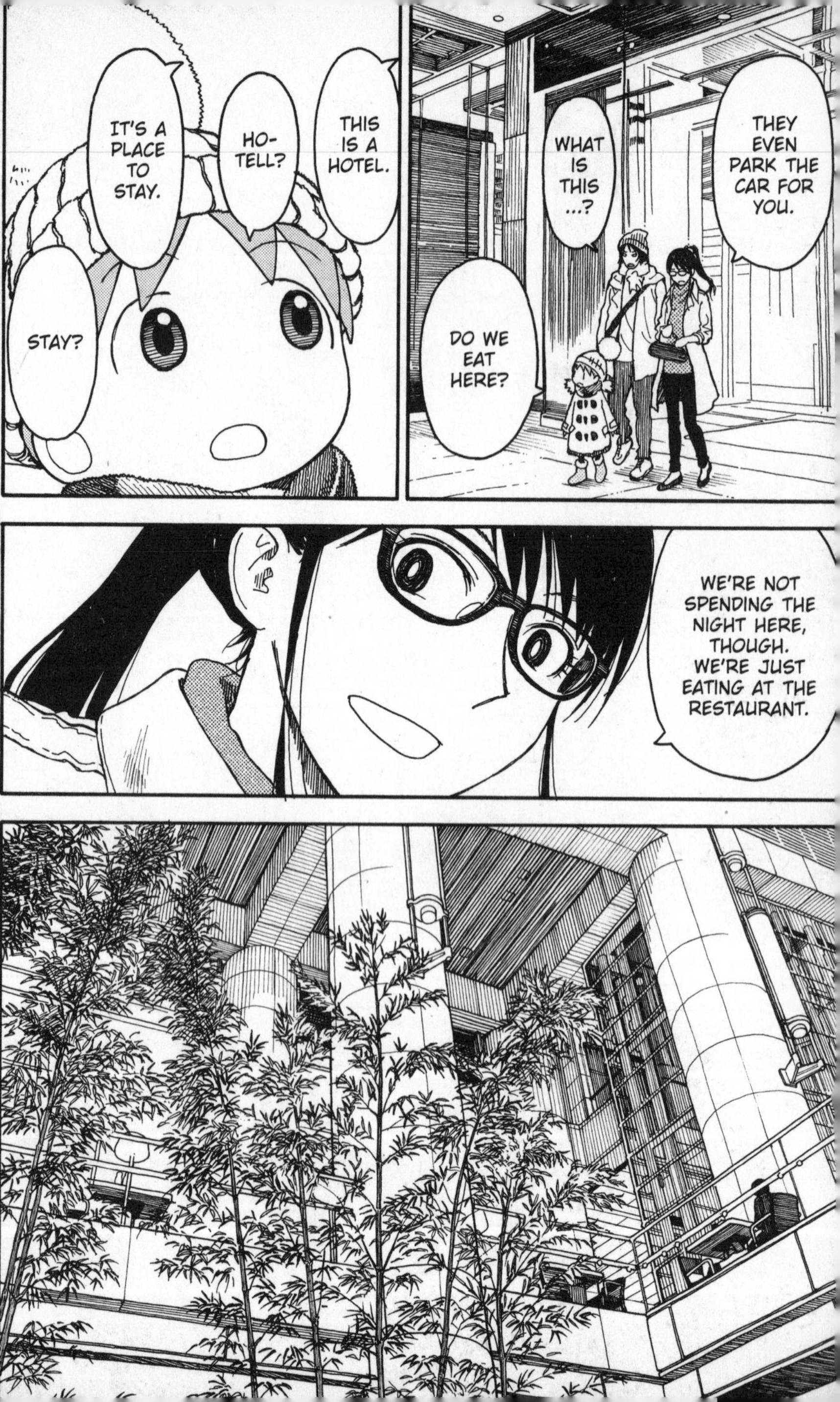
THEY EVEN PARK THE CAR FOR YOU.
WHAT IS THIS ...?
DO WE EAT HERE?
THIS IS A HOTEL.
HO-TELL?
IT'S A PLACE TO STAY.
STAY?
WE'RE NOT SPENDING THE NIGHT HERE, THOUGH. WE'RE JUST EATING AT THE RESTAURANT.

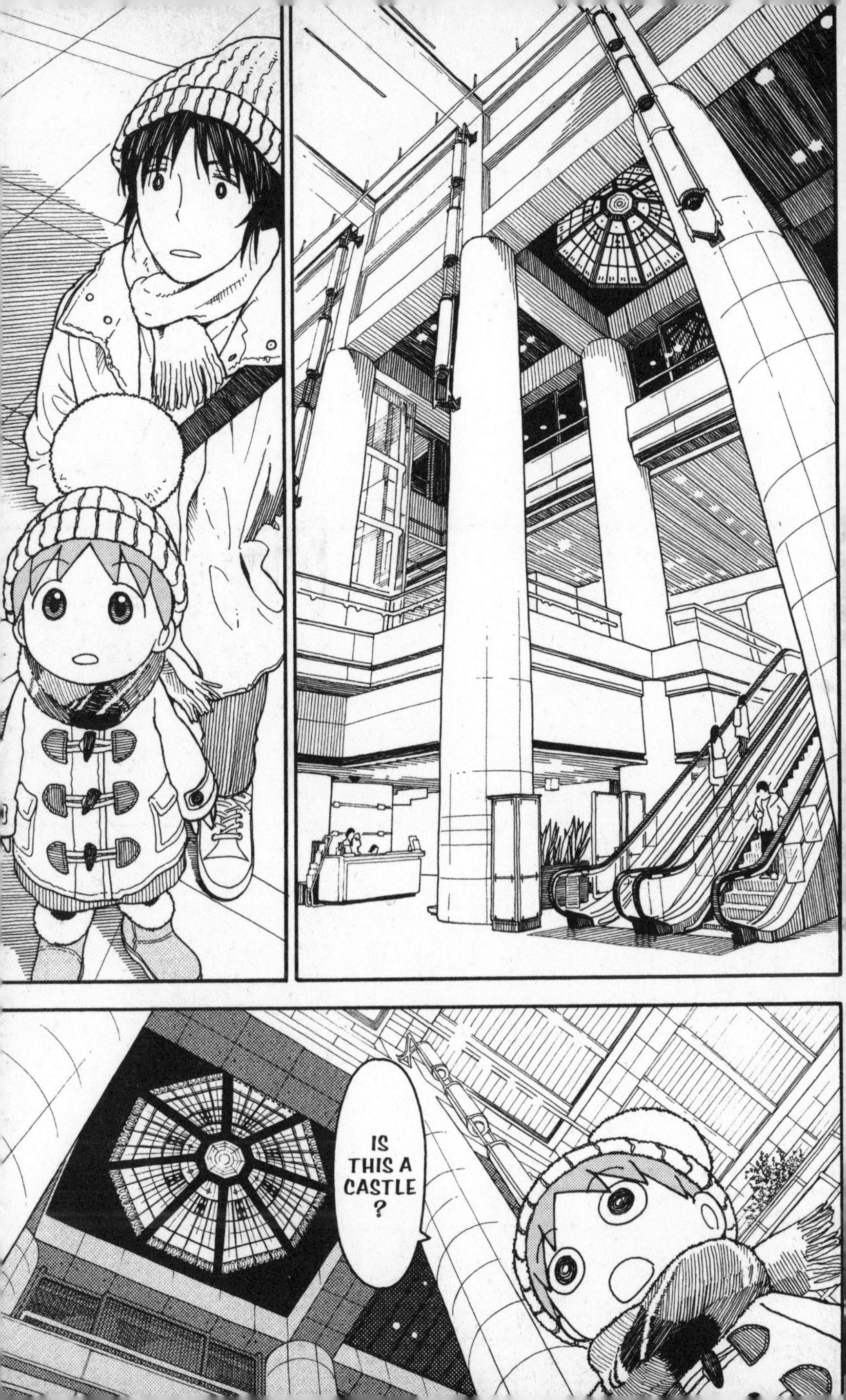
IS THIS A CASTLE?

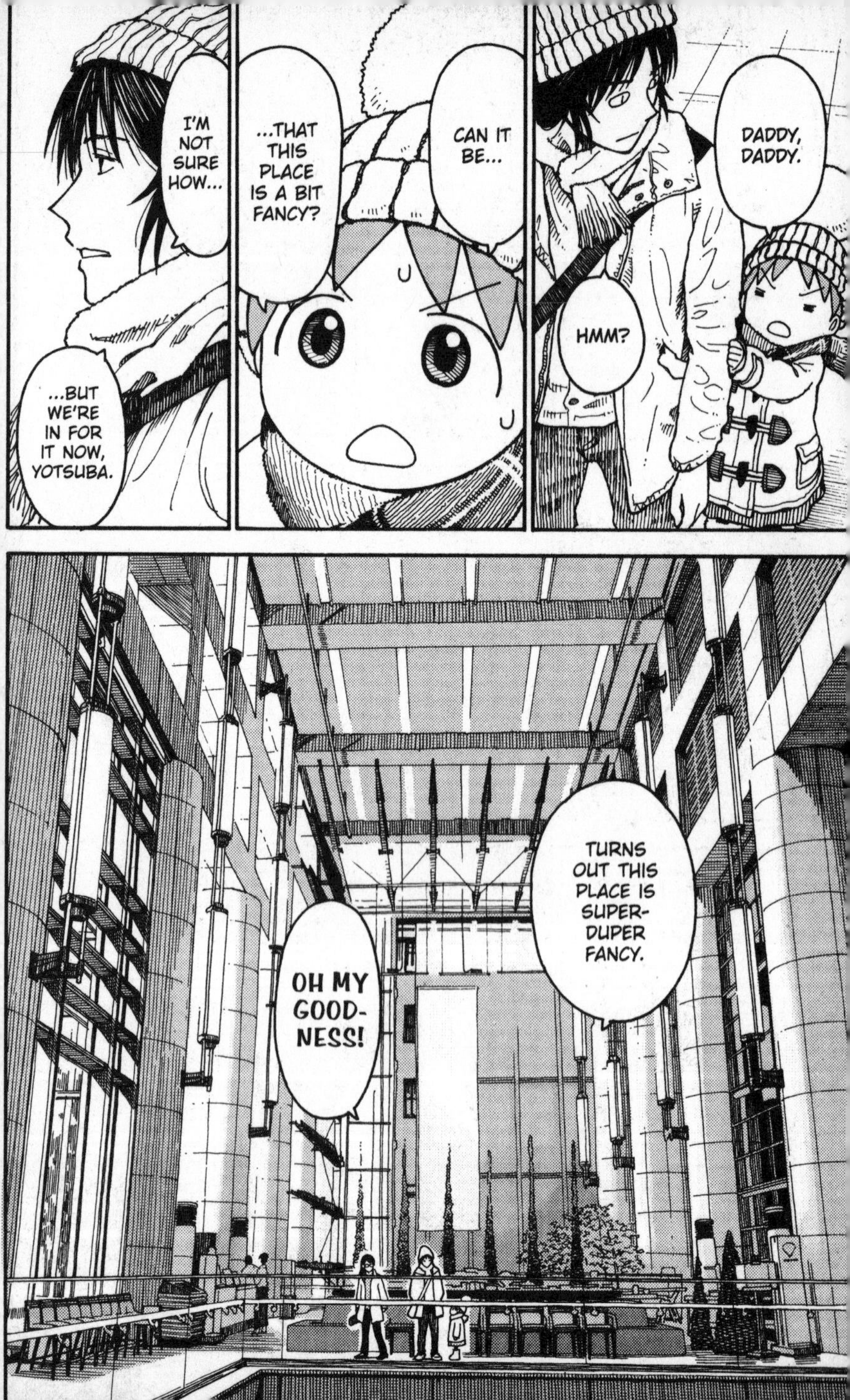
DADDY, DADDY.
HMM?
CAN IT BE...
...THAT THIS PLACE IS A BIT FANCY?
I'M NOT SURE HOW...
...BUT WE'RE IN FOR IT NOW, YOTSUBA.
TURNS OUT THIS PLACE IS SUPER-DUPER FANCY.
OH MY GOODNESS!

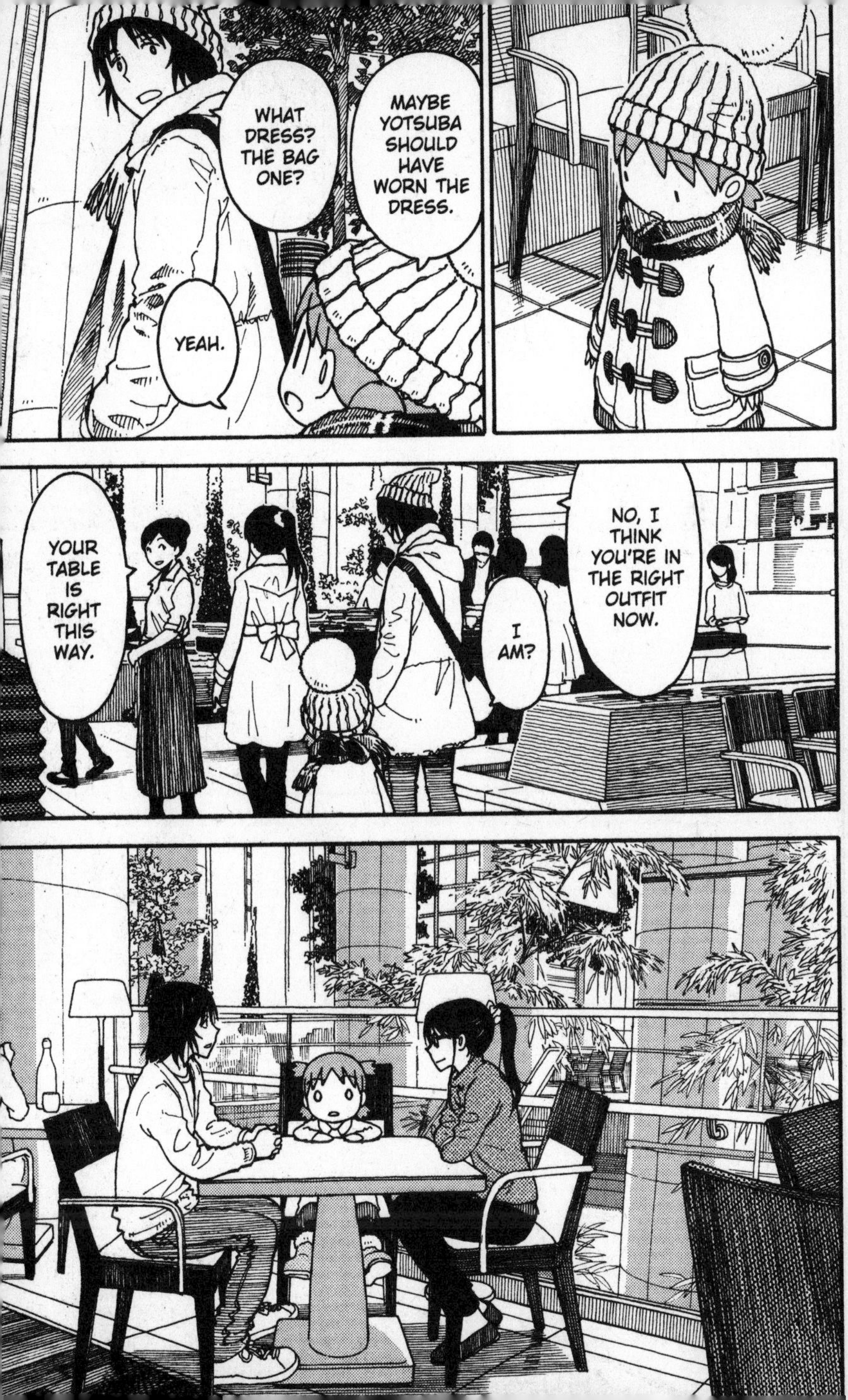
MAYBE YOTSUBA SHOULD HAVE WORN THE DRESS.
WHAT DRESS? THE BAG ONE?
YEAH.
NO, I THINK YOU'RE IN THE RIGHT OUTFIT NOW.
I AM?
YOUR TABLE IS RIGHT THIS WAY.

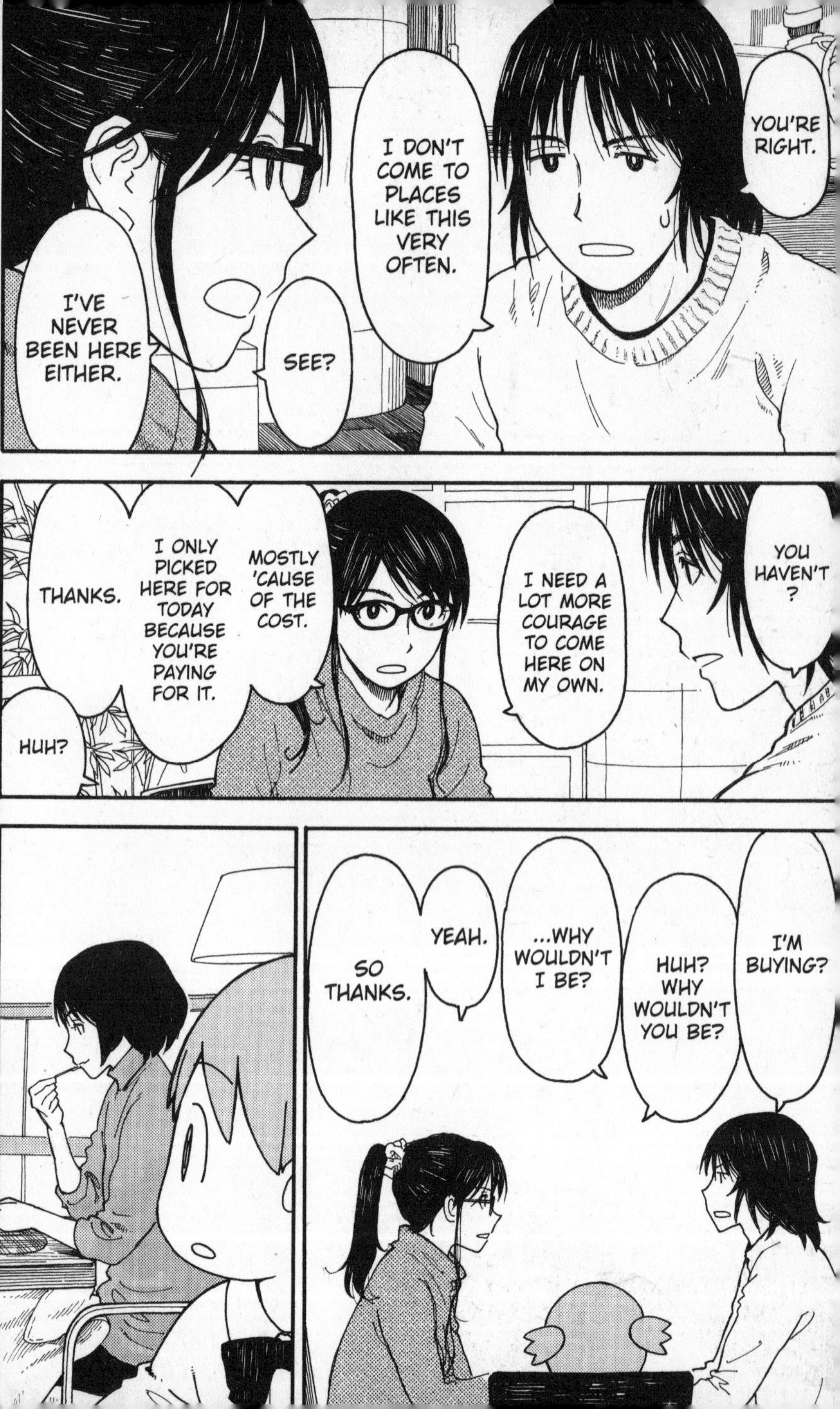
YOU'RE RIGHT.
I DON'T COME TO PLACES LIKE THIS VERY OFTEN.
SEE?
I'VE NEVER BEEN HERE EITHER.
YOU HAVEN'T?
I NEED A LOT MORE COURAGE TO COME HERE ON MY OWN.
MOSTLY 'CAUSE OF THE COST.
I ONLY PICKED HERE FOR TODAY BECAUSE YOU'RE PAYING FOR IT.
THANKS.
HUH?
I'M BUYING?
HUH? WHY WOULDN'T YOU BE?
...WHY WOULDN'T I BE?
YEAH.
SO THANKS.

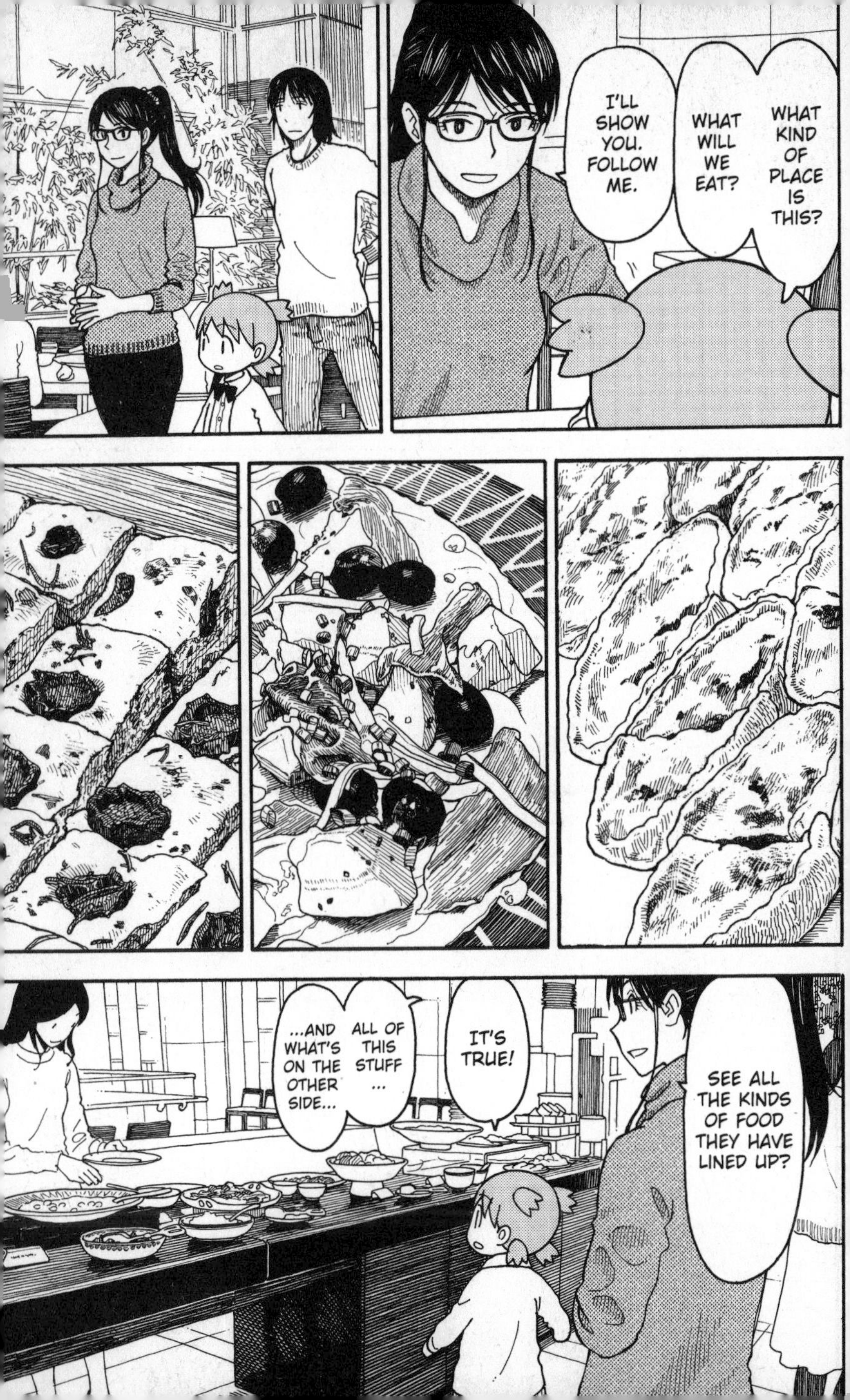
WHAT KIND OF PLACE IS THIS?
WHAT WILL WE EAT?
I'LL SHOW YOU. FOLLOW ME.
SEE ALL THE KINDS OF FOOD THEY HAVE LINED UP?
IT'S TRUE!
ALL OF THIS STUFF ...
...AND WHAT'S ON THE OTHER SIDE...

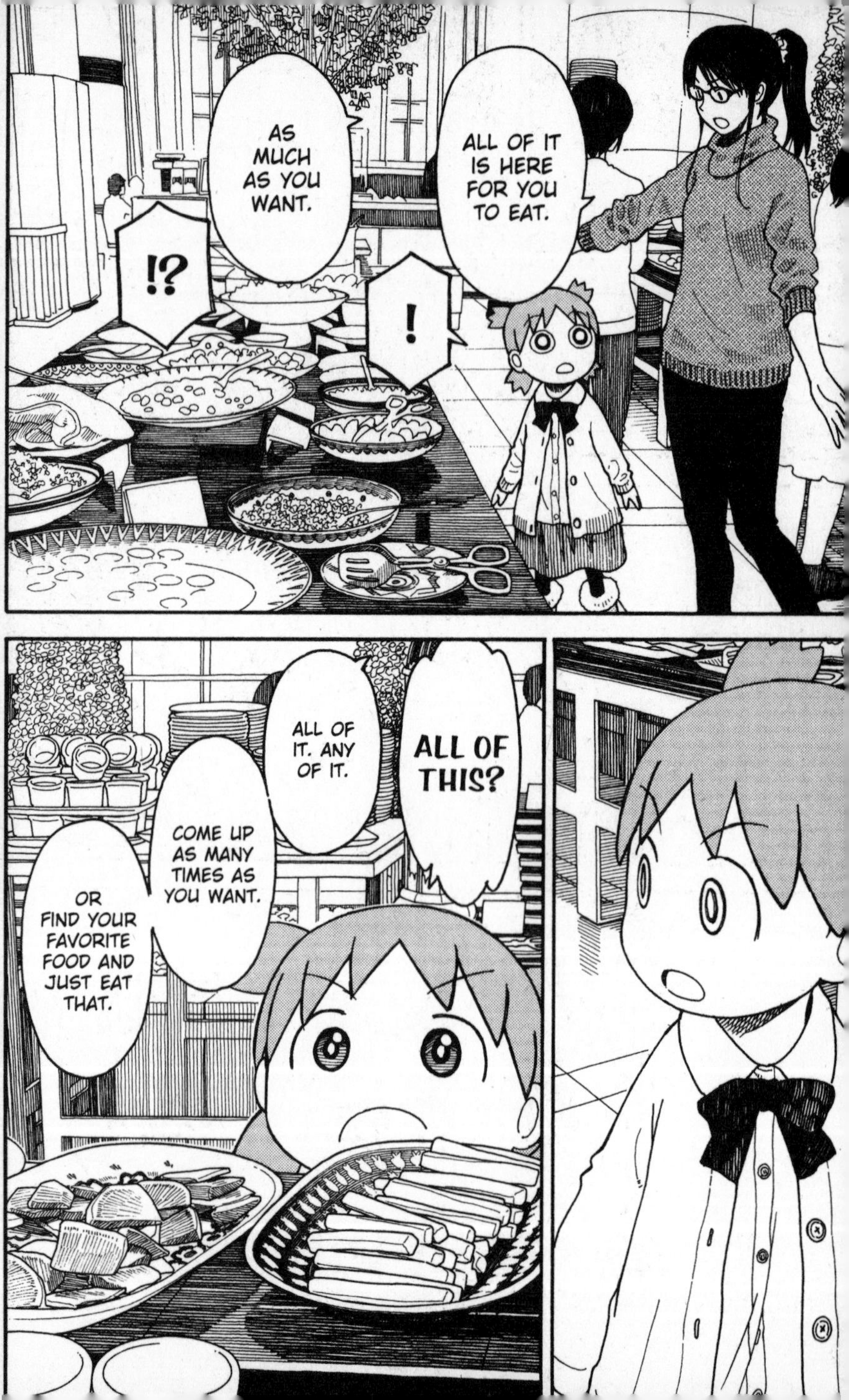
ALL OF IT IS HERE FOR YOU TO EAT.
AS MUCH AS YOU WANT.
!
!?
ALL OF THIS?
ALL OF IT. ANY OF IT.
COME UP AS MANY TIMES AS YOU WANT.
OR FIND YOUR FAVORITE FOOD AND JUST EAT THAT.

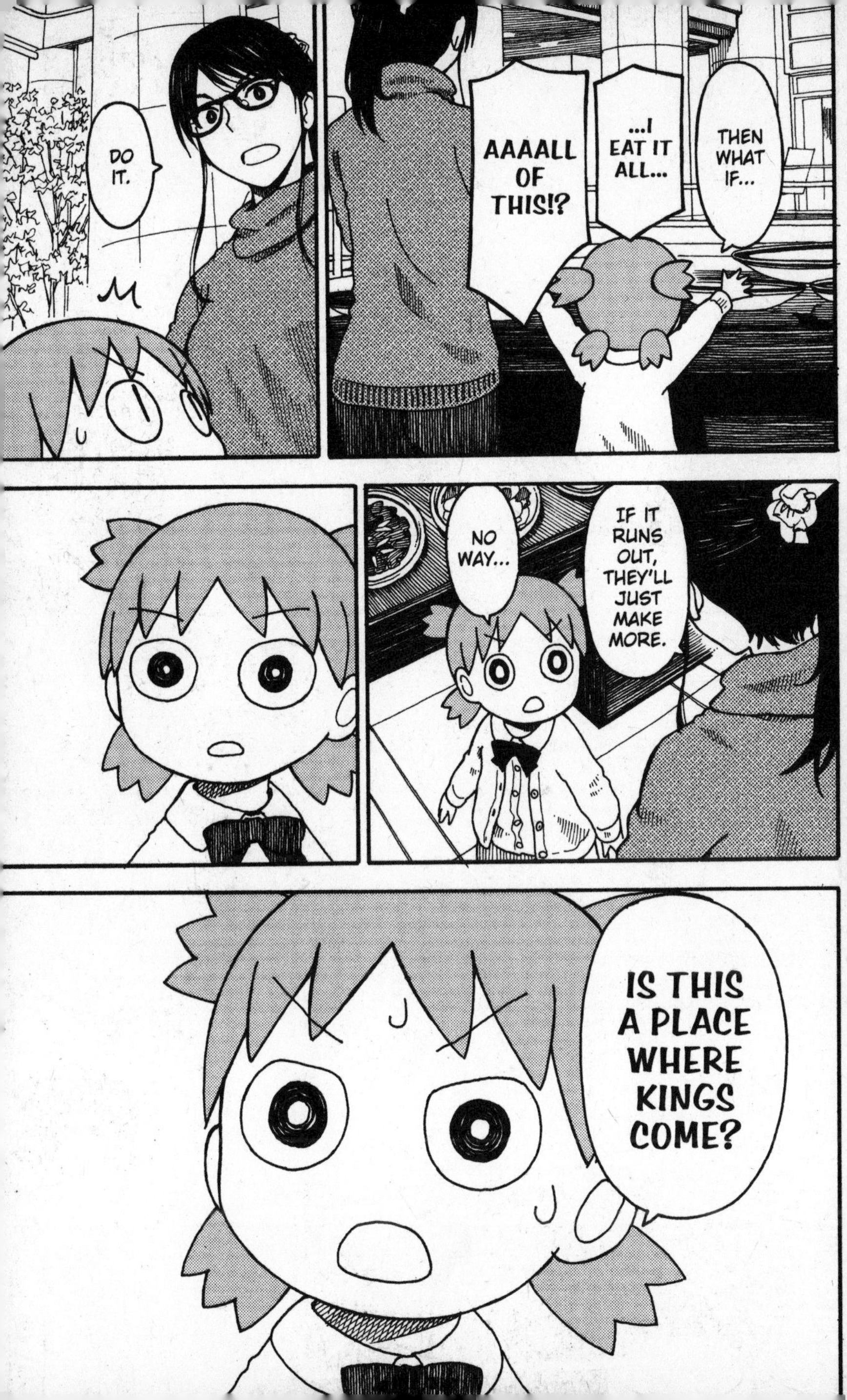
THEN WHAT IF...
...I EAT IT ALL...
AAAALL OF THIS!?
DO IT.
IF IT RUNS OUT, THEY'LL JUST MAKE MORE.
NO WAY...
IS THIS A PLACE WHERE KINGS COME?

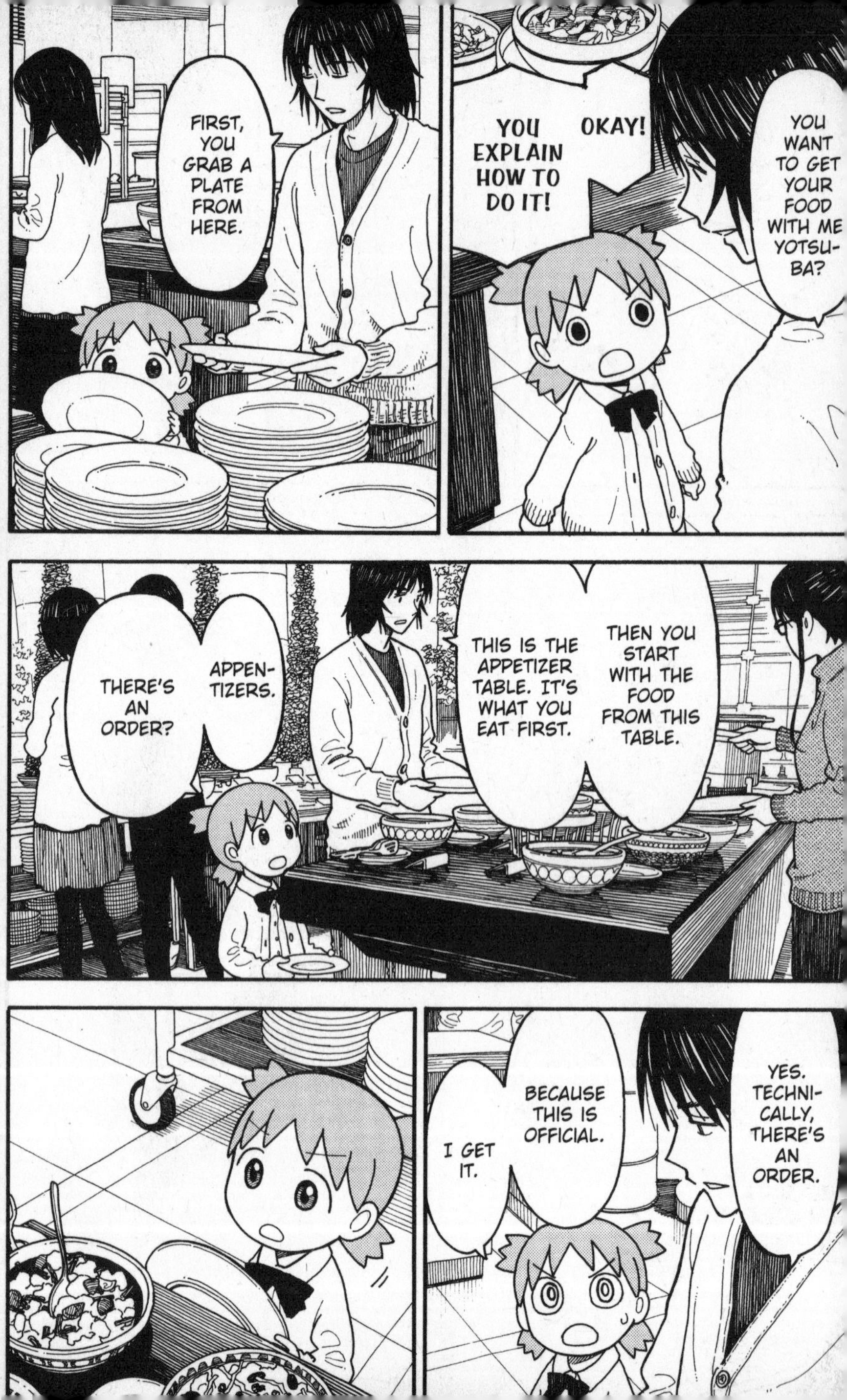
YOU WANT TO GET YOUR FOOD WITH ME YOTSUBA?
OKAY!
YOU EXPLAIN HOW TO DO IT!
FIRST, YOU GRAB A PLATE FROM HERE.
THEN YOU START WITH THE FOOD FROM THIS TABLE.
THIS IS THE APPETIZER TABLE. IT'S WHAT YOU EAT FIRST.
APPEN-TIZERS.
THERE'S AN ORDER?
YES. TECHNI-CALLY, THERE'S AN ORDER.
BECAUSE THIS IS OFFICIAL.
I GET IT.

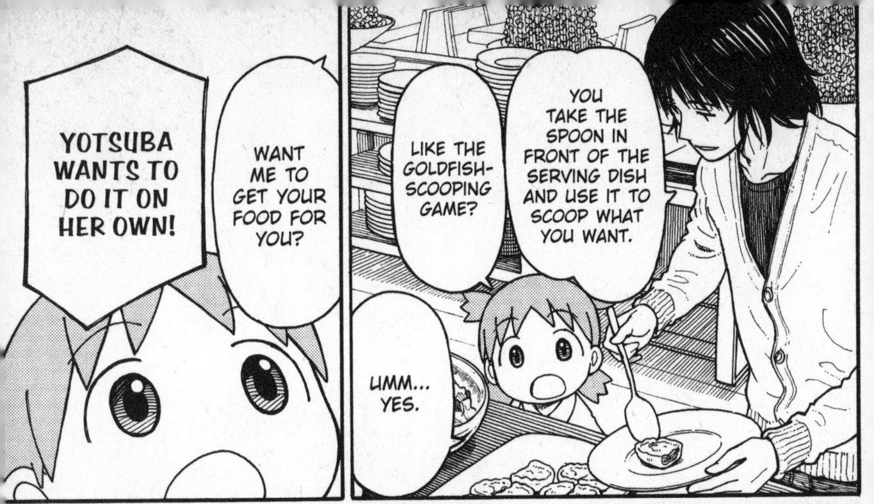
YOU TAKE THE SPOON IN FRONT OF THE SERVING DISH AND USE IT TO SCOOP WHAT YOU WANT.
LIKE THE GOLDFISH-SCOOPING GAME?
UMM... YES.
WANT ME TO GET YOUR FOOD FOR YOU?
YOTSUBA WANTS TO DO IT ON HER OWN!

NOTE: GOLDFISH SCOOPING IS A POPULAR FESTIVAL GAME WHERE PLAYERS ATTEMPT TO SCOOP FISH FROM A BASIN USING FRAGILE PAPER NETS.

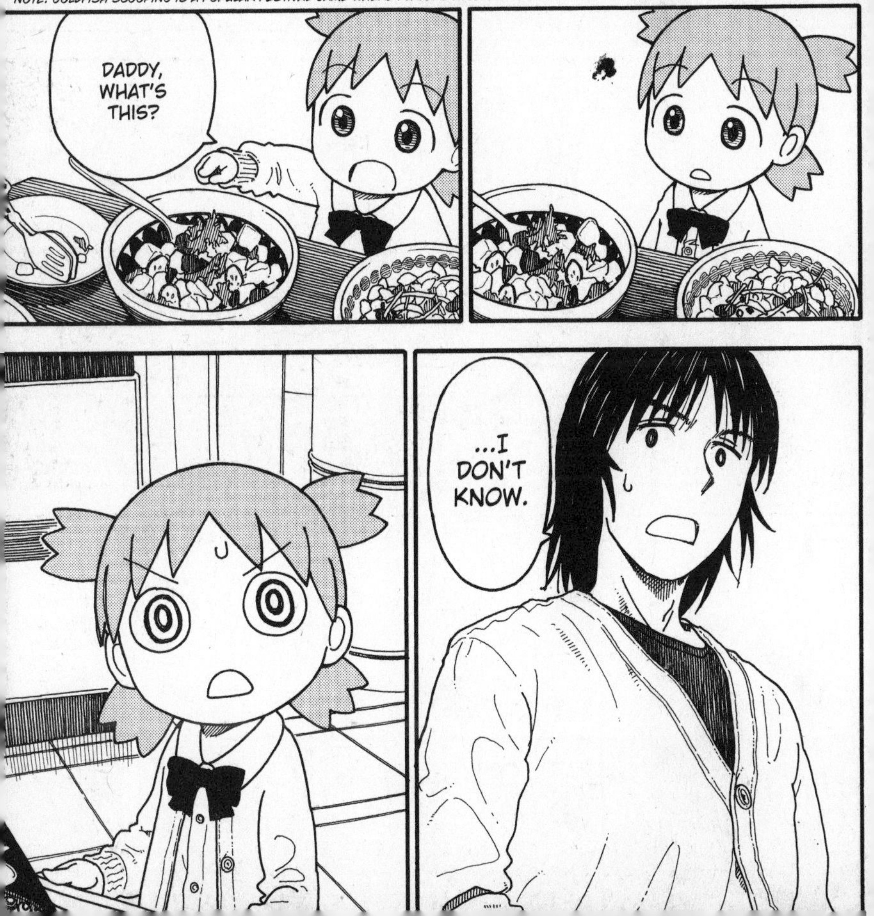
DADDY, WHAT'S THIS?
...I DON'T KNOW.

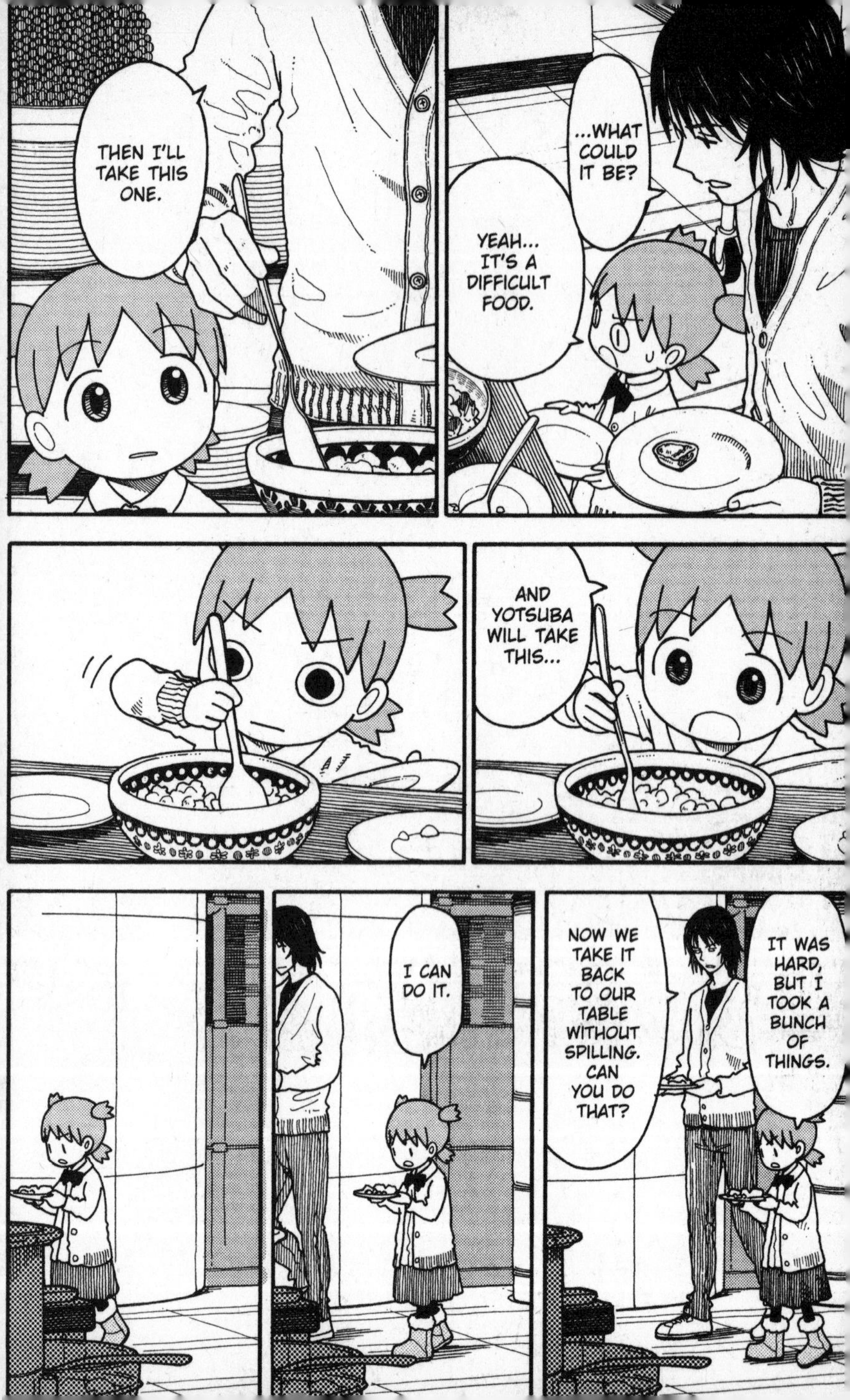
...WHAT COULD IT BE?
YEAH... IT'S A DIFFICULT FOOD.
THEN I'LL TAKE THIS ONE.
AND YOTSUBA WILL TAKE THIS...
IT WAS HARD, BUT I TOOK A BUNCH OF THINGS.
NOW WE TAKE IT BACK TO OUR TABLE WITHOUT SPILLING. CAN YOU DO THAT?
I CAN DO IT.

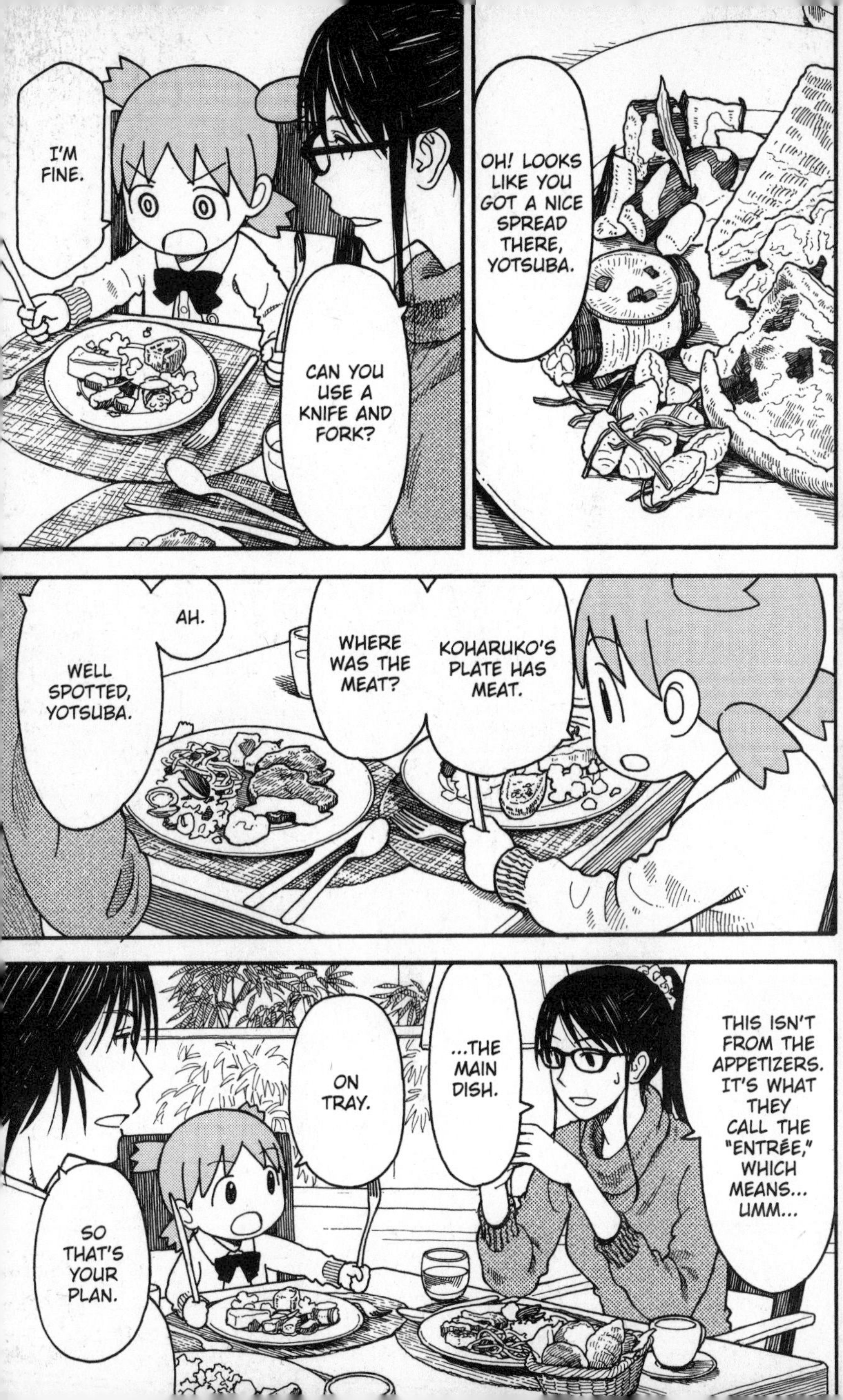
OH! LOOKS LIKE YOU GOT A NICE SPREAD THERE, YOTSUBA.
CAN YOU USE A KNIFE AND FORK?
I'M FINE.
KOHARUKO'S PLATE HAS MEAT.
WHERE WAS THE MEAT?
AH.
WELL SPOTTED, YOTSUBA.
THIS ISN'T FROM THE APPETIZERS. IT'S WHAT THEY CALL THE "ENTRÉE," WHICH MEANS... UMM...
...THE MAIN DISH.
ON TRAY.
SO THAT'S YOUR PLAN.

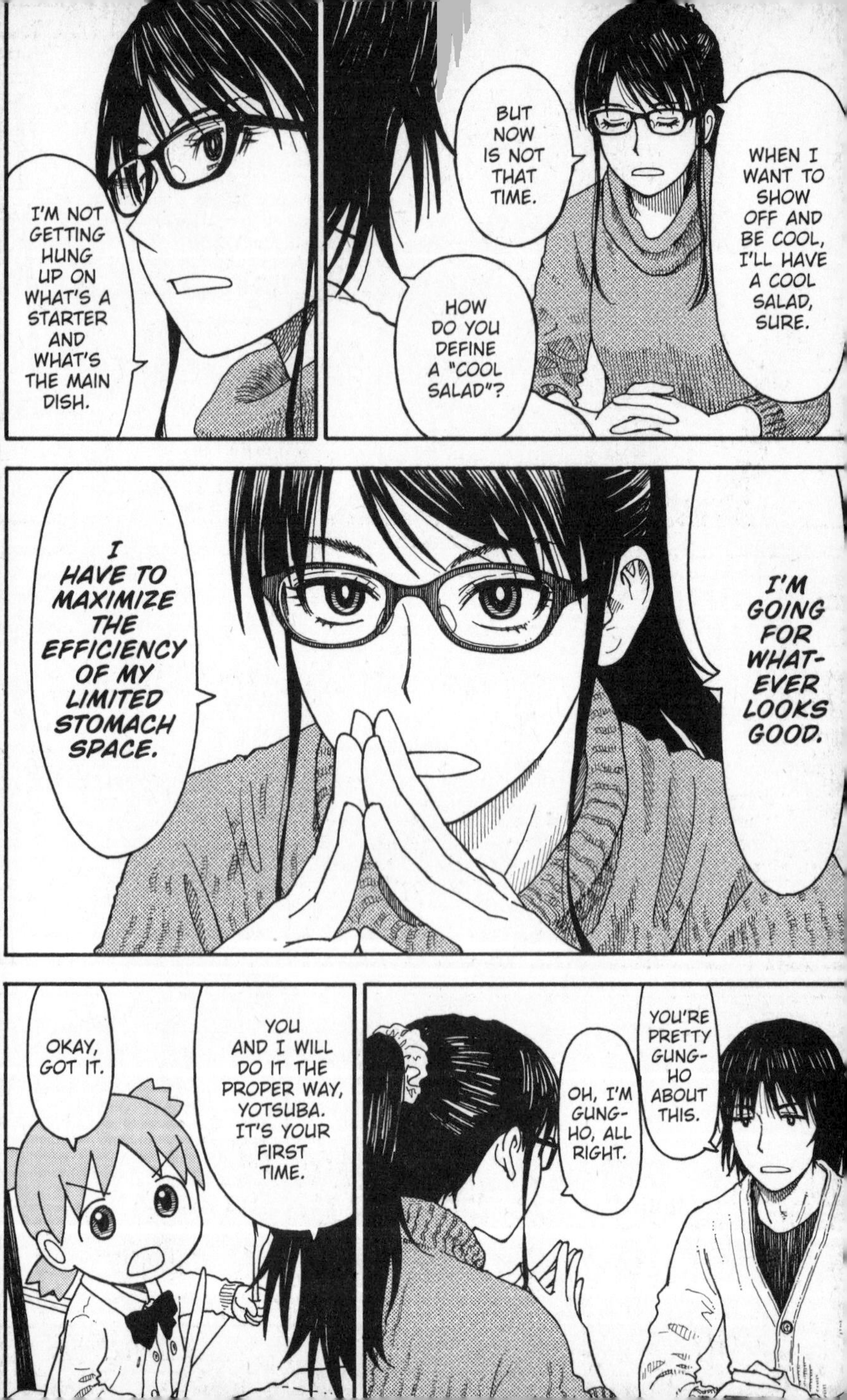
WHEN I WANT TO SHOW OFF AND BE COOL, I'LL HAVE A COOL SALAD, SURE.
BUT NOW IS NOT THAT TIME.
HOW DO YOU DEFINE A "COOL SALAD"?
I'M NOT GETTING HUNG UP ON WHAT'S A STARTER AND WHAT'S THE MAIN DISH.
I'M GOING FOR WHAT-EVER LOOKS GOOD.
I HAVE TO MAXIMIZE THE EFFICIENCY OF MY LIMITED STOMACH SPACE.
YOU'RE PRETTY GUNG-HO ABOUT THIS.
OH, I'M GUNG-HO, ALL RIGHT.
YOU AND I WILL DO IT THE PROPER WAY, YOTSUBA. IT'S YOUR FIRST TIME.
OKAY, GOT IT.

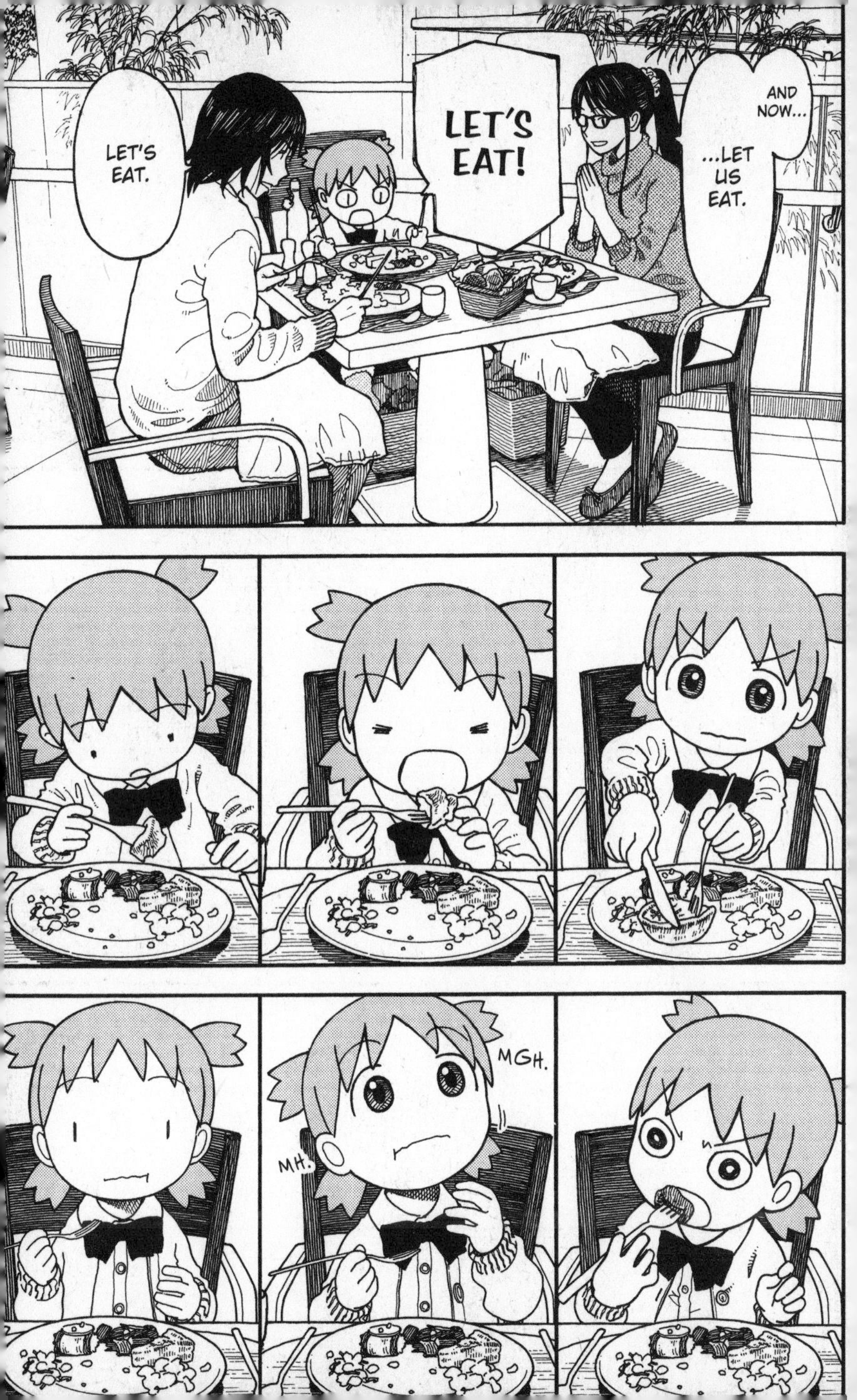
AND NOW... ...LET US EAT.
LET'S EAT!
LET'S EAT.
MGH.
MH.

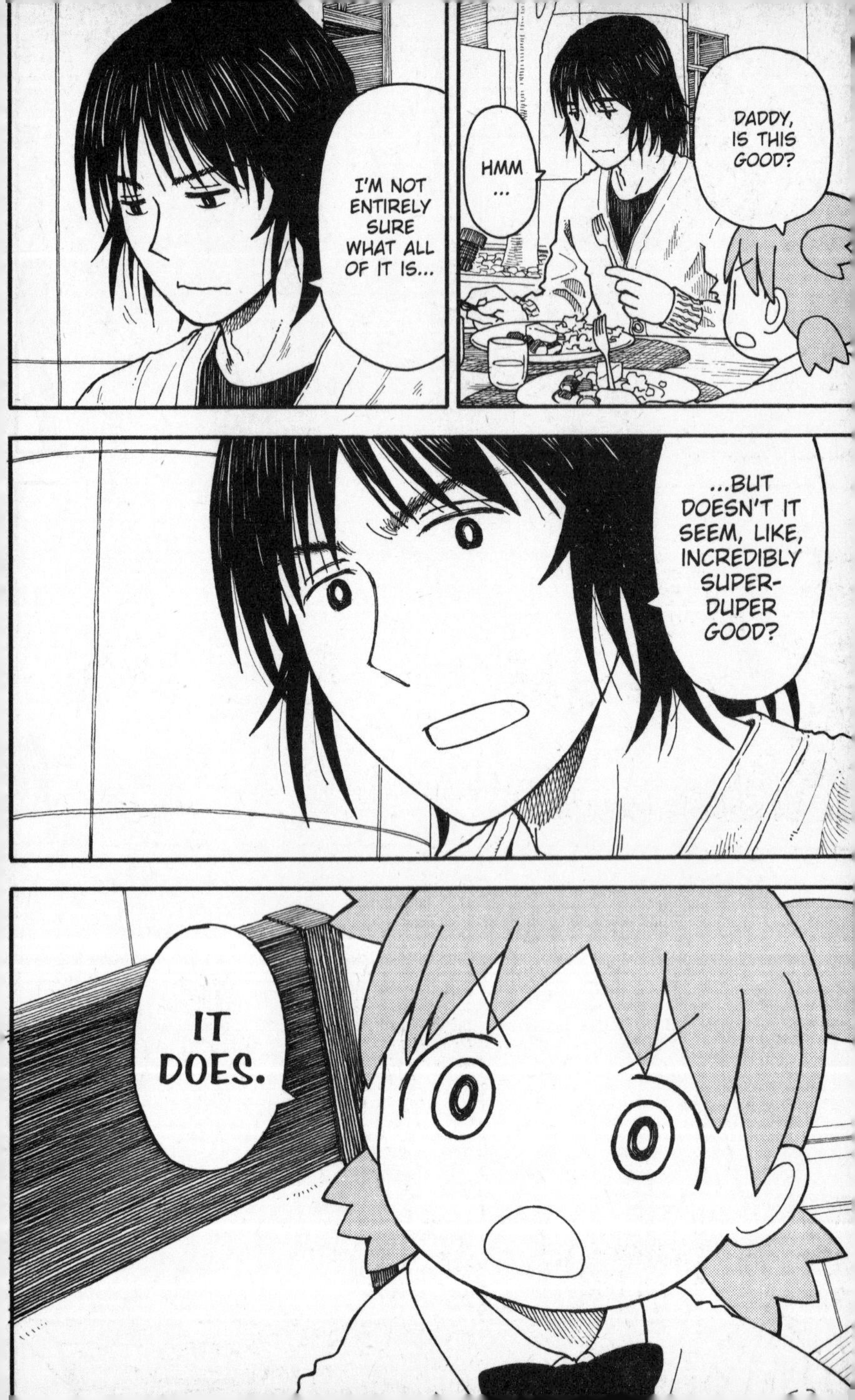
DADDY, IS THIS GOOD?
HMM ...
I'M NOT ENTIRELY SURE WHAT ALL OF IT IS...
...BUT DOESN'T IT SEEM, LIKE, INCREDIBLY SUPER-DUPER GOOD?
IT DOES.

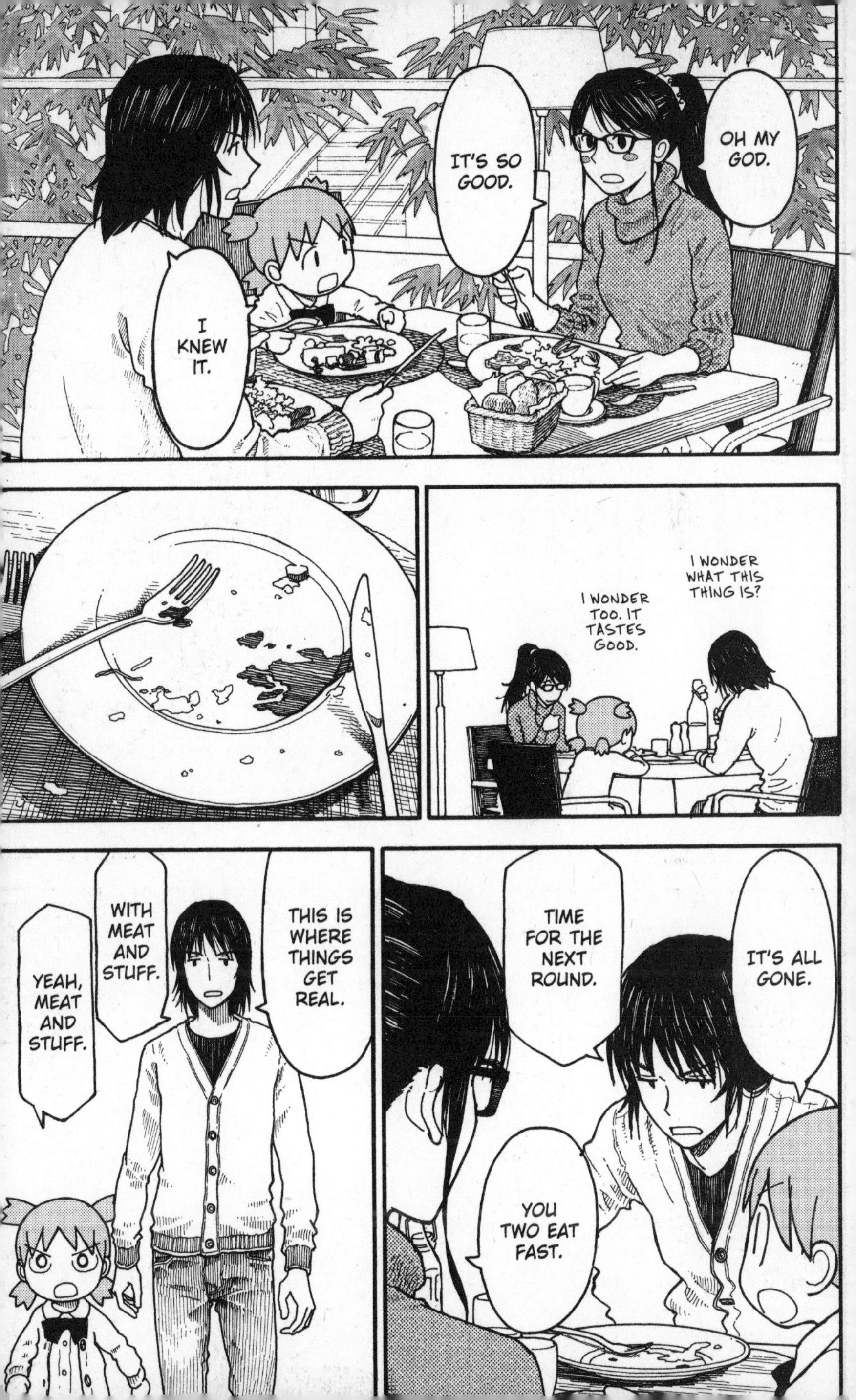
OH MY GOD.
IT'S SO GOOD.
I KNEW IT.
I WONDER WHAT THIS THING IS?
I WONDER TOO. IT TASTES GOOD.
IT'S ALL GONE.
TIME FOR THE NEXT ROUND.
YOU TWO EAT FAST.
THIS IS WHERE THINGS GET REAL.
WITH MEAT AND STUFF.
YEAH, MEAT AND STUFF.

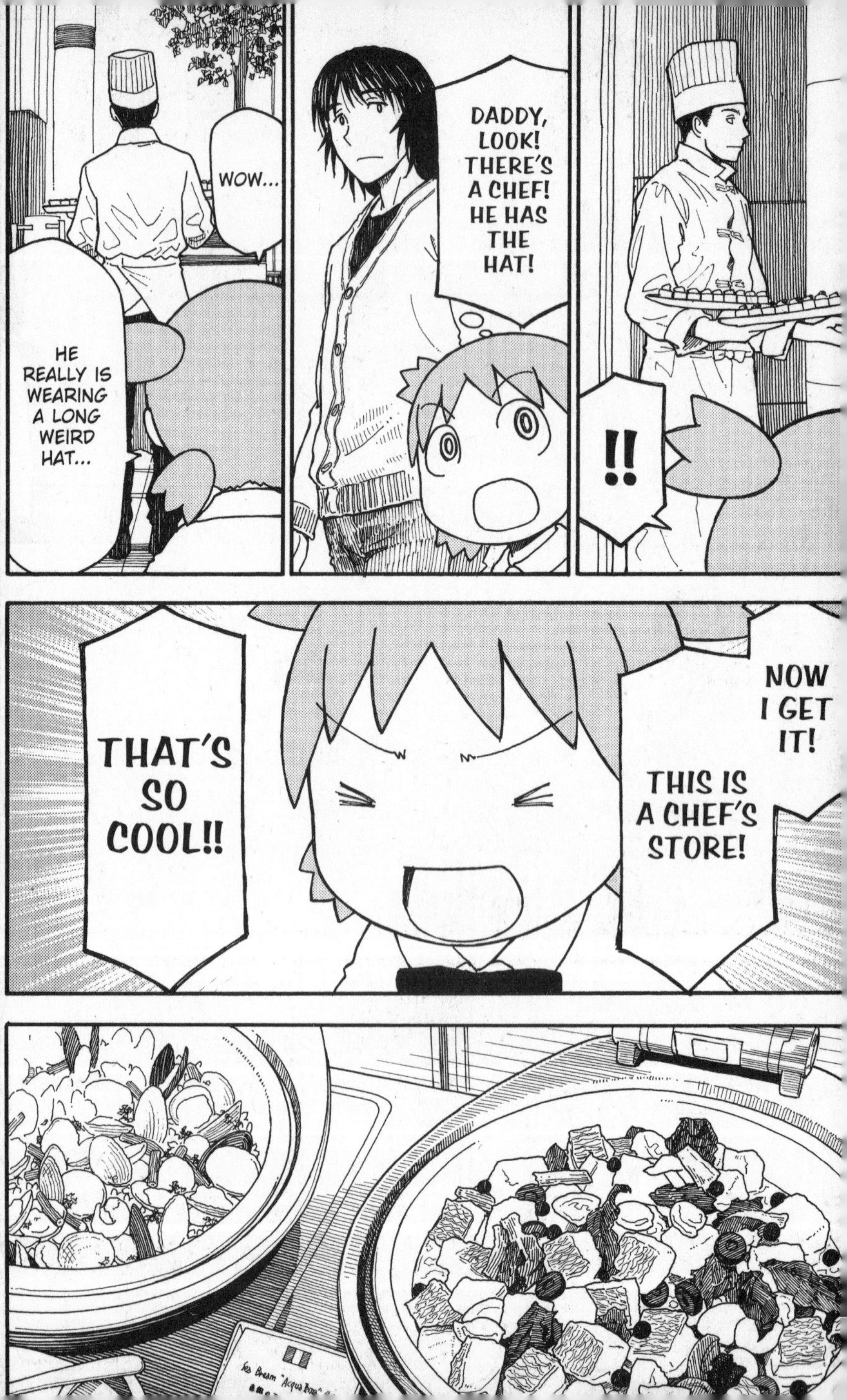
!!
DADDY, LOOK! THERE'S A CHEF! HE HAS THE HAT!
WOW...
HE REALLY IS WEARING A LONG WEIRD HAT...
NOW I GET IT!
THIS IS A CHEF'S STORE!
THAT'S SO COOL!!

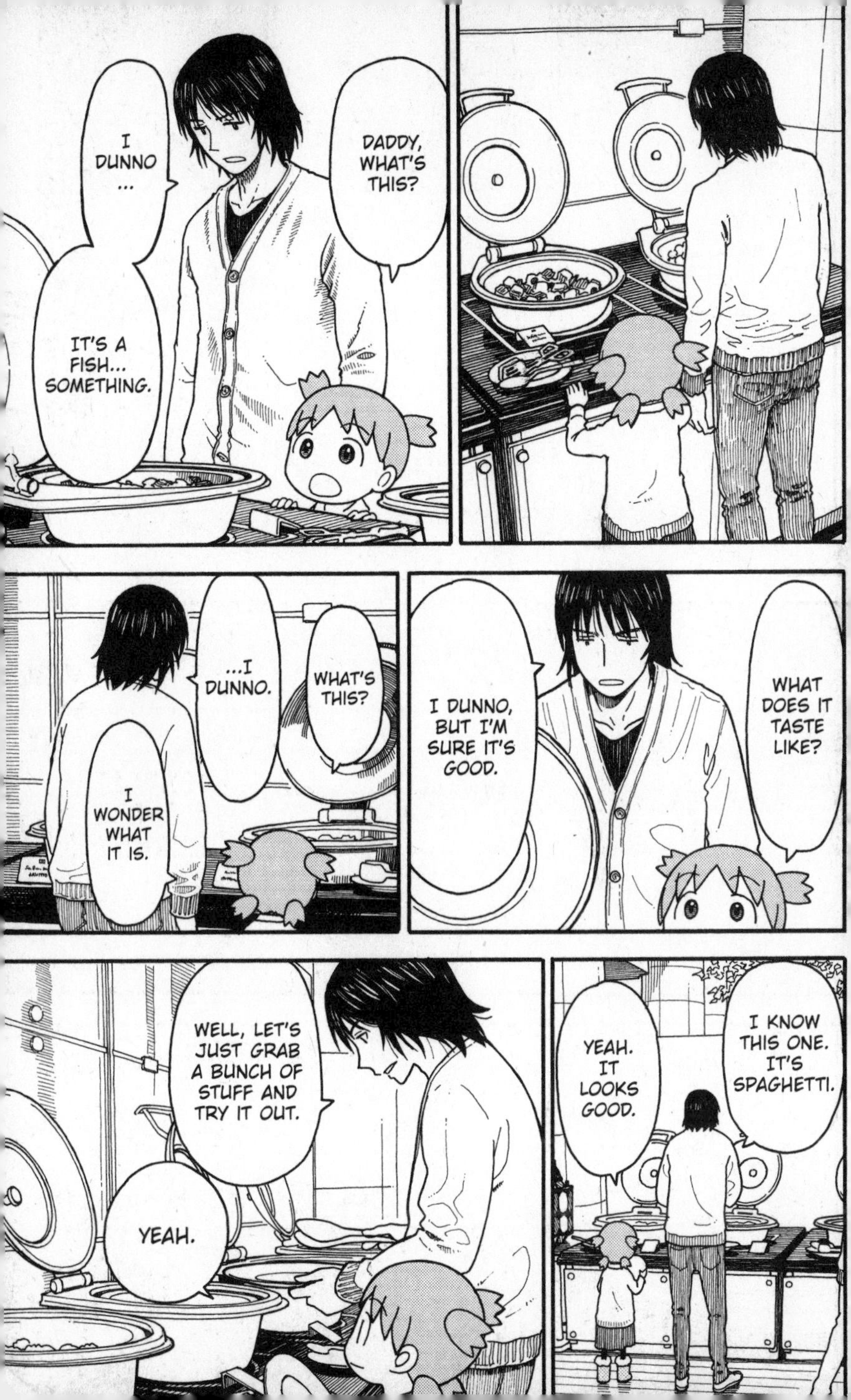
DADDY, WHAT'S THIS?
I DUNNO ...
IT'S A FISH... SOMETHING.
WHAT DOES IT TASTE LIKE?
I DUNNO, BUT I'M SURE IT'S GOOD.
WHAT'S THIS?
...I DUNNO.
I WONDER WHAT IT IS.
I KNOW THIS ONE. IT'S SPAGHETTI.
YEAH. IT LOOKS GOOD.
WELL, LET'S JUST GRAB A BUNCH OF STUFF AND TRY IT OUT.
YEAH.

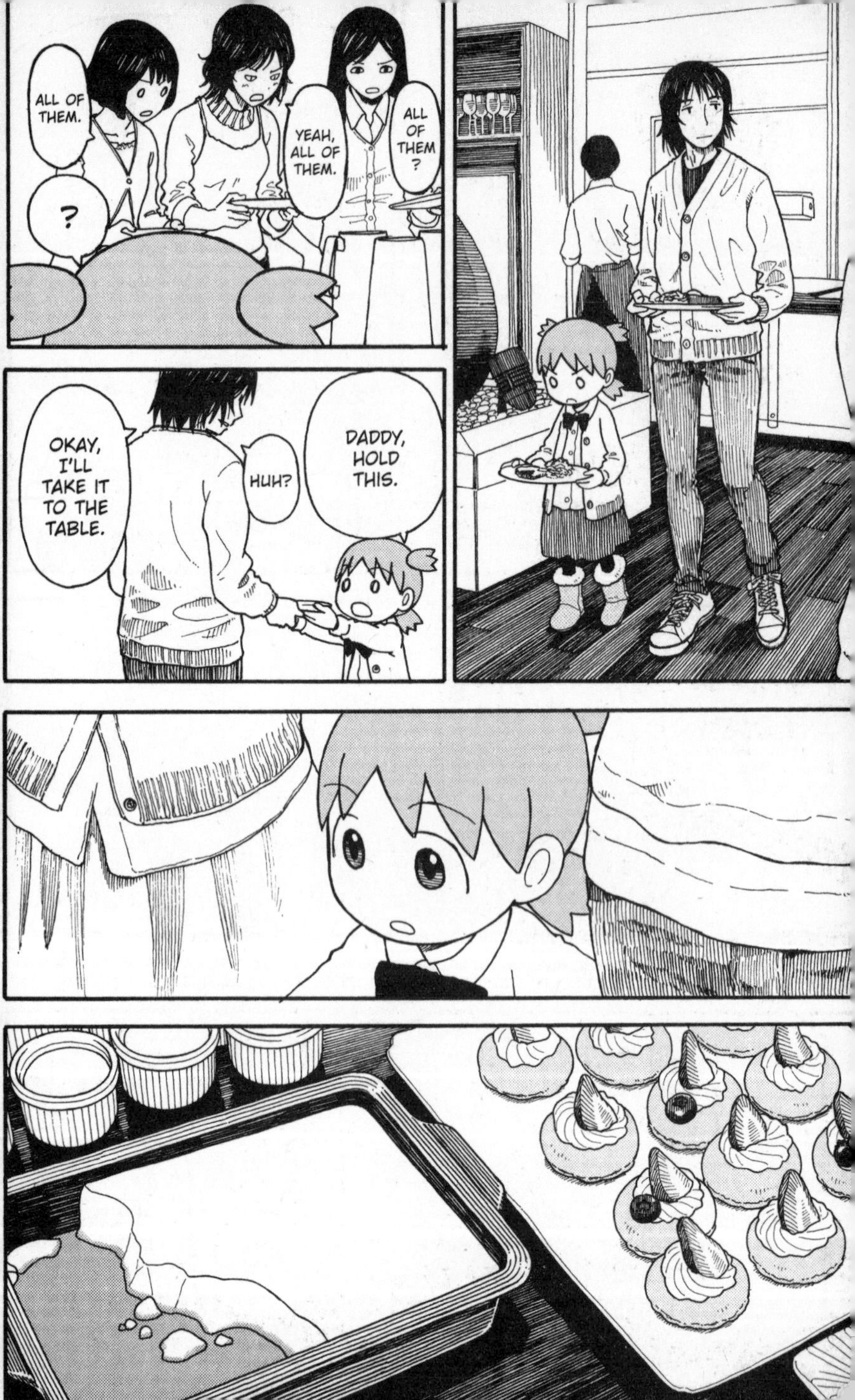
ALL OF THEM?
YEAH, ALL OF THEM.
ALL OF THEM.
?
DADDY, HOLD THIS.
HUH?
OKAY, I'LL TAKE IT TO THE TABLE.

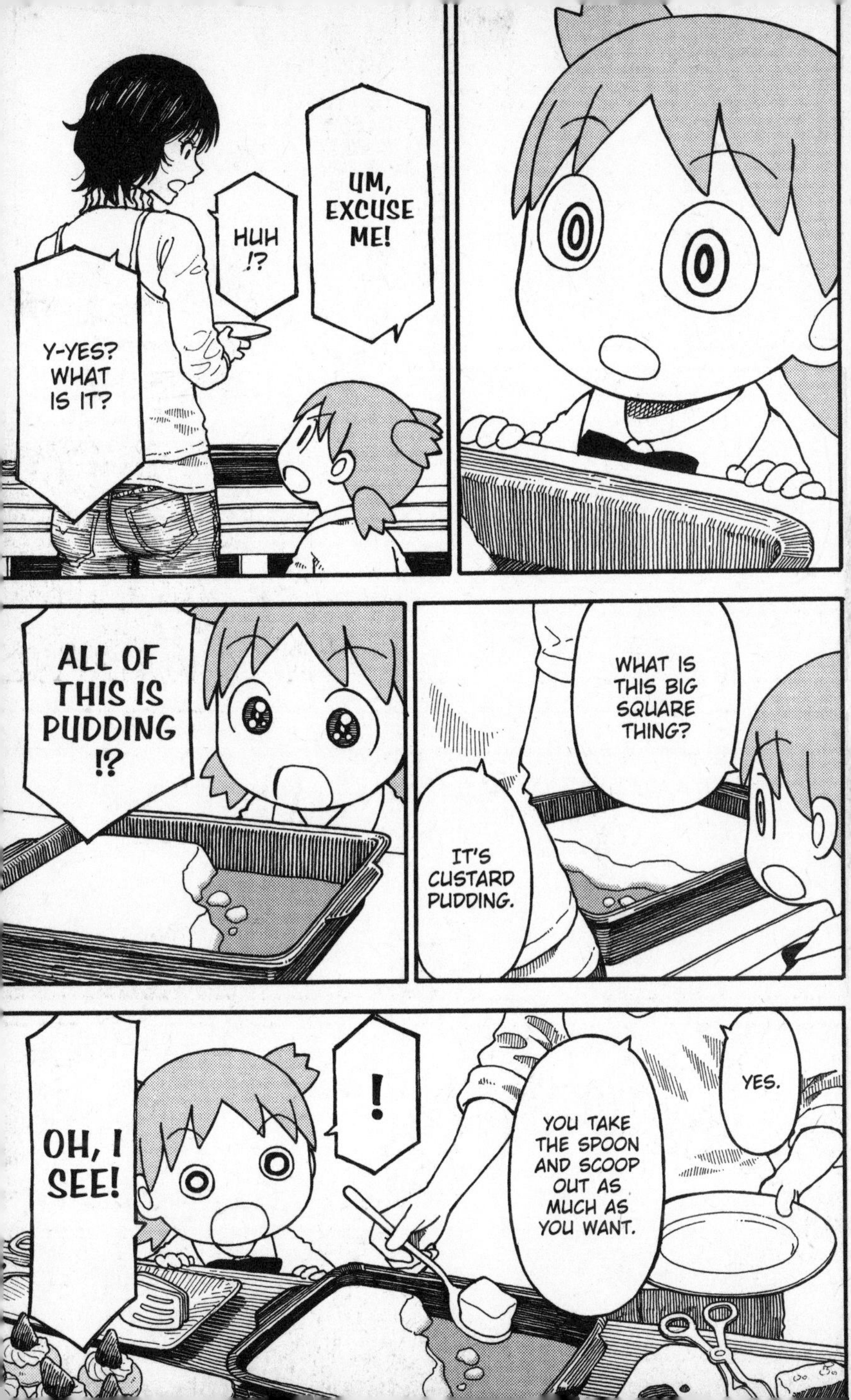
UM, EXCUSE ME!
HUH !?
Y-YES? WHAT IS IT?
WHAT IS THIS BIG SQUARE THING?
IT'S CUSTARD PUDDING.
ALL OF THIS IS PUDDING !?
YES.
YOU TAKE THE SPOON AND SCOOP OUT AS MUCH AS YOU WANT.
!
OH, I SEE!

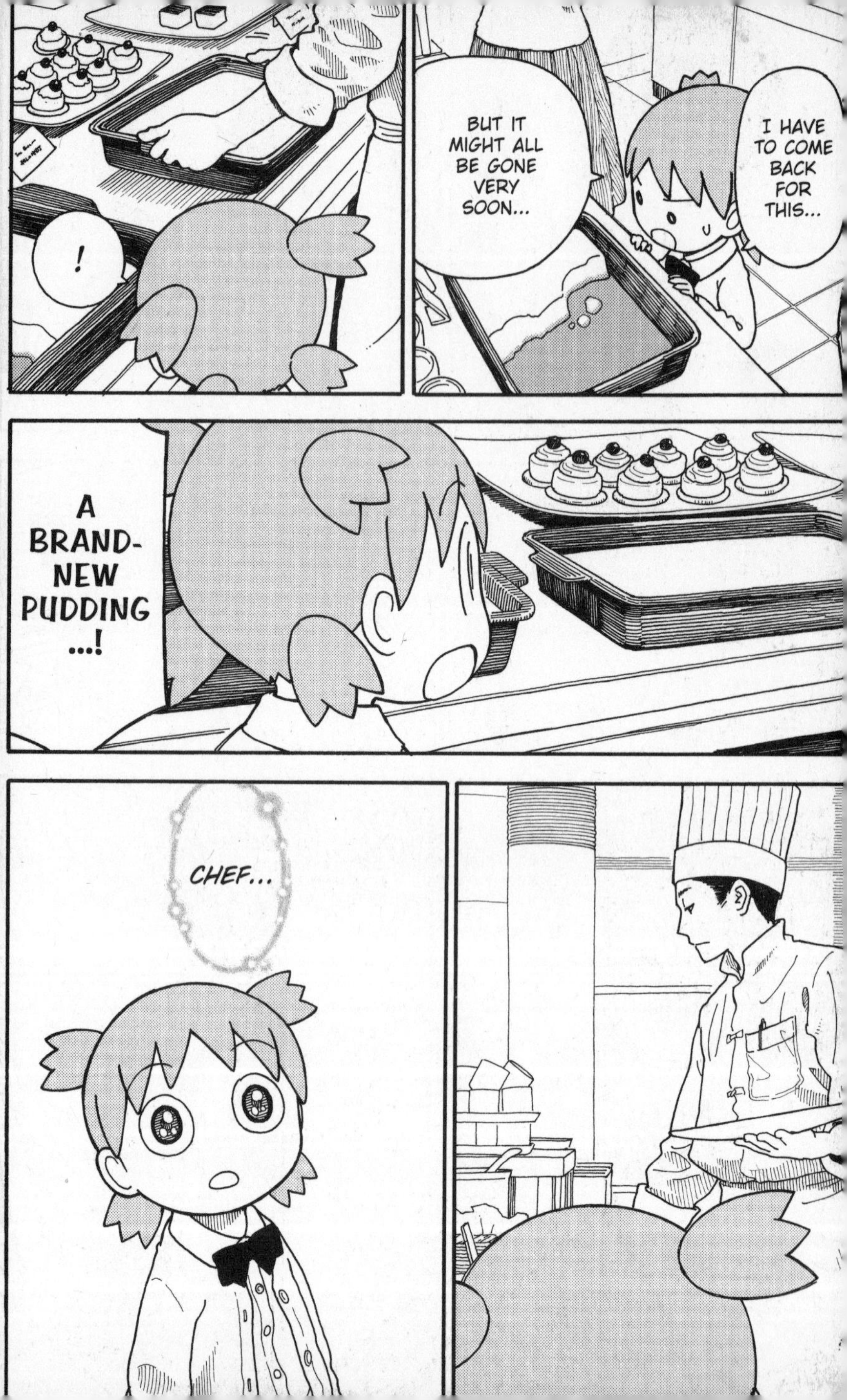
I HAVE TO COME BACK FOR THIS...
BUT IT MIGHT ALL BE GONE VERY SOON...
!
A BRAND-NEW PUDDING ...!
CHEF...

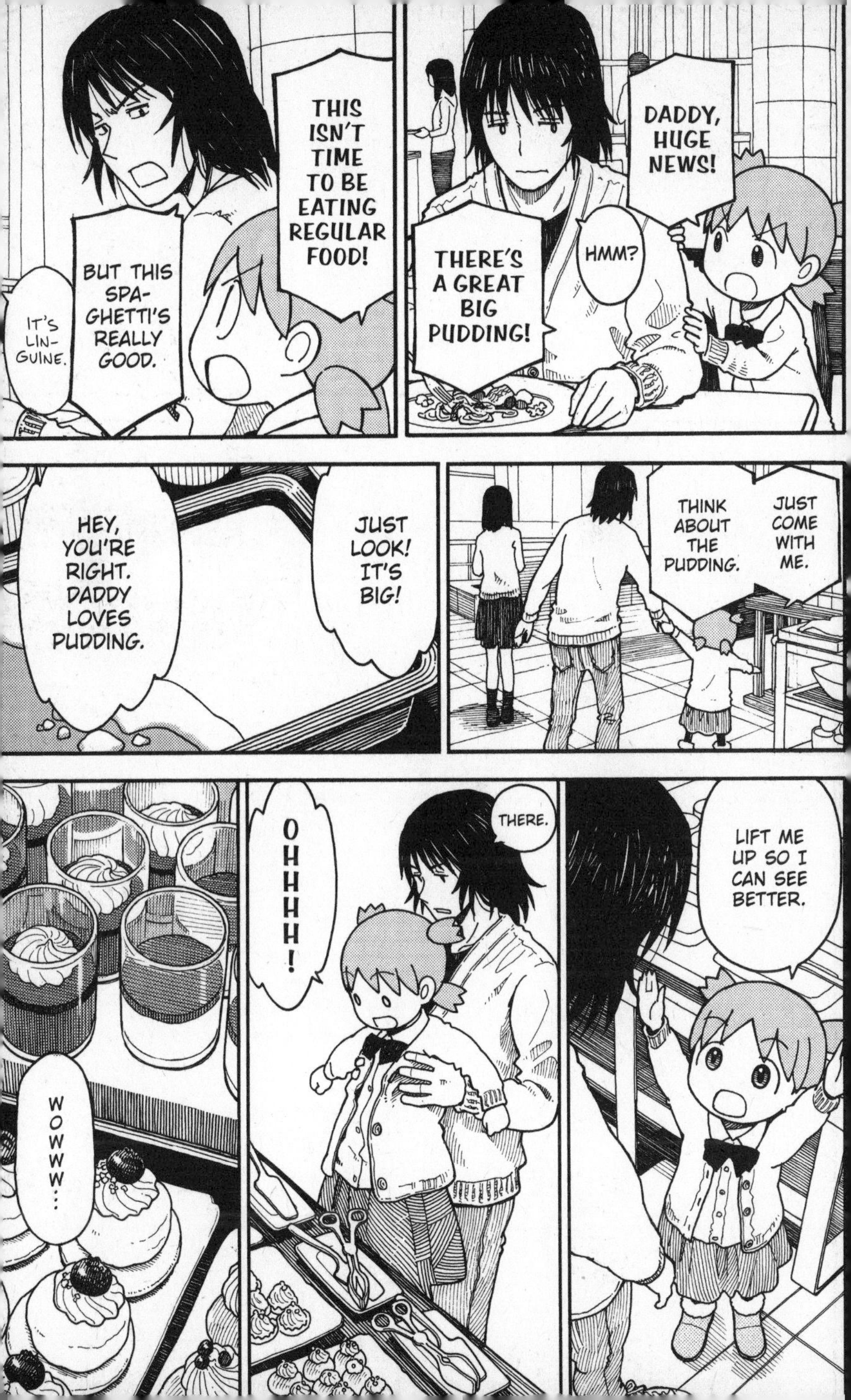
DADDY, HUGE NEWS!
HMM?
THERE'S A GREAT BIG PUDDING!
THIS ISN'T TIME TO BE EATING REGULAR FOOD!
BUT THIS SPA-GHETTI'S REALLY GOOD.
IT'S LIN-GUINE.
JUST COME WITH ME.
THINK ABOUT THE PUDDING.
JUST LOOK! IT'S BIG!
HEY, YOU'RE RIGHT. DADDY LOVES PUDDING.
LIFT ME UP SO I CAN SEE BETTER.
THERE.
OHHHHH!
WOWWWW...

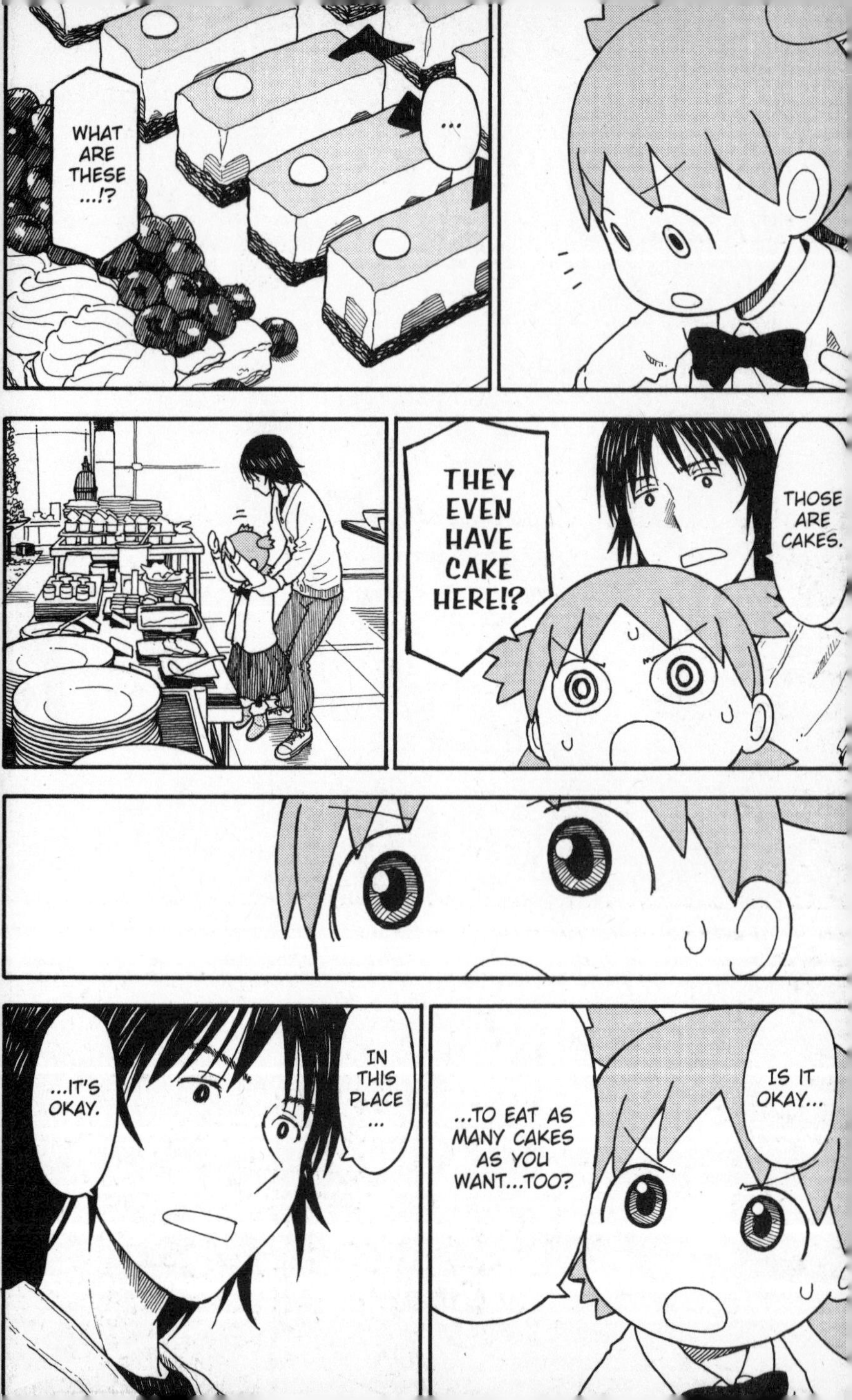
...
WHAT ARE THESE ...!?
THOSE ARE CAKES.
THEY EVEN HAVE CAKE HERE!?
IS IT OKAY...
...TO EAT AS MANY CAKES AS YOU WANT...TOO?
IN THIS PLACE ...
...IT'S OKAY.

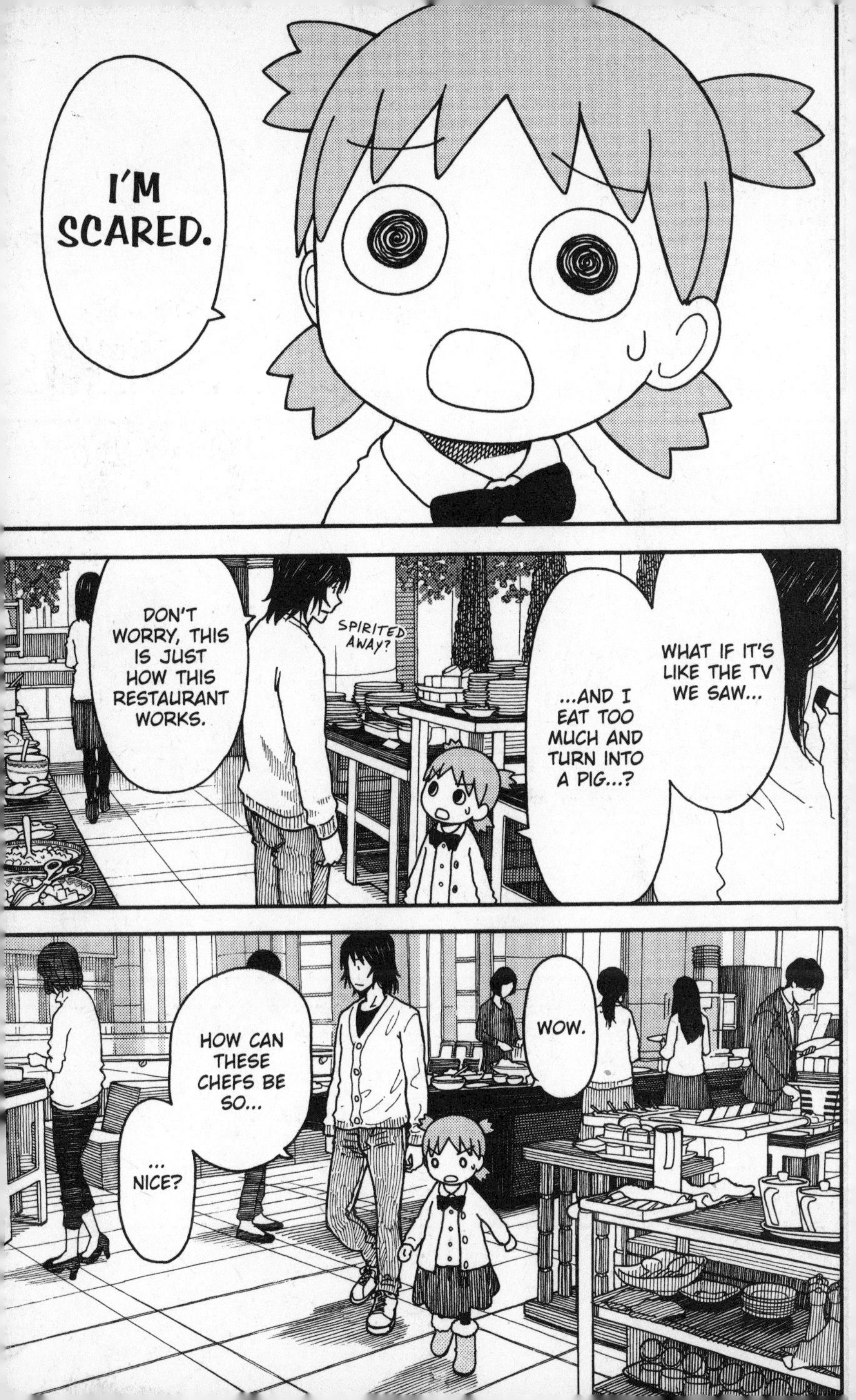
I'M SCARED.
WHAT IF IT'S LIKE THE TV WE SAW...
...AND I EAT TOO MUCH AND TURN INTO A PIG...?
SPIRITED AWAY?
DON'T WORRY, THIS IS JUST HOW THIS RESTAURANT WORKS.
WOW.
HOW CAN THESE CHEFS BE SO...
...NICE?

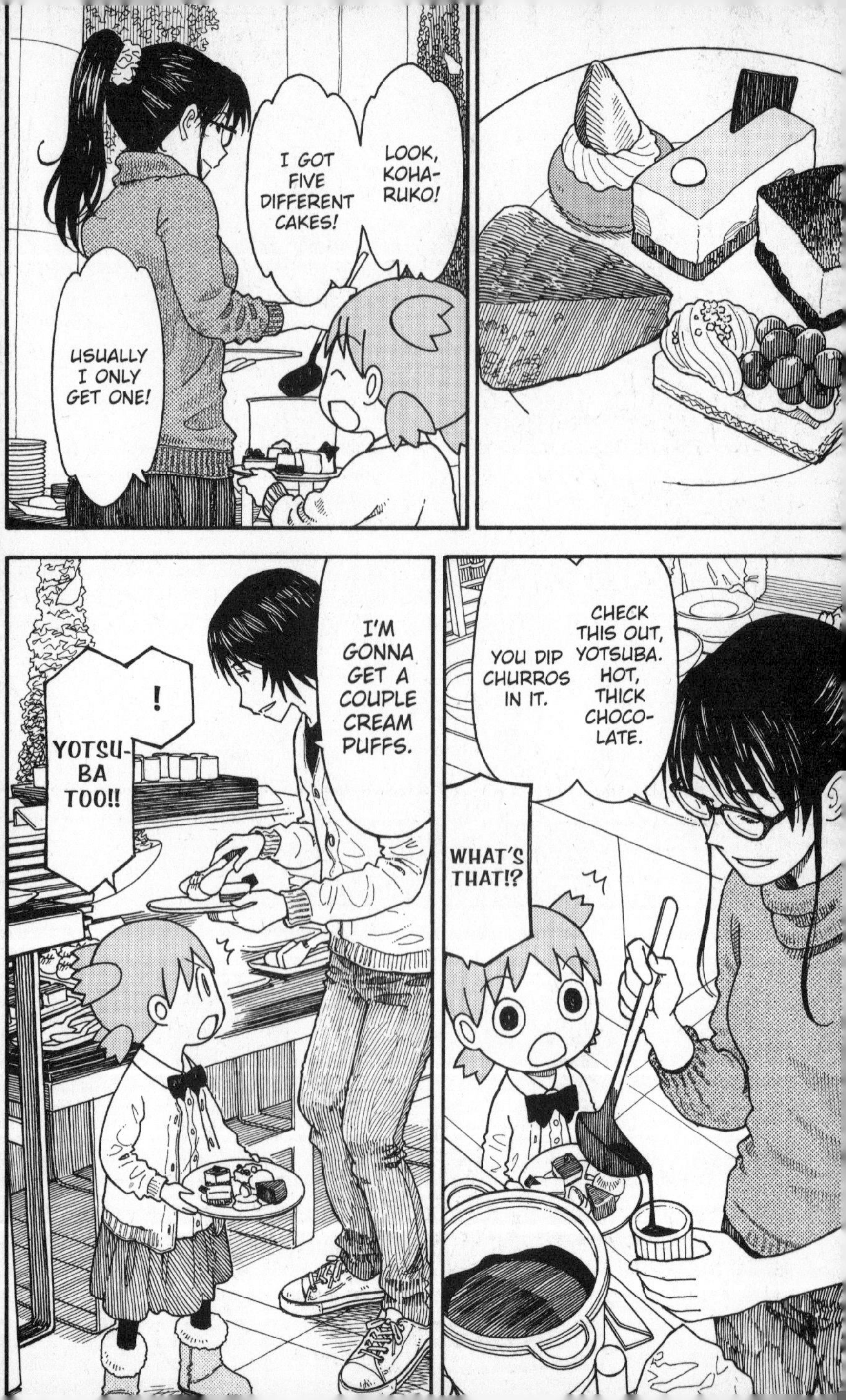
LOOK, KOHA-RUKO!
I GOT FIVE DIFFERENT CAKES!
USUALLY I ONLY GET ONE!
CHECK THIS OUT, YOTSUBA. HOT, THICK CHOCO-LATE.
YOU DIP CHURROS IN IT.
WHAT'S THAT!?
I'M GONNA GET A COUPLE CREAM PUFFS.
!
YOTSU-BA TOO!!

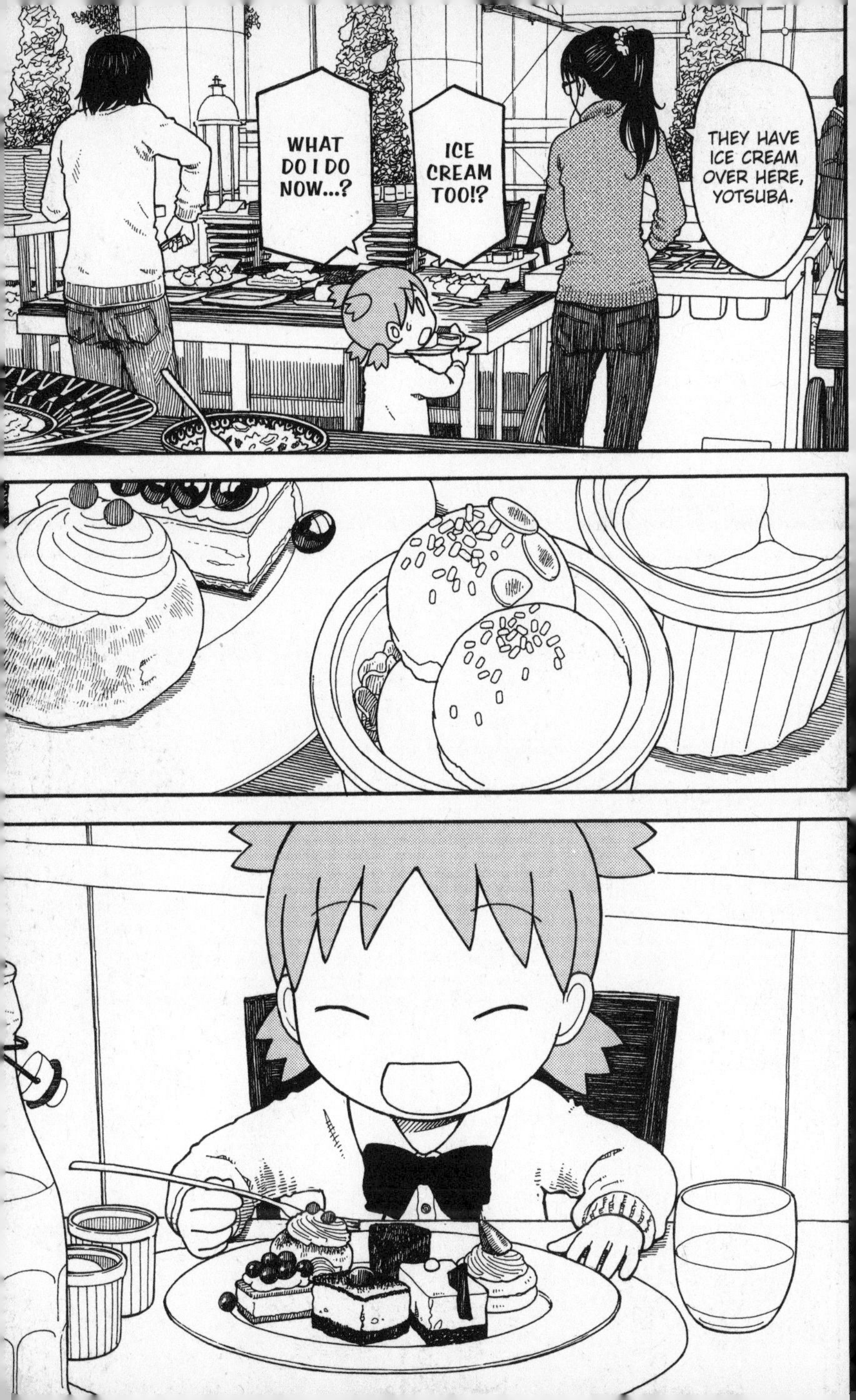
THEY HAVE ICE CREAM OVER HERE, YOTSUBA.
ICE CREAM TOO!?
WHAT DO I DO NOW...?

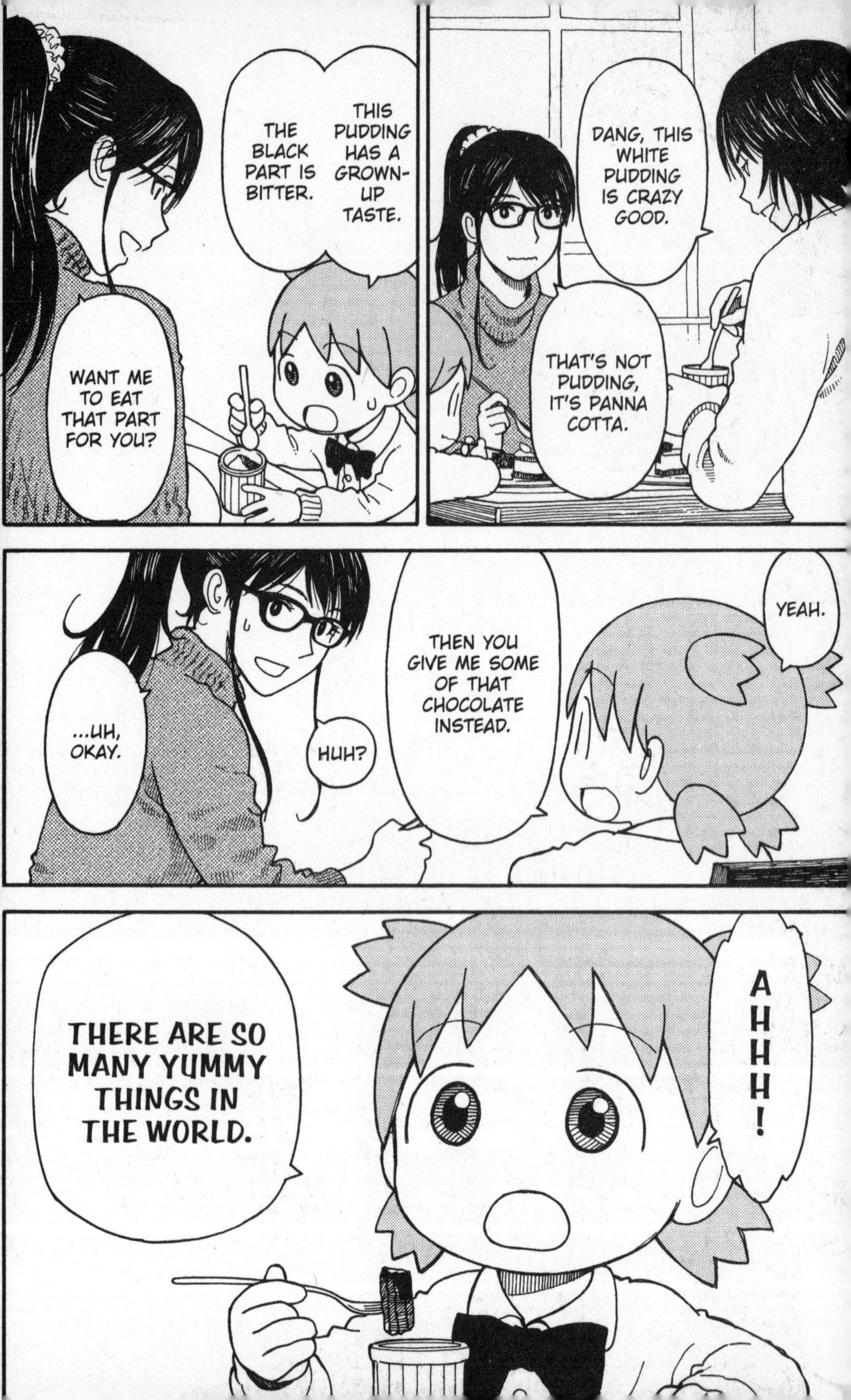
DANG, THIS WHITE PUDDING IS CRAZY GOOD.
THAT'S NOT PUDDING, IT'S PANNA COTTA.
THIS PUDDING HAS A GROWN-UP TASTE.
THE BLACK PART IS BITTER.
WANT ME TO EAT THAT PART FOR YOU?
YEAH.
THEN YOU GIVE ME SOME OF THAT CHOCOLATE INSTEAD.
HUH?
...UH, OKAY.
AHHH!
THERE ARE SO MANY YUMMY THINGS IN THE WORLD.

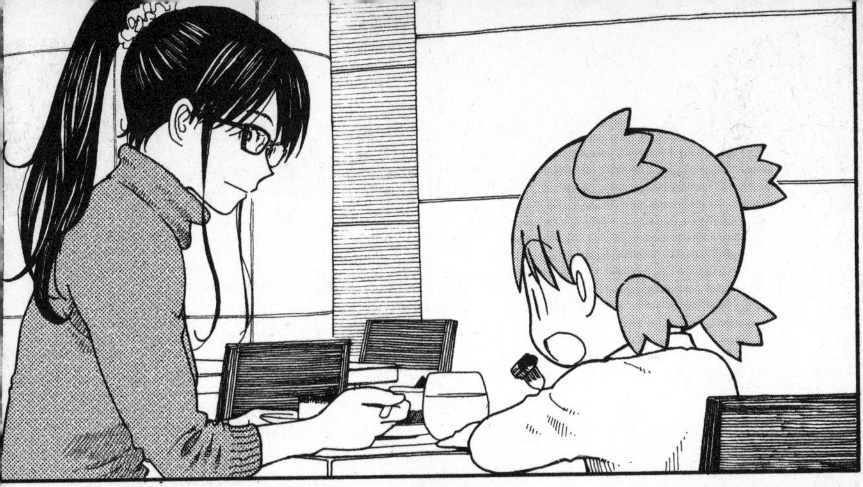

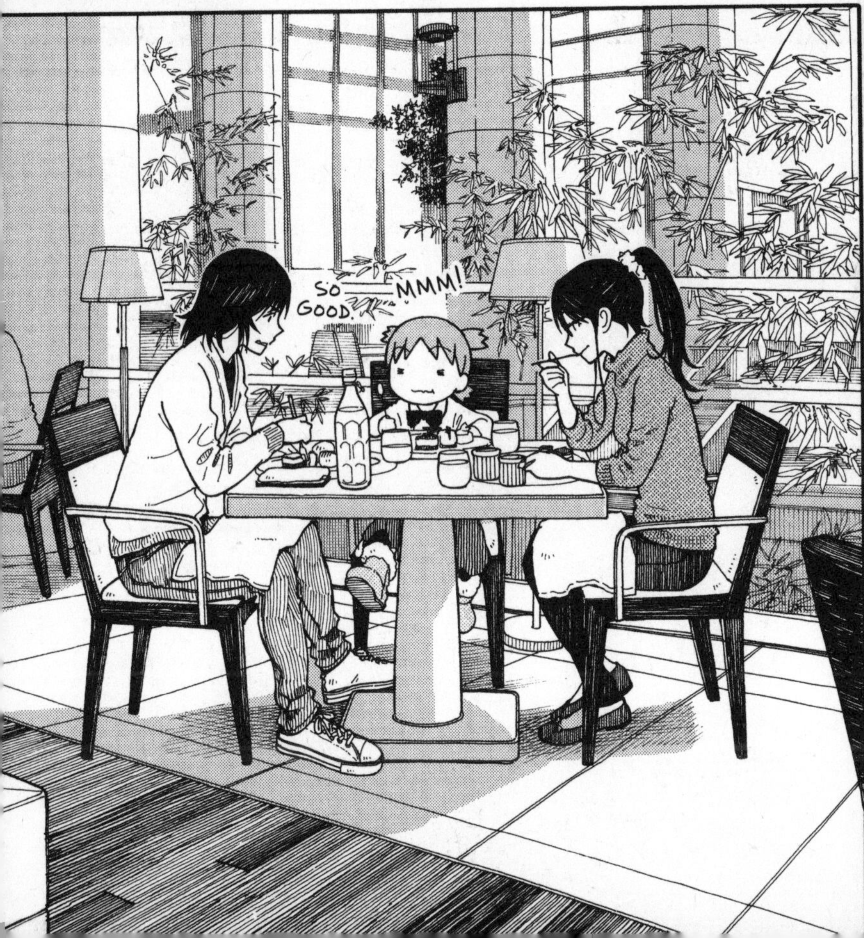
MMM!
SO GOOD.

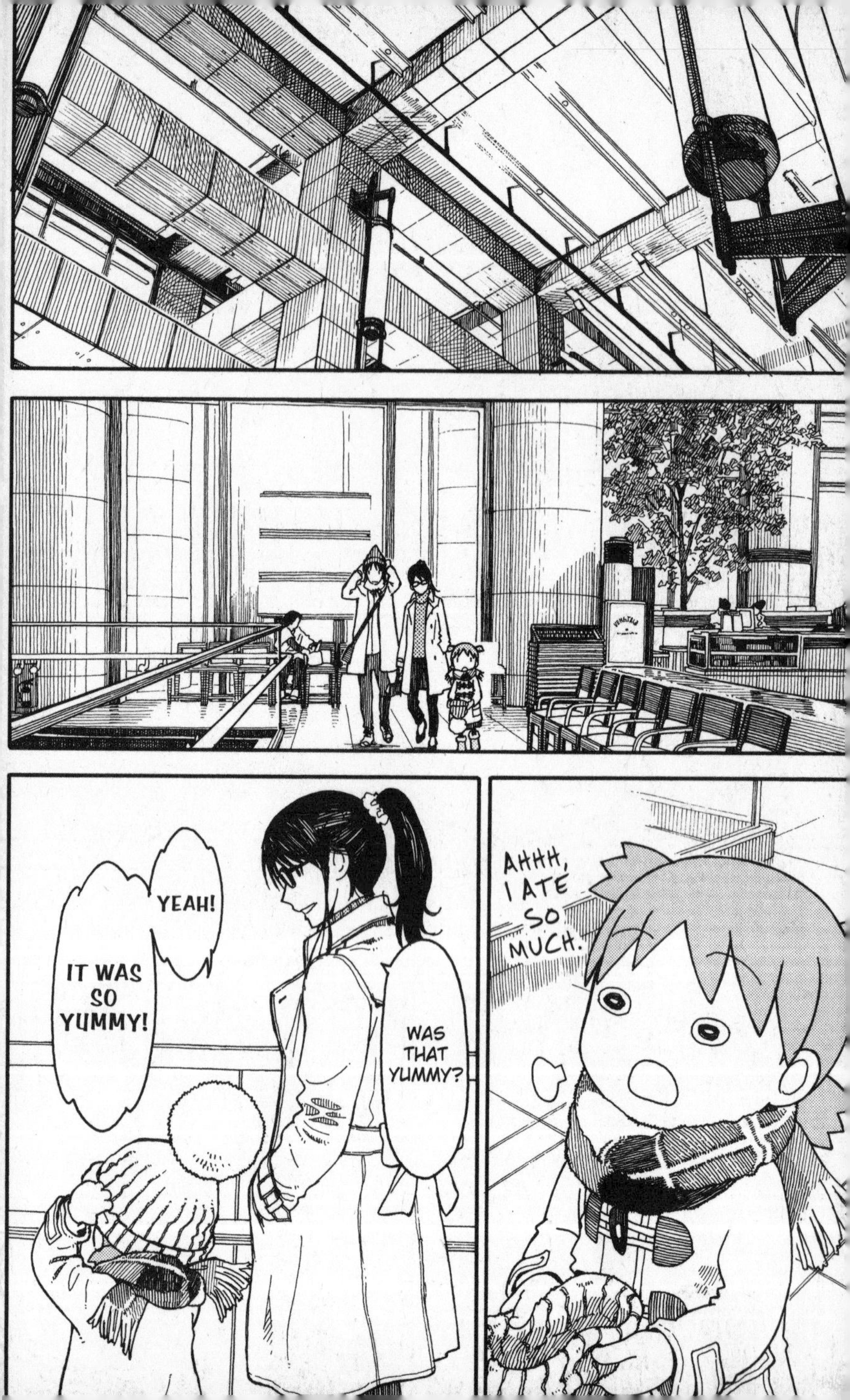
AHHH, I ATE SO MUCH.
WAS THAT YUMMY?
YEAH!
IT WAS SO YUMMY!

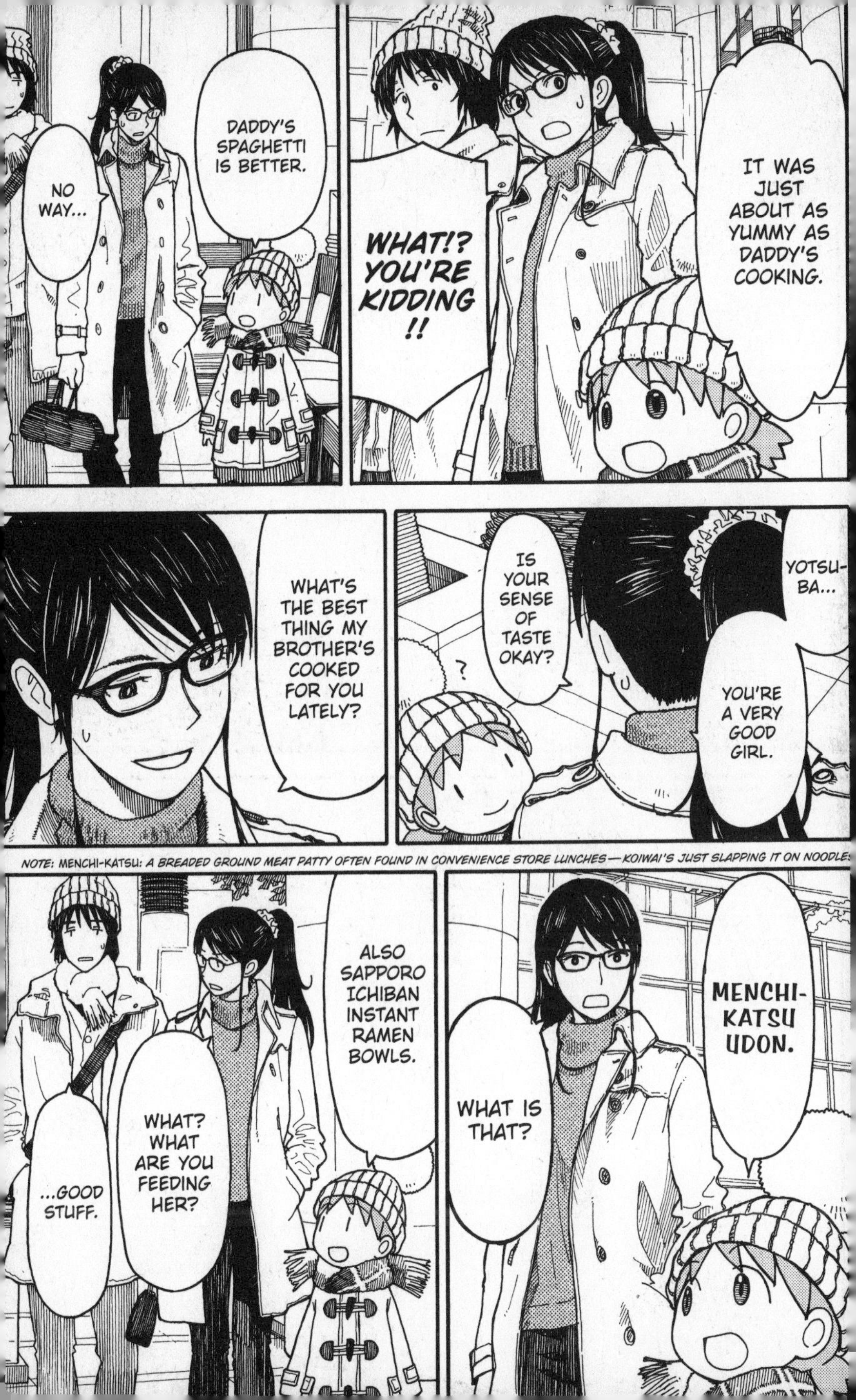
IT WAS JUST ABOUT AS YUMMY AS DADDY'S COOKING.
WHAT!? YOU'RE KIDDING!!
DADDY'S SPAGHETTI IS BETTER.
NO WAY...
YOTSUBA...
YOU'RE A VERY GOOD GIRL.
IS YOUR SENSE OF TASTE OKAY?
?
WHAT'S THE BEST THING MY BROTHER'S COOKED FOR YOU LATELY?
NOTE: MENCHI-KATSU: A BREADED GROUND MEAT PATTY OFTEN FOUND IN CONVENIENCE STORE LUNCHES—KOIWAI'S JUST SLAPPING IT ON NOODLES
MENCHI-KATSU UDON.
WHAT IS THAT?
ALSO SAPPORO ICHIBAN INSTANT RAMEN BOWLS.
WHAT? WHAT ARE YOU FEEDING HER?
...GOOD STUFF.

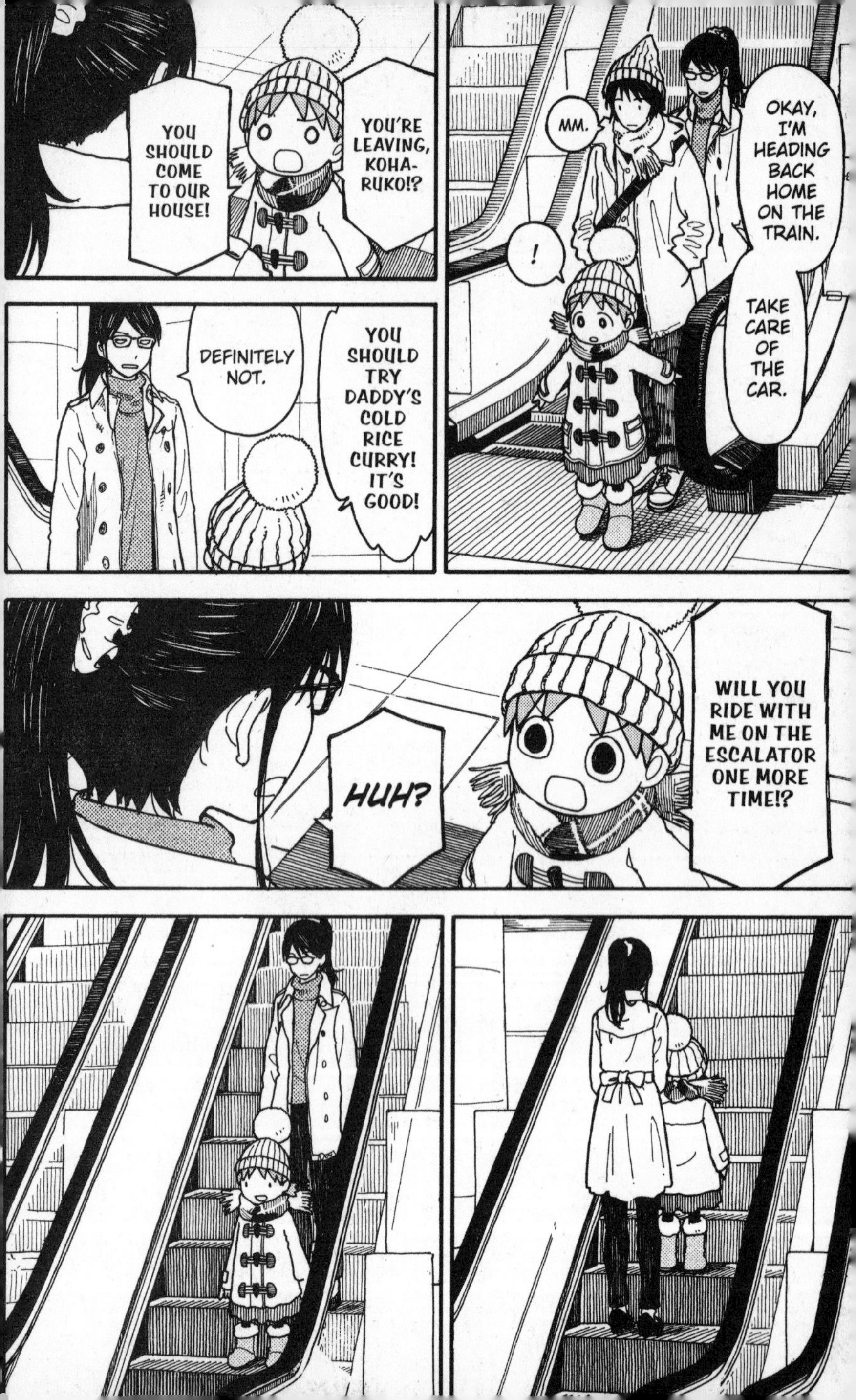
OKAY, I'M HEADING BACK HOME ON THE TRAIN.
MM.
!
TAKE CARE OF THE CAR.
YOU'RE LEAVING, KOHARUKO!?
YOU SHOULD COME TO OUR HOUSE!
YOU SHOULD TRY DADDY'S COLD RICE CURRY! IT'S GOOD!
DEFINITELY NOT.
WILL YOU RIDE WITH ME ON THE ESCALATOR ONE MORE TIME!?
HUH?

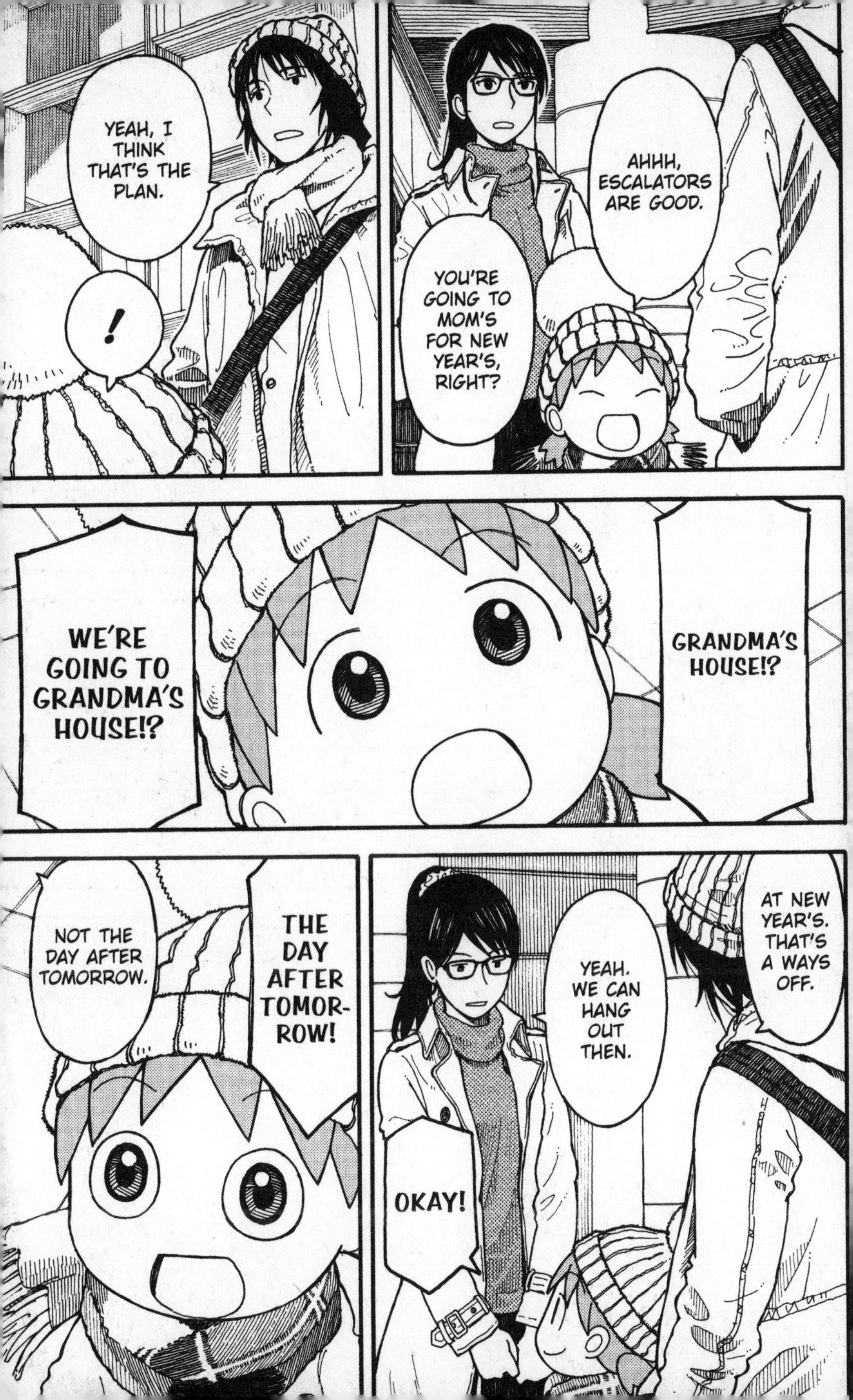
AHHH, ESCALATORS ARE GOOD.
YOU'RE GOING TO MOM'S FOR NEW YEAR'S, RIGHT?
YEAH, I THINK THAT'S THE PLAN.
!
GRANDMA'S HOUSE!?
WE'RE GOING TO GRANDMA'S HOUSE!?
AT NEW YEAR'S. THAT'S A WAYS OFF.
YEAH. WE CAN HANG OUT THEN.
OKAY!
THE DAY AFTER TOMOR-ROW!
NOT THE DAY AFTER TOMORROW.

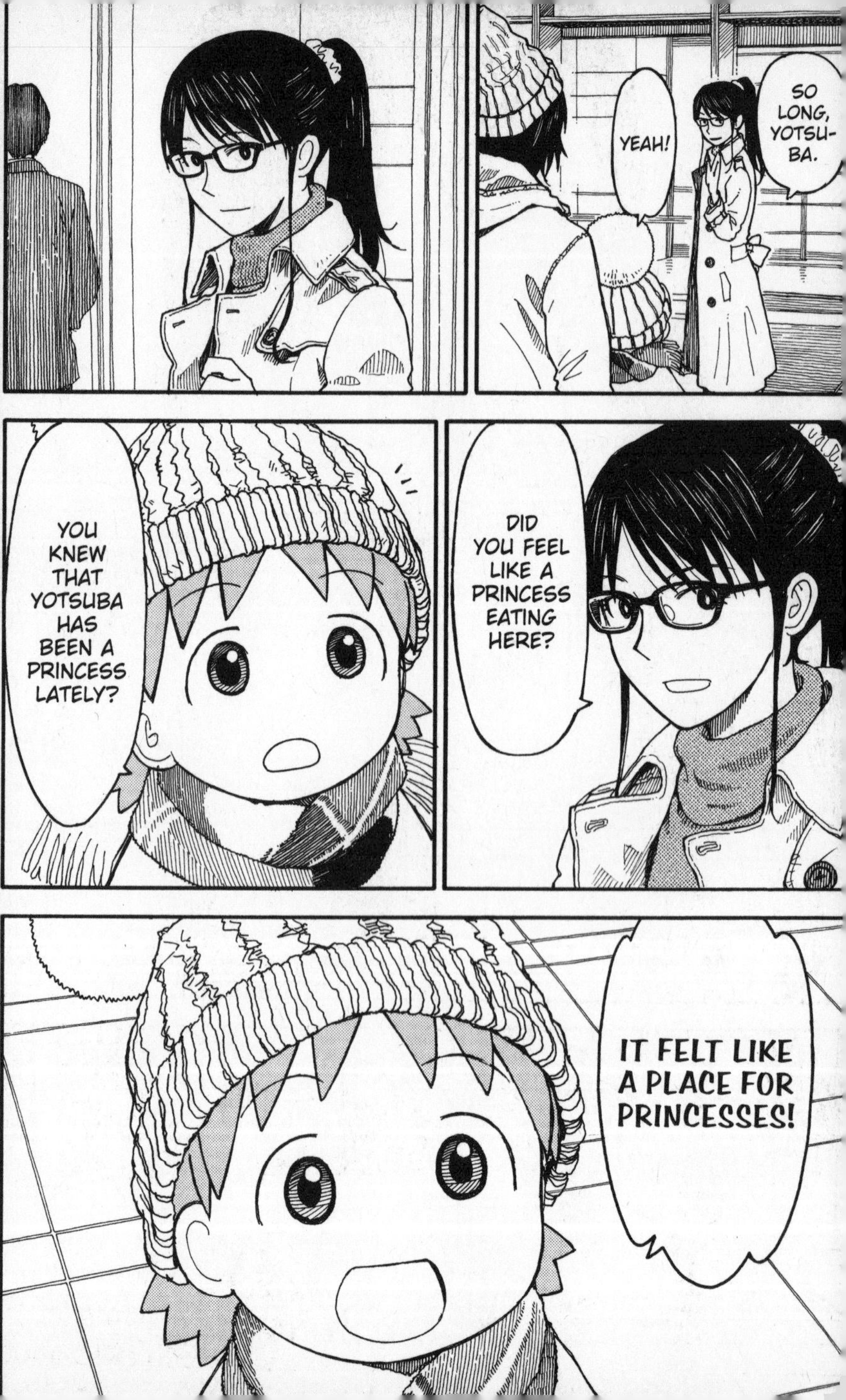
SO LONG, YOTSUBA.
YEAH!
DID YOU FEEL LIKE A PRINCESS EATING HERE?
YOU KNEW THAT YOTSUBA HAS BEEN A PRINCESS LATELY?
IT FELT LIKE A PLACE FOR PRINCESSES!

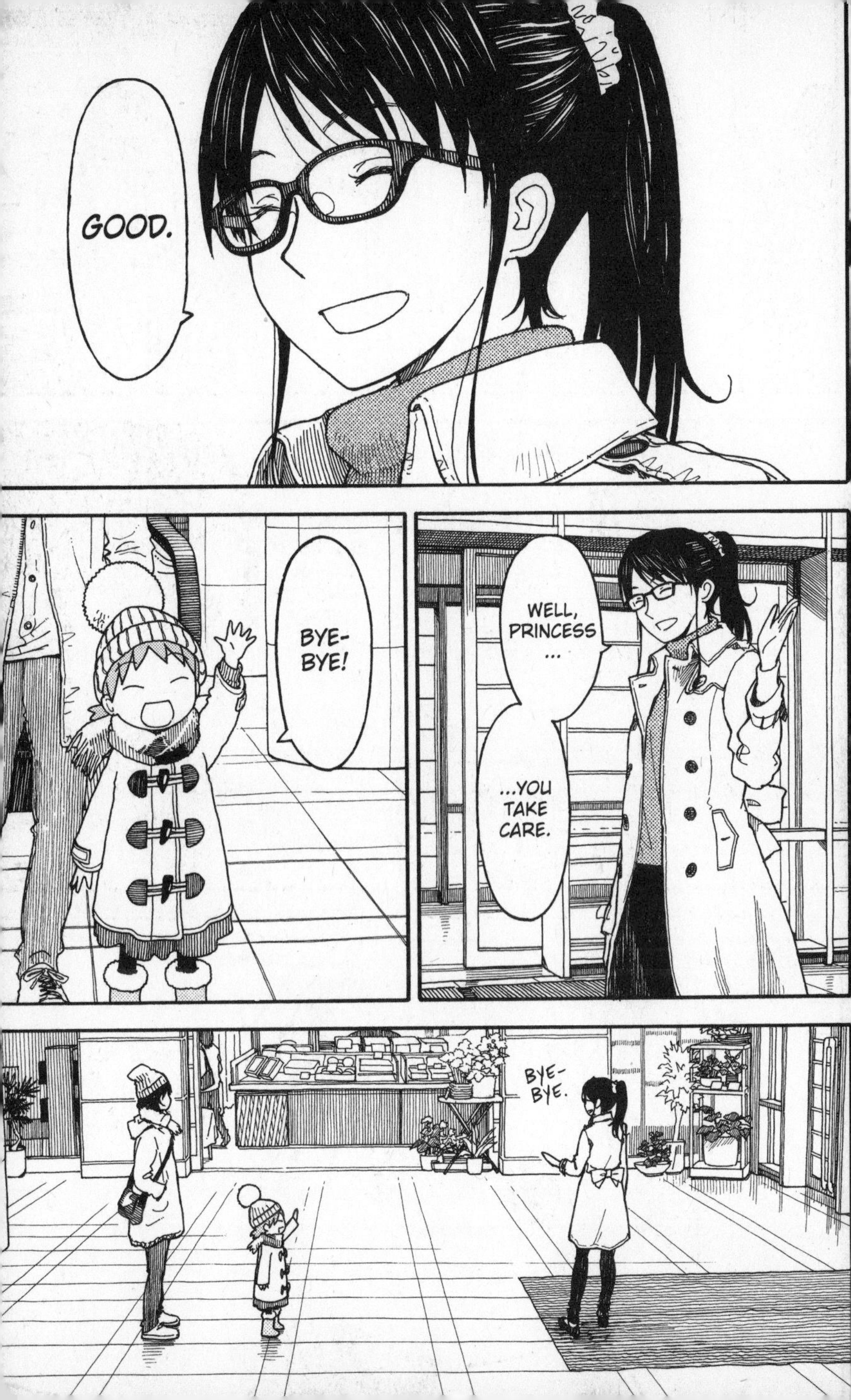
GOOD.
WELL, PRINCESS...
...YOU TAKE CARE.
BYE-BYE!
BYE-BYE.

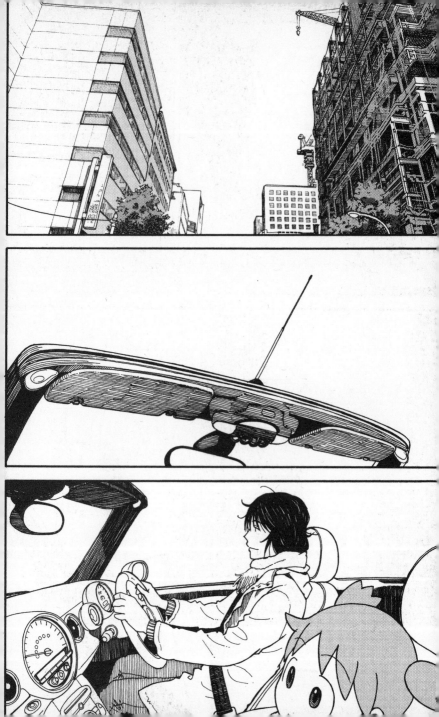

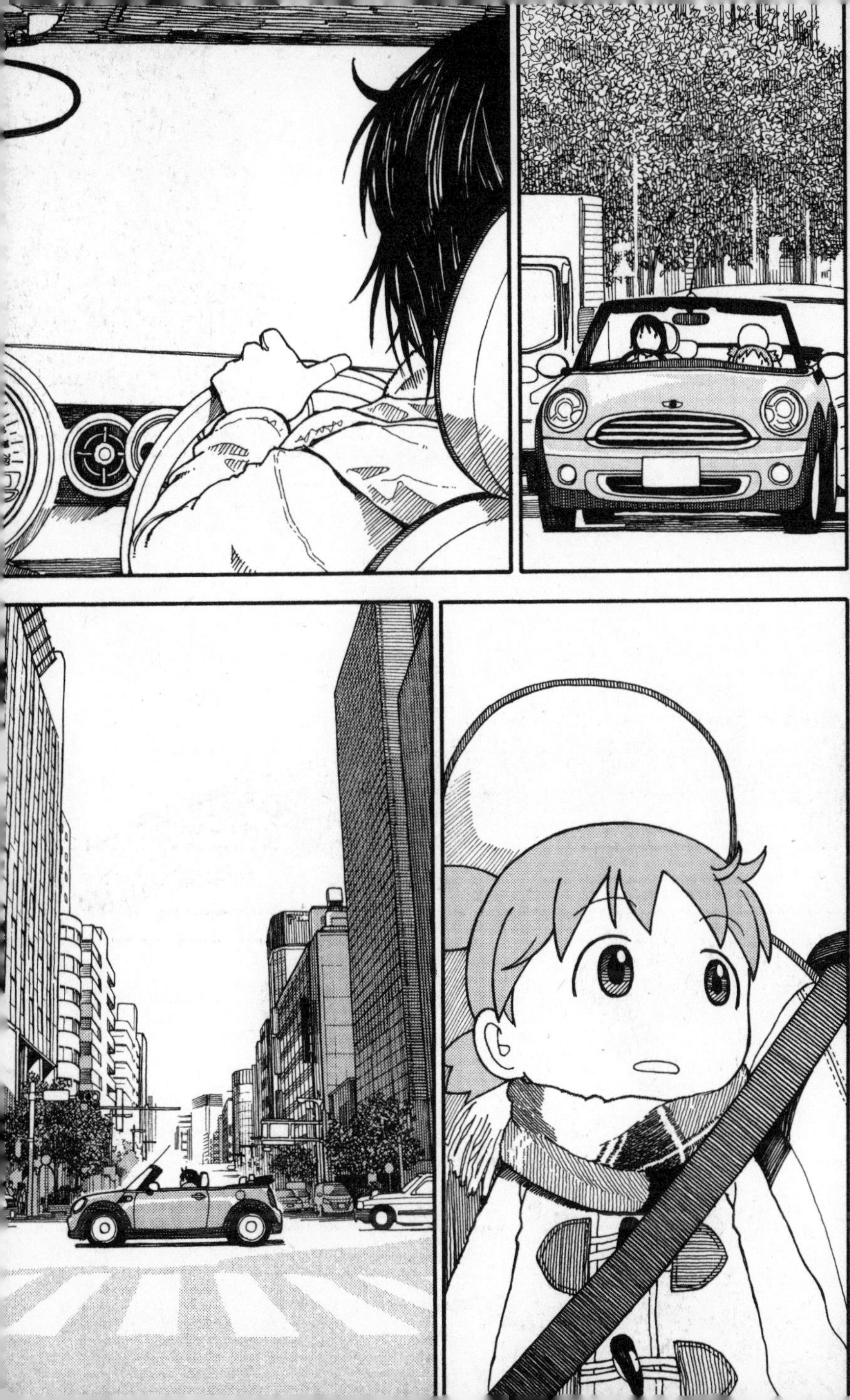

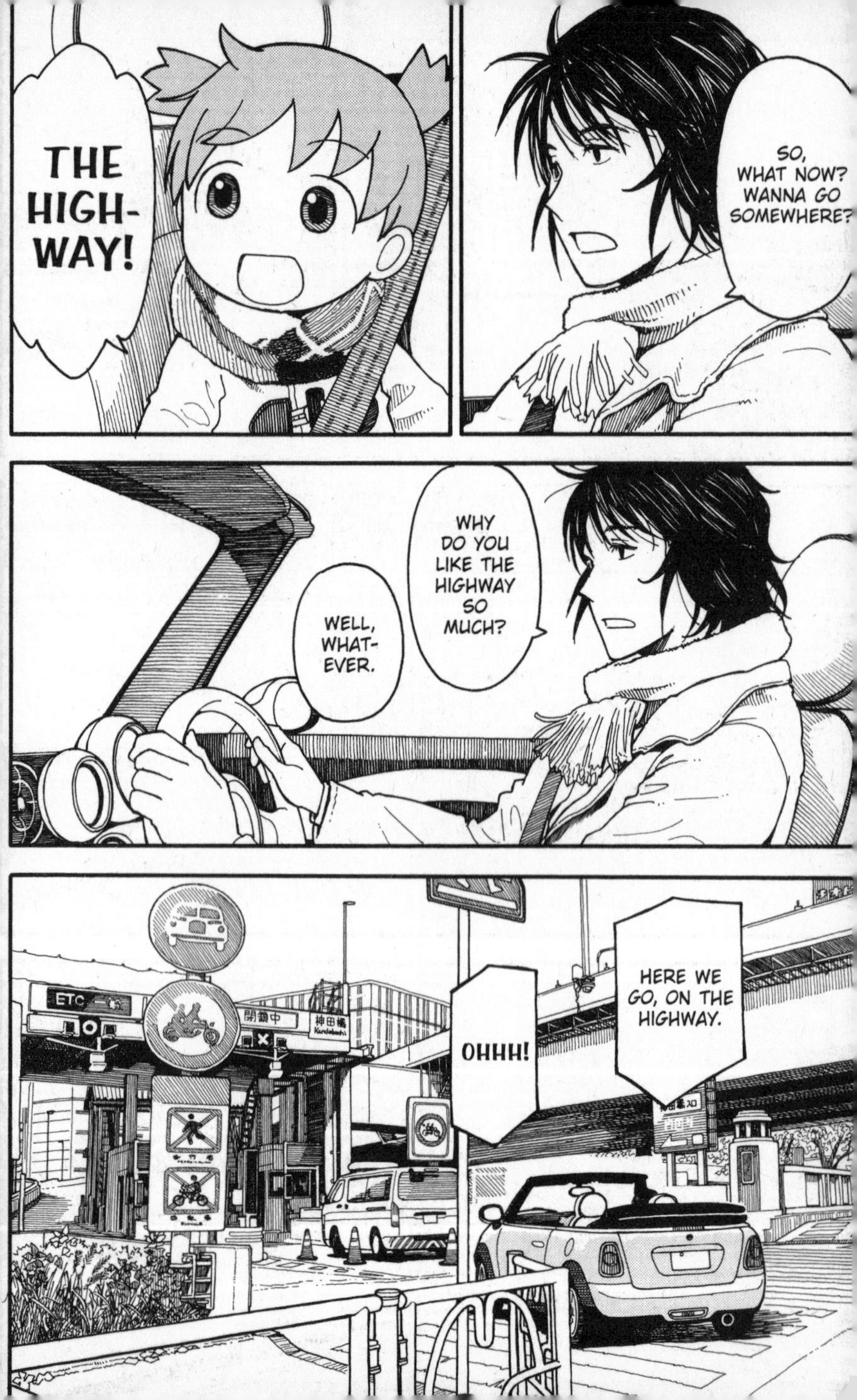
SO, WHAT NOW? WANNA GO SOMEWHERE?
THE HIGH-WAY!
WHY DO YOU LIKE THE HIGHWAY SO MUCH?
WELL, WHAT-EVER.
HERE WE GO, ON THE HIGHWAY.
OHHH!
ETC
開鎖中
神田橋
Kandabashi

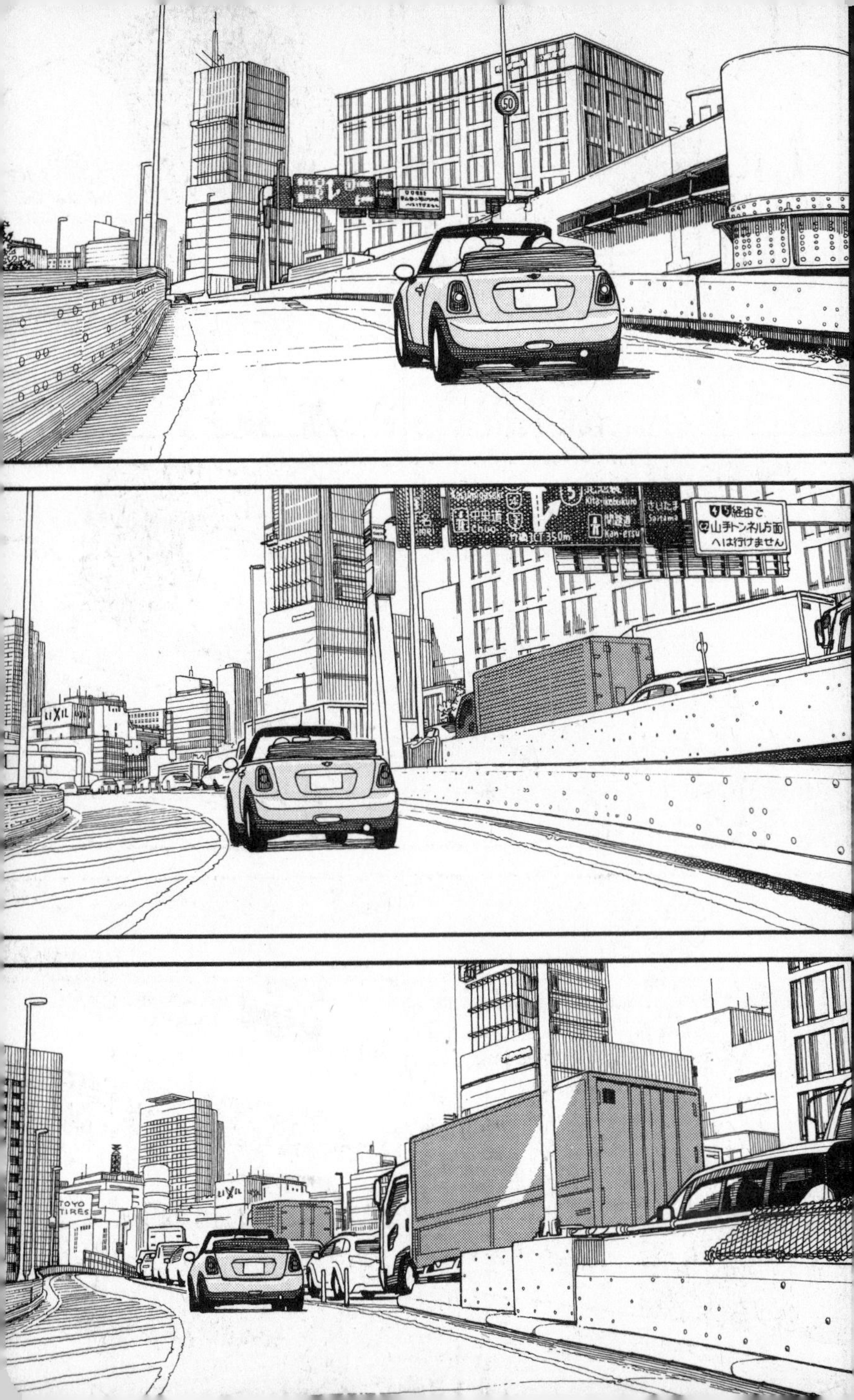
50
中央道
Chuo
竹橋JCT 350m
Kita-ikebukuro
関越道
Kan-etsu
さいたま
Saitama
経由で
山手トンネル方面
へは行けません
LIXIL
TOYO
TIRES

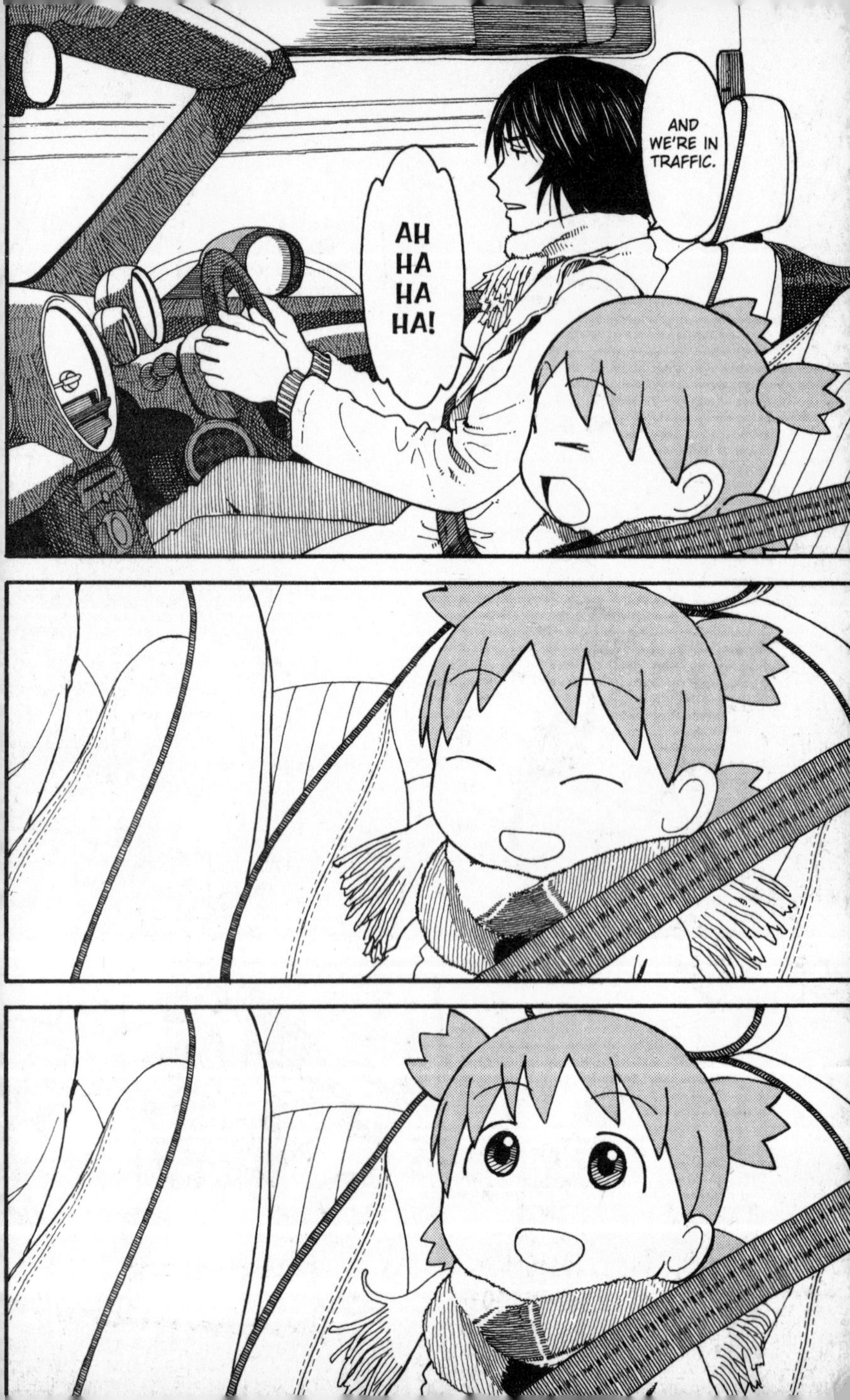
AND WE'RE IN TRAFFIC.
AH HA HA HA!

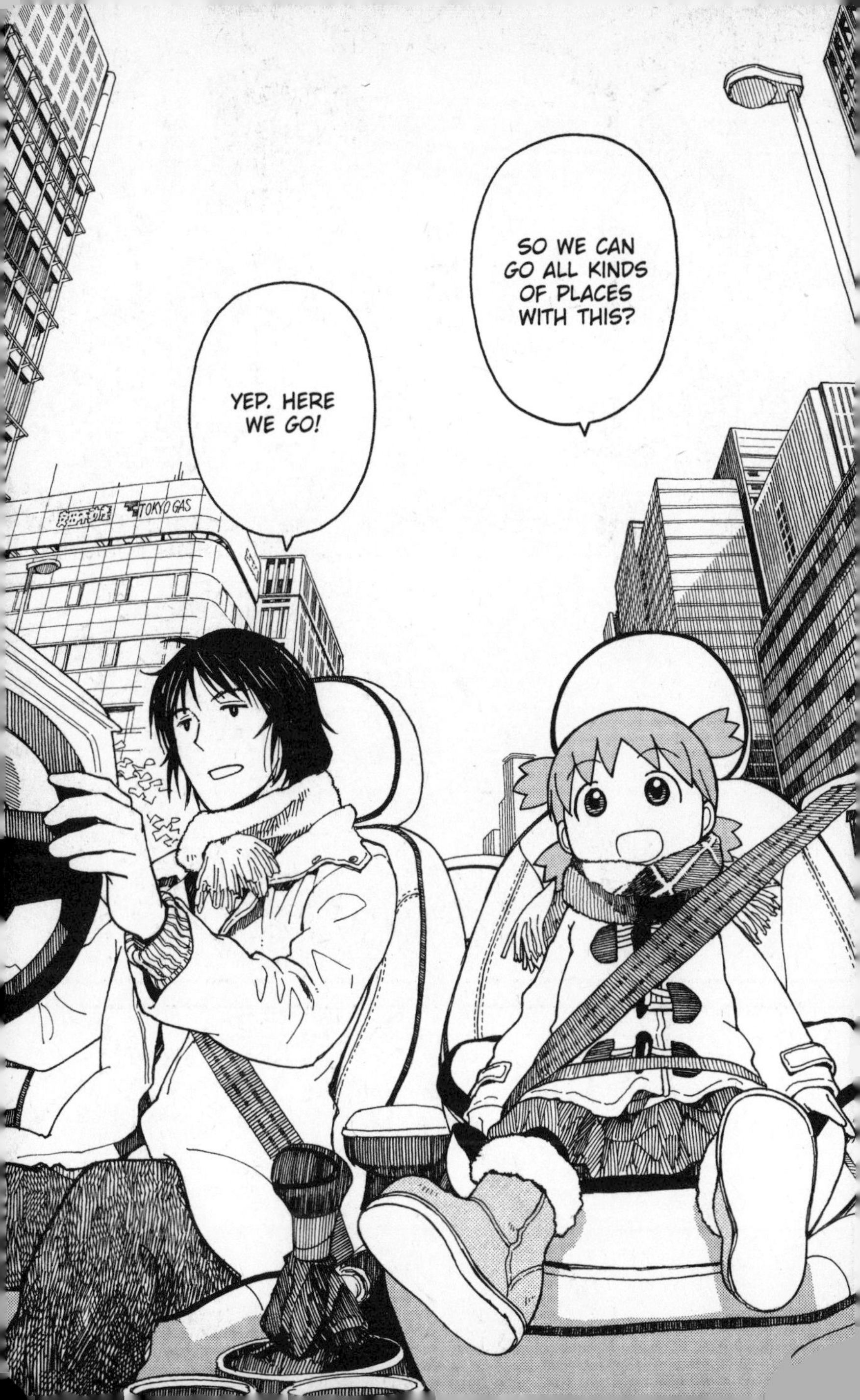
SO WE CAN GO ALL KINDS OF PLACES WITH THIS?
YEP. HERE WE GO!
TOKYO GAS

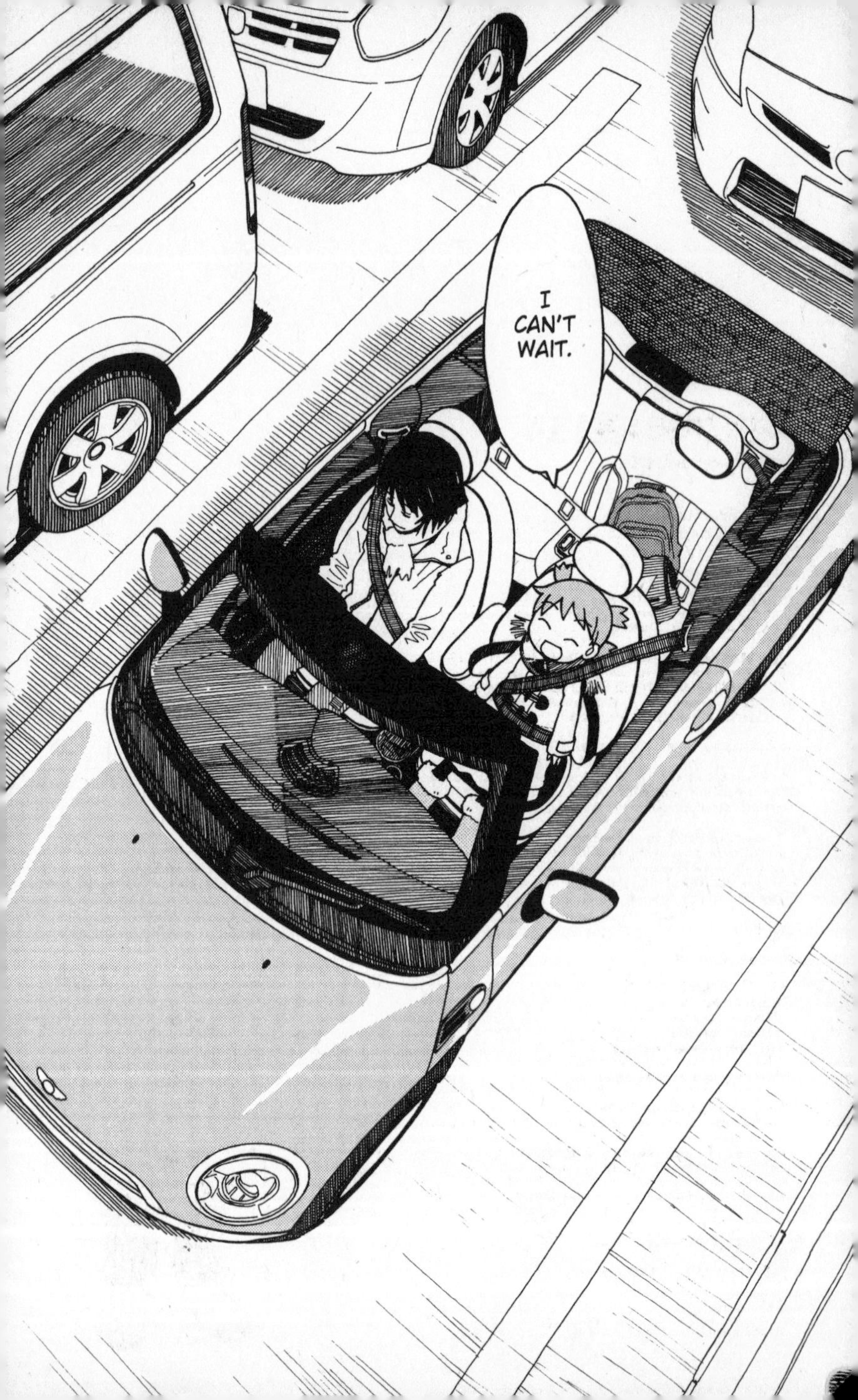
I CAN'T WAIT.

YOTSUBA&! 14

KIYOHIKO AZUMA

Translation: Stephen Paul
Lettering: Abigail Blackman

YOTSUBA&! Vol. 14 © KIYOHIKO AZUMA / YOTUBA SUTAZIO 2018 First published in Japan in 2018 by KADOKAWA CORPORATION, Tokyo. English translation rights in USA, Canada, and UK arranged with KADOKAWA CORPORATION, Tokyo through Tuttle-Mori Agency, Inc., Tokyo.

English translation © 2018 by Yen Press, LLC

Yen Press
1290 Avenue of the Americas
New York, NY 10104

Visit us at yenpress.com
facebook.com/yenpress
twitter.com/yenpress
yenpress.tumblr.com
instagram.com/yenpress

First Yen Press Edition: November 2018

Yen Press is an imprint of Yen Press, LLC.
The Yen Press name and logo are trademarks of Yen Press, LLC.

Library of Congress Control Number: 2016932334

ISBNs: 978-1-9753-2818-4 (paperback)
        978-1-9753-8312-1 (ebook)

10 9 8 7 6 5 4 3 2 1

WOR

Printed in the United States of America

YOTSUBA&!

ENJOY EVERYTHING.

TO BE CONTINUED!